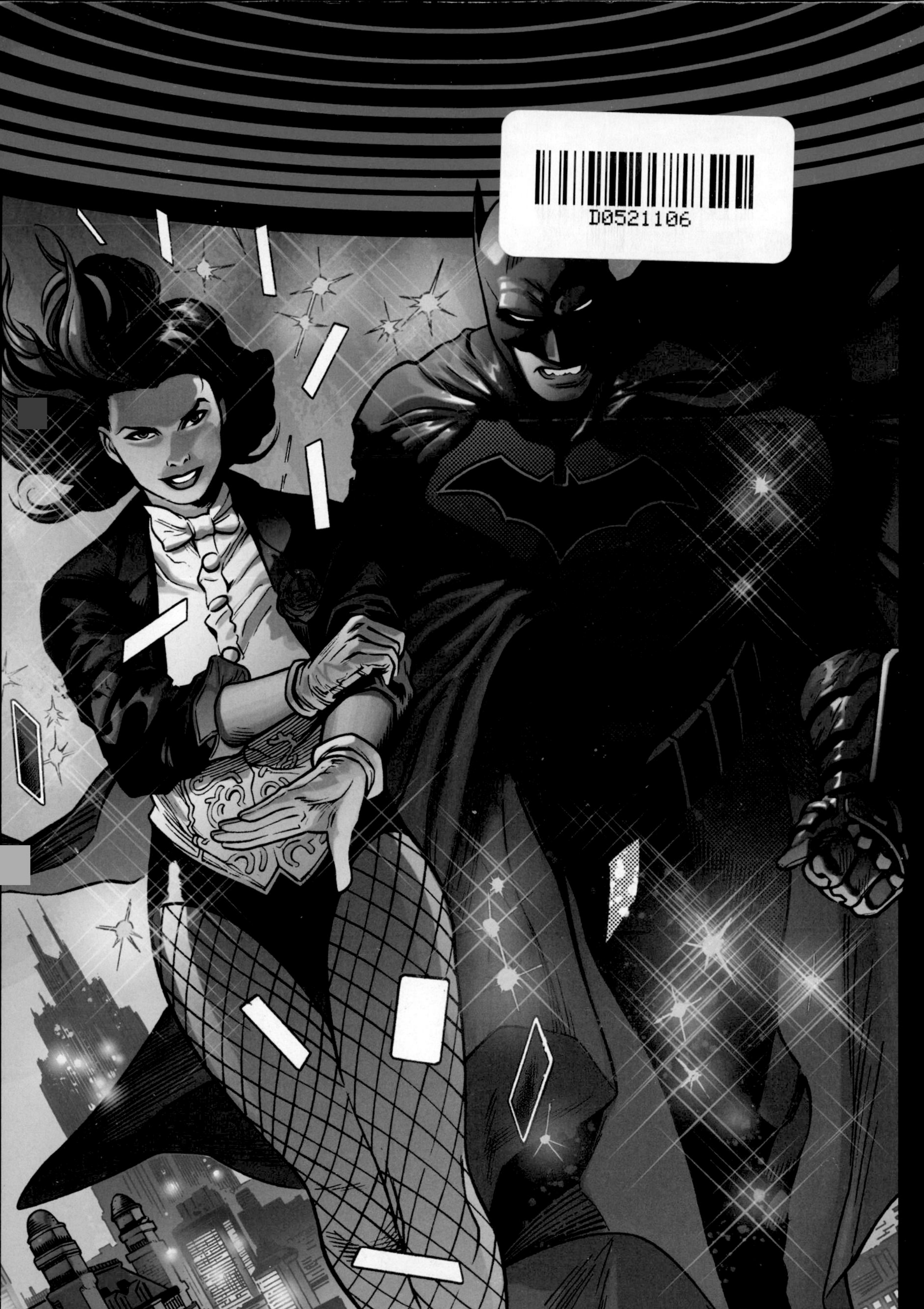

BATMAN: DETECTIVE COMICS

VOL.4 DEUS EX MACHINA

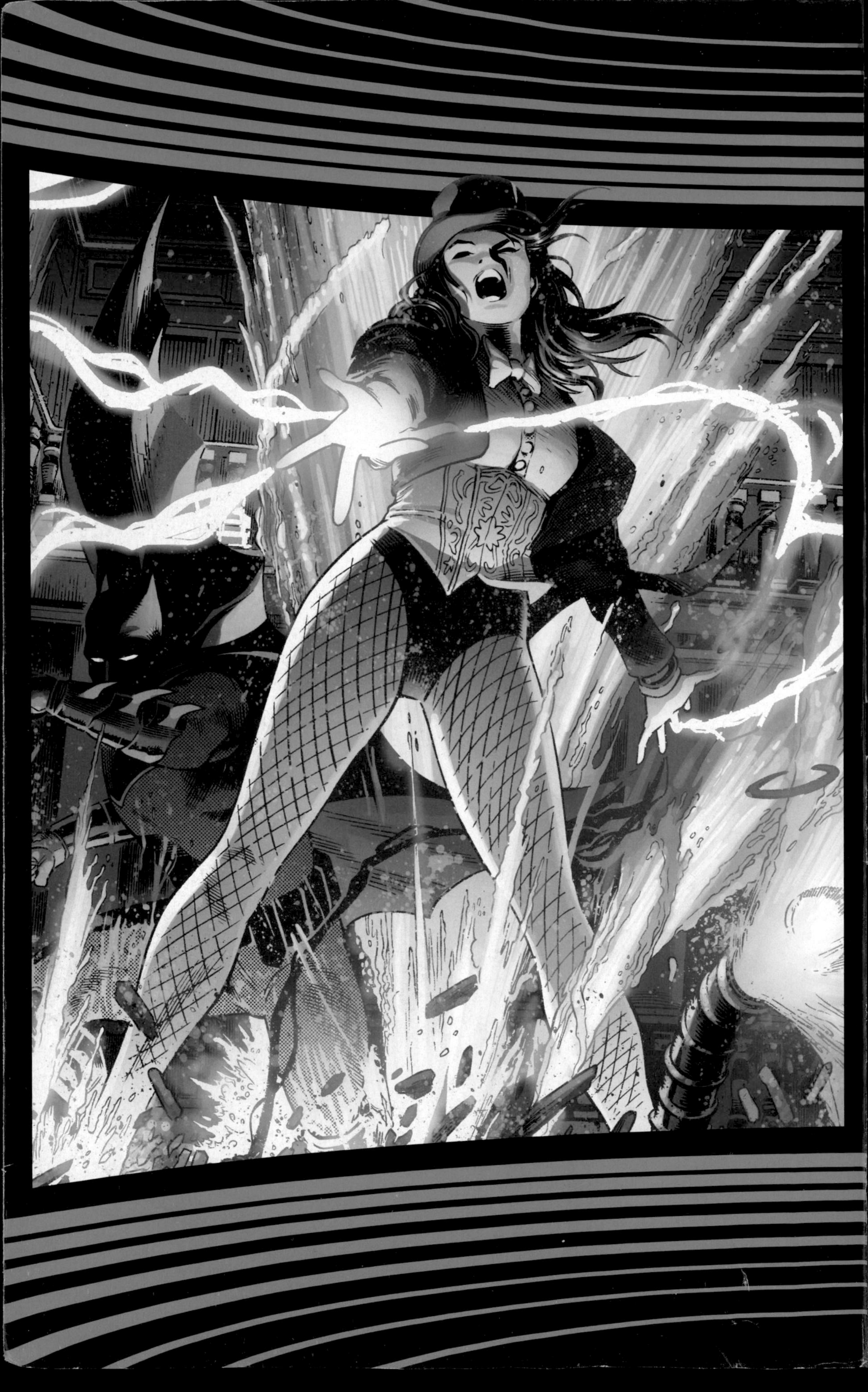

BATMAN: DETECTIVE COMICS
VOL.4 DEUS EX MACHINA

JAMES TYNION IV
CHRISTOPHER SEBELA
writers

ALVARO MARTINEZ
CARMEN CARNERO
pencillers

RAÚL FERNÁNDEZ
KARL STORY * RICHARD FRIEND * CARMEN CARNERO
inkers

BRAD ANDERSON
JAVIER MENA
colorists

SAL CIPRIANO
letterer

YASMINE PUTRI
collection cover artist

BATMAN created by BOB KANE with BILL FINGER
ZATANNA created by GARDNER FOX and MURPHY ANDERSON
SPOILER created by CHUCK DIXON and TOM LYLE

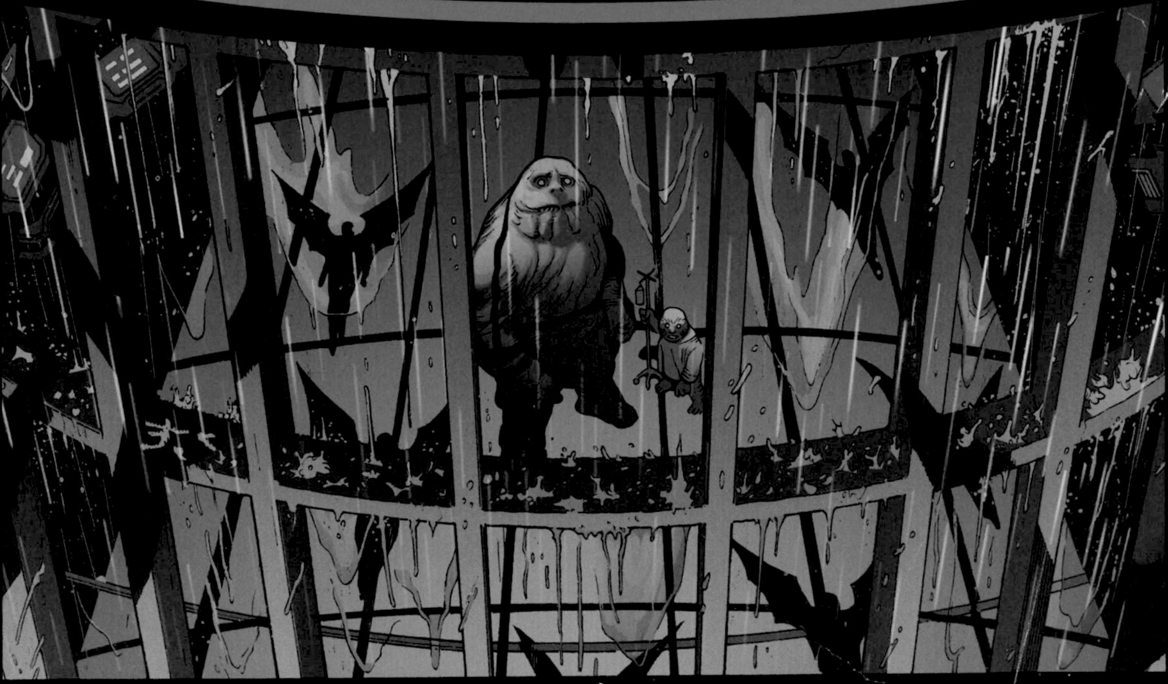

CHRIS CONROY Editor - Original Series • **DAVE WIELGOSZ** Assistant Editor - Original Series
JEB WOODARD Group Editor - Collected Editions • **ROBIN WILDMAN** Editor - Collected Edition
STEVE COOK Design Director - Books • **MONIQUE NARBONETA** Publication Design

BOB HARRAS Senior VP - Editor-in-Chief, DC Comics
PAT McCALLUM Executive Editor, DC Comics

DIANE NELSON President • **DAN DiDIO** Publisher • **JIM LEE** Publisher • **GEOFF JOHNS** President & Chief Creative Officer
AMIT DESAI Executive VP - Business & Marketing Strategy, Direct to Consumer & Global Franchise Management
SAM ADES Senior VP & General Manager, Digital Services • **BOBBIE CHASE** VP & Executive Editor, Young Reader & Talent Development
MARK CHIARELLO Senior VP - Art, Design & Collected Editions • **JOHN CUNNINGHAM** Senior VP - Sales & Trade Marketing
ANNE DePIES Senior VP - Business Strategy, Finance & Administration • **DON FALLETTI** VP - Manufacturing Operations
LAWRENCE GANEM VP - Editorial Administration & Talent Relations • **ALISON GILL** Senior VP - Manufacturing & Operations
HANK KANALZ Senior VP - Editorial Strategy & Administration • **JAY KOGAN** VP - Legal Affairs • **JACK MAHAN** VP - Business Affairs
NICK J. NAPOLITANO VP - Manufacturing Administration • **EDDIE SCANNELL** VP - Consumer Marketing
COURTNEY SIMMONS Senior VP - Publicity & Communications • **JIM (SKI) SOKOLOWSKI** VP - Comic Book Specialty Sales & Trade Marketing
NANCY SPEARS VP - Mass, Book, Digital Sales & Trade Marketing • **MICHELE R. WELLS** VP - Content Strategy

BATMAN: DETECTIVE COMICS VOL. 4–DEUS EX MACHINA

DC Comics, 2900 West Alameda Ave., Burbank, CA 91505
Printed by LSC Communications, Kendallville, IN, USA. 11/17/17. First Printing.
ISBN: 978-1-4012-7497-9

Library of Congress Cataloging-in-Publication Data is available.

PEFC Certified
Printed on paper from sustainably managed forests, controlled sources
PEFC
PEFC/29-31-337
www.pefc.org

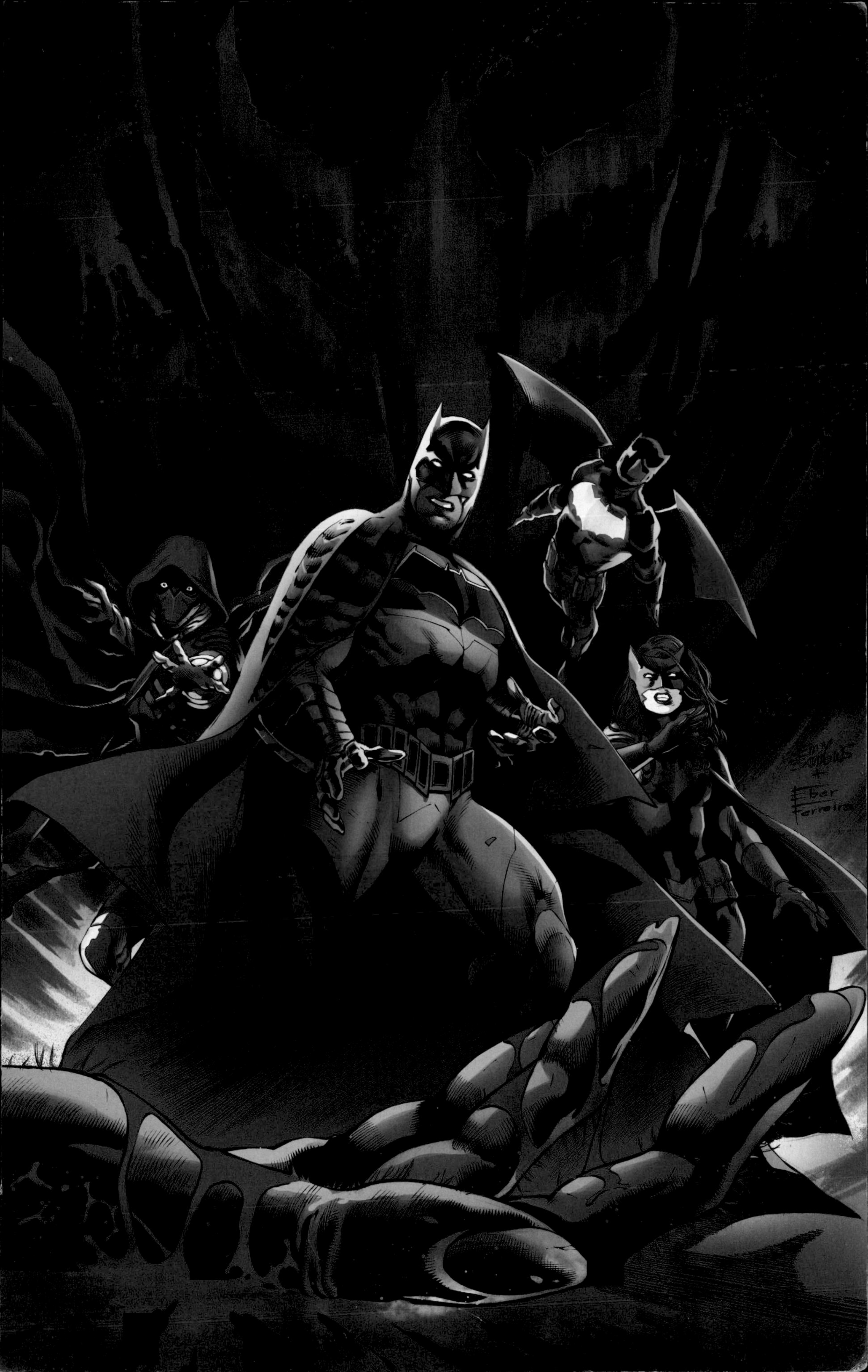

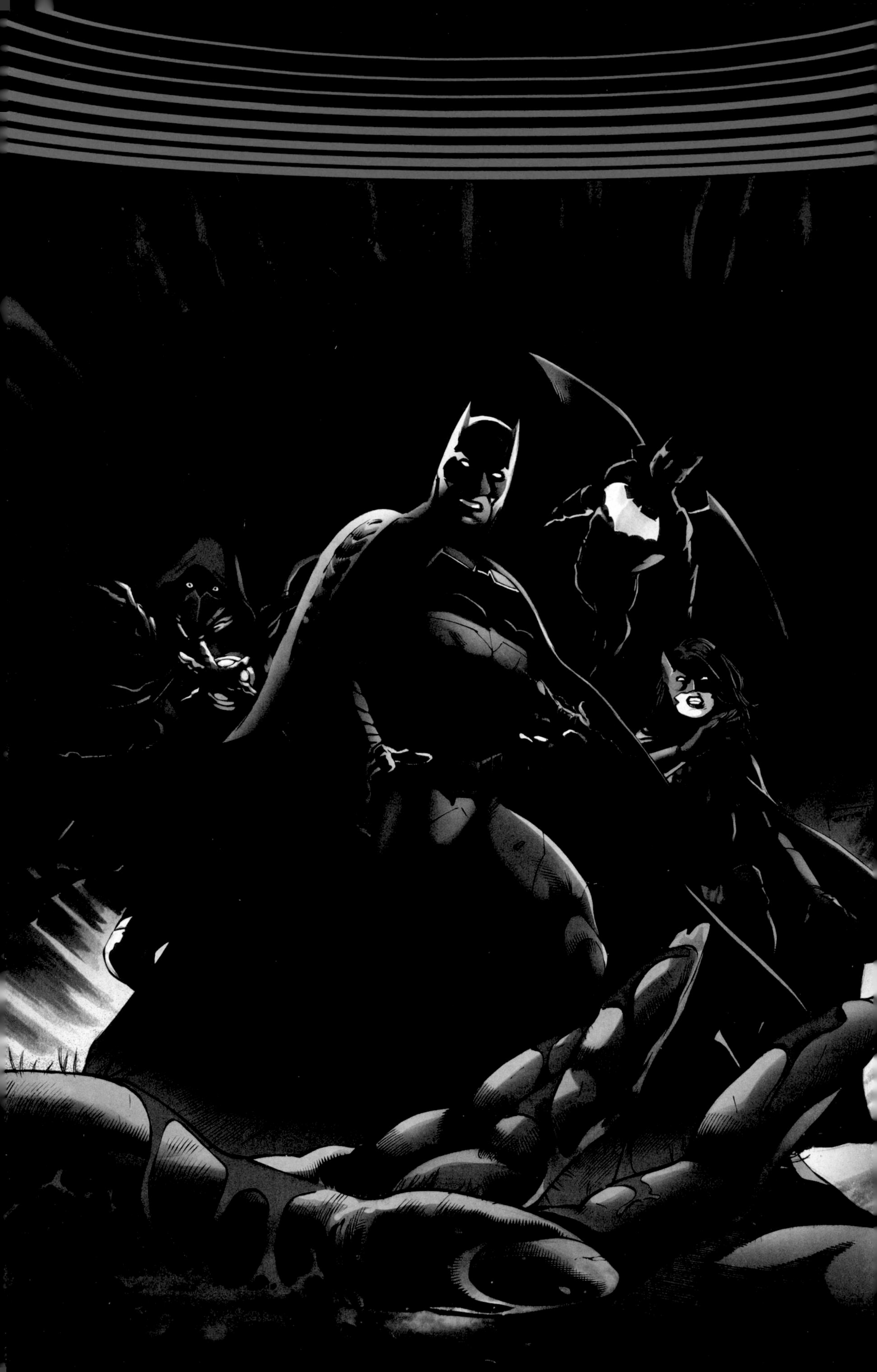

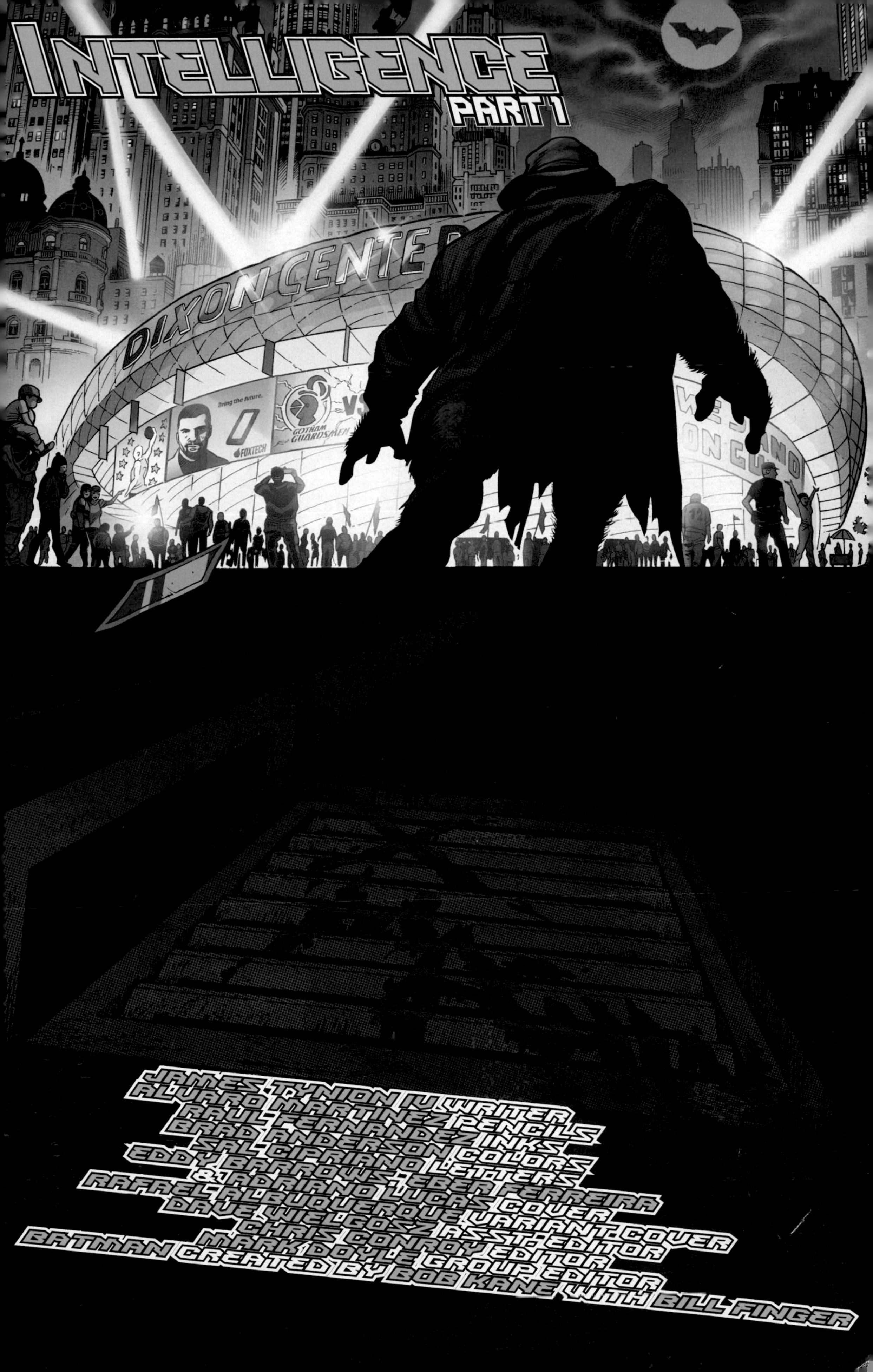
INTELLIGENCE
PART 1
DIXON CENTER
Bring the future.
FOXTECH
GOTHAM GUARDSMEN
VS
JAMES TYNION IV WRITER
ALVARO MARTINEZ PENCILS
RAUL FERNANDEZ INKS
BRAD ANDERSON COLORS
SAL CIPRIANO LETTERS
EDDY BARROWS, EBER FERREIRA
& ADRIANO LUCAS COVER
RAFAEL ALBUQUERQUE VARIANT COVER
DAVE WIELGOSZ ASST. EDITOR
CHRIS CONROY EDITOR
MARK DOYLE GROUP EDITOR
BATMAN CREATED BY BOB KANE WITH BILL FINGER

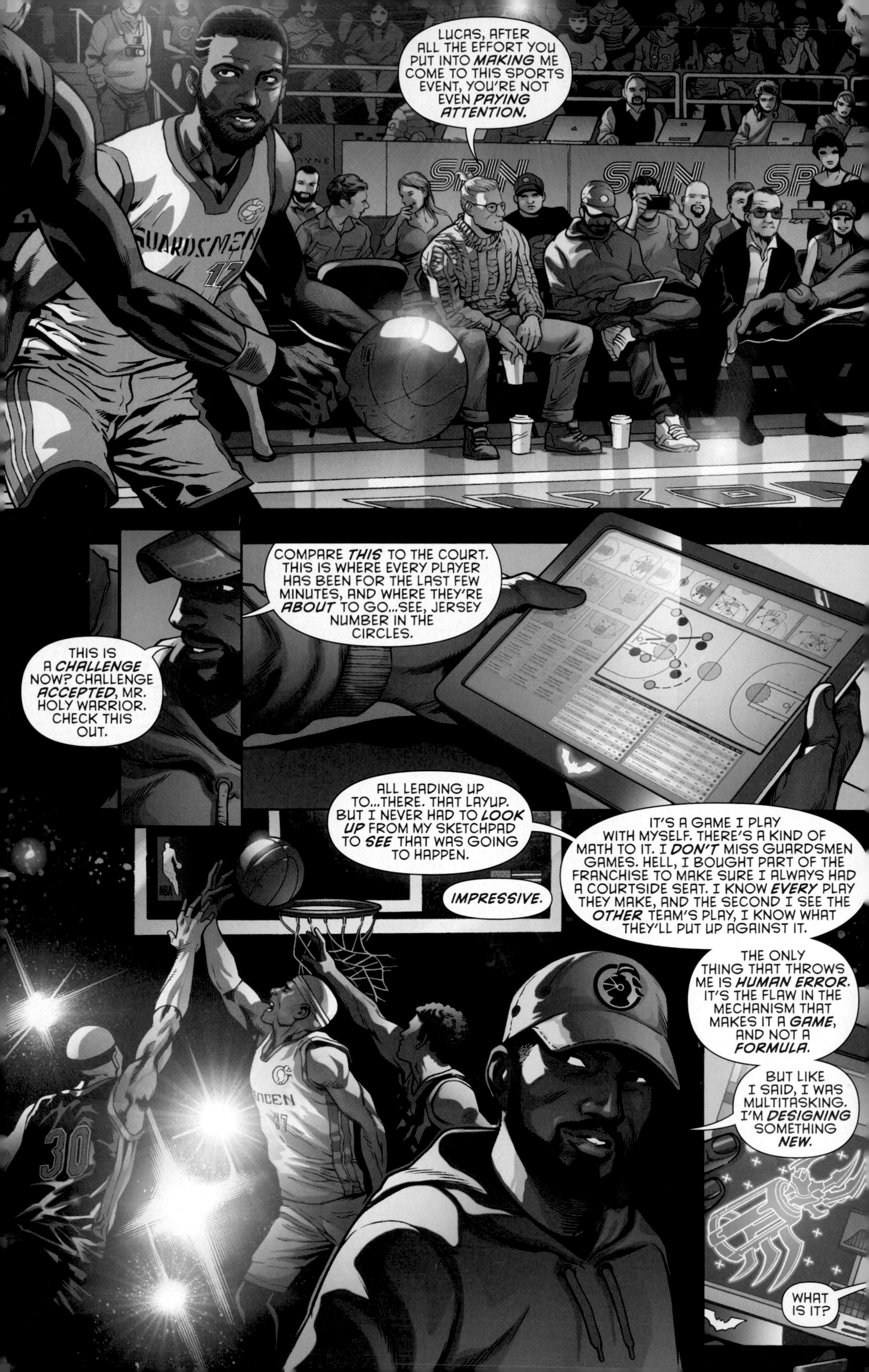
LUCAS, AFTER ALL THE EFFORT YOU PUT INTO *MAKING* ME COME TO THIS SPORTS EVENT, YOU'RE NOT EVEN *PAYING ATTENTION.*
SPIN
GUARDSMEN
THIS IS A *CHALLENGE* NOW? CHALLENGE *ACCEPTED*, MR. HOLY WARRIOR. CHECK THIS OUT.
COMPARE *THIS* TO THE COURT. THIS IS WHERE EVERY PLAYER HAS BEEN FOR THE LAST FEW MINUTES, AND WHERE THEY'RE *ABOUT* TO GO...SEE, JERSEY NUMBER IN THE CIRCLES.
ALL LEADING UP TO...THERE. THAT LAYUP. BUT I NEVER HAD TO *LOOK UP* FROM MY SKETCHPAD TO *SEE* THAT WAS GOING TO HAPPEN.
IMPRESSIVE.
IT'S A GAME I PLAY WITH MYSELF. THERE'S A KIND OF MATH TO IT. *I DON'T* MISS GUARDSMEN GAMES. HELL, I BOUGHT PART OF THE FRANCHISE TO MAKE SURE I ALWAYS HAD A COURTSIDE SEAT. I KNOW *EVERY* PLAY THEY MAKE, AND THE SECOND I SEE THE *OTHER* TEAM'S PLAY, I KNOW WHAT THEY'LL PUT UP AGAINST IT.
THE ONLY THING THAT THROWS ME IS *HUMAN ERROR.* IT'S THE FLAW IN THE MECHANISM THAT MAKES IT A *GAME*, AND NOT A *FORMULA.*
BUT LIKE I SAID, I WAS MULTITASKING. I'M *DESIGNING* SOMETHING *NEW.*
WHAT IS IT?

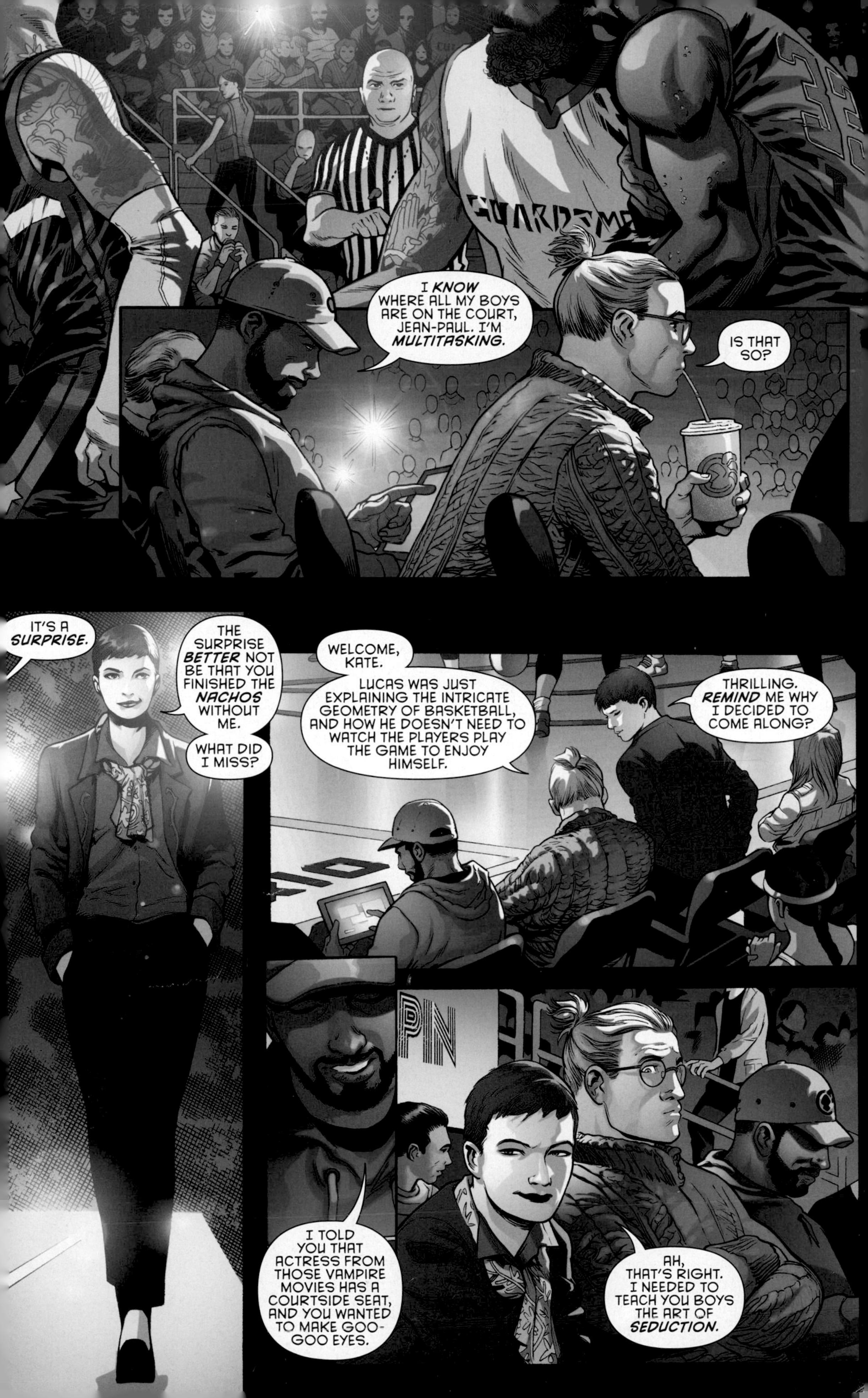

GUARDSME
I KNOW WHERE ALL MY BOYS ARE ON THE COURT, JEAN-PAUL. I'M MULTITASKING.
IS THAT SO?
IT'S A SURPRISE.
THE SURPRISE BETTER NOT BE THAT YOU FINISHED THE NACHOS WITHOUT ME.
WHAT DID I MISS?
WELCOME, KATE.
LUCAS WAS JUST EXPLAINING THE INTRICATE GEOMETRY OF BASKETBALL, AND HOW HE DOESN'T NEED TO WATCH THE PLAYERS PLAY THE GAME TO ENJOY HIMSELF.
THRILLING. REMIND ME WHY I DECIDED TO COME ALONG?
I TOLD YOU THAT ACTRESS FROM THOSE VAMPIRE MOVIES HAS A COURTSIDE SEAT, AND YOU WANTED TO MAKE GOO-GOO EYES.
AH, THAT'S RIGHT. I NEEDED TO TEACH YOU BOYS THE ART OF SEDUCTION.

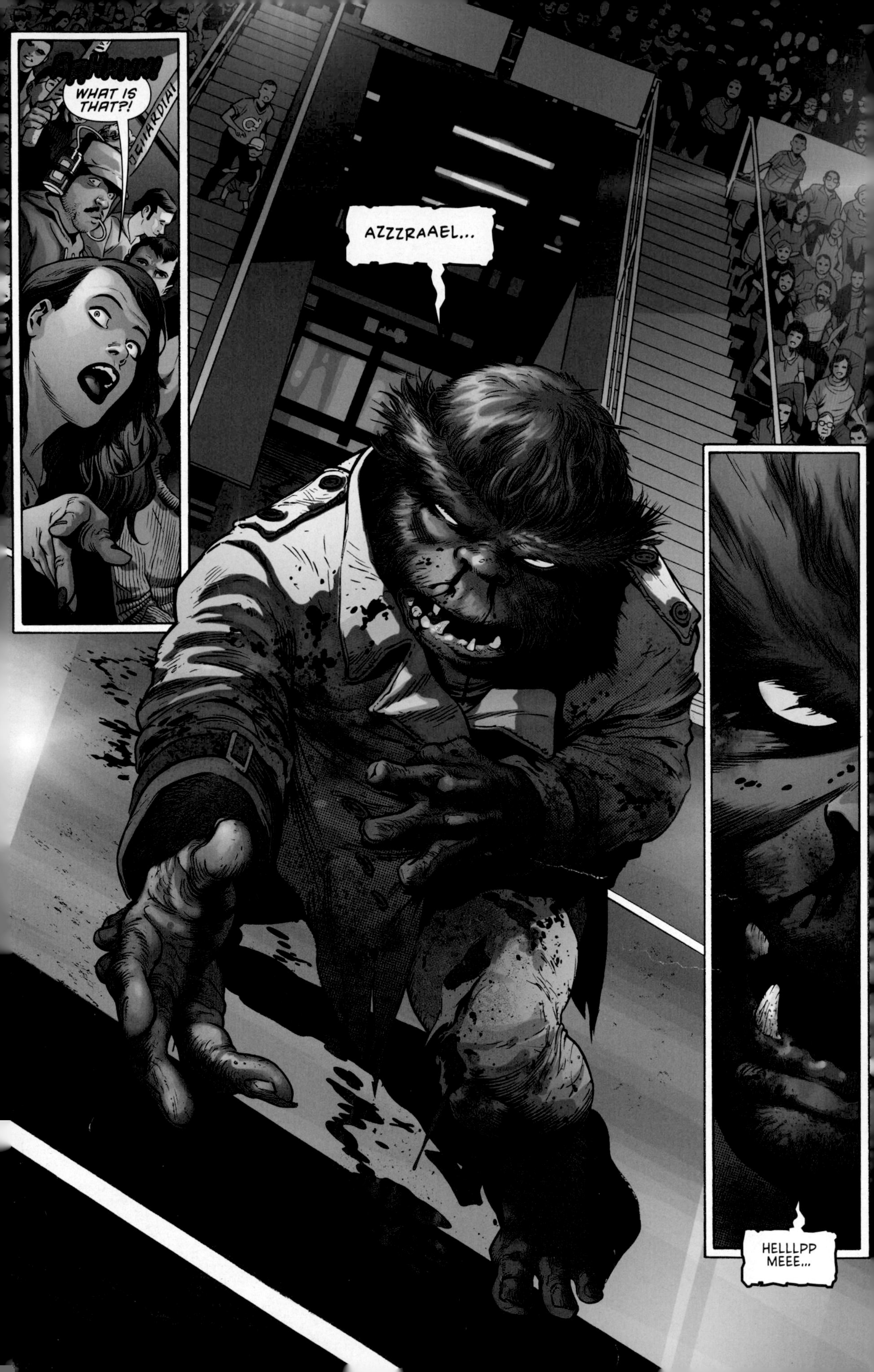
WHAT IS THAT?!
AZZZRAAEL...
HELLLPP MEEE...

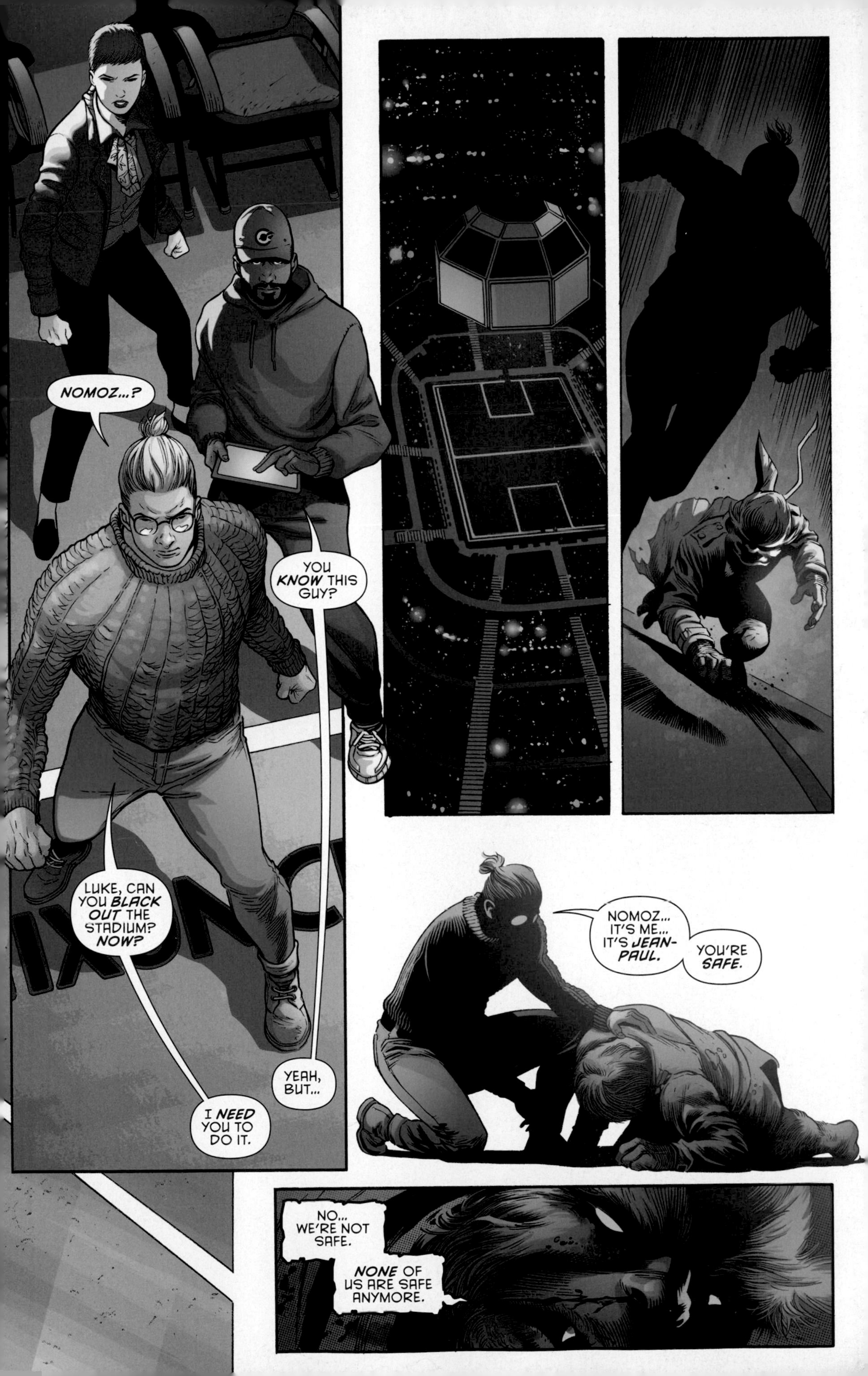
NOMOZ...?
YOU KNOW THIS GUY?
LUKE, CAN YOU BLACK OUT THE STADIUM? NOW?
YEAH, BUT...
I NEED YOU TO DO IT.
NOMOZ... IT'S ME... IT'S JEAN-PAUL.
YOU'RE SAFE.
NO... WE'RE NOT SAFE.
NONE OF US ARE SAFE ANYMORE.

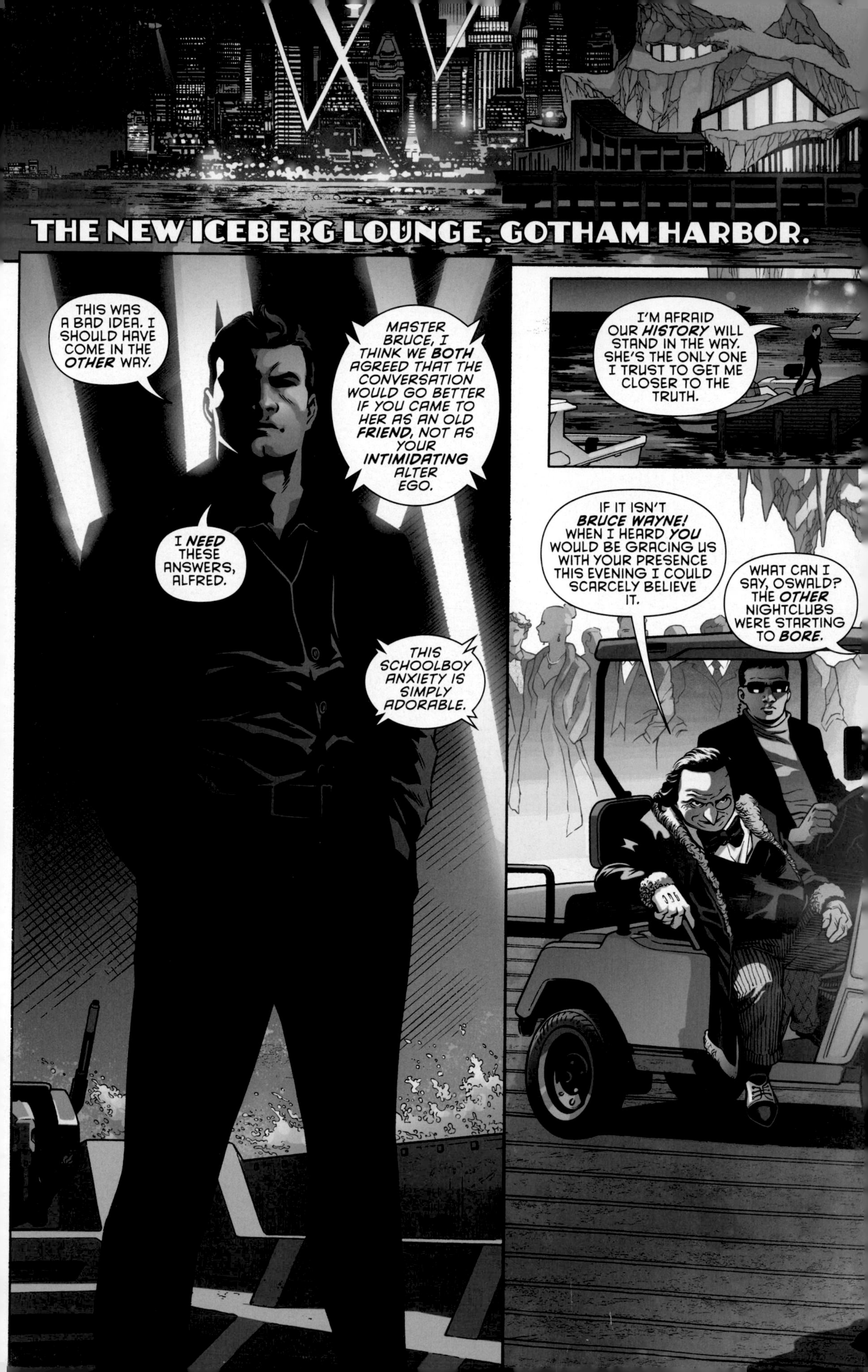
THE NEW ICEBERG LOUNGE. GOTHAM HARBOR.
THIS WAS A BAD IDEA. I SHOULD HAVE COME IN THE OTHER WAY.
MASTER BRUCE, I THINK WE BOTH AGREED THAT THE CONVERSATION WOULD GO BETTER IF YOU CAME TO HER AS AN OLD FRIEND, NOT AS YOUR INTIMIDATING ALTER EGO.
I NEED THESE ANSWERS, ALFRED.
THIS SCHOOLBOY ANXIETY IS SIMPLY ADORABLE.
I'M AFRAID OUR HISTORY WILL STAND IN THE WAY. SHE'S THE ONLY ONE I TRUST TO GET ME CLOSER TO THE TRUTH.
IF IT ISN'T BRUCE WAYNE! WHEN I HEARD YOU WOULD BE GRACING US WITH YOUR PRESENCE THIS EVENING I COULD SCARCELY BELIEVE IT.
WHAT CAN I SAY, OSWALD? THE OTHER NIGHTCLUBS WERE STARTING TO BORE.

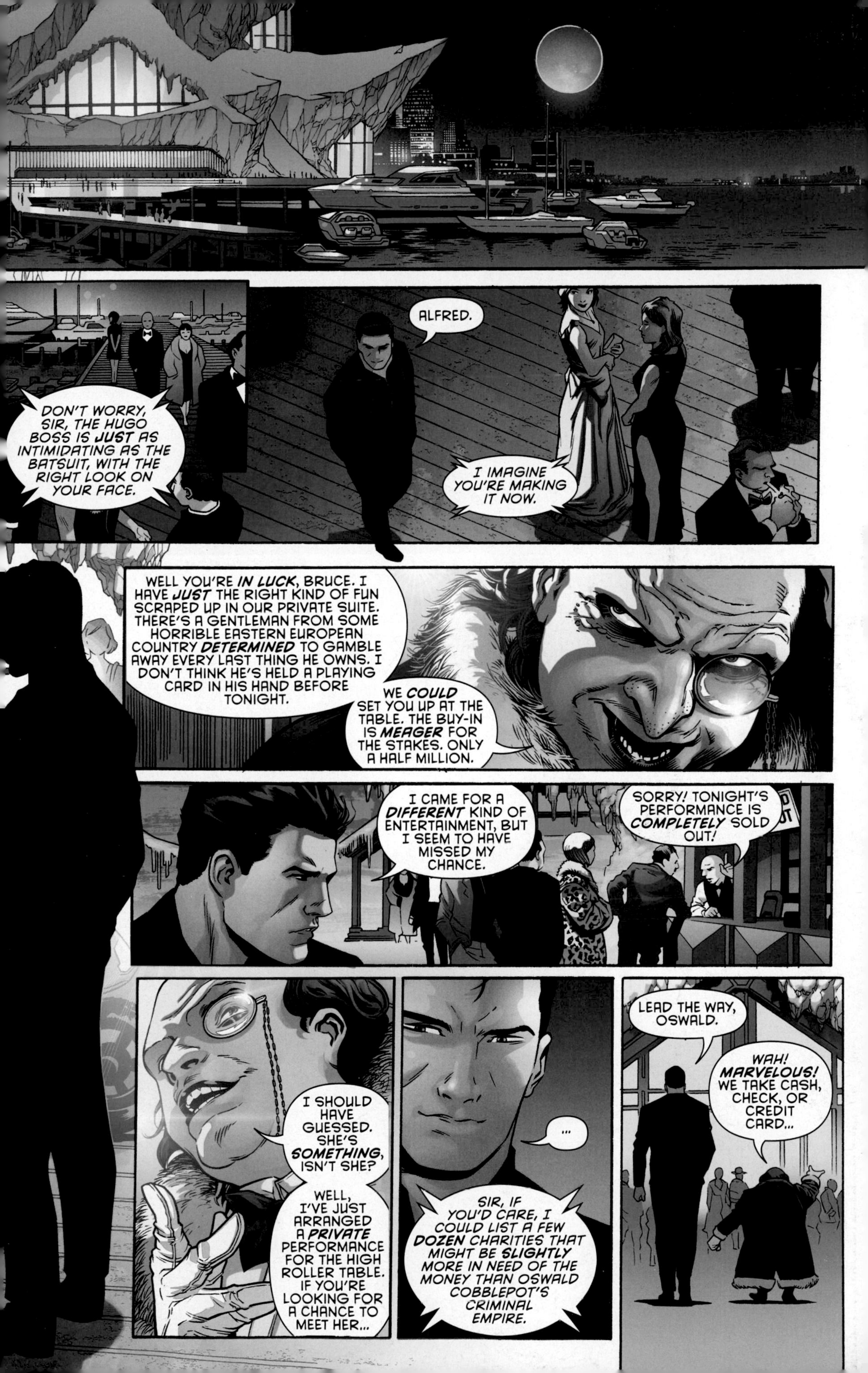

ALFRED.
DON'T WORRY, SIR, THE HUGO BOSS IS JUST AS INTIMIDATING AS THE BATSUIT, WITH THE RIGHT LOOK ON YOUR FACE.
I IMAGINE YOU'RE MAKING IT NOW.
WELL YOU'RE IN LUCK, BRUCE. I HAVE JUST THE RIGHT KIND OF FUN SCRAPED UP IN OUR PRIVATE SUITE. THERE'S A GENTLEMAN FROM SOME HORRIBLE EASTERN EUROPEAN COUNTRY DETERMINED TO GAMBLE AWAY EVERY LAST THING HE OWNS. I DON'T THINK HE'S HELD A PLAYING CARD IN HIS HAND BEFORE TONIGHT.
WE COULD SET YOU UP AT THE TABLE. THE BUY-IN IS MEAGER FOR THE STAKES. ONLY A HALF MILLION.
I CAME FOR A DIFFERENT KIND OF ENTERTAINMENT, BUT I SEEM TO HAVE MISSED MY CHANCE.
SORRY! TONIGHT'S PERFORMANCE IS COMPLETELY SOLD OUT!
I SHOULD HAVE GUESSED. SHE'S SOMETHING, ISN'T SHE?
WELL, I'VE JUST ARRANGED A PRIVATE PERFORMANCE FOR THE HIGH ROLLER TABLE. IF YOU'RE LOOKING FOR A CHANCE TO MEET HER...
...
SIR, IF YOU'D CARE, I COULD LIST A FEW DOZEN CHARITIES THAT MIGHT BE SLIGHTLY MORE IN NEED OF THE MONEY THAN OSWALD COBBLEPOT'S CRIMINAL EMPIRE.
LEAD THE WAY, OSWALD.
WAH! MARVELOUS! WE TAKE CASH, CHECK, OR CREDIT CARD...

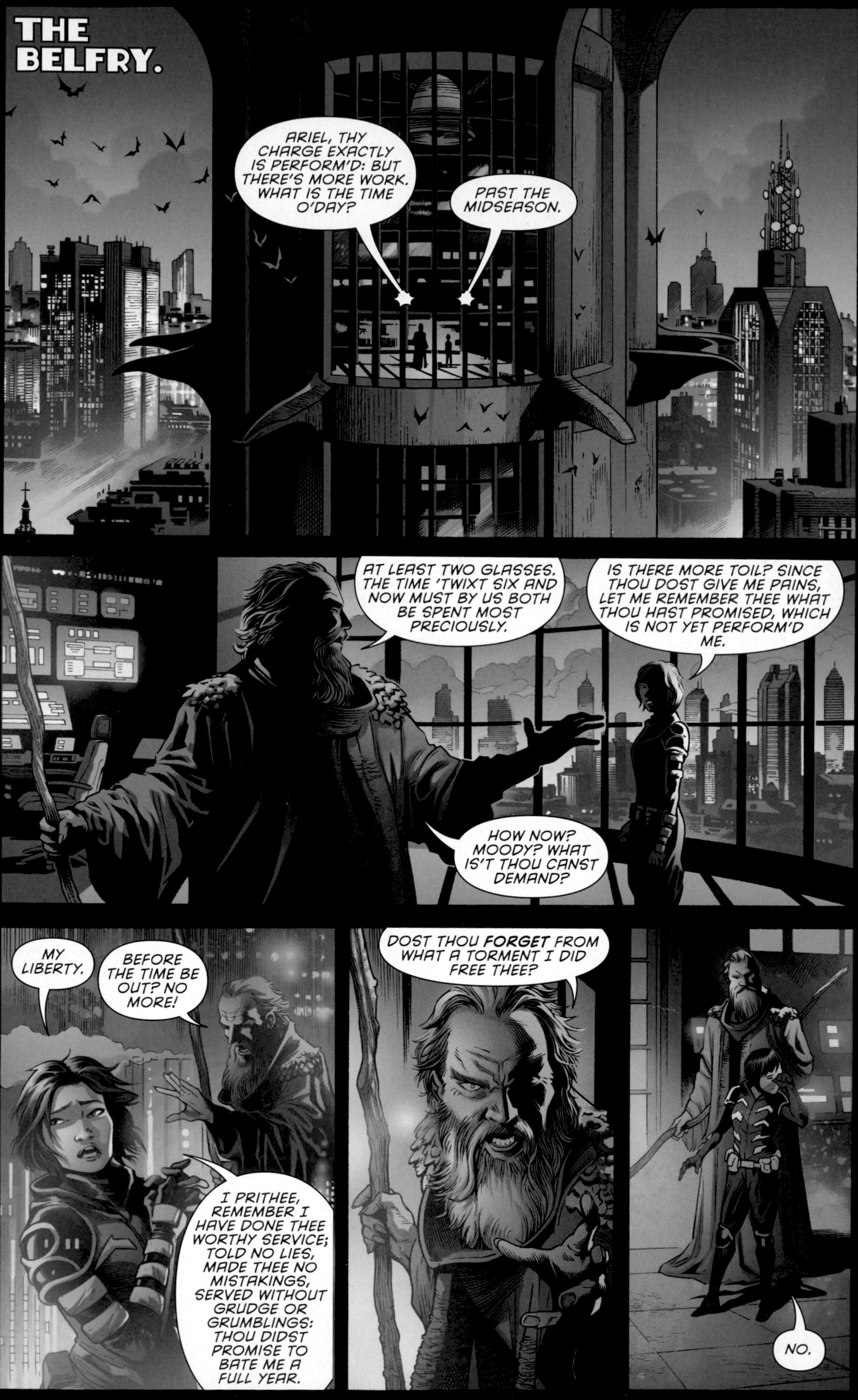
THE BELFRY.
ARIEL, THY CHARGE EXACTLY IS PERFORM'D: BUT THERE'S MORE WORK. WHAT IS THE TIME O'DAY?
PAST THE MIDSEASON.
AT LEAST TWO GLASSES. THE TIME 'TWIXT SIX AND NOW MUST BY US BOTH BE SPENT MOST PRECIOUSLY.
IS THERE MORE TOIL? SINCE THOU DOST GIVE ME PAINS, LET ME REMEMBER THEE WHAT THOU HAST PROMISED, WHICH IS NOT YET PERFORM'D ME.
HOW NOW? MOODY? WHAT IS'T THOU CANST DEMAND?
MY LIBERTY.
BEFORE THE TIME BE OUT? NO MORE!
I PRITHEE, REMEMBER I HAVE DONE THEE WORTHY SERVICE; TOLD NO LIES, MADE THEE NO MISTAKINGS, SERVED WITHOUT GRUDGE OR GRUMBLINGS: THOU DIDST PROMISE TO BATE ME A FULL YEAR.
DOST THOU **FORGET** FROM WHAT A TORMENT I DID FREE THEE?
NO.

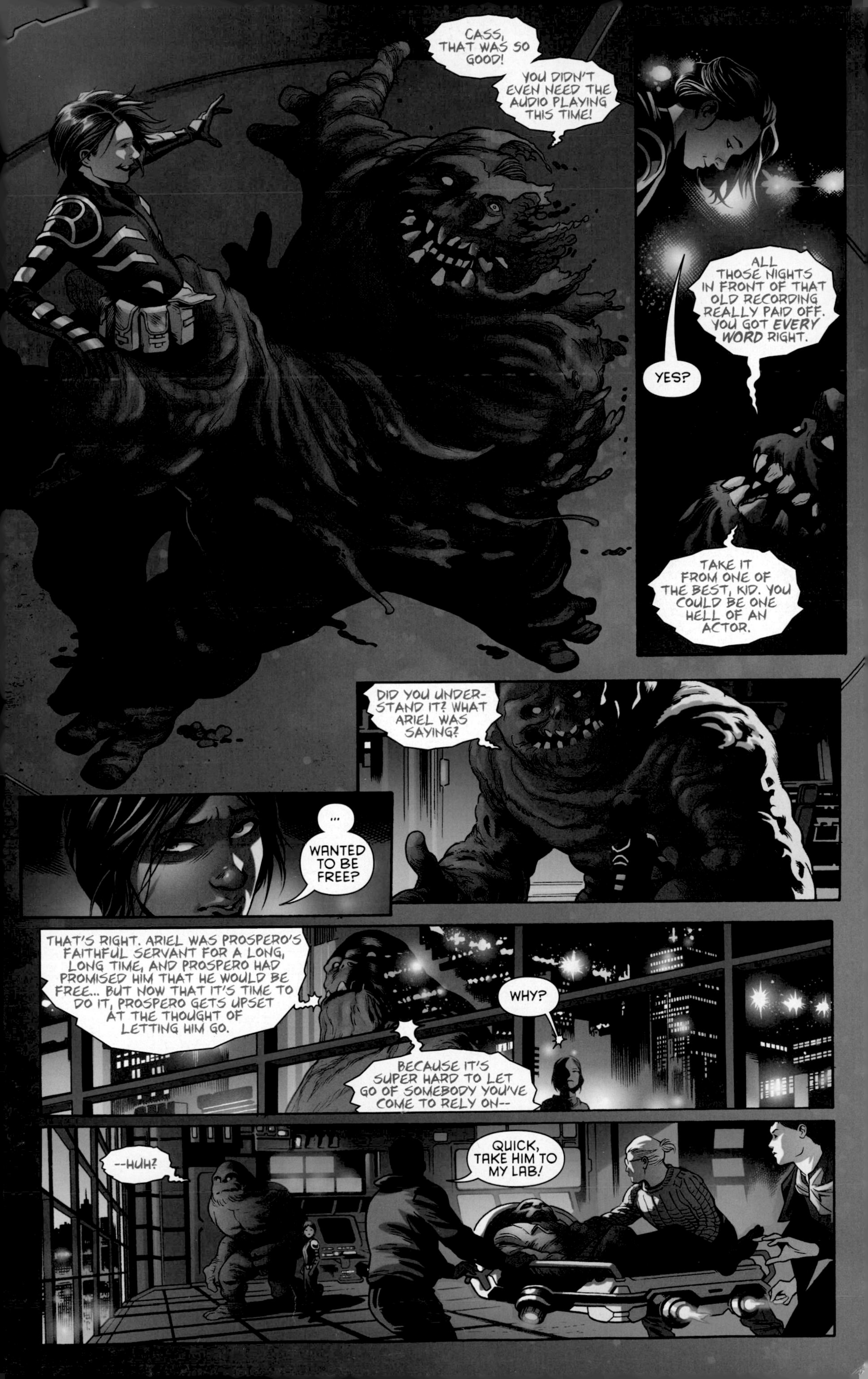
CASS, THAT WAS SO GOOD!
YOU DIDN'T EVEN NEED THE AUDIO PLAYING THIS TIME!
ALL THOSE NIGHTS IN FRONT OF THAT OLD RECORDING REALLY PAID OFF. YOU GOT EVERY WORD RIGHT.
YES?
TAKE IT FROM ONE OF THE BEST, KID. YOU COULD BE ONE HELL OF AN ACTOR.
DID YOU UNDER-STAND IT? WHAT ARIEL WAS SAYING?
...
WANTED TO BE FREE?
THAT'S RIGHT. ARIEL WAS PROSPERO'S FAITHFUL SERVANT FOR A LONG, LONG TIME, AND PROSPERO HAD PROMISED HIM THAT HE WOULD BE FREE... BUT NOW THAT IT'S TIME TO DO IT, PROSPERO GETS UPSET AT THE THOUGHT OF LETTING HIM GO.
WHY?
BECAUSE IT'S SUPER HARD TO LET GO OF SOMEBODY YOU'VE COME TO RELY ON--
--HUH?
QUICK, TAKE HIM TO MY LAB!

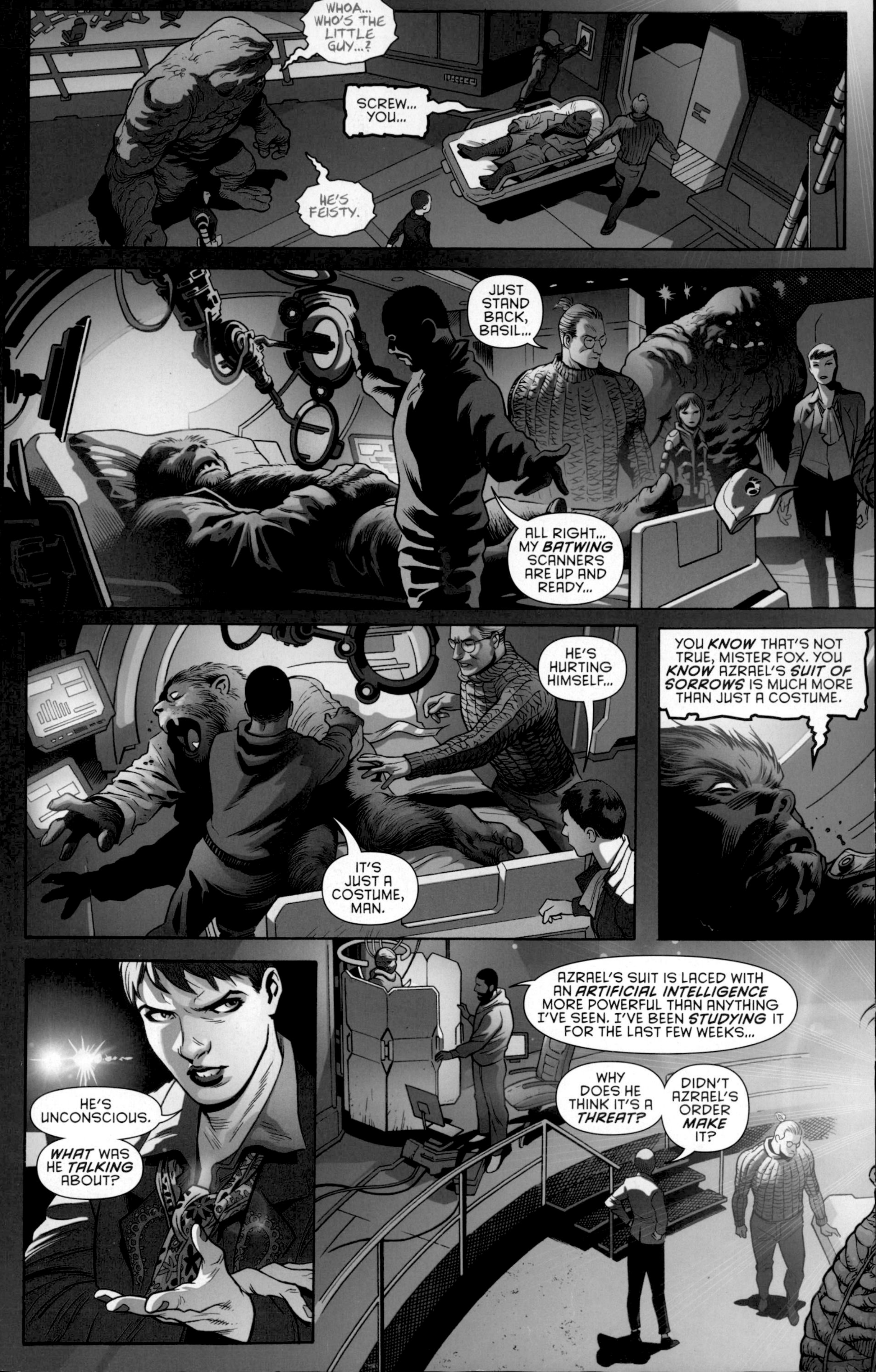
WHOA... WHO'S THE LITTLE GUY...?
SCREW... YOU...
HE'S FEISTY.
JUST STAND BACK, BASIL...
ALL RIGHT... MY BATWING SCANNERS ARE UP AND READY...
HE'S HURTING HIMSELF...
IT'S JUST A COSTUME, MAN.
YOU KNOW THAT'S NOT TRUE, MISTER FOX. YOU KNOW AZRAEL'S SUIT OF SORROWS IS MUCH MORE THAN JUST A COSTUME.
HE'S UNCONSCIOUS.
WHAT WAS HE TALKING ABOUT?
AZRAEL'S SUIT IS LACED WITH AN ARTIFICIAL INTELLIGENCE MORE POWERFUL THAN ANYTHING I'VE SEEN. I'VE BEEN STUDYING IT FOR THE LAST FEW WEEKS...
WHY DOES HE THINK IT'S A THREAT?
DIDN'T AZRAEL'S ORDER MAKE IT?

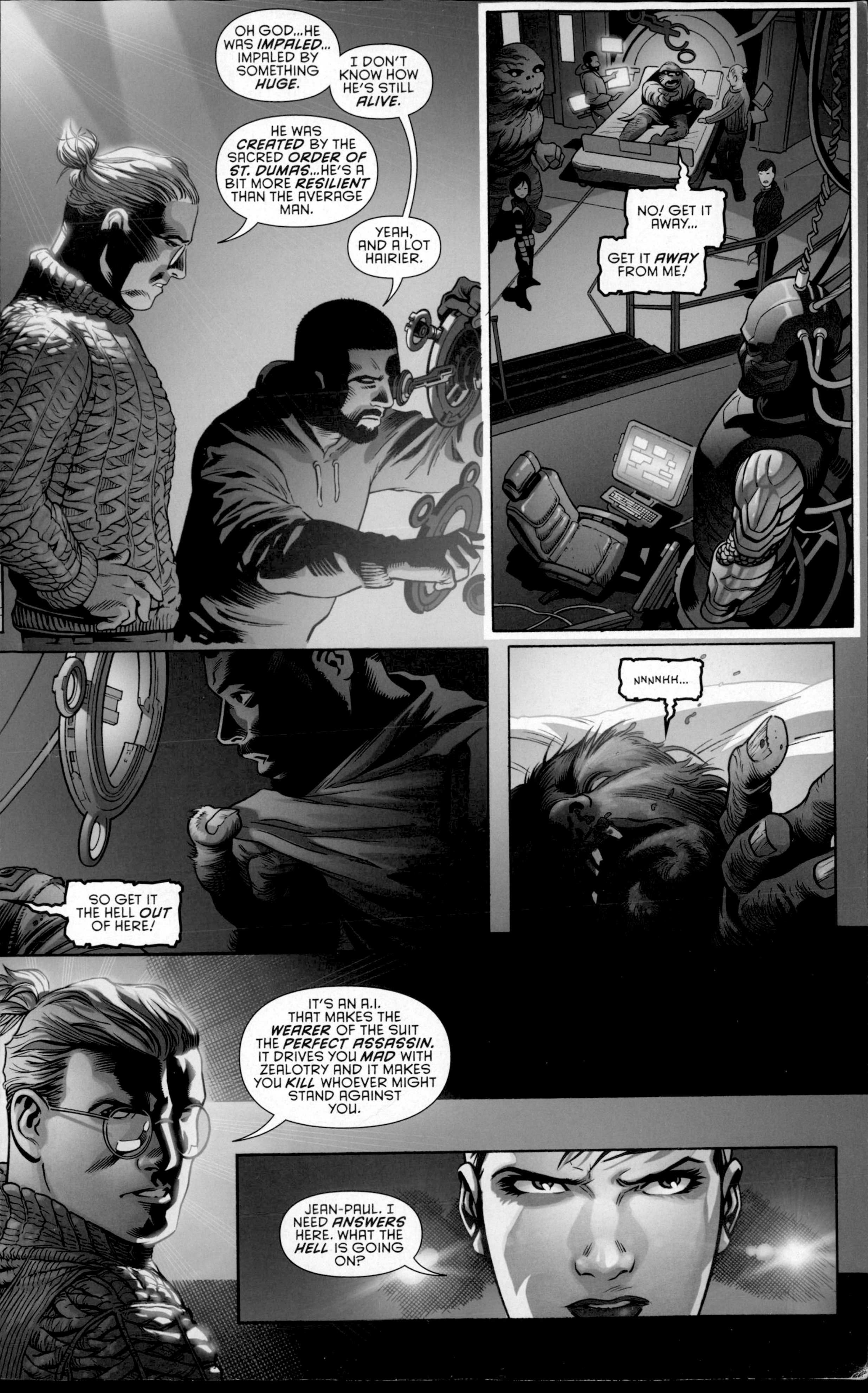
OH GOD...HE WAS IMPALED... IMPALED BY SOMETHING HUGE.
I DON'T KNOW HOW HE'S STILL ALIVE.
HE WAS CREATED BY THE SACRED ORDER OF ST. DUMAS...HE'S A BIT MORE RESILIENT THAN THE AVERAGE MAN.
YEAH, AND A LOT HAIRIER.
NO! GET IT AWAY...
GET IT AWAY FROM ME!
SO GET IT THE HELL OUT OF HERE!
NNNNHH...
IT'S AN A.I. THAT MAKES THE WEARER OF THE SUIT THE PERFECT ASSASSIN. IT DRIVES YOU MAD WITH ZEALOTRY AND IT MAKES YOU KILL WHOEVER MIGHT STAND AGAINST YOU.
JEAN-PAUL. I NEED ANSWERS HERE. WHAT THE HELL IS GOING ON?

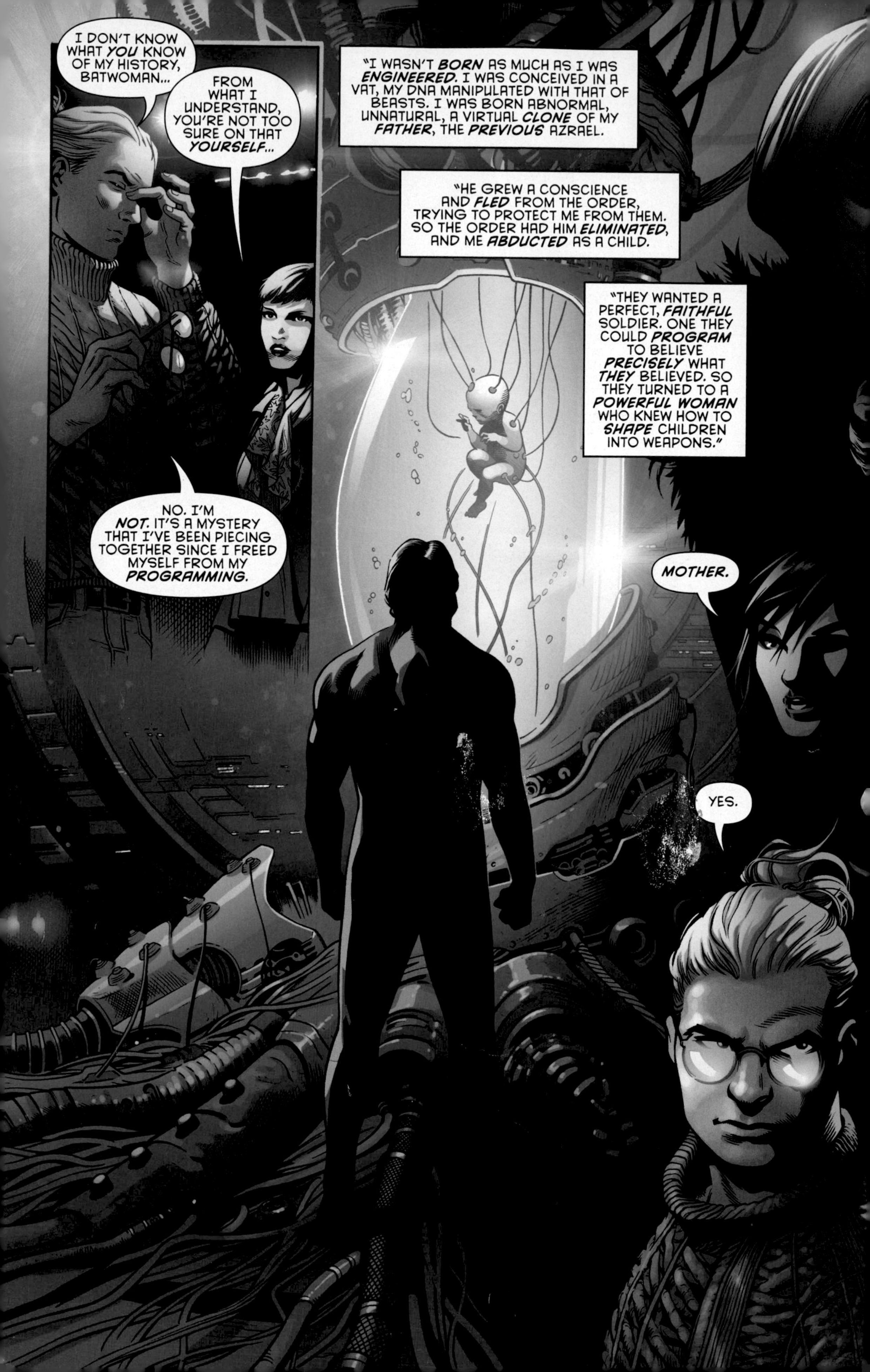

I DON'T KNOW WHAT *YOU* KNOW OF MY HISTORY, BATWOMAN...
FROM WHAT I UNDERSTAND, YOU'RE NOT TOO SURE ON THAT *YOURSELF*...
NO. I'M *NOT*. IT'S A MYSTERY THAT I'VE BEEN PIECING TOGETHER SINCE I FREED MYSELF FROM MY *PROGRAMMING*.
"I WASN'T *BORN* AS MUCH AS I WAS *ENGINEERED*. I WAS CONCEIVED IN A VAT, MY DNA MANIPULATED WITH THAT OF BEASTS. I WAS BORN ABNORMAL, UNNATURAL, A VIRTUAL *CLONE* OF MY *FATHER*, THE *PREVIOUS* AZRAEL.
"HE GREW A CONSCIENCE AND *FLED* FROM THE ORDER, TRYING TO PROTECT ME FROM THEM. SO THE ORDER HAD HIM *ELIMINATED*, AND ME *ABDUCTED* AS A CHILD.
"THEY WANTED A PERFECT, *FAITHFUL* SOLDIER. ONE THEY COULD *PROGRAM* TO BELIEVE *PRECISELY* WHAT *THEY* BELIEVED. SO THEY TURNED TO A *POWERFUL WOMAN* WHO KNEW HOW TO *SHAPE* CHILDREN INTO WEAPONS."
MOTHER.
YES.

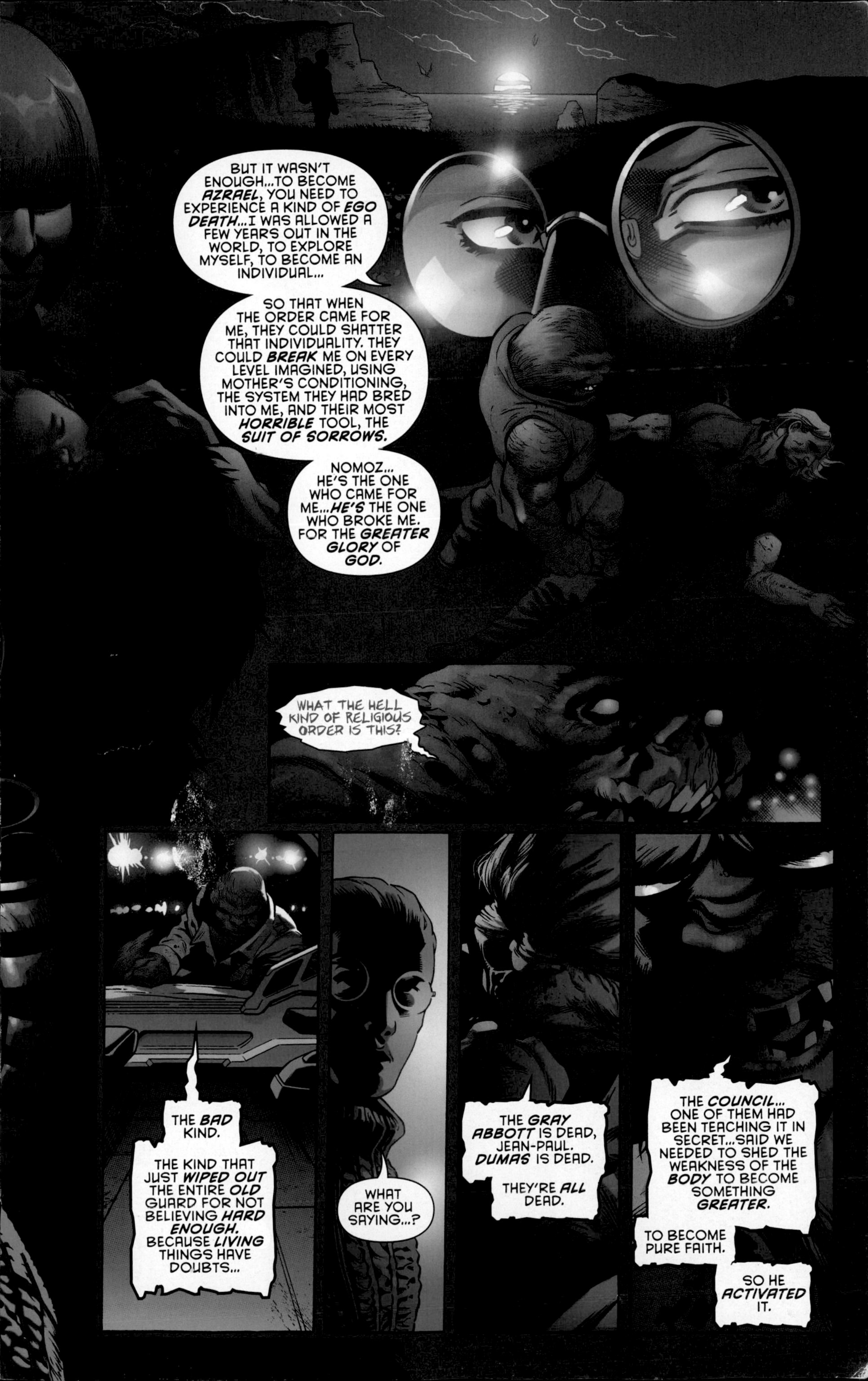
BUT IT WASN'T ENOUGH...TO BECOME AZRAEL, YOU NEED TO EXPERIENCE A KIND OF EGO DEATH...I WAS ALLOWED A FEW YEARS OUT IN THE WORLD, TO EXPLORE MYSELF, TO BECOME AN INDIVIDUAL...
SO THAT WHEN THE ORDER CAME FOR ME, THEY COULD SHATTER THAT INDIVIDUALITY. THEY COULD BREAK ME ON EVERY LEVEL IMAGINED, USING MOTHER'S CONDITIONING, THE SYSTEM THEY HAD BRED INTO ME, AND THEIR MOST HORRIBLE TOOL, THE SUIT OF SORROWS.
NOMOZ... HE'S THE ONE WHO CAME FOR ME...HE'S THE ONE WHO BROKE ME. FOR THE GREATER GLORY OF GOD.
WHAT THE HELL KIND OF RELIGIOUS ORDER IS THIS?
THE BAD KIND.
THE KIND THAT JUST WIPED OUT THE ENTIRE OLD GUARD FOR NOT BELIEVING HARD ENOUGH. BECAUSE LIVING THINGS HAVE DOUBTS...
WHAT ARE YOU SAYING...?
THE GRAY ABBOTT IS DEAD, JEAN-PAUL. DUMAS IS DEAD.
THEY'RE ALL DEAD.
THE COUNCIL... ONE OF THEM HAD BEEN TEACHING IT IN SECRET...SAID WE NEEDED TO SHED THE WEAKNESS OF THE BODY TO BECOME SOMETHING GREATER.
TO BECOME PURE FAITH.
SO HE ACTIVATED IT.

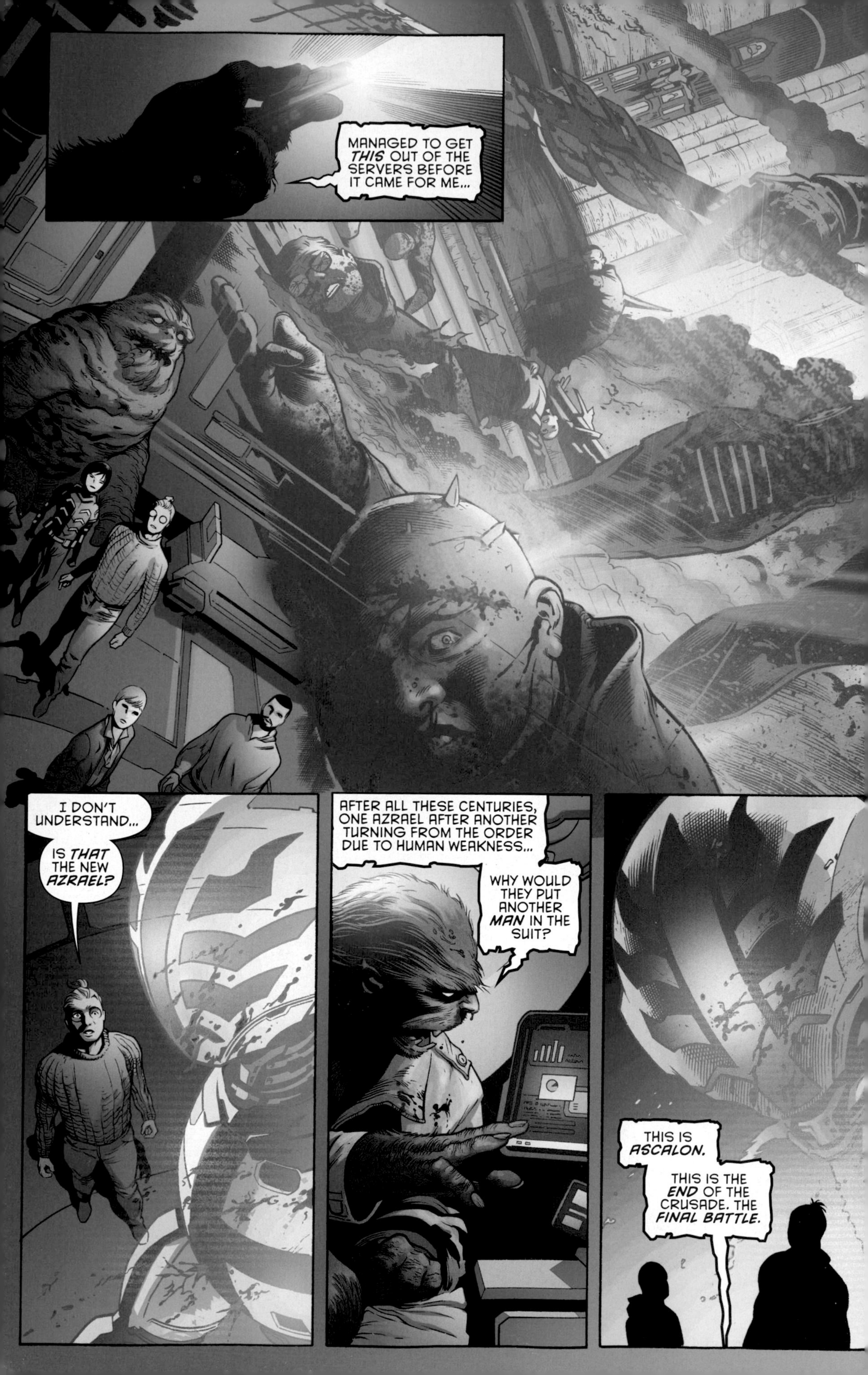
MANAGED TO GET *THIS* OUT OF THE SERVERS BEFORE IT CAME FOR ME...
I DON'T UNDERSTAND...
IS *THAT* THE NEW *AZRAEL?*
AFTER ALL THESE CENTURIES, ONE AZRAEL AFTER ANOTHER TURNING FROM THE ORDER DUE TO HUMAN WEAKNESS...
WHY WOULD THEY PUT ANOTHER *MAN* IN THE SUIT?
THIS IS *ASCALON.*
THIS IS THE *END* OF THE CRUSADE. THE *FINAL BATTLE.*

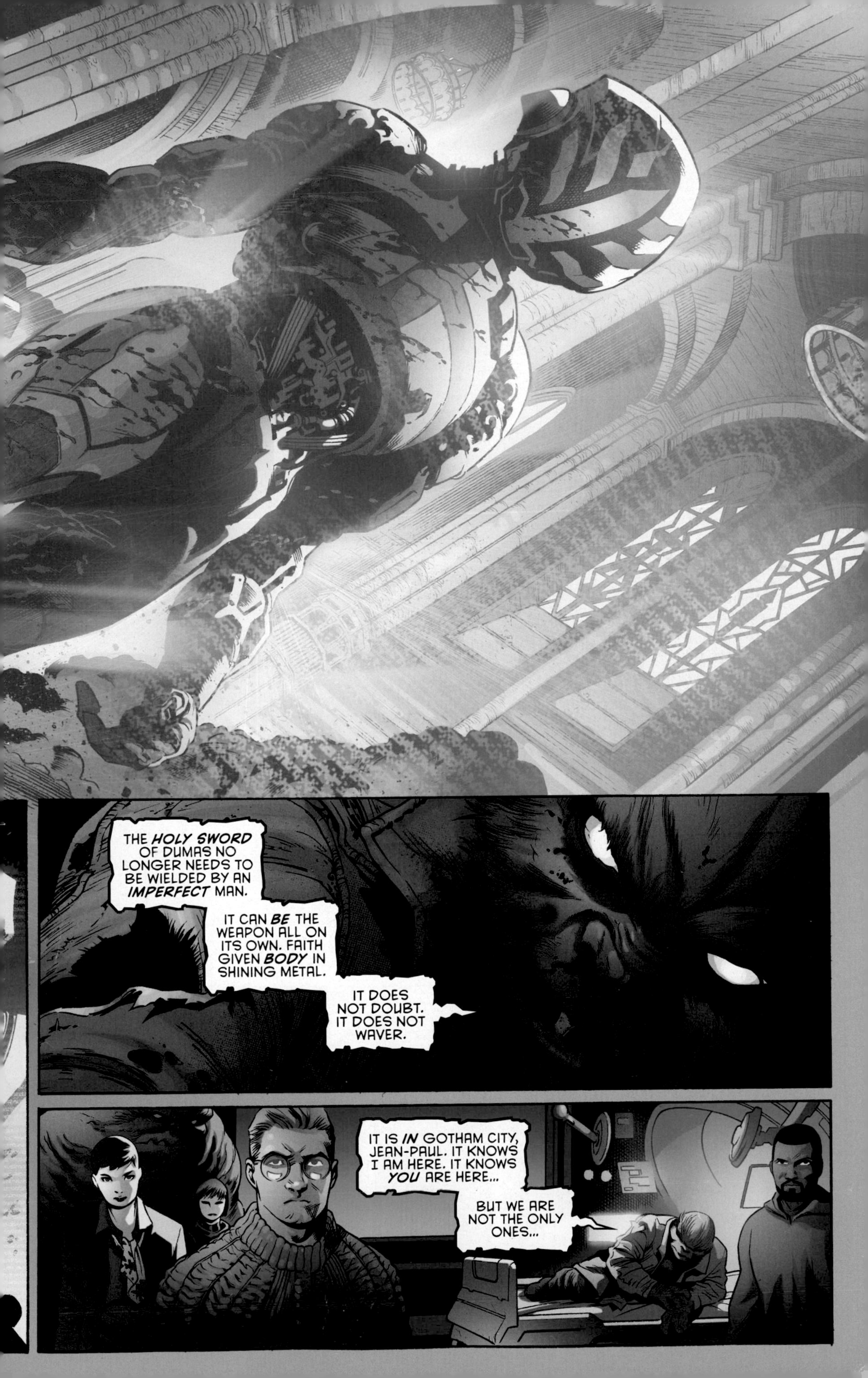

THE HOLY SWORD OF DUMAS NO LONGER NEEDS TO BE WIELDED BY AN IMPERFECT MAN.
IT CAN BE THE WEAPON ALL ON ITS OWN. FAITH GIVEN BODY IN SHINING METAL.
IT DOES NOT DOUBT. IT DOES NOT WAVER.
IT IS IN GOTHAM CITY, JEAN-PAUL. IT KNOWS I AM HERE. IT KNOWS YOU ARE HERE...
BUT WE ARE NOT THE ONLY ONES...

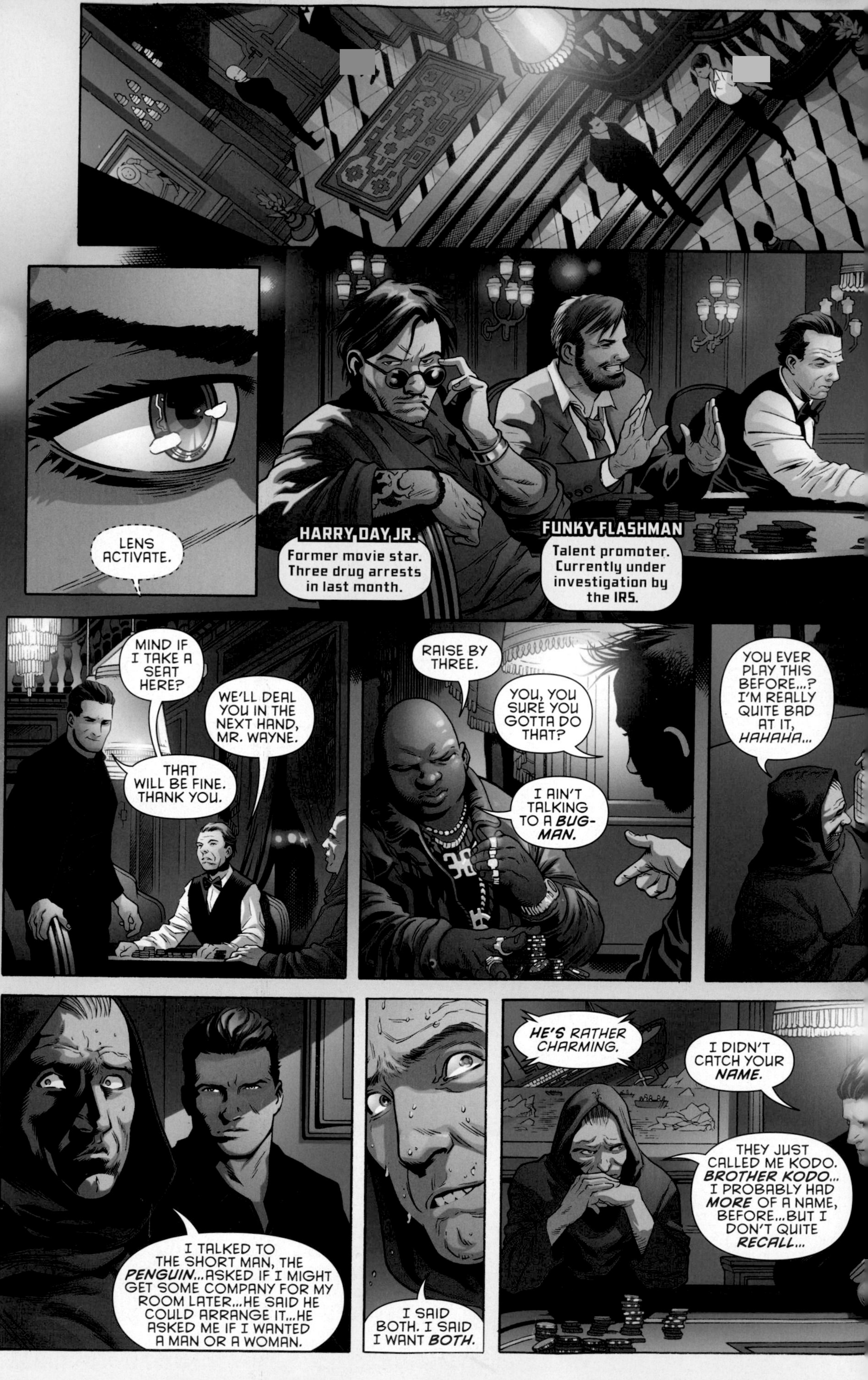
LENS ACTIVATE.
HARRY DAY JR.
Former movie star. Three drug arrests in last month.
FUNKY FLASHMAN
Talent promoter. Currently under investigation by the IRS.
MIND IF I TAKE A SEAT HERE?
WE'LL DEAL YOU IN THE NEXT HAND, MR. WAYNE.
THAT WILL BE FINE. THANK YOU.
RAISE BY THREE.
YOU, YOU SURE YOU GOTTA DO THAT?
I AIN'T TALKING TO A BUG-MAN.
YOU EVER PLAY THIS BEFORE...? I'M REALLY QUITE BAD AT IT, HAHAHA...
I TALKED TO THE SHORT MAN, THE PENGUIN...ASKED IF I MIGHT GET SOME COMPANY FOR MY ROOM LATER...HE SAID HE COULD ARRANGE IT...HE ASKED ME IF I WANTED A MAN OR A WOMAN.
I SAID BOTH. I SAID I WANT BOTH.
HE'S RATHER CHARMING.
I DIDN'T CATCH YOUR NAME.
THEY JUST CALLED ME KODO. BROTHER KODO... I PROBABLY HAD MORE OF A NAME, BEFORE...BUT I DON'T QUITE RECALL...

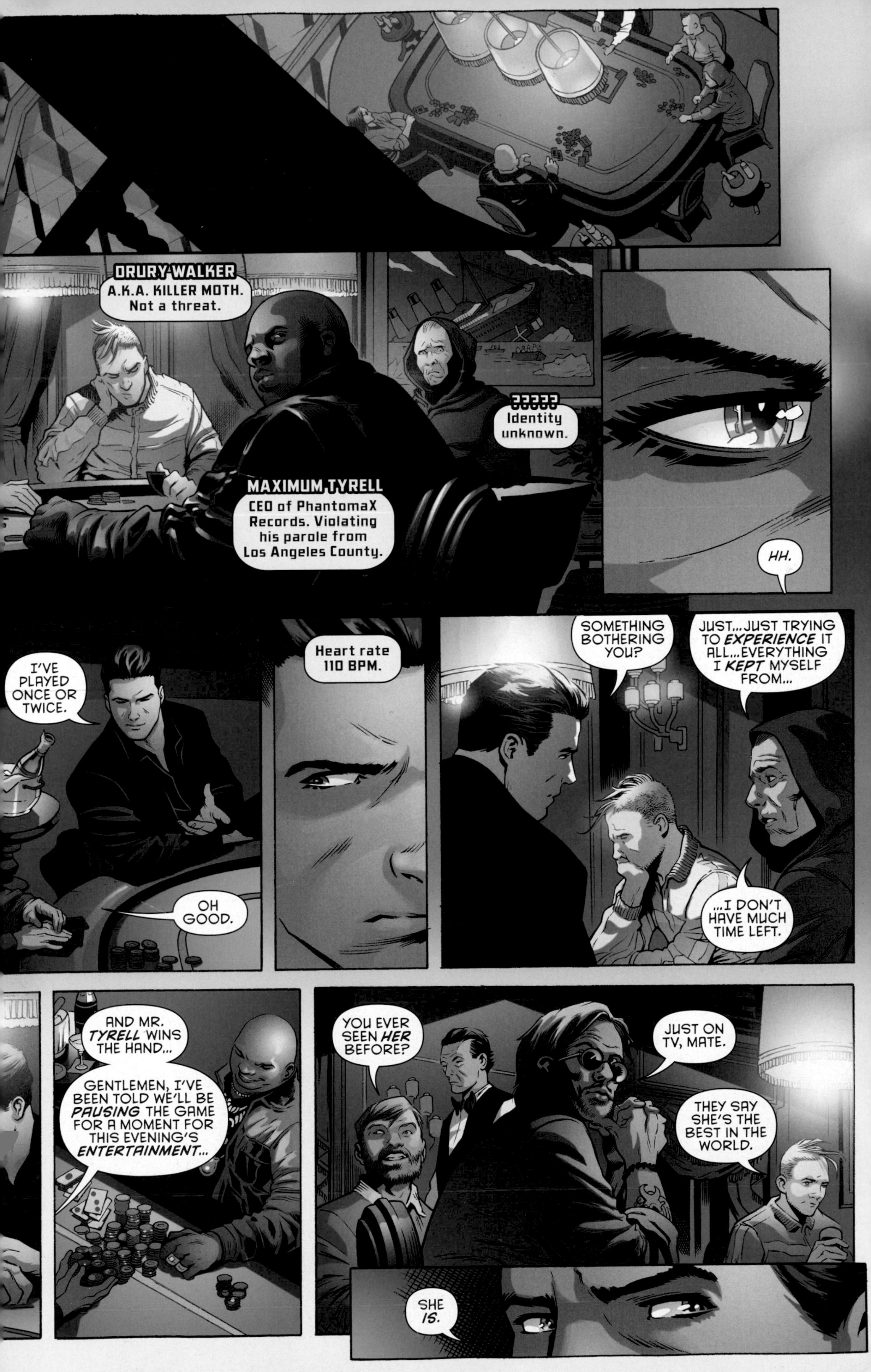

DRURY WALKER
A.K.A. KILLER MOTH. Not a threat.
MAXIMUM TYRELL
CEO of PhantomaX Records. Violating his parole from Los Angeles County.
Identity unknown.
HH.
I'VE PLAYED ONCE OR TWICE.
OH GOOD.
Heart rate 110 BPM.
SOMETHING BOTHERING YOU?
JUST... JUST TRYING TO EXPERIENCE IT ALL... EVERYTHING I KEPT MYSELF FROM...
...I DON'T HAVE MUCH TIME LEFT.
AND MR. TYRELL WINS THE HAND...
GENTLEMEN, I'VE BEEN TOLD WE'LL BE PAUSING THE GAME FOR A MOMENT FOR THIS EVENING'S ENTERTAINMENT...
YOU EVER SEEN HER BEFORE?
JUST ON TV, MATE.
THEY SAY SHE'S THE BEST IN THE WORLD.
SHE IS.

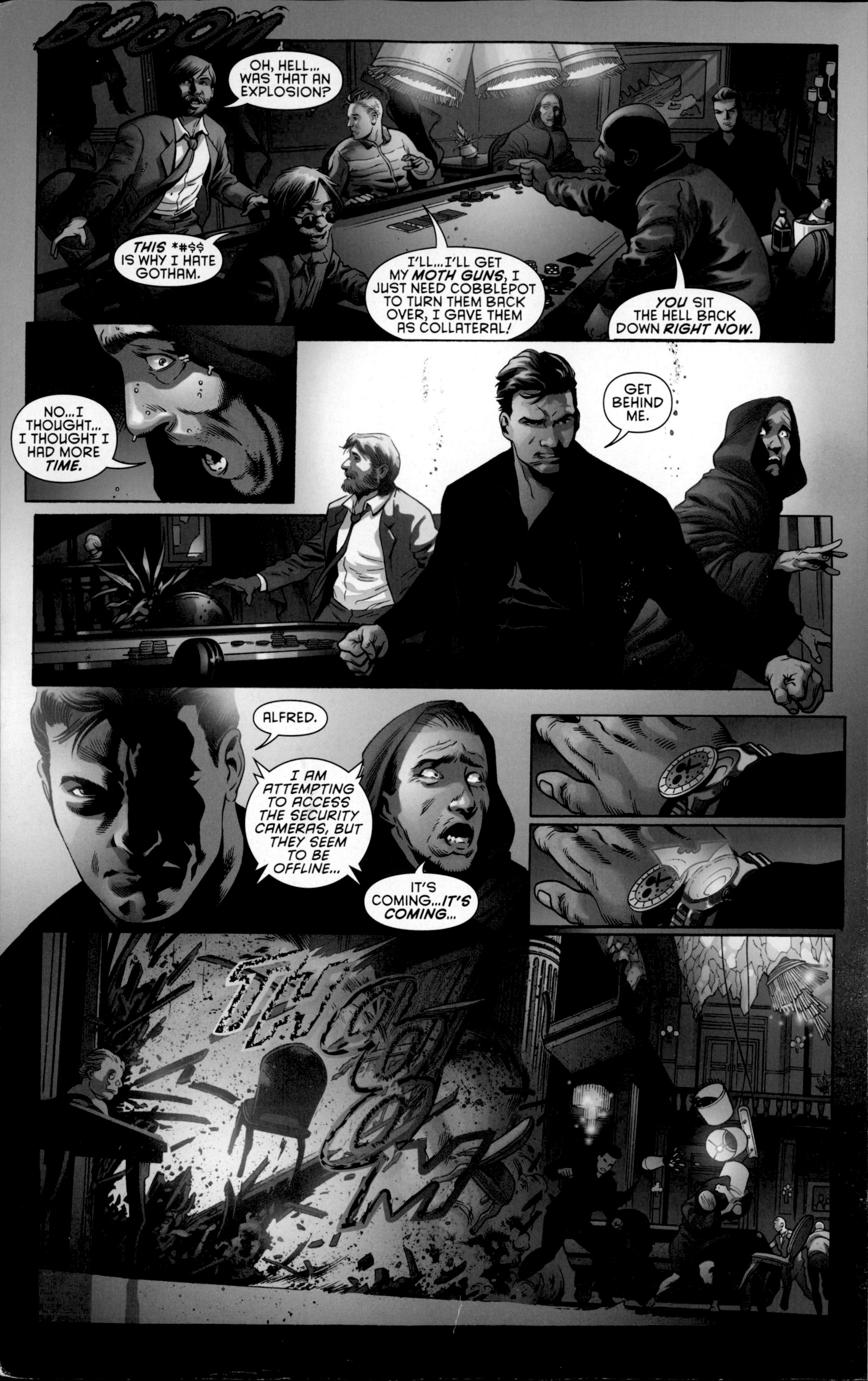
BOOOM
OH, HELL... WAS THAT AN EXPLOSION?
THIS *#$$ IS WHY I HATE GOTHAM.
I'LL...I'LL GET MY MOTH GUNS, I JUST NEED COBBLEPOT TO TURN THEM BACK OVER, I GAVE THEM AS COLLATERAL!
YOU SIT THE HELL BACK DOWN RIGHT NOW.
NO...I THOUGHT... I THOUGHT I HAD MORE TIME.
GET BEHIND ME.
ALFRED.
I AM ATTEMPTING TO ACCESS THE SECURITY CAMERAS, BUT THEY SEEM TO BE OFFLINE...
IT'S COMING...IT'S COMING...

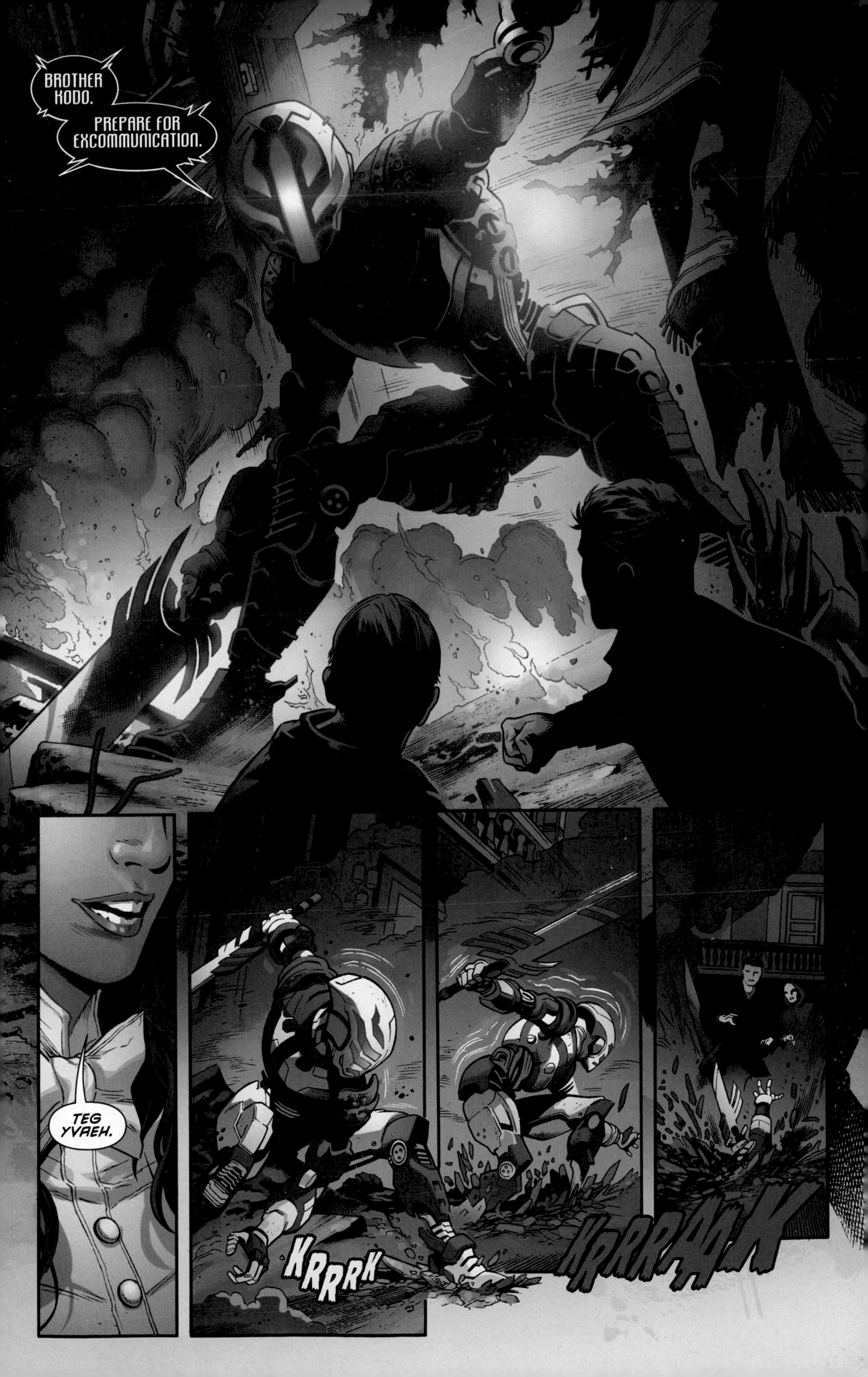
BROTHER KODO.
PREPARE FOR EXCOMMUNICATION.
TEG YVAEH.
KRRRK
KRRRAAK

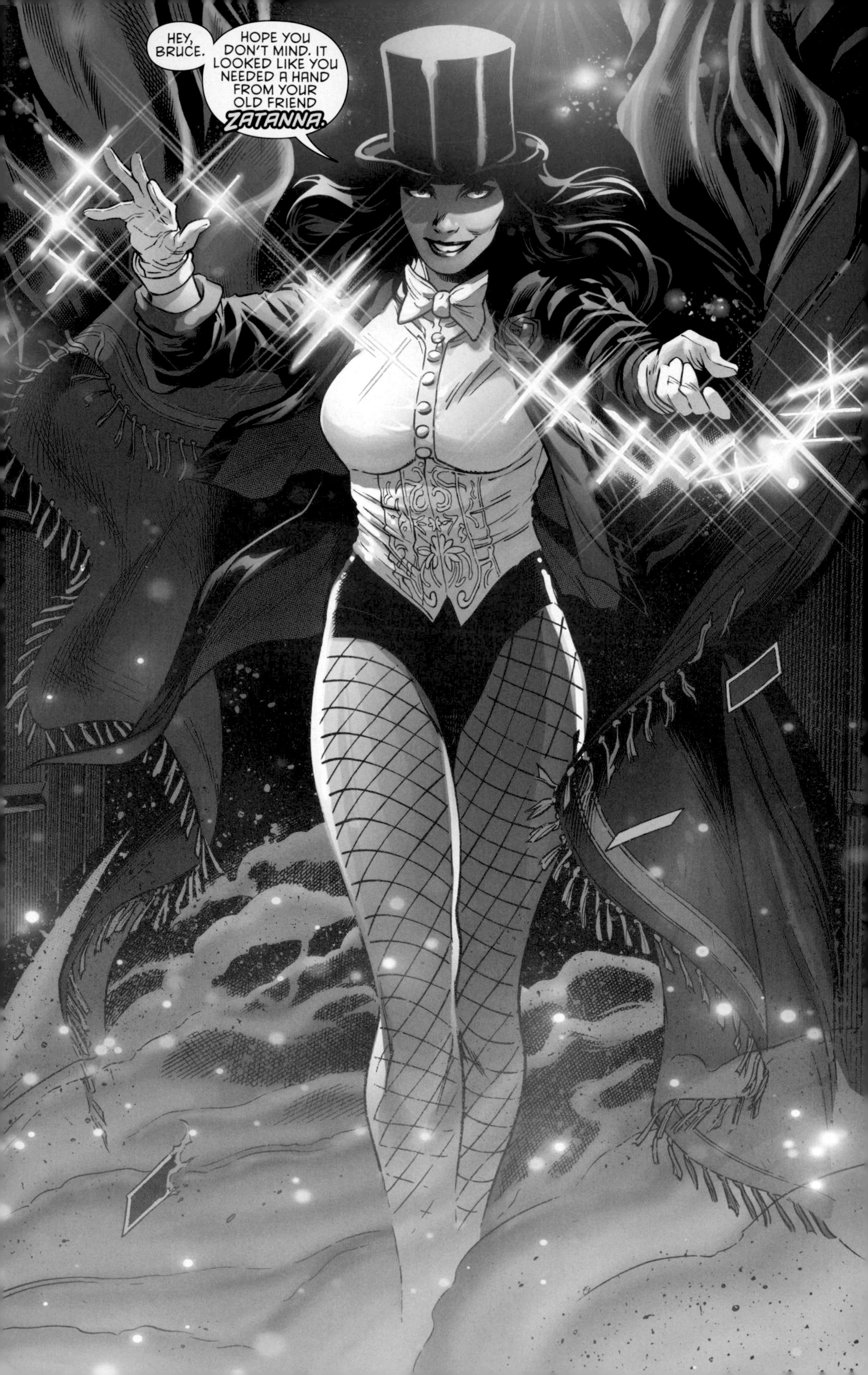
HEY, BRUCE.
HOPE YOU DON'T MIND. IT LOOKED LIKE YOU NEEDED A HAND FROM YOUR OLD FRIEND ZATANNA.

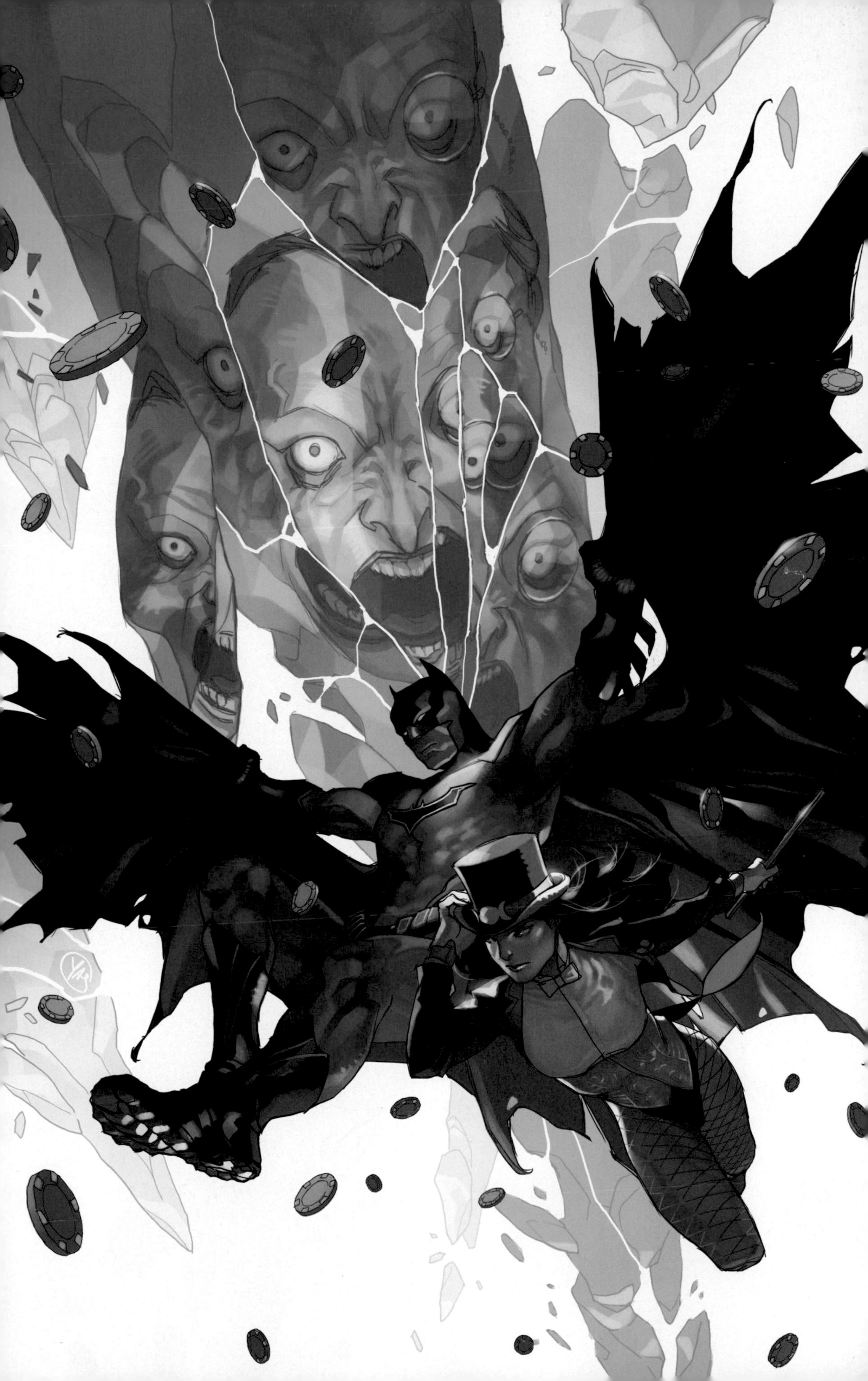

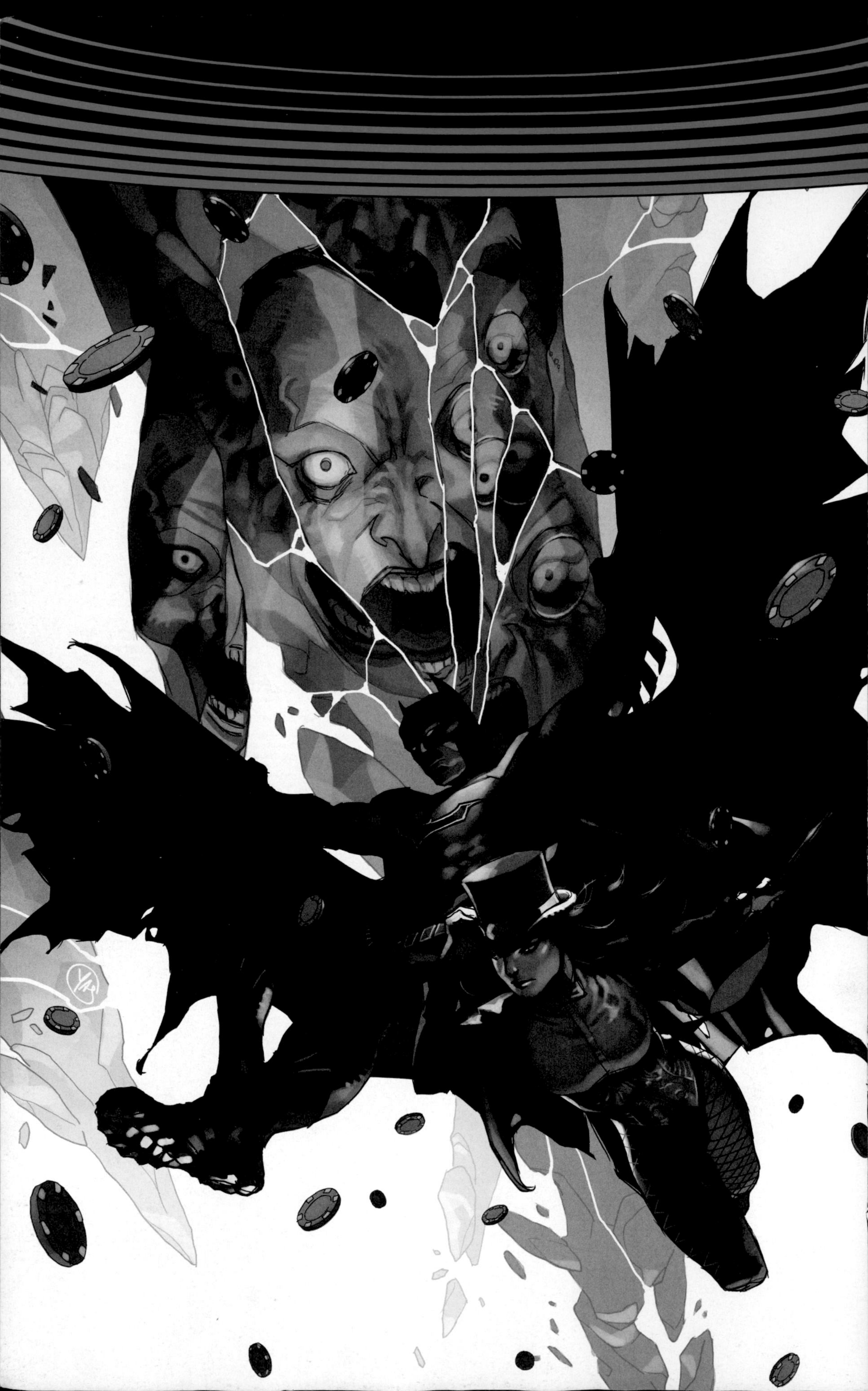

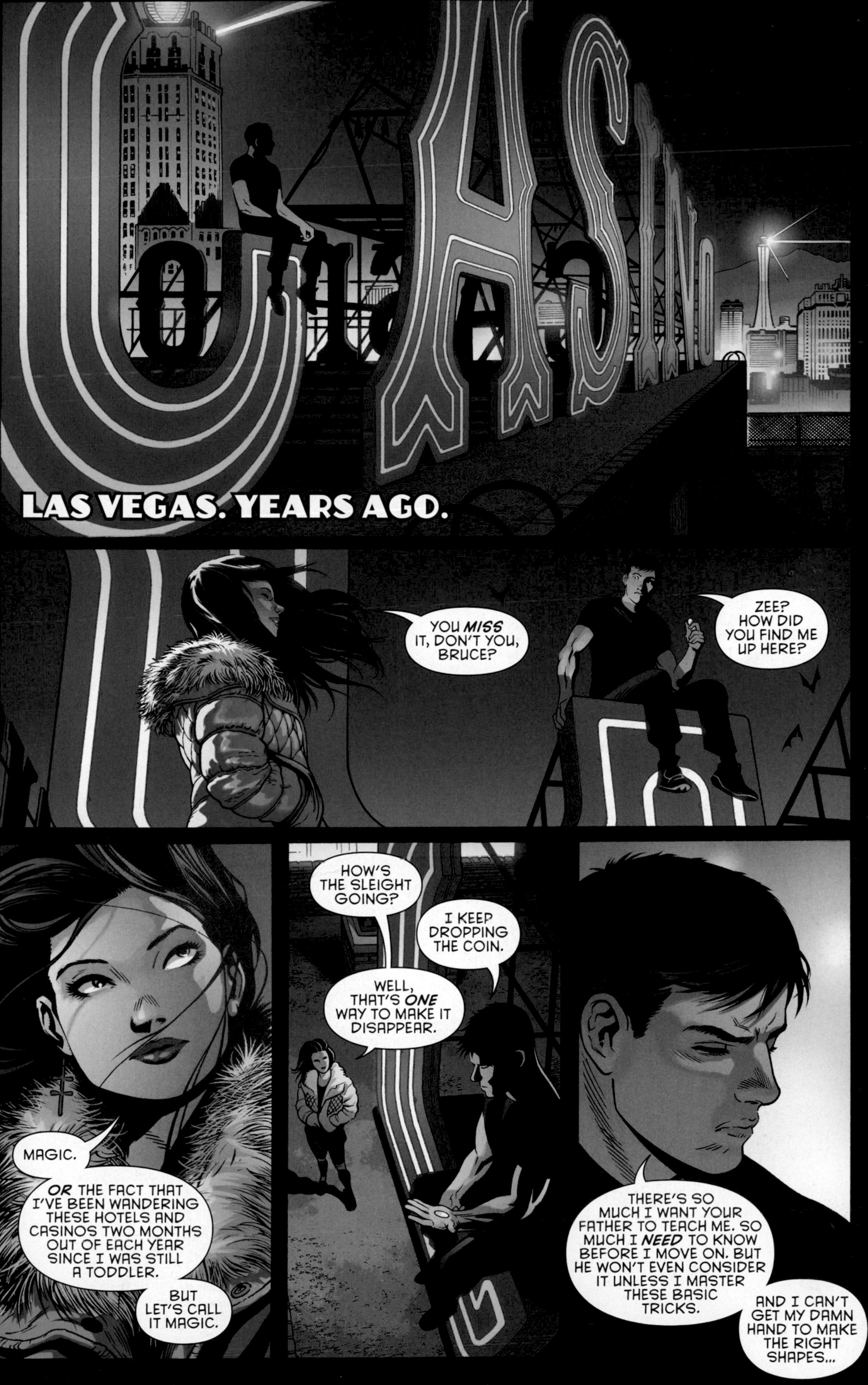
LAS VEGAS. YEARS AGO.
YOU *MISS* IT, DON'T YOU, BRUCE?
ZEE? HOW DID YOU FIND ME UP HERE?
MAGIC.
OR THE FACT THAT I'VE BEEN WANDERING THESE HOTELS AND CASINOS TWO MONTHS OUT OF EACH YEAR SINCE I WAS STILL A TODDLER.
BUT LET'S CALL IT MAGIC.
HOW'S THE SLEIGHT GOING?
I KEEP DROPPING THE COIN.
WELL, THAT'S *ONE* WAY TO MAKE IT DISAPPEAR.
THERE'S SO MUCH I WANT YOUR FATHER TO TEACH ME. SO MUCH I *NEED* TO KNOW BEFORE I MOVE ON. BUT HE WON'T EVEN CONSIDER IT UNLESS I MASTER THESE BASIC TRICKS.
AND I CAN'T GET MY DAMN HAND TO MAKE THE RIGHT SHAPES...

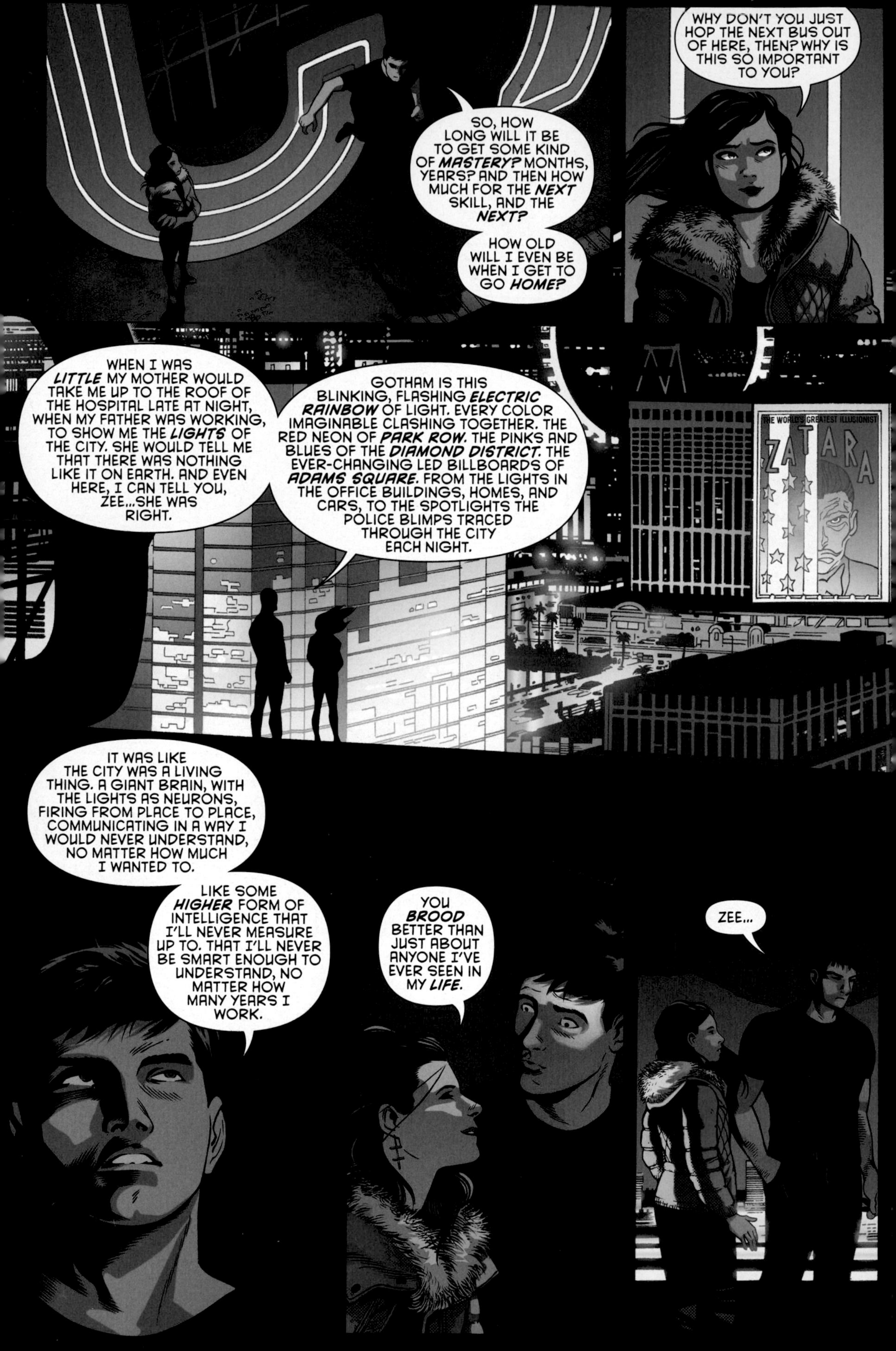
SO, HOW LONG WILL IT BE TO GET SOME KIND OF MASTERY? MONTHS, YEARS? AND THEN HOW MUCH FOR THE NEXT SKILL, AND THE NEXT?
HOW OLD WILL I EVEN BE WHEN I GET TO GO HOME?
WHY DON'T YOU JUST HOP THE NEXT BUS OUT OF HERE, THEN? WHY IS THIS SO IMPORTANT TO YOU?
WHEN I WAS LITTLE MY MOTHER WOULD TAKE ME UP TO THE ROOF OF THE HOSPITAL LATE AT NIGHT, WHEN MY FATHER WAS WORKING, TO SHOW ME THE LIGHTS OF THE CITY. SHE WOULD TELL ME THAT THERE WAS NOTHING LIKE IT ON EARTH. AND EVEN HERE, I CAN TELL YOU, ZEE...SHE WAS RIGHT.
GOTHAM IS THIS BLINKING, FLASHING ELECTRIC RAINBOW OF LIGHT. EVERY COLOR IMAGINABLE CLASHING TOGETHER. THE RED NEON OF PARK ROW. THE PINKS AND BLUES OF THE DIAMOND DISTRICT. THE EVER-CHANGING LED BILLBOARDS OF ADAMS SQUARE. FROM THE LIGHTS IN THE OFFICE BUILDINGS, HOMES, AND CARS, TO THE SPOTLIGHTS THE POLICE BLIMPS TRACED THROUGH THE CITY EACH NIGHT.
THE WORLD'S GREATEST ILLUSIONIST
ZATARA
IT WAS LIKE THE CITY WAS A LIVING THING. A GIANT BRAIN, WITH THE LIGHTS AS NEURONS, FIRING FROM PLACE TO PLACE, COMMUNICATING IN A WAY I WOULD NEVER UNDERSTAND, NO MATTER HOW MUCH I WANTED TO.
LIKE SOME HIGHER FORM OF INTELLIGENCE THAT I'LL NEVER MEASURE UP TO. THAT I'LL NEVER BE SMART ENOUGH TO UNDERSTAND, NO MATTER HOW MANY YEARS I WORK.
YOU BROOD BETTER THAN JUST ABOUT ANYONE I'VE EVER SEEN IN MY LIFE.
ZEE...

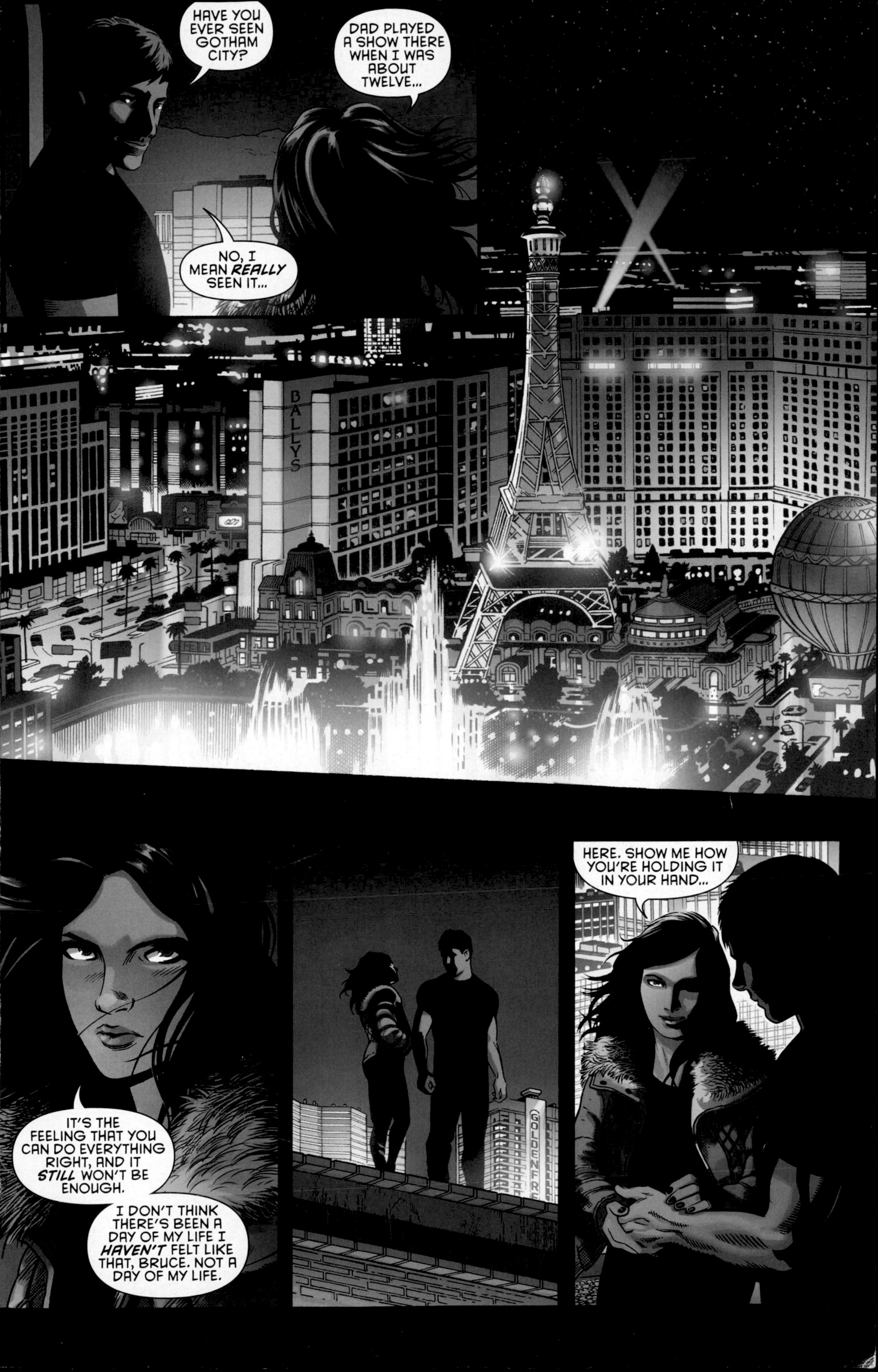
HAVE YOU EVER SEEN GOTHAM CITY?
DAD PLAYED A SHOW THERE WHEN I WAS ABOUT TWELVE...
NO, I MEAN *REALLY* SEEN IT...
BALLYS
IT'S THE FEELING THAT YOU CAN DO EVERYTHING RIGHT, AND IT *STILL* WON'T BE ENOUGH.
I DON'T THINK THERE'S BEEN A DAY OF MY LIFE I *HAVEN'T* FELT LIKE THAT, BRUCE. NOT A DAY OF MY LIFE.
HERE. SHOW ME HOW YOU'RE HOLDING IT IN YOUR HAND...

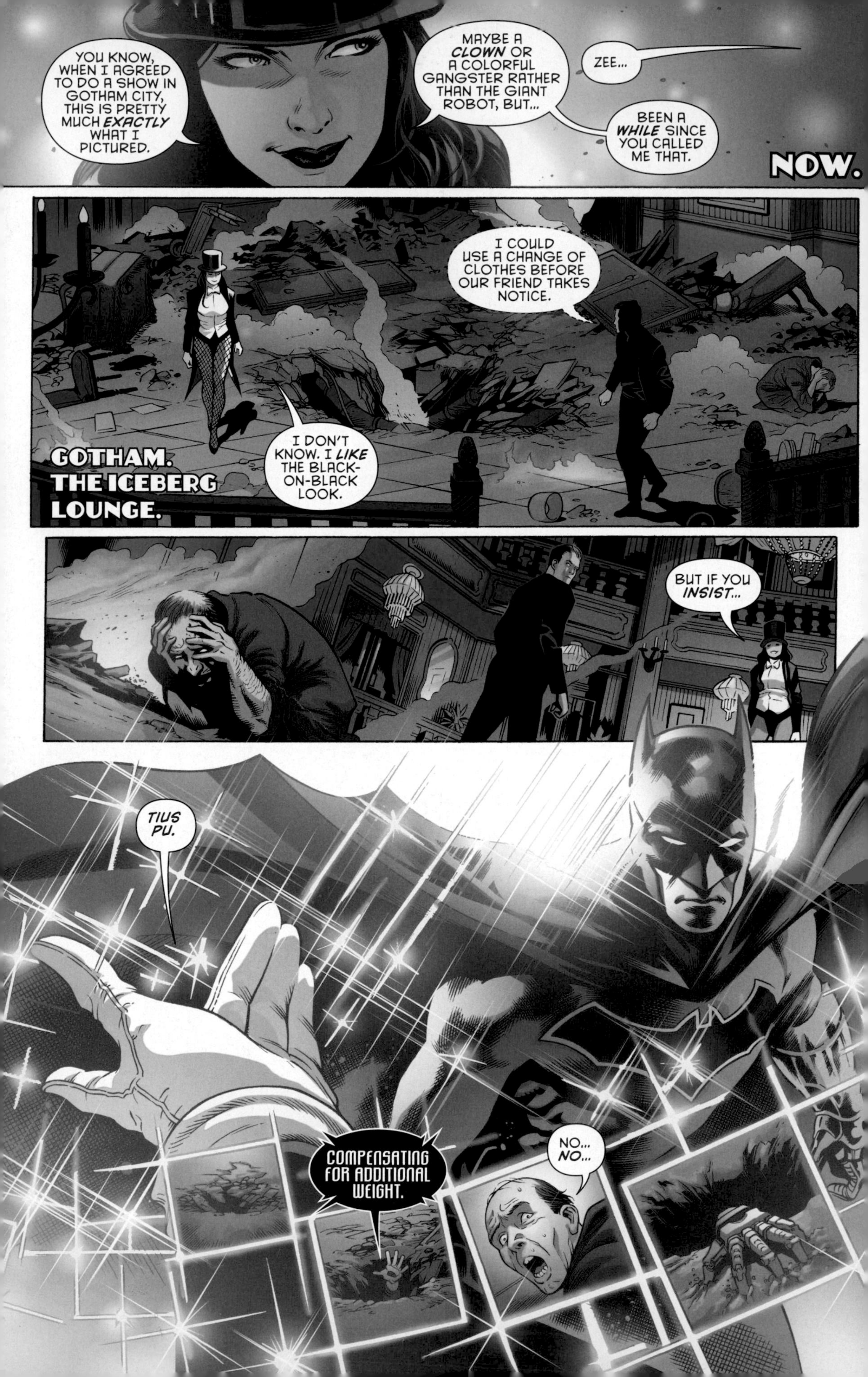
YOU KNOW, WHEN I AGREED TO DO A SHOW IN GOTHAM CITY, THIS IS PRETTY MUCH *EXACTLY* WHAT I PICTURED.
MAYBE A *CLOWN* OR A COLORFUL GANGSTER RATHER THAN THE GIANT ROBOT, BUT...
ZEE...
BEEN A *WHILE* SINCE YOU CALLED ME THAT.
NOW.
GOTHAM. THE ICEBERG LOUNGE.
I COULD USE A CHANGE OF CLOTHES BEFORE OUR FRIEND TAKES NOTICE.
I DON'T KNOW. I *LIKE* THE BLACK-ON-BLACK LOOK.
BUT IF YOU *INSIST*...
TIUS PU.
COMPENSATING FOR ADDITIONAL WEIGHT.
NO... *NO*...

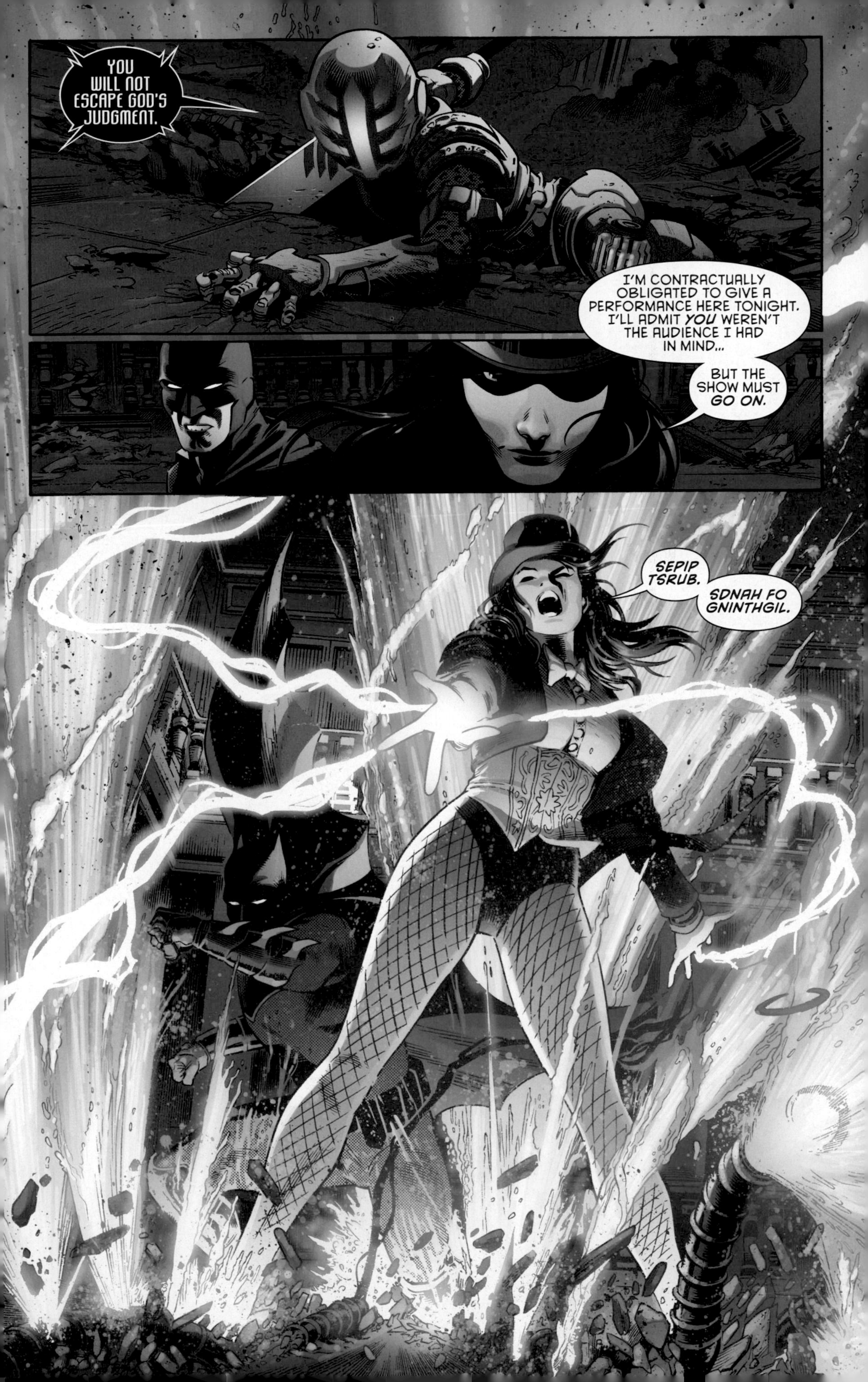
YOU WILL NOT ESCAPE GOD'S JUDGMENT.
I'M CONTRACTUALLY OBLIGATED TO GIVE A PERFORMANCE HERE TONIGHT. I'LL ADMIT *YOU* WEREN'T THE AUDIENCE I HAD IN MIND...
BUT THE SHOW MUST *GO ON.*
SEPIP TSRUB.
SDNAH FO GNINTHGIL.

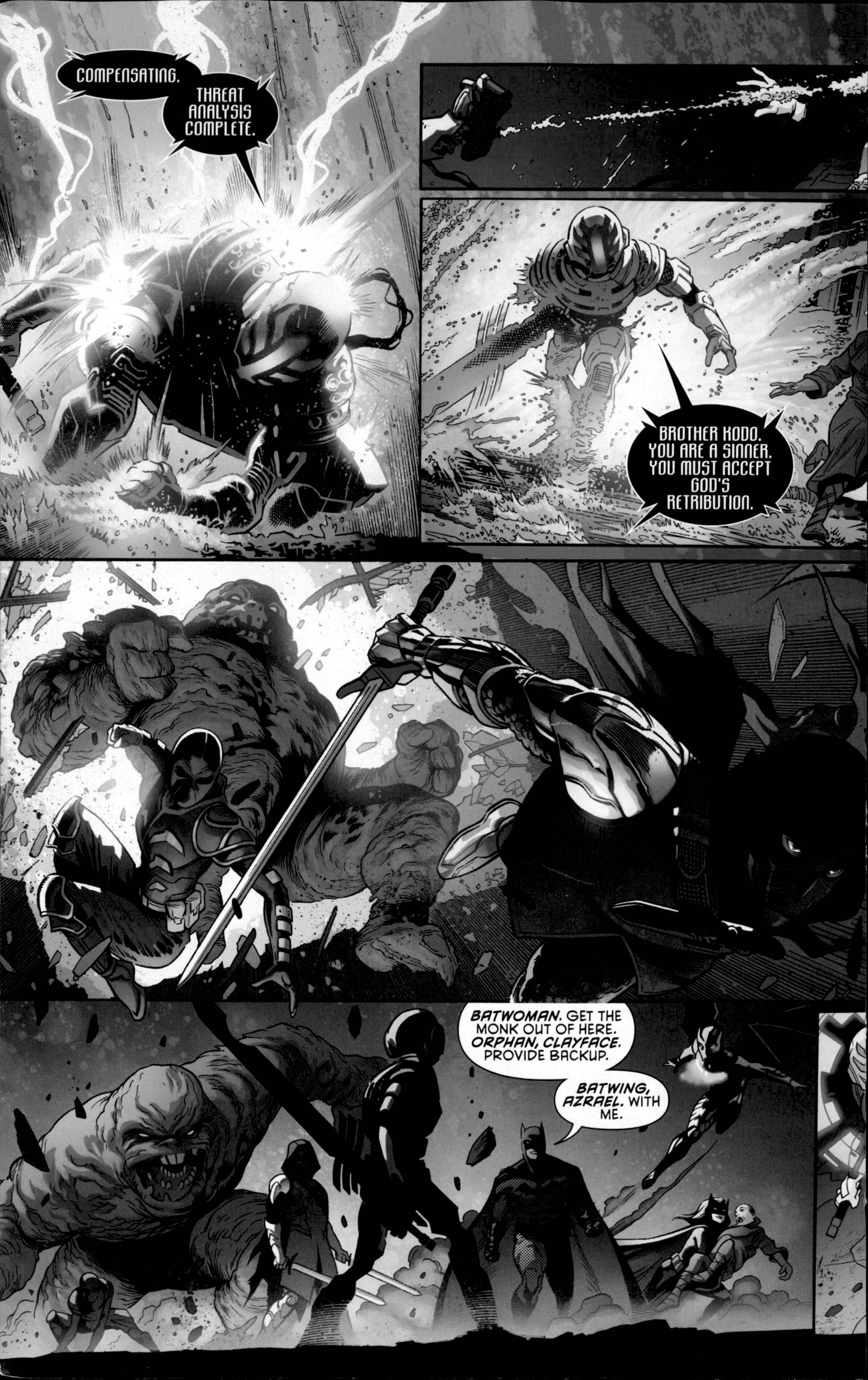
COMPENSATING.
THREAT ANALYSIS COMPLETE.
BROTHER KODO. YOU ARE A SINNER. YOU MUST ACCEPT GOD'S RETRIBUTION.
BATWOMAN. GET THE MONK OUT OF HERE. *ORPHAN, CLAYFACE.* PROVIDE BACKUP.
BATWING, AZRAEL. WITH ME.

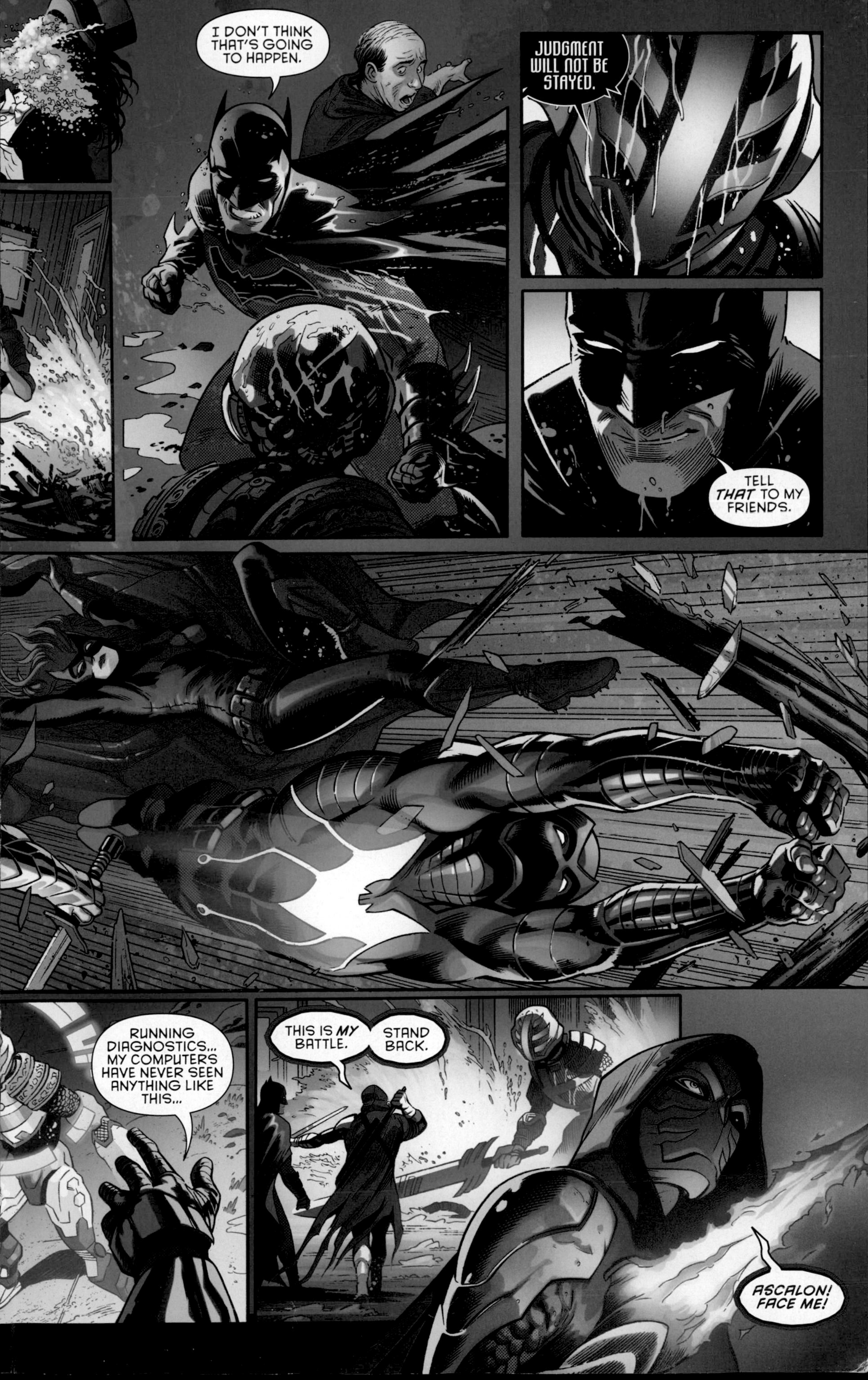
I DON'T THINK THAT'S GOING TO HAPPEN.
JUDGMENT WILL NOT BE STAYED.
TELL *THAT* TO MY FRIENDS.
RUNNING DIAGNOSTICS... MY COMPUTERS HAVE NEVER SEEN ANYTHING LIKE THIS...
THIS IS *MY* BATTLE.
STAND BACK.
ASCALON! FACE ME!

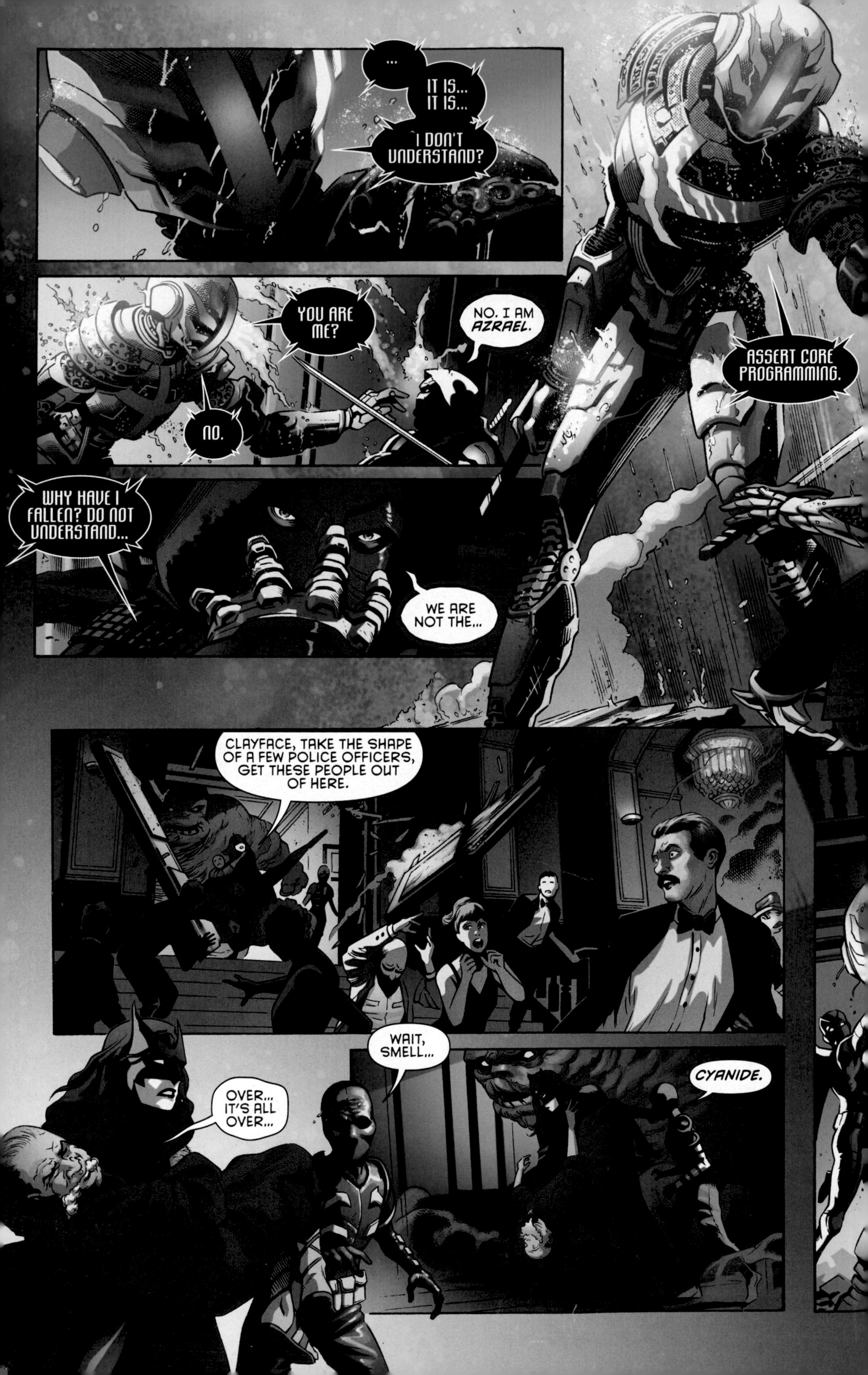
...
IT IS... IT IS...
I DON'T UNDERSTAND?
YOU ARE ME?
NO.
NO. I AM AZRAEL.
ASSERT CORE PROGRAMMING.
WHY HAVE I FALLEN? DO NOT UNDERSTAND...
WE ARE NOT THE...
CLAYFACE, TAKE THE SHAPE OF A FEW POLICE OFFICERS, GET THESE PEOPLE OUT OF HERE.
OVER... IT'S ALL OVER...
WAIT, SMELL...
CYANIDE.

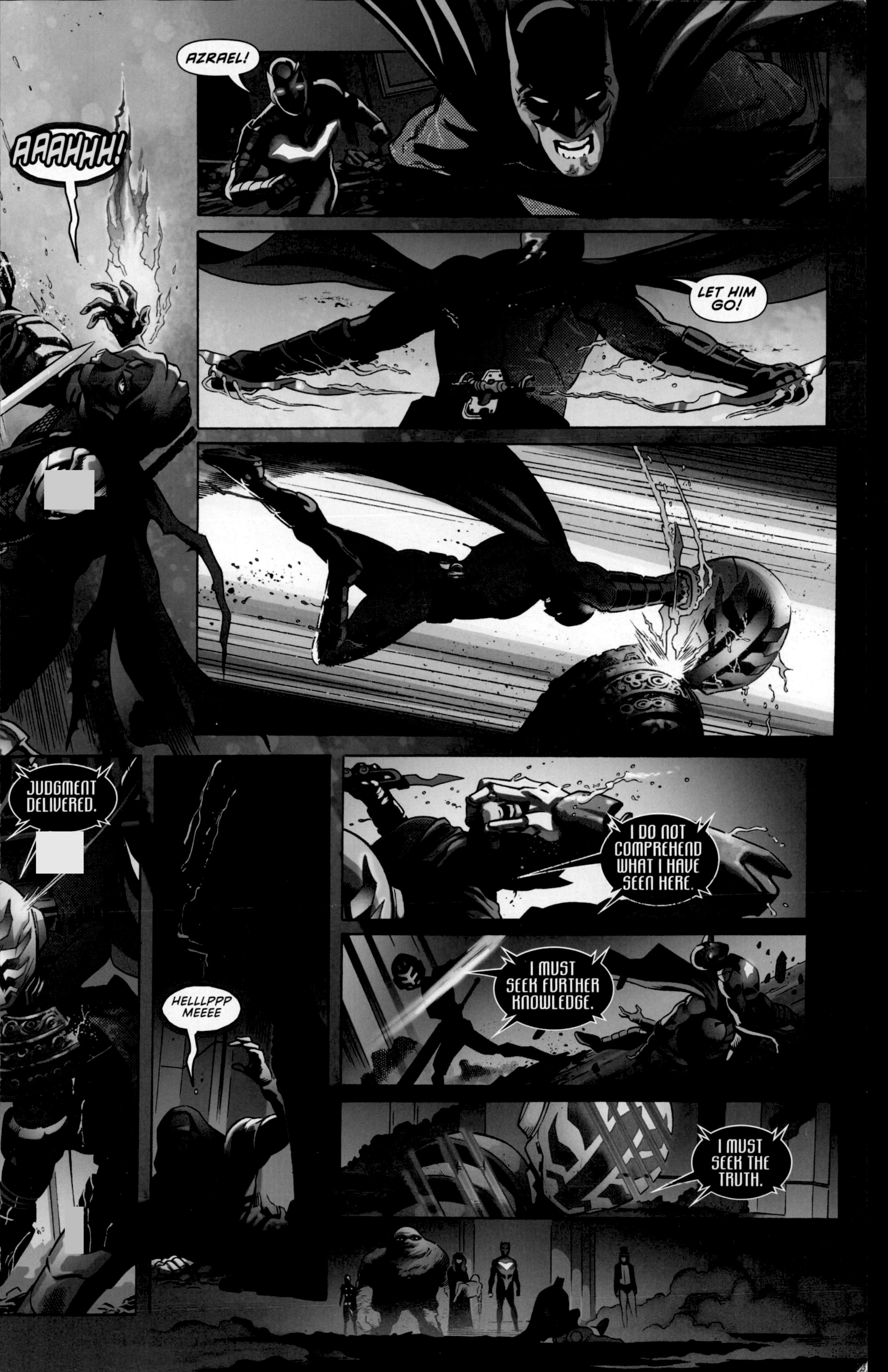
AZRAEL!
AAAHHH!
LET HIM GO!
JUDGMENT DELIVERED.
I DO NOT COMPREHEND WHAT I HAVE SEEN HERE.
HELLLPPP MEEEE
I MUST SEEK FURTHER KNOWLEDGE.
I MUST SEEK THE TRUTH.

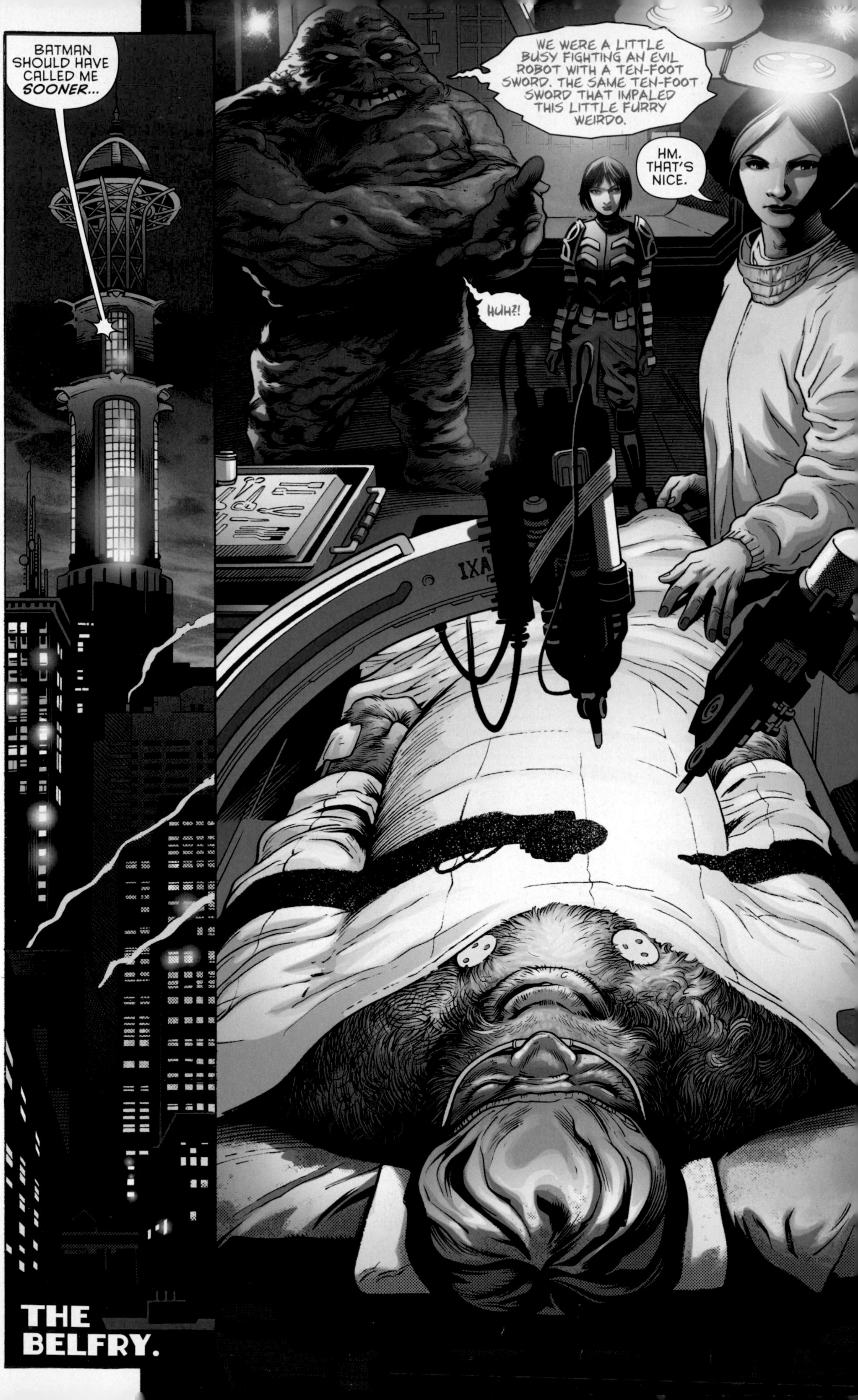
BATMAN SHOULD HAVE CALLED ME SOONER...
WE WERE A LITTLE BUSY FIGHTING AN EVIL ROBOT WITH A TEN-FOOT SWORD. THE SAME TEN-FOOT SWORD THAT IMPALED THIS LITTLE FURRY WEIRDO.
HM. THAT'S NICE.
HUH?!
IXA
THE BELFRY.

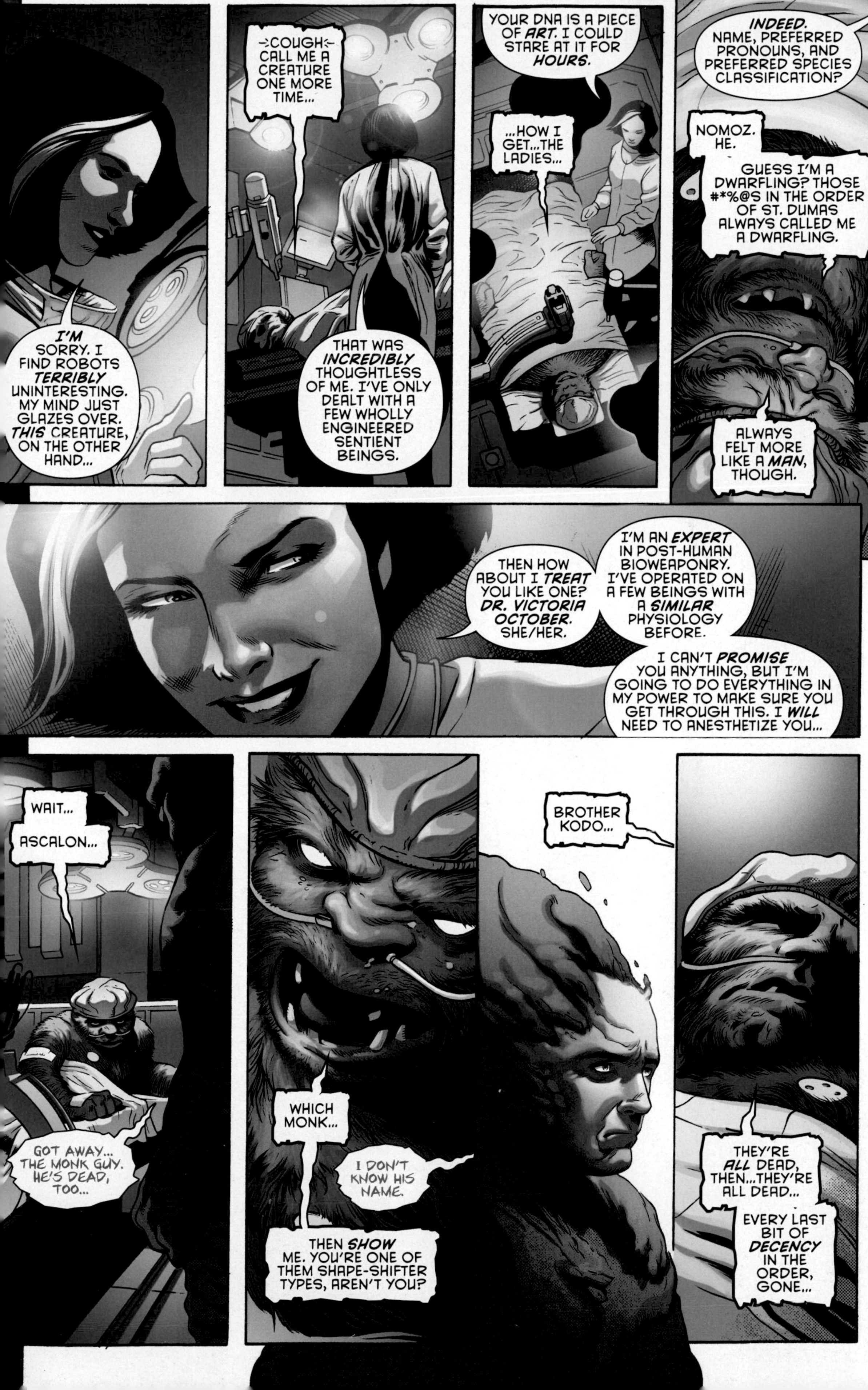
I'M SORRY. I FIND ROBOTS TERRIBLY UNINTERESTING. MY MIND JUST GLAZES OVER. THIS CREATURE, ON THE OTHER HAND...
-COUGH- CALL ME A CREATURE ONE MORE TIME...
THAT WAS INCREDIBLY THOUGHTLESS OF ME. I'VE ONLY DEALT WITH A FEW WHOLLY ENGINEERED SENTIENT BEINGS.
YOUR DNA IS A PIECE OF ART. I COULD STARE AT IT FOR HOURS.
...HOW I GET...THE LADIES...
INDEED. NAME, PREFERRED PRONOUNS, AND PREFERRED SPECIES CLASSIFICATION?
NOMOZ. HE.
GUESS I'M A DWARFLING? THOSE #*%@S IN THE ORDER OF ST. DUMAS ALWAYS CALLED ME A DWARFLING.
ALWAYS FELT MORE LIKE A MAN, THOUGH.
THEN HOW ABOUT I TREAT YOU LIKE ONE? DR. VICTORIA OCTOBER. SHE/HER.
I'M AN EXPERT IN POST-HUMAN BIOWEAPONRY. I'VE OPERATED ON A FEW BEINGS WITH A SIMILAR PHYSIOLOGY BEFORE.
I CAN'T PROMISE YOU ANYTHING, BUT I'M GOING TO DO EVERYTHING IN MY POWER TO MAKE SURE YOU GET THROUGH THIS. I WILL NEED TO ANESTHETIZE YOU...
WAIT...
ASCALON...
GOT AWAY... THE MONK GUY. HE'S DEAD, TOO...
WHICH MONK...
I DON'T KNOW HIS NAME.
THEN SHOW ME. YOU'RE ONE OF THEM SHAPE-SHIFTER TYPES, AREN'T YOU?
BROTHER KODO...
THEY'RE ALL DEAD, THEN...THEY'RE ALL DEAD...
EVERY LAST BIT OF DECENCY IN THE ORDER, GONE...

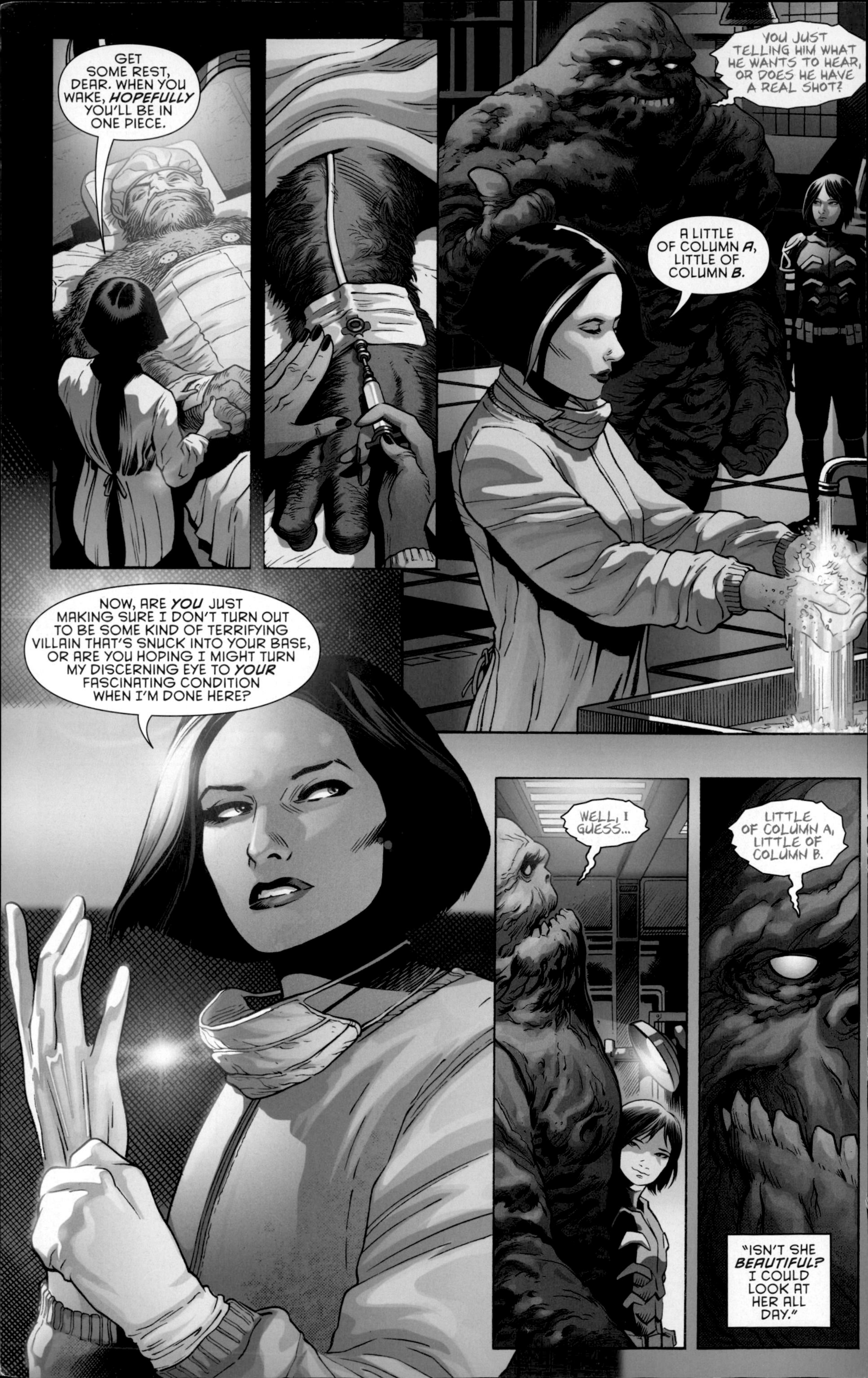

GET SOME REST, DEAR. WHEN YOU WAKE, *HOPEFULLY* YOU'LL BE IN ONE PIECE.
YOU JUST TELLING HIM WHAT HE WANTS TO HEAR, OR DOES HE HAVE A REAL SHOT?
A LITTLE OF COLUMN *A*, LITTLE OF COLUMN *B*.
NOW, ARE *YOU* JUST MAKING SURE I DON'T TURN OUT TO BE SOME KIND OF TERRIFYING VILLAIN THAT'S SNUCK INTO YOUR BASE, OR ARE YOU HOPING I MIGHT TURN MY DISCERNING EYE TO *YOUR* FASCINATING CONDITION WHEN I'M DONE HERE?
WELL, I GUESS...
LITTLE OF COLUMN A, LITTLE OF COLUMN B.
"ISN'T SHE *BEAUTIFUL?* I COULD LOOK AT HER ALL DAY."

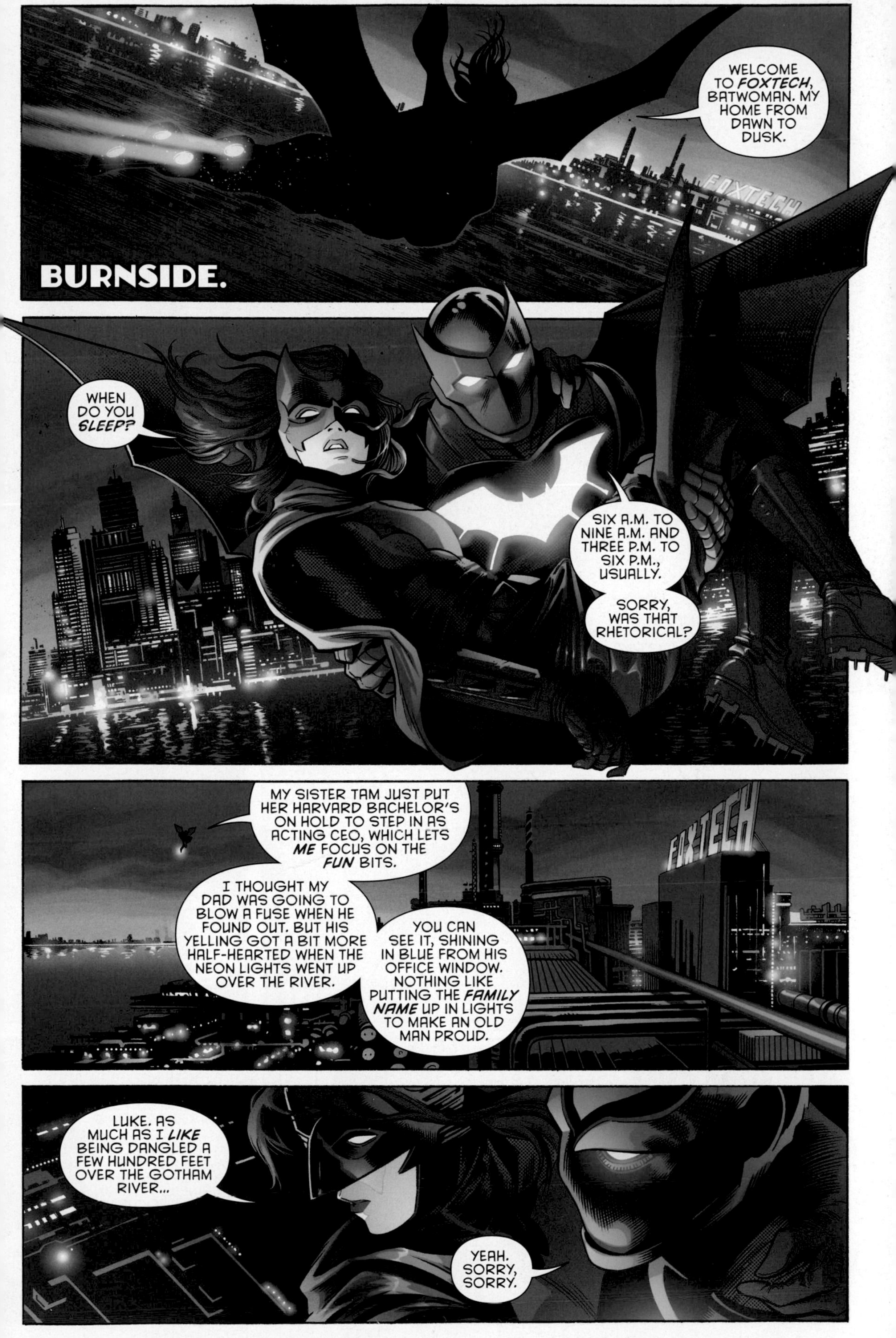
WELCOME TO FOXTECH, BATWOMAN. MY HOME FROM DAWN TO DUSK.
FOXTECH
BURNSIDE.
WHEN DO YOU SLEEP?
SIX A.M. TO NINE A.M. AND THREE P.M. TO SIX P.M., USUALLY.
SORRY, WAS THAT RHETORICAL?
MY SISTER TAM JUST PUT HER HARVARD BACHELOR'S ON HOLD TO STEP IN AS ACTING CEO, WHICH LETS ME FOCUS ON THE FUN BITS.
I THOUGHT MY DAD WAS GOING TO BLOW A FUSE WHEN HE FOUND OUT. BUT HIS YELLING GOT A BIT MORE HALF-HEARTED WHEN THE NEON LIGHTS WENT UP OVER THE RIVER.
YOU CAN SEE IT, SHINING IN BLUE FROM HIS OFFICE WINDOW. NOTHING LIKE PUTTING THE FAMILY NAME UP IN LIGHTS TO MAKE AN OLD MAN PROUD.
FOXTECH
LUKE. AS MUCH AS I LIKE BEING DANGLED A FEW HUNDRED FEET OVER THE GOTHAM RIVER...
YEAH. SORRY, SORRY.

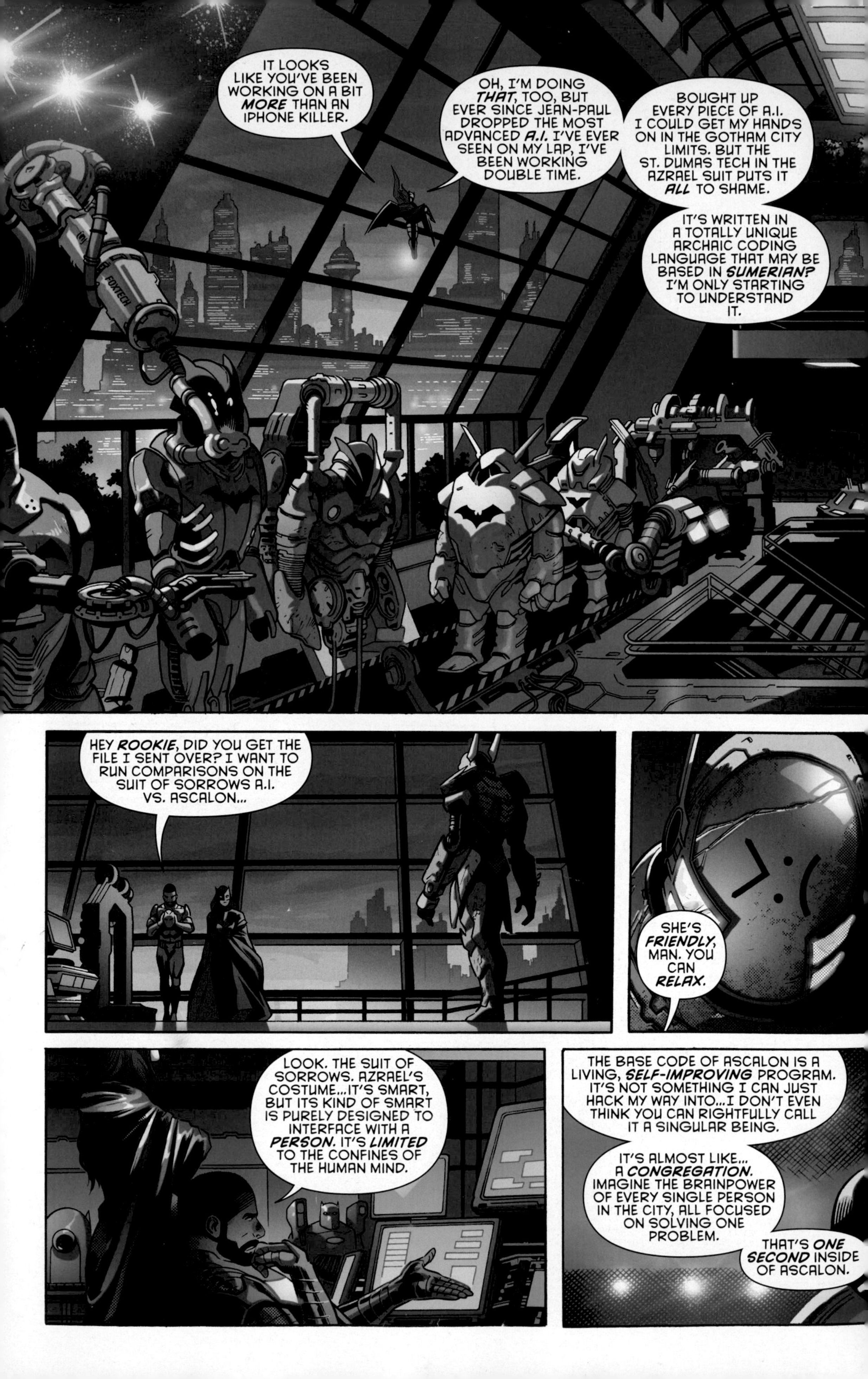
IT LOOKS LIKE YOU'VE BEEN WORKING ON A BIT MORE THAN AN IPHONE KILLER.
OH, I'M DOING THAT, TOO, BUT EVER SINCE JEAN-PAUL DROPPED THE MOST ADVANCED A.I. I'VE EVER SEEN ON MY LAP, I'VE BEEN WORKING DOUBLE TIME.
BOUGHT UP EVERY PIECE OF A.I. I COULD GET MY HANDS ON IN THE GOTHAM CITY LIMITS. BUT THE ST. DUMAS TECH IN THE AZRAEL SUIT PUTS IT ALL TO SHAME.
IT'S WRITTEN IN A TOTALLY UNIQUE ARCHAIC CODING LANGUAGE THAT MAY BE BASED IN SUMERIAN? I'M ONLY STARTING TO UNDERSTAND IT.
FOXTECH
HEY ROOKIE, DID YOU GET THE FILE I SENT OVER? I WANT TO RUN COMPARISONS ON THE SUIT OF SORROWS A.I. VS. ASCALON...
SHE'S FRIENDLY, MAN. YOU CAN RELAX.
LOOK. THE SUIT OF SORROWS. AZRAEL'S COSTUME...IT'S SMART, BUT ITS KIND OF SMART IS PURELY DESIGNED TO INTERFACE WITH A PERSON. IT'S LIMITED TO THE CONFINES OF THE HUMAN MIND.
THE BASE CODE OF ASCALON IS A LIVING, SELF-IMPROVING PROGRAM. IT'S NOT SOMETHING I CAN JUST HACK MY WAY INTO...I DON'T EVEN THINK YOU CAN RIGHTFULLY CALL IT A SINGULAR BEING.
IT'S ALMOST LIKE... A CONGREGATION. IMAGINE THE BRAINPOWER OF EVERY SINGLE PERSON IN THE CITY, ALL FOCUSED ON SOLVING ONE PROBLEM.
THAT'S ONE SECOND INSIDE OF ASCALON.

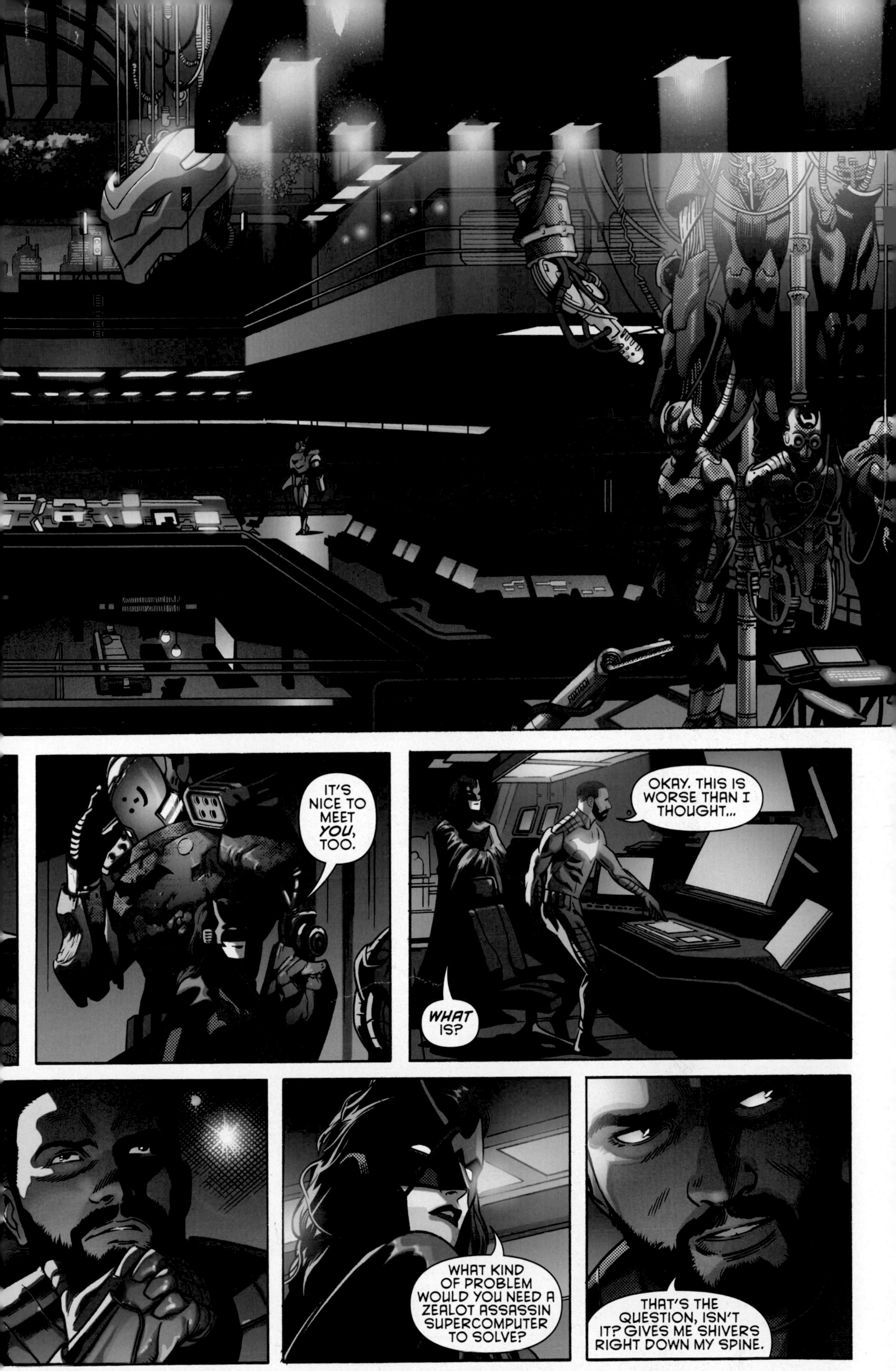

IT'S NICE TO MEET *YOU*, TOO.
OKAY. THIS IS WORSE THAN I THOUGHT...
WHAT IS?
WHAT KIND OF PROBLEM WOULD YOU NEED A ZEALOT ASSASSIN SUPERCOMPUTER TO SOLVE?
THAT'S THE QUESTION, ISN'T IT? GIVES ME SHIVERS RIGHT DOWN MY SPINE.

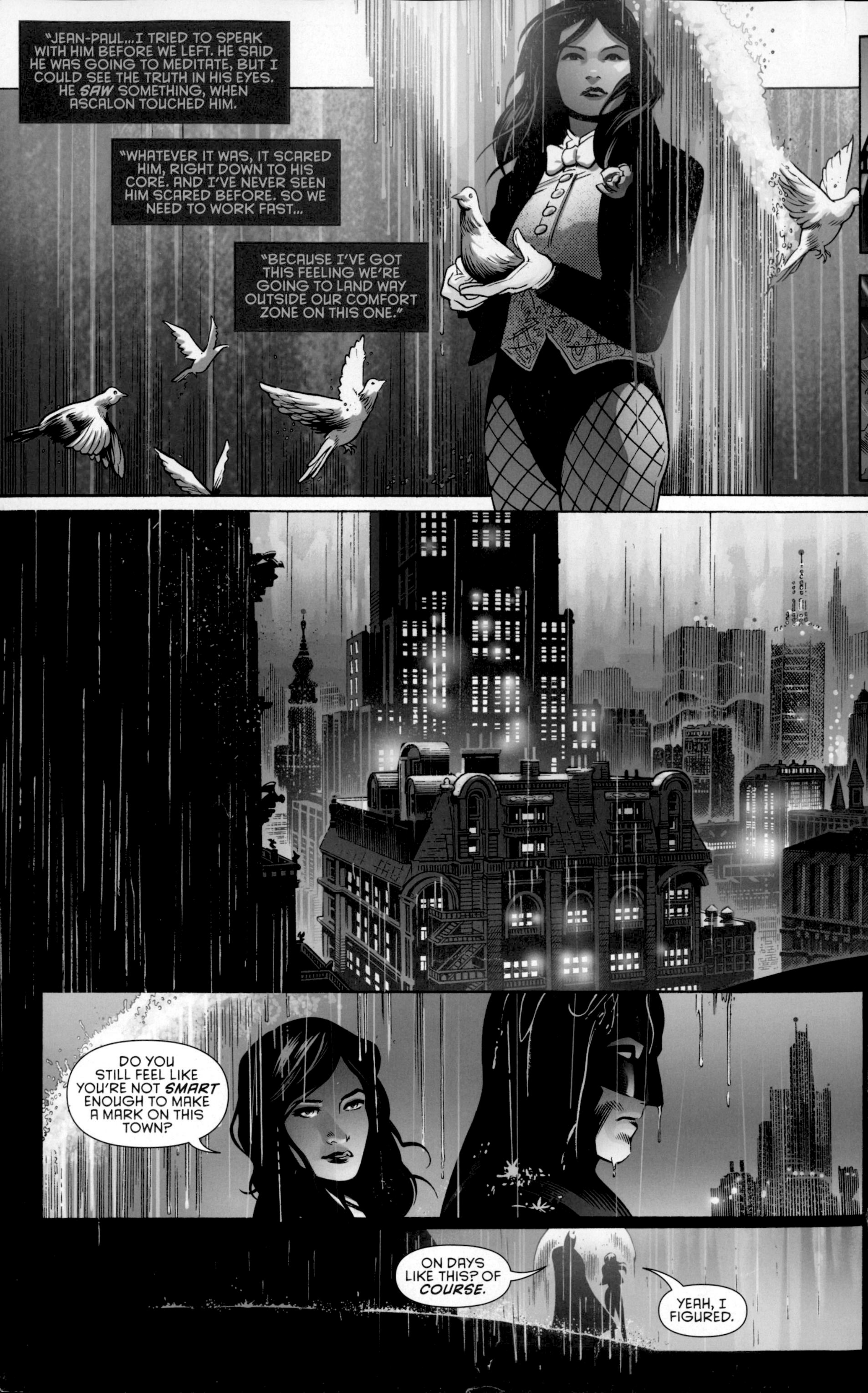
"JEAN-PAUL...I TRIED TO SPEAK WITH HIM BEFORE WE LEFT. HE SAID HE WAS GOING TO MEDITATE, BUT I COULD SEE THE TRUTH IN HIS EYES. HE *SAW* SOMETHING, WHEN ASCALON TOUCHED HIM.
"WHATEVER IT WAS, IT SCARED HIM, RIGHT DOWN TO HIS CORE. AND I'VE NEVER SEEN HIM SCARED BEFORE. SO WE NEED TO WORK FAST...
"BECAUSE I'VE GOT THIS FEELING WE'RE GOING TO LAND WAY OUTSIDE OUR COMFORT ZONE ON THIS ONE."
DO YOU STILL FEEL LIKE YOU'RE NOT **SMART** ENOUGH TO MAKE A MARK ON THIS TOWN?
ON DAYS LIKE THIS? OF ***COURSE.***
YEAH, I FIGURED.

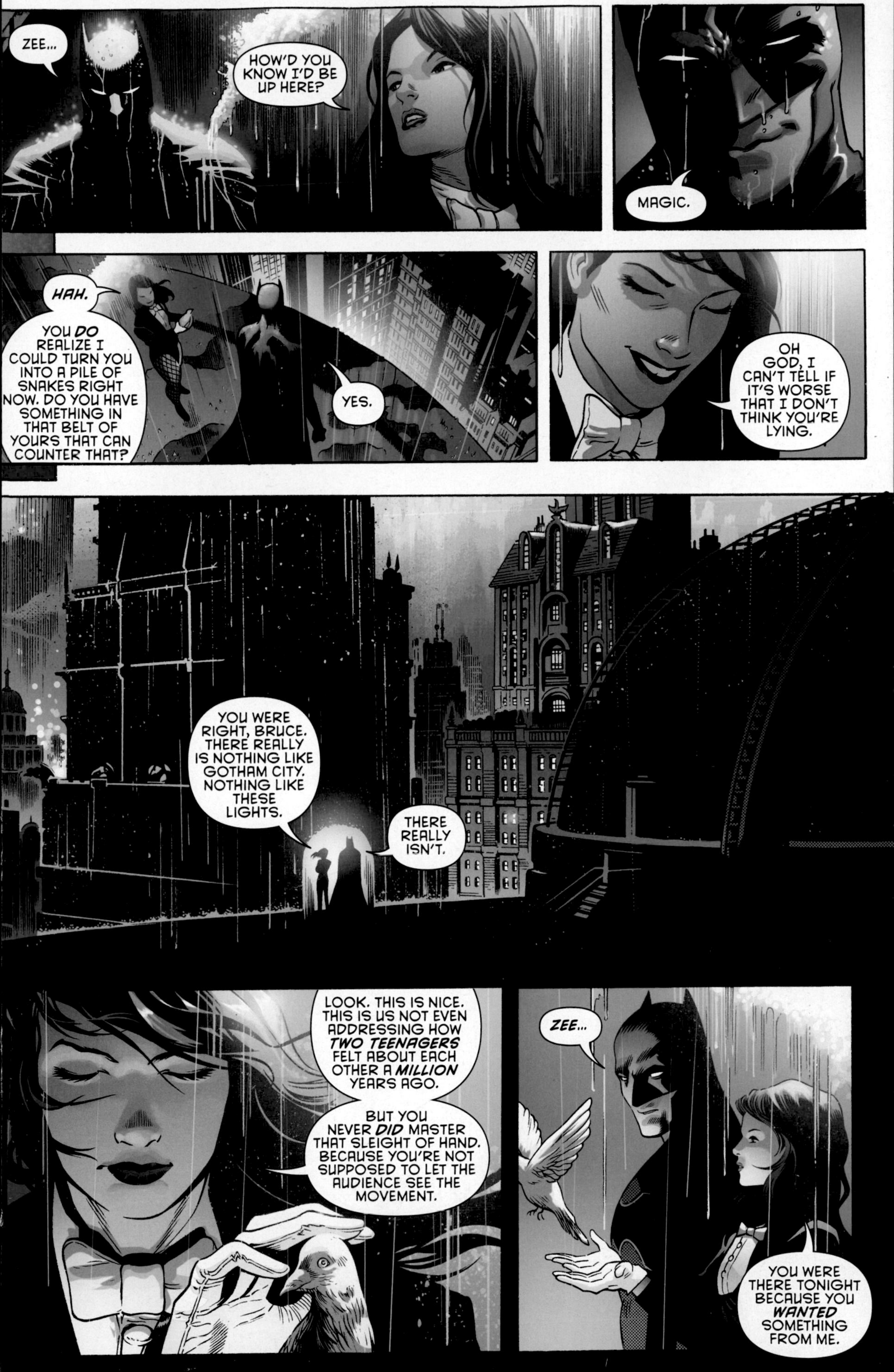
ZEE...
HOW'D YOU KNOW I'D BE UP HERE?
MAGIC.
HAH.
YOU DO REALIZE I COULD TURN YOU INTO A PILE OF SNAKES RIGHT NOW. DO YOU HAVE SOMETHING IN THAT BELT OF YOURS THAT CAN COUNTER THAT?
YES.
OH GOD, I CAN'T TELL IF IT'S WORSE THAT I DON'T THINK YOU'RE LYING.
YOU WERE RIGHT, BRUCE. THERE REALLY IS NOTHING LIKE GOTHAM CITY. NOTHING LIKE THESE LIGHTS.
THERE REALLY ISN'T.
LOOK. THIS IS NICE. THIS IS US NOT EVEN ADDRESSING HOW TWO TEENAGERS FELT ABOUT EACH OTHER A MILLION YEARS AGO.
BUT YOU NEVER DID MASTER THAT SLEIGHT OF HAND. BECAUSE YOU'RE NOT SUPPOSED TO LET THE AUDIENCE SEE THE MOVEMENT.
ZEE...
YOU WERE THERE TONIGHT BECAUSE YOU WANTED SOMETHING FROM ME.

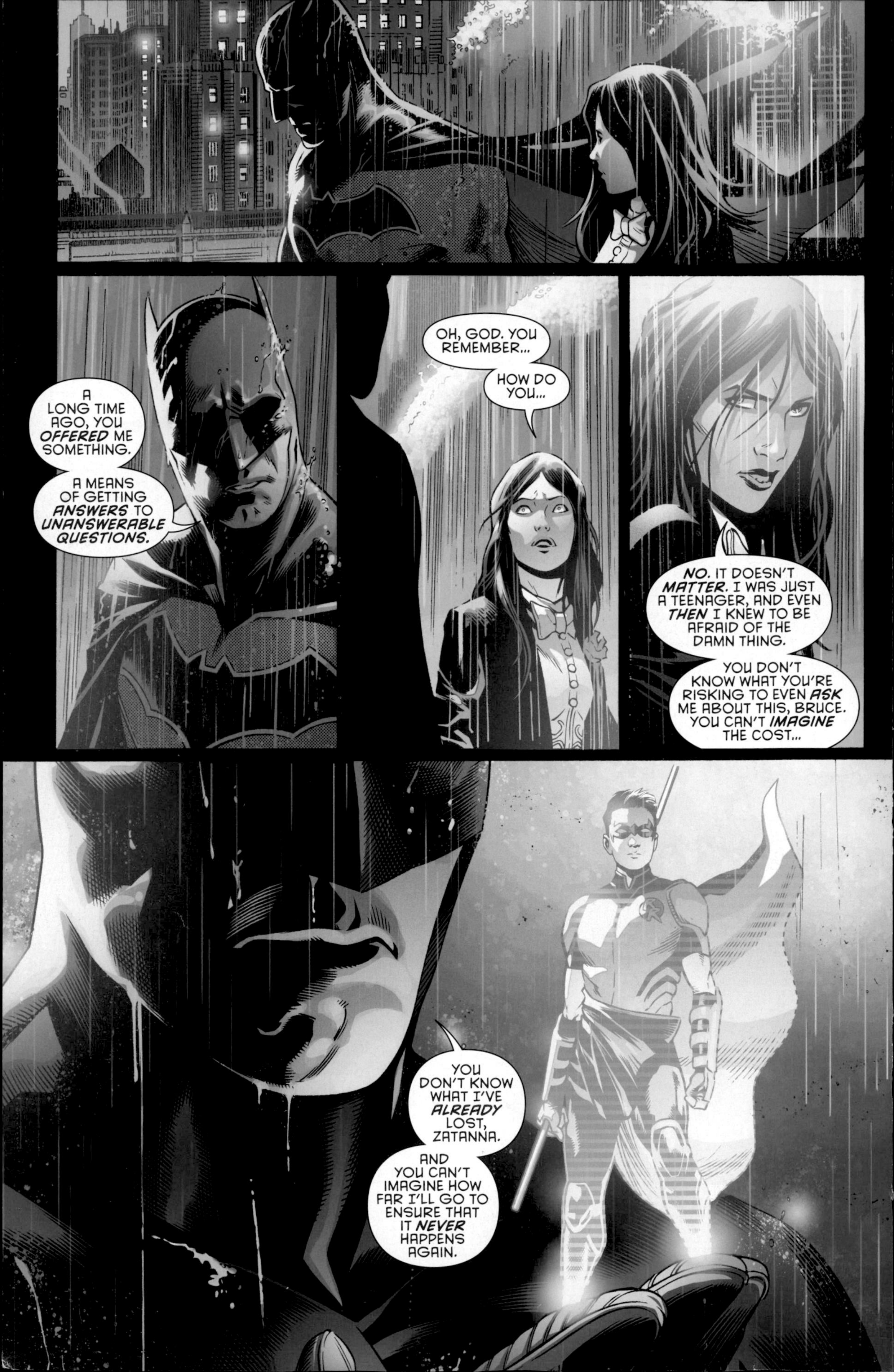
A LONG TIME AGO, YOU OFFERED ME SOMETHING.
A MEANS OF GETTING ANSWERS TO UNANSWERABLE QUESTIONS.
OH, GOD. YOU REMEMBER...
HOW DO YOU...
NO. IT DOESN'T MATTER. I WAS JUST A TEENAGER, AND EVEN THEN I KNEW TO BE AFRAID OF THE DAMN THING.
YOU DON'T KNOW WHAT YOU'RE RISKING TO EVEN ASK ME ABOUT THIS, BRUCE. YOU CAN'T IMAGINE THE COST...
YOU DON'T KNOW WHAT I'VE ALREADY LOST, ZATANNA.
AND YOU CAN'T IMAGINE HOW FAR I'LL GO TO ENSURE THAT IT NEVER HAPPENS AGAIN.

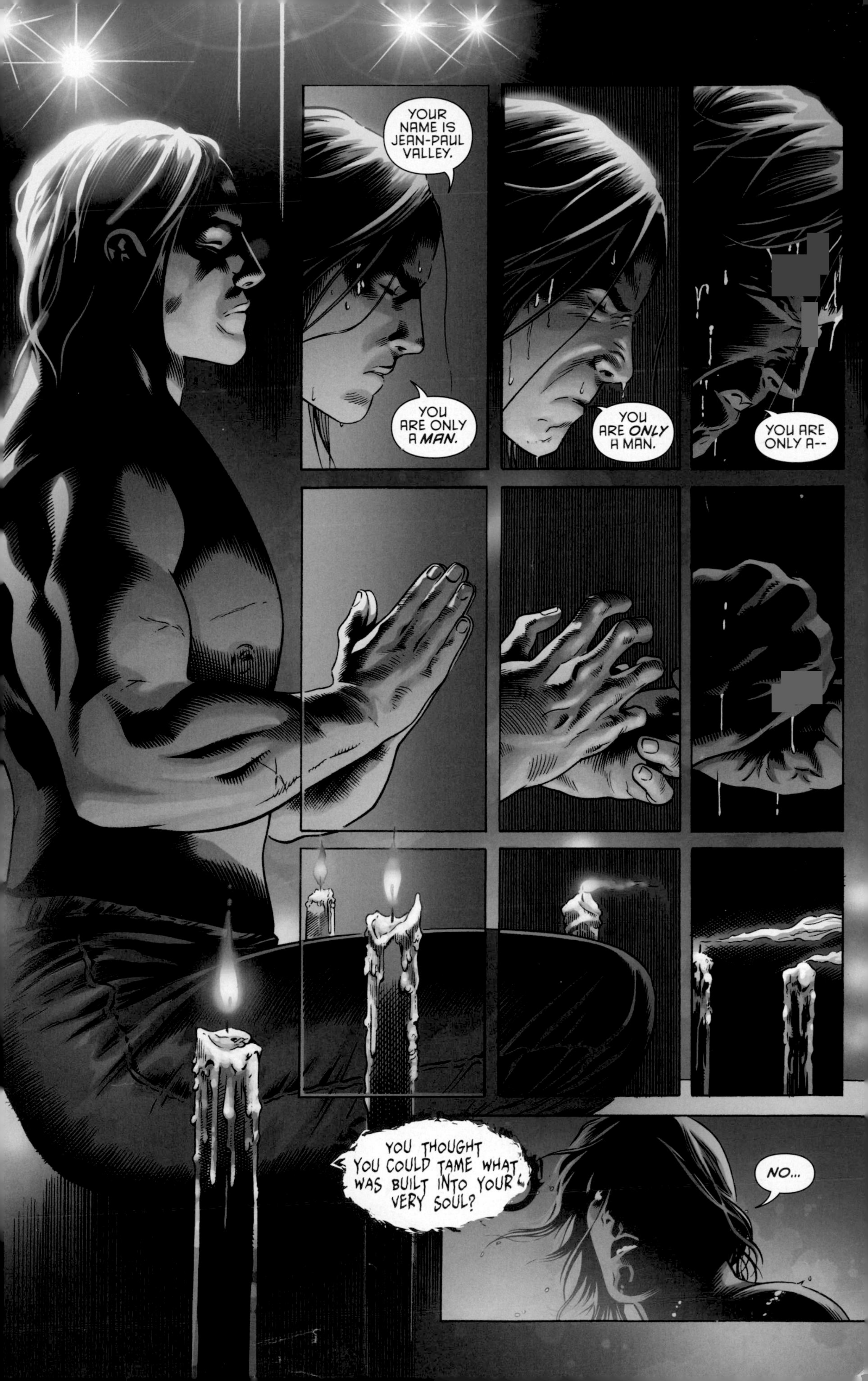
YOUR NAME IS JEAN-PAUL VALLEY.
YOU ARE ONLY A MAN.
YOU ARE ONLY A MAN.
YOU ARE ONLY A--
YOU THOUGHT YOU COULD TAME WHAT WAS BUILT INTO YOUR VERY SOUL?
NO...

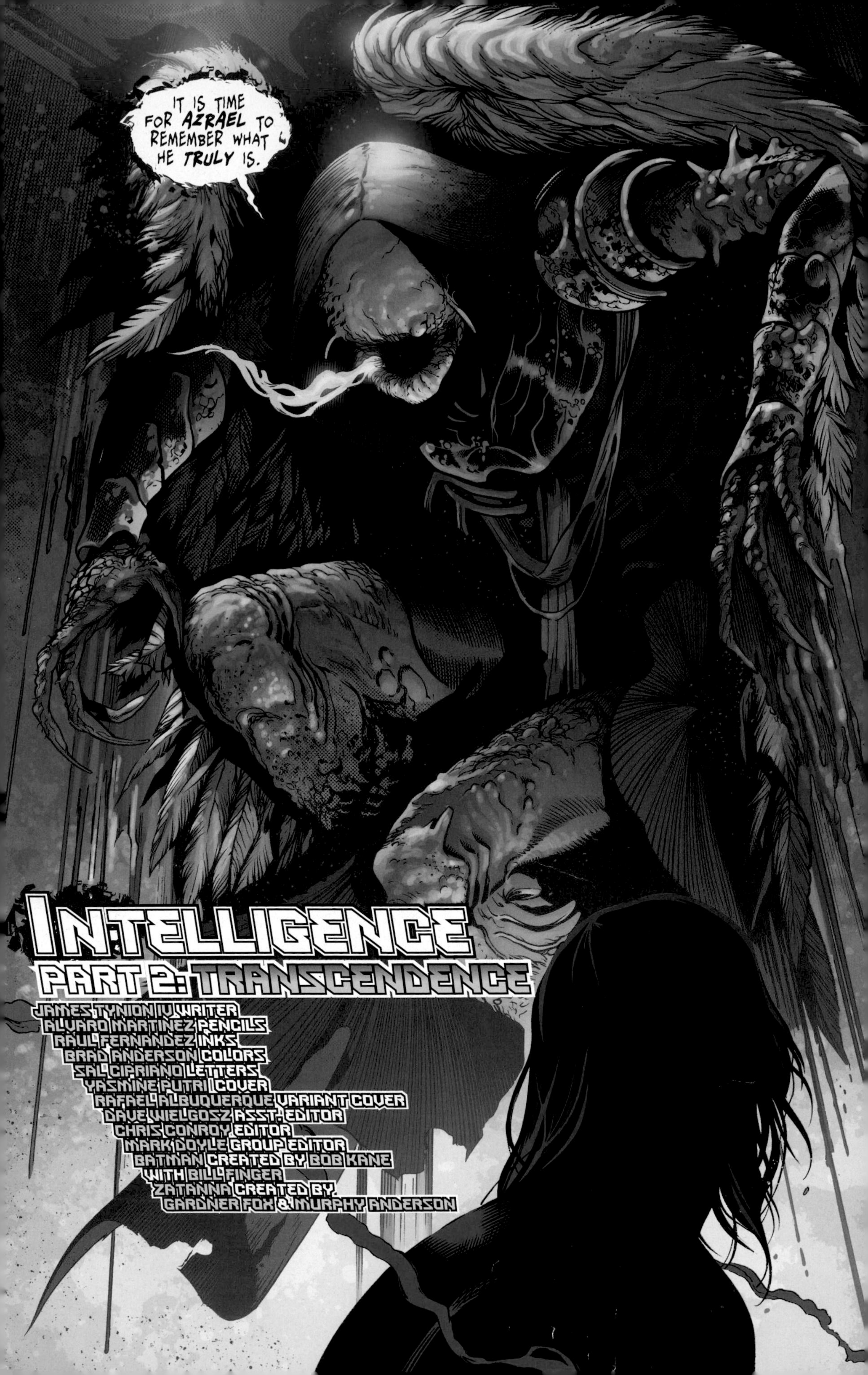
IT IS TIME FOR AZRAEL TO REMEMBER WHAT HE TRULY IS.
INTELLIGENCE
PART 2: TRANSCENDENCE
JAMES TYNION IV WRITER
ALVARO MARTINEZ PENCILS
RAUL FERNANDEZ INKS
BRAD ANDERSON COLORS
SAL CIPRIANO LETTERS
YASMINE PUTRI COVER
RAFAEL ALBUQUERQUE VARIANT COVER
DAVE WIELGOSZ ASST. EDITOR
CHRIS CONROY EDITOR
MARK DOYLE GROUP EDITOR
BATMAN CREATED BY BOB KANE WITH BILL FINGER
ZATANNA CREATED BY GARDNER FOX & MURPHY ANDERSON

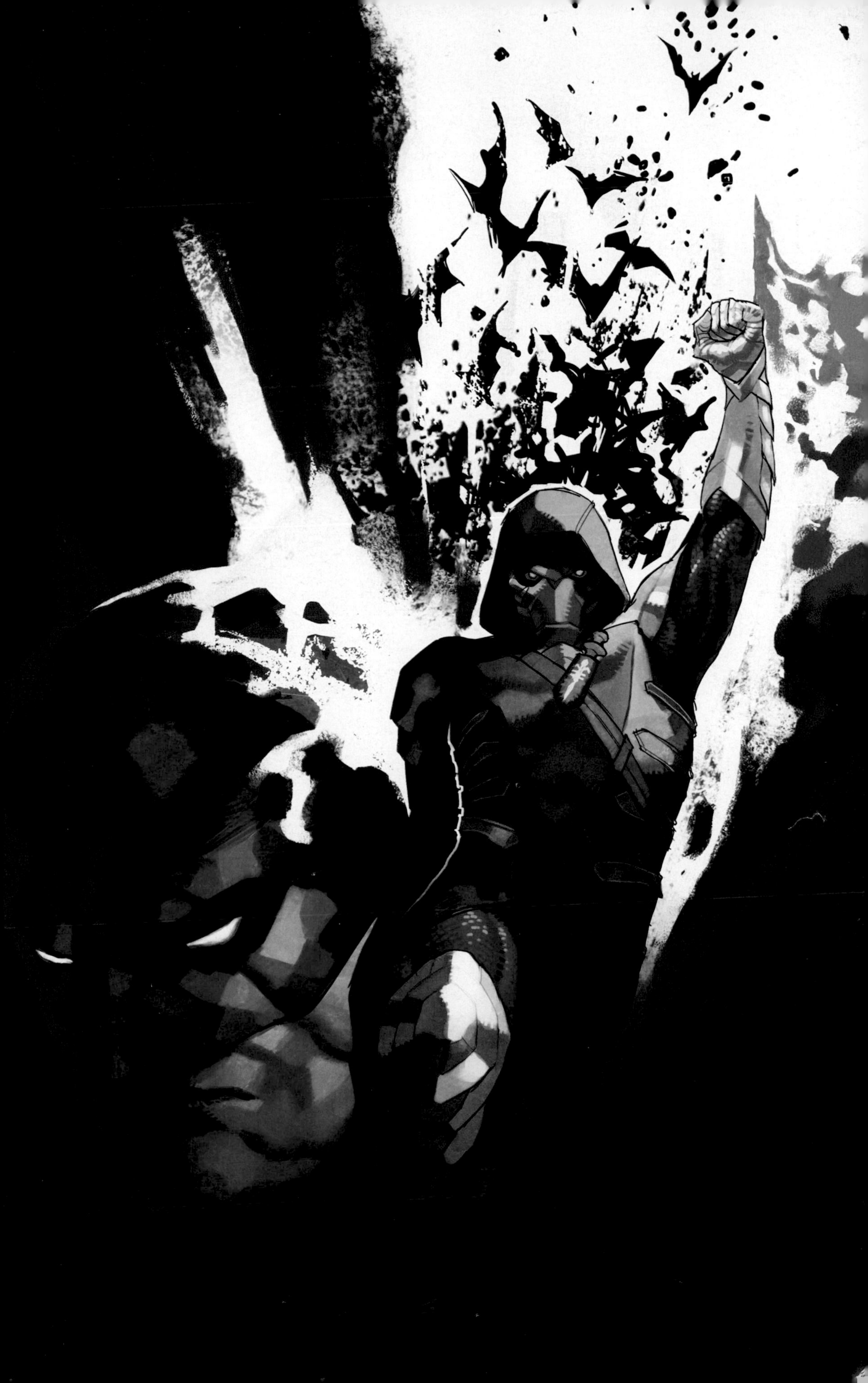

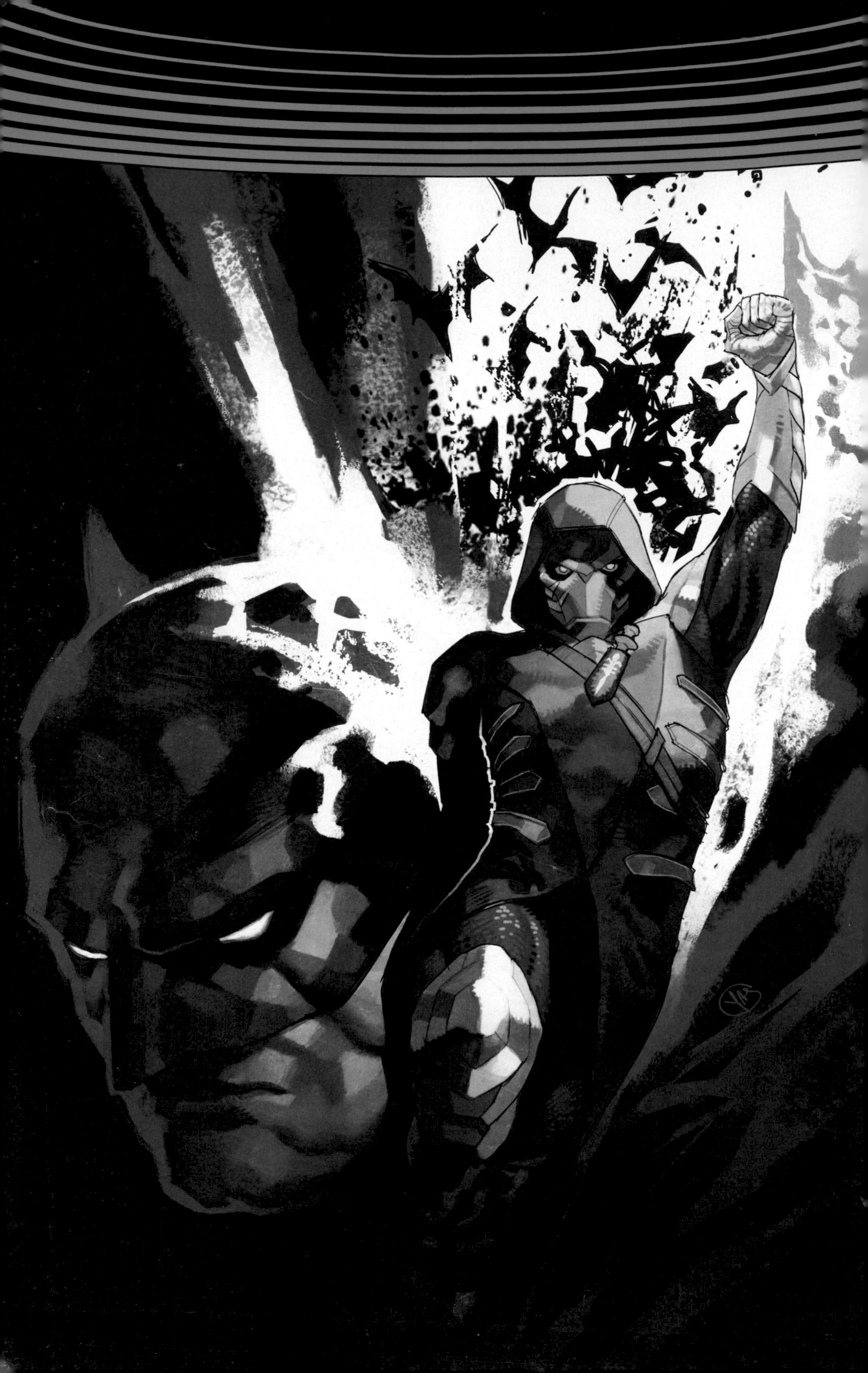

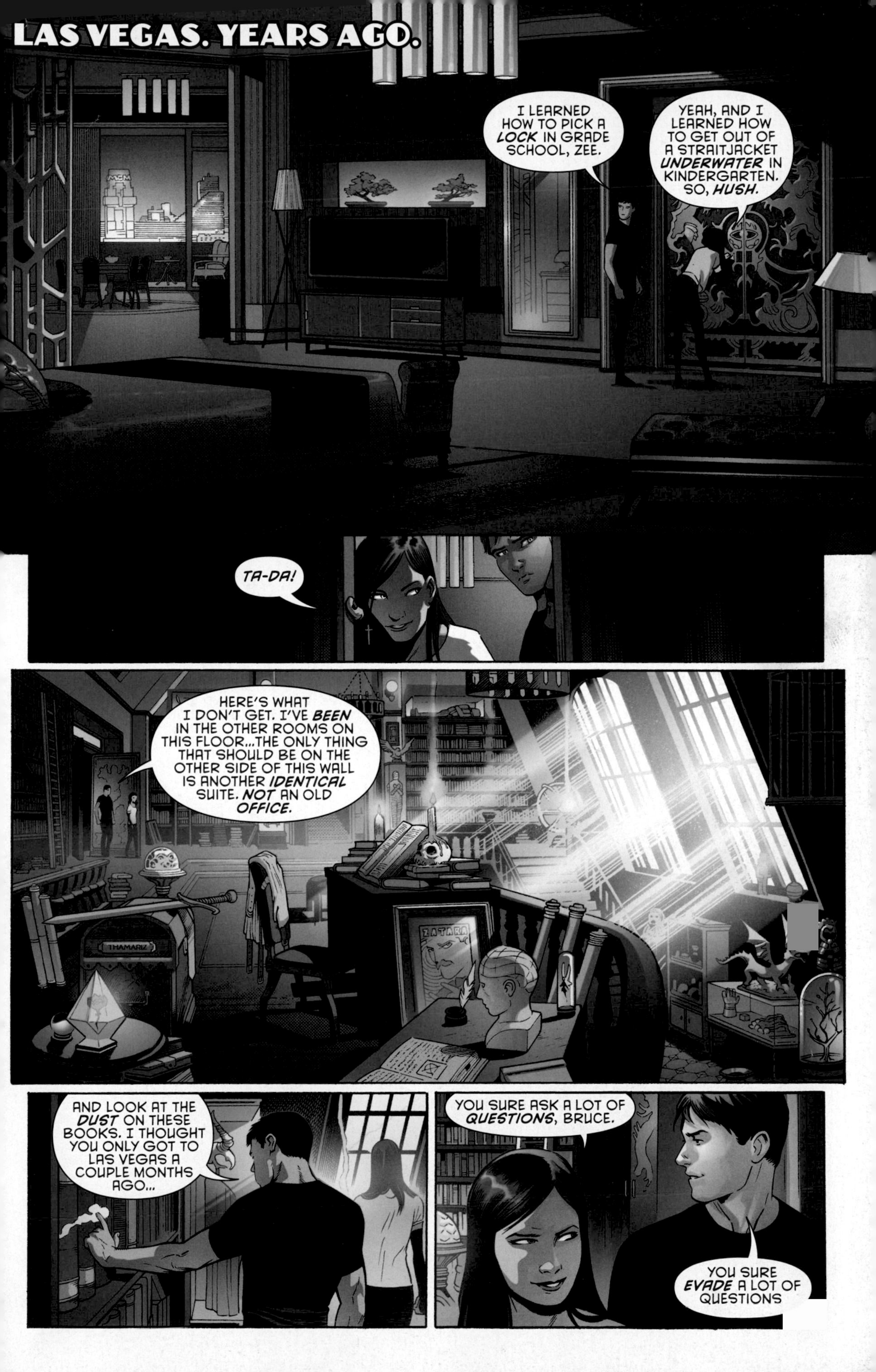
LAS VEGAS. YEARS AGO.
I LEARNED HOW TO PICK A LOCK IN GRADE SCHOOL, ZEE.
YEAH, AND I LEARNED HOW TO GET OUT OF A STRAITJACKET UNDERWATER IN KINDERGARTEN. SO, HUSH.
TA-DA!
HERE'S WHAT I DON'T GET. I'VE BEEN IN THE OTHER ROOMS ON THIS FLOOR...THE ONLY THING THAT SHOULD BE ON THE OTHER SIDE OF THIS WALL IS ANOTHER IDENTICAL SUITE. NOT AN OLD OFFICE.
ZATARA
THAMARIZ
AND LOOK AT THE DUST ON THESE BOOKS. I THOUGHT YOU ONLY GOT TO LAS VEGAS A COUPLE MONTHS AGO...
YOU SURE ASK A LOT OF QUESTIONS, BRUCE.
YOU SURE EVADE A LOT OF QUESTIONS

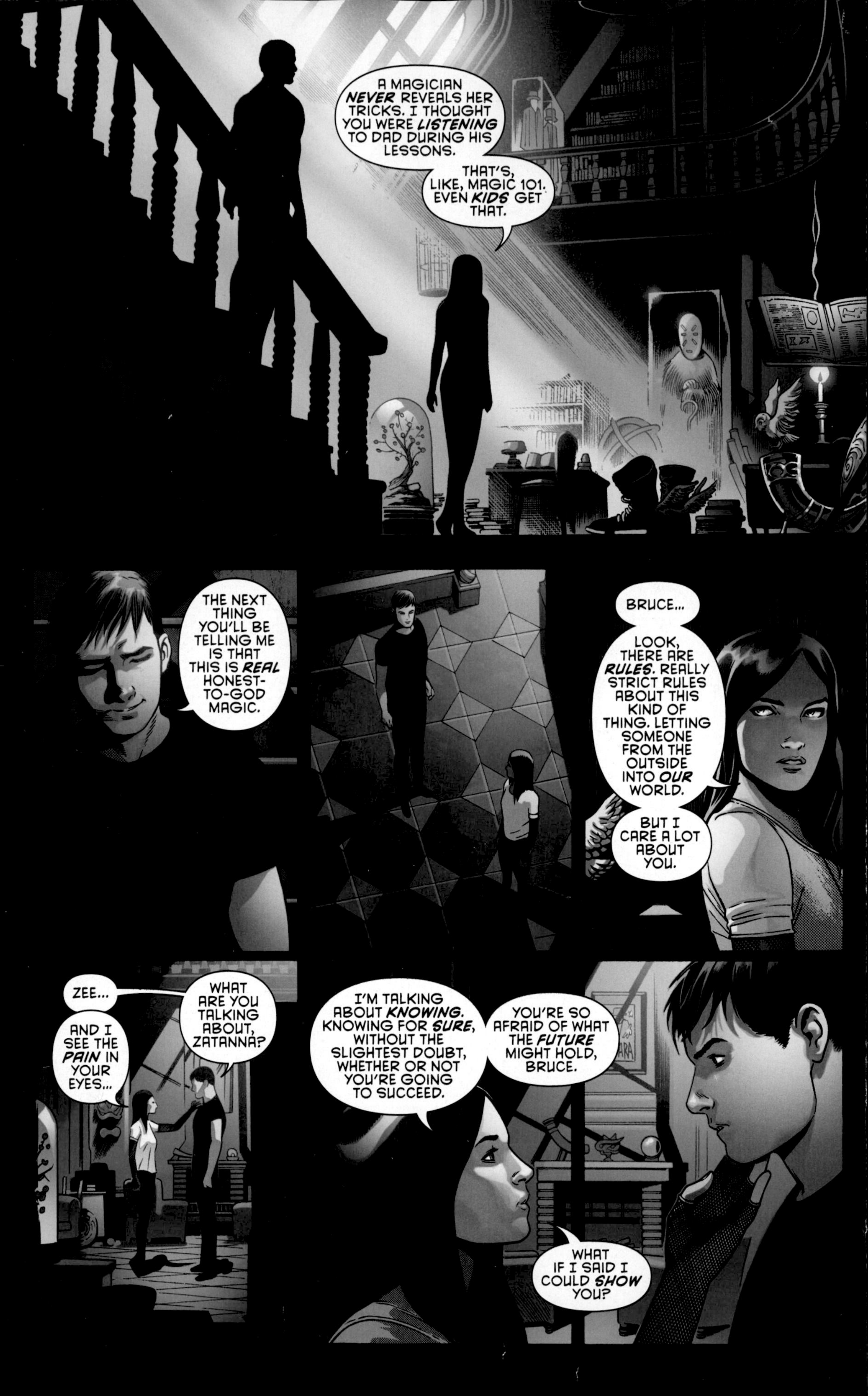
A MAGICIAN NEVER REVEALS HER TRICKS. I THOUGHT YOU WERE LISTENING TO DAD DURING HIS LESSONS.
THAT'S, LIKE, MAGIC 101. EVEN KIDS GET THAT.
THE NEXT THING YOU'LL BE TELLING ME IS THAT THIS IS REAL HONEST-TO-GOD MAGIC.
BRUCE...
LOOK, THERE ARE RULES. REALLY STRICT RULES ABOUT THIS KIND OF THING. LETTING SOMEONE FROM THE OUTSIDE INTO OUR WORLD.
BUT I CARE A LOT ABOUT YOU.
ZEE...
AND I SEE THE PAIN IN YOUR EYES...
WHAT ARE YOU TALKING ABOUT, ZATANNA?
I'M TALKING ABOUT KNOWING. KNOWING FOR SURE, WITHOUT THE SLIGHTEST DOUBT, WHETHER OR NOT YOU'RE GOING TO SUCCEED.
YOU'RE SO AFRAID OF WHAT THE FUTURE MIGHT HOLD, BRUCE.
WHAT IF I SAID I COULD SHOW YOU?

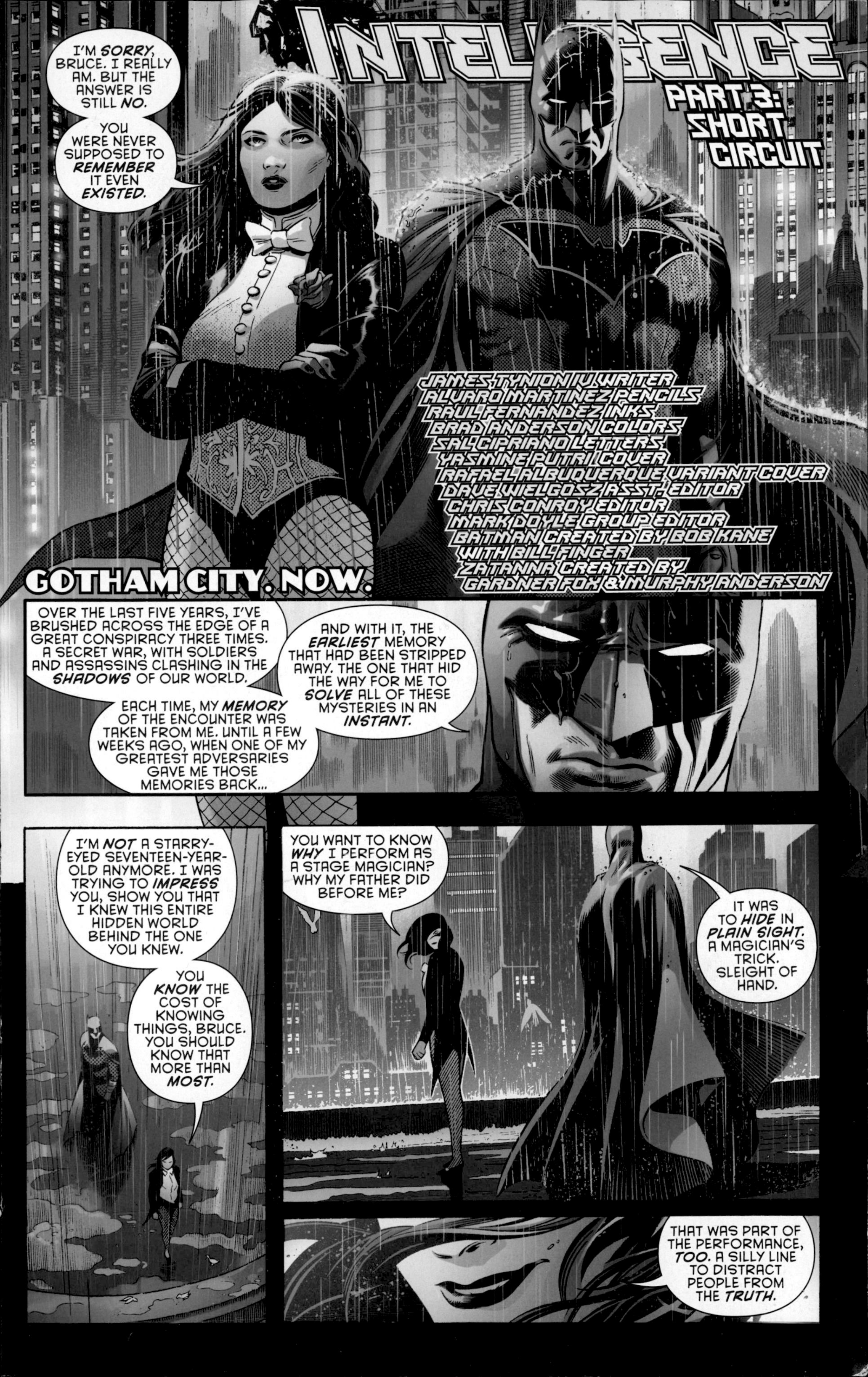

INTELLIGENCE
PART 3: SHORT CIRCUIT
I'M SORRY, BRUCE. I REALLY AM. BUT THE ANSWER IS STILL NO.
YOU WERE NEVER SUPPOSED TO REMEMBER IT EVEN EXISTED.
JAMES TYNION IV WRITER
ALVARO MARTINEZ PENCILS
RAUL FERNANDEZ INKS
BRAD ANDERSON COLORS
SAL CIPRIANO LETTERS
YASMINE PUTRI COVER
RAFAEL ALBUQUERQUE VARIANT COVER
DAVE WIELGOSZ ASST. EDITOR
CHRIS CONROY EDITOR
MARK DOYLE GROUP EDITOR
BATMAN CREATED BY BOB KANE WITH BILL FINGER
ZATANNA CREATED BY GARDNER FOX & MURPHY ANDERSON
GOTHAM CITY. NOW.
OVER THE LAST FIVE YEARS, I'VE BRUSHED ACROSS THE EDGE OF A GREAT CONSPIRACY THREE TIMES. A SECRET WAR, WITH SOLDIERS AND ASSASSINS CLASHING IN THE SHADOWS OF OUR WORLD.
EACH TIME, MY MEMORY OF THE ENCOUNTER WAS TAKEN FROM ME. UNTIL A FEW WEEKS AGO, WHEN ONE OF MY GREATEST ADVERSARIES GAVE ME THOSE MEMORIES BACK...
AND WITH IT, THE EARLIEST MEMORY THAT HAD BEEN STRIPPED AWAY. THE ONE THAT HID THE WAY FOR ME TO SOLVE ALL OF THESE MYSTERIES IN AN INSTANT.
I'M NOT A STARRY-EYED SEVENTEEN-YEAR-OLD ANYMORE. I WAS TRYING TO IMPRESS YOU, SHOW YOU THAT I KNEW THIS ENTIRE HIDDEN WORLD BEHIND THE ONE YOU KNEW.
YOU KNOW THE COST OF KNOWING THINGS, BRUCE. YOU SHOULD KNOW THAT MORE THAN MOST.
YOU WANT TO KNOW WHY I PERFORM AS A STAGE MAGICIAN? WHY MY FATHER DID BEFORE ME?
IT WAS TO HIDE IN PLAIN SIGHT. A MAGICIAN'S TRICK. SLEIGHT OF HAND.
THAT WAS PART OF THE PERFORMANCE, TOO. A SILLY LINE TO DISTRACT PEOPLE FROM THE TRUTH.

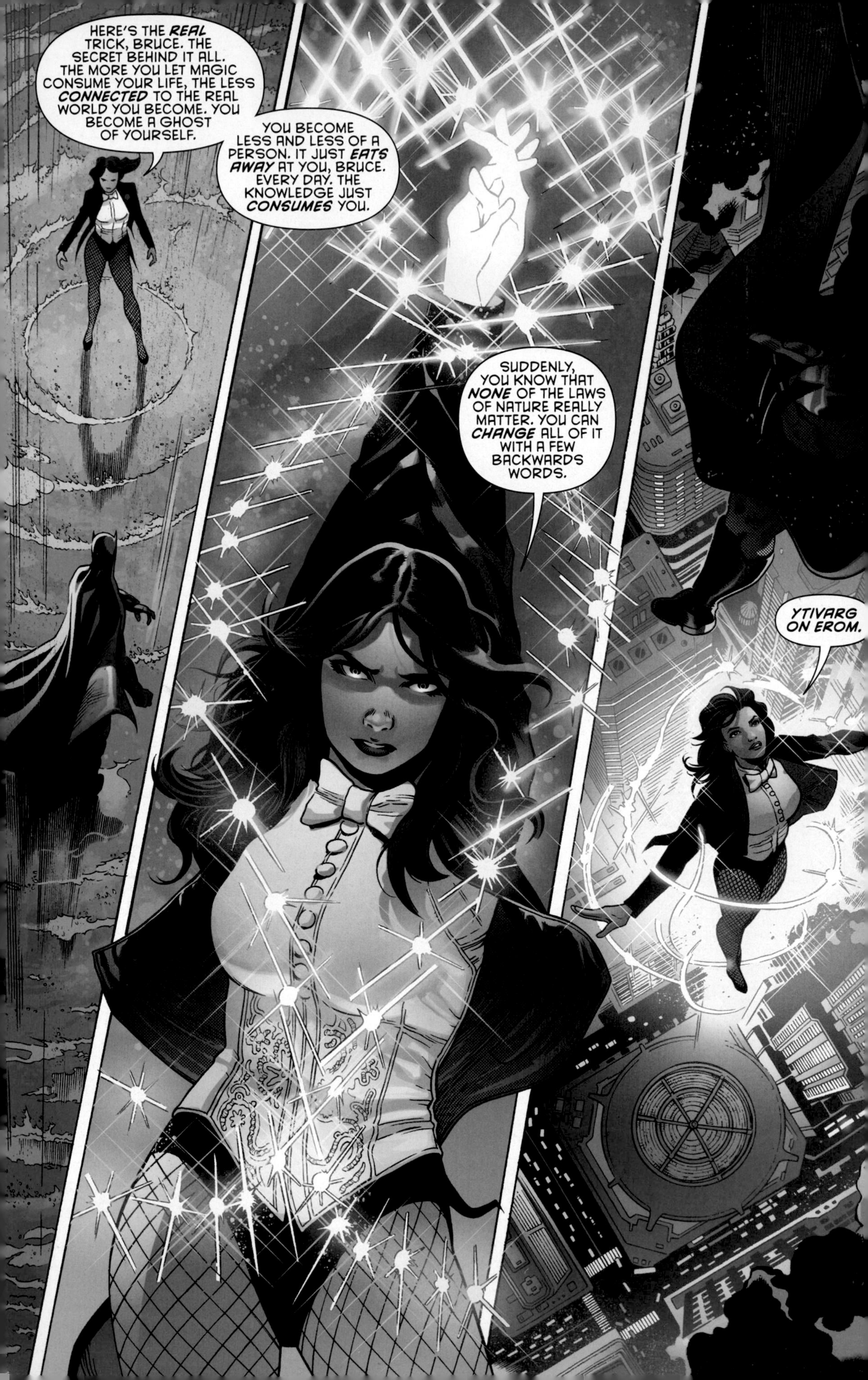
HERE'S THE REAL TRICK, BRUCE. THE SECRET BEHIND IT ALL. THE MORE YOU LET MAGIC CONSUME YOUR LIFE, THE LESS CONNECTED TO THE REAL WORLD YOU BECOME. YOU BECOME A GHOST OF YOURSELF.
YOU BECOME LESS AND LESS OF A PERSON. IT JUST EATS AWAY AT YOU, BRUCE. EVERY DAY. THE KNOWLEDGE JUST CONSUMES YOU.
SUDDENLY, YOU KNOW THAT NONE OF THE LAWS OF NATURE REALLY MATTER. YOU CAN CHANGE ALL OF IT WITH A FEW BACKWARDS WORDS.
YTIVARG ON EROM.

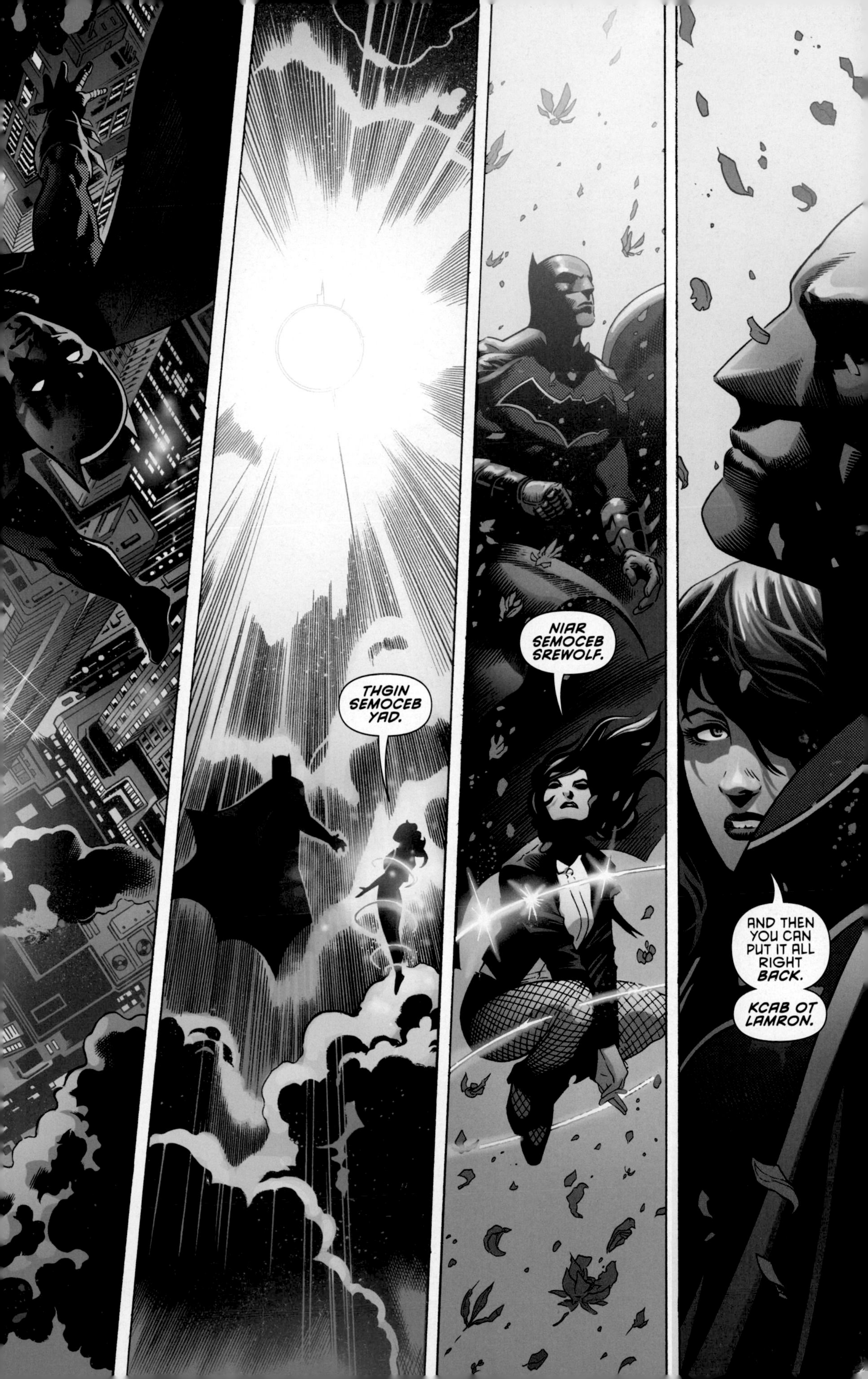
THGIN SEMOCEB YAD.
NIAR SEMOCEB SREWOLF.
AND THEN YOU CAN PUT IT ALL RIGHT BACK.
KCAB OT LAMRON.

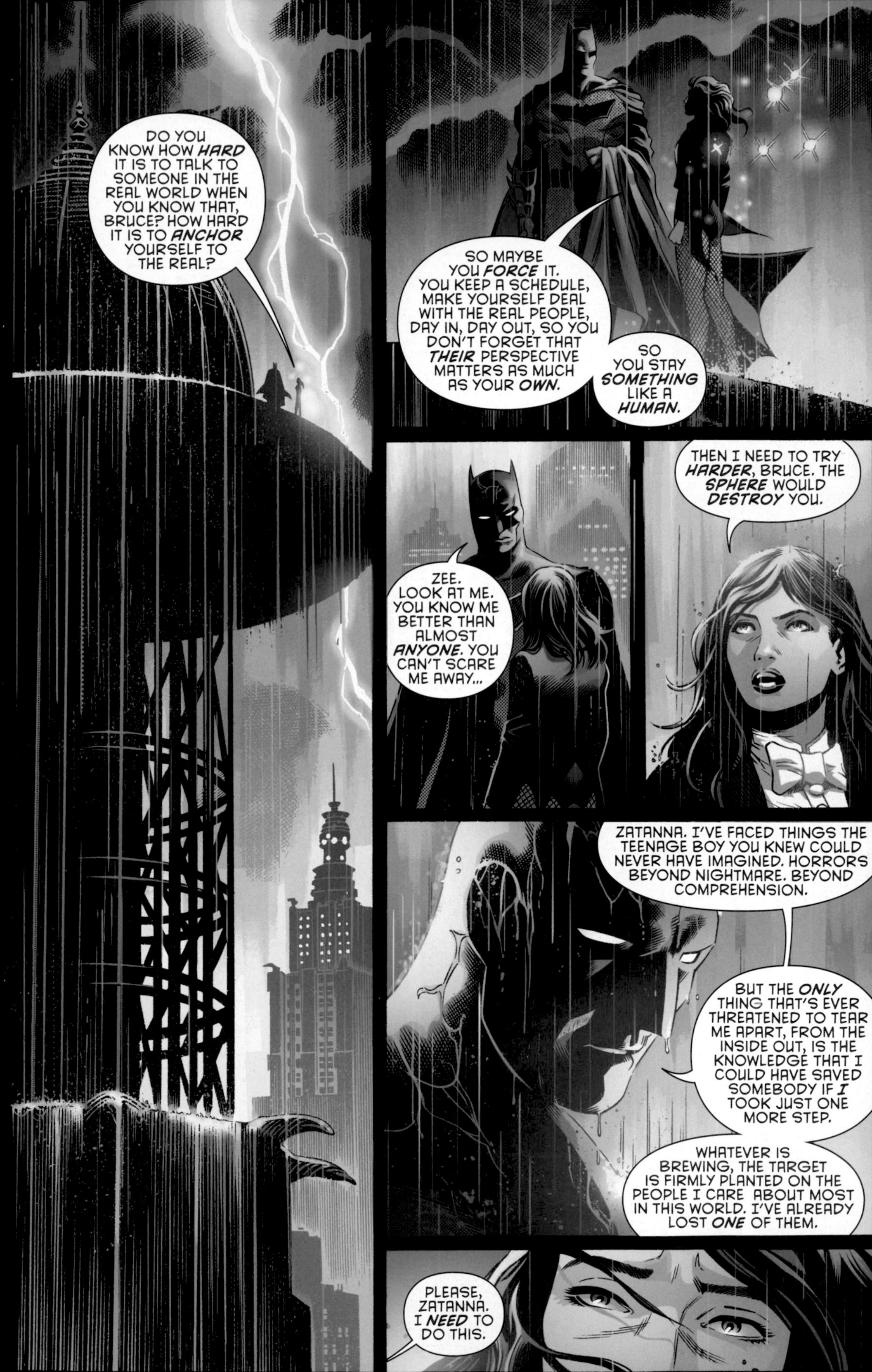
DO YOU KNOW HOW HARD IT IS TO TALK TO SOMEONE IN THE REAL WORLD WHEN YOU KNOW THAT, BRUCE? HOW HARD IT IS TO ANCHOR YOURSELF TO THE REAL?
SO MAYBE YOU FORCE IT. YOU KEEP A SCHEDULE, MAKE YOURSELF DEAL WITH THE REAL PEOPLE, DAY IN, DAY OUT, SO YOU DON'T FORGET THAT THEIR PERSPECTIVE MATTERS AS MUCH AS YOUR OWN.
SO YOU STAY SOMETHING LIKE A HUMAN.
ZEE. LOOK AT ME. YOU KNOW ME BETTER THAN ALMOST ANYONE. YOU CAN'T SCARE ME AWAY...
THEN I NEED TO TRY HARDER, BRUCE. THE SPHERE WOULD DESTROY YOU.
ZATANNA. I'VE FACED THINGS THE TEENAGE BOY YOU KNEW COULD NEVER HAVE IMAGINED. HORRORS BEYOND NIGHTMARE. BEYOND COMPREHENSION.
BUT THE ONLY THING THAT'S EVER THREATENED TO TEAR ME APART, FROM THE INSIDE OUT, IS THE KNOWLEDGE THAT I COULD HAVE SAVED SOMEBODY IF I TOOK JUST ONE MORE STEP.
WHATEVER IS BREWING, THE TARGET IS FIRMLY PLANTED ON THE PEOPLE I CARE ABOUT MOST IN THIS WORLD. I'VE ALREADY LOST ONE OF THEM.
PLEASE, ZATANNA. I NEED TO DO THIS.

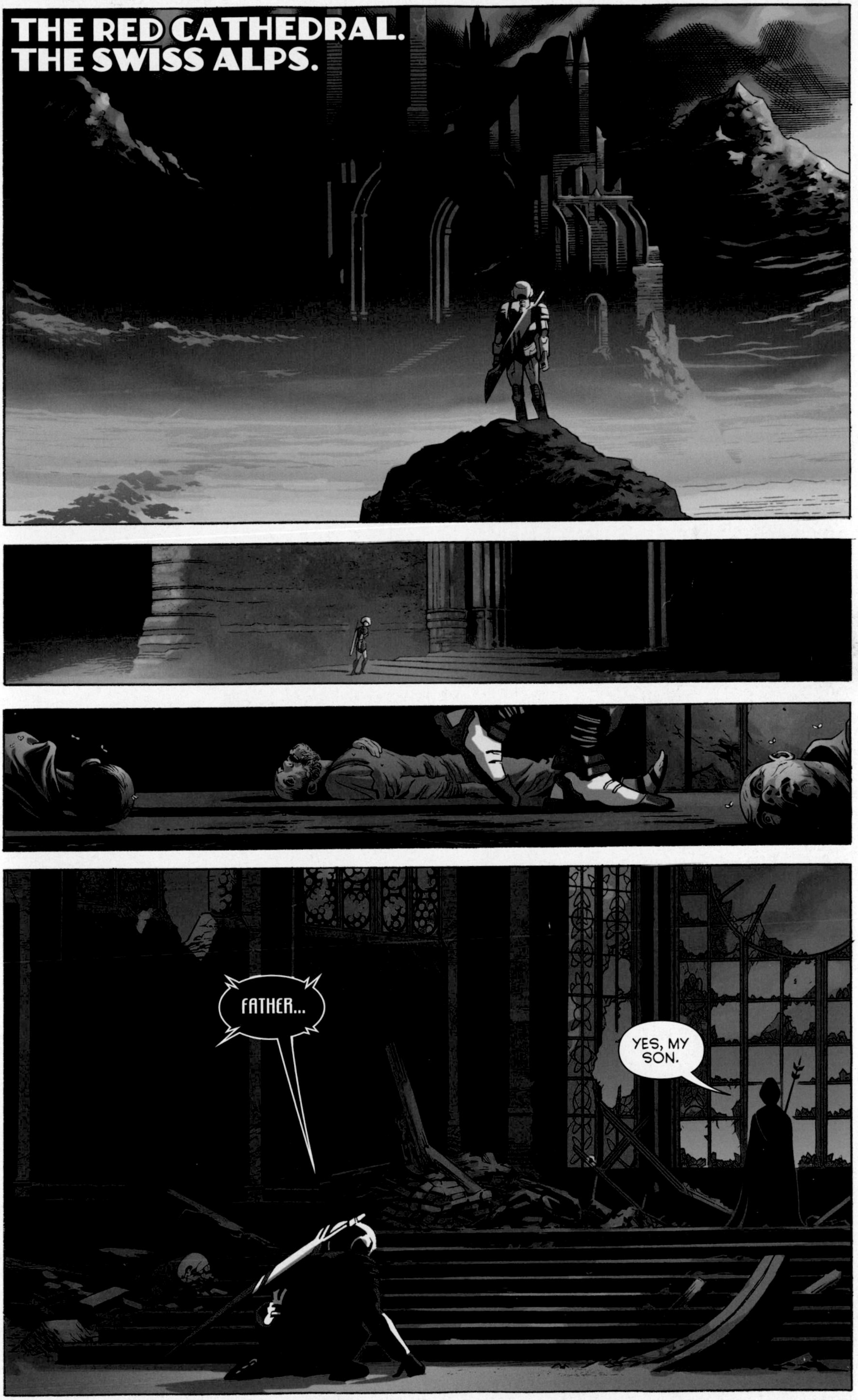
THE RED CATHEDRAL.
THE SWISS ALPS.
FATHER...
YES, MY SON.

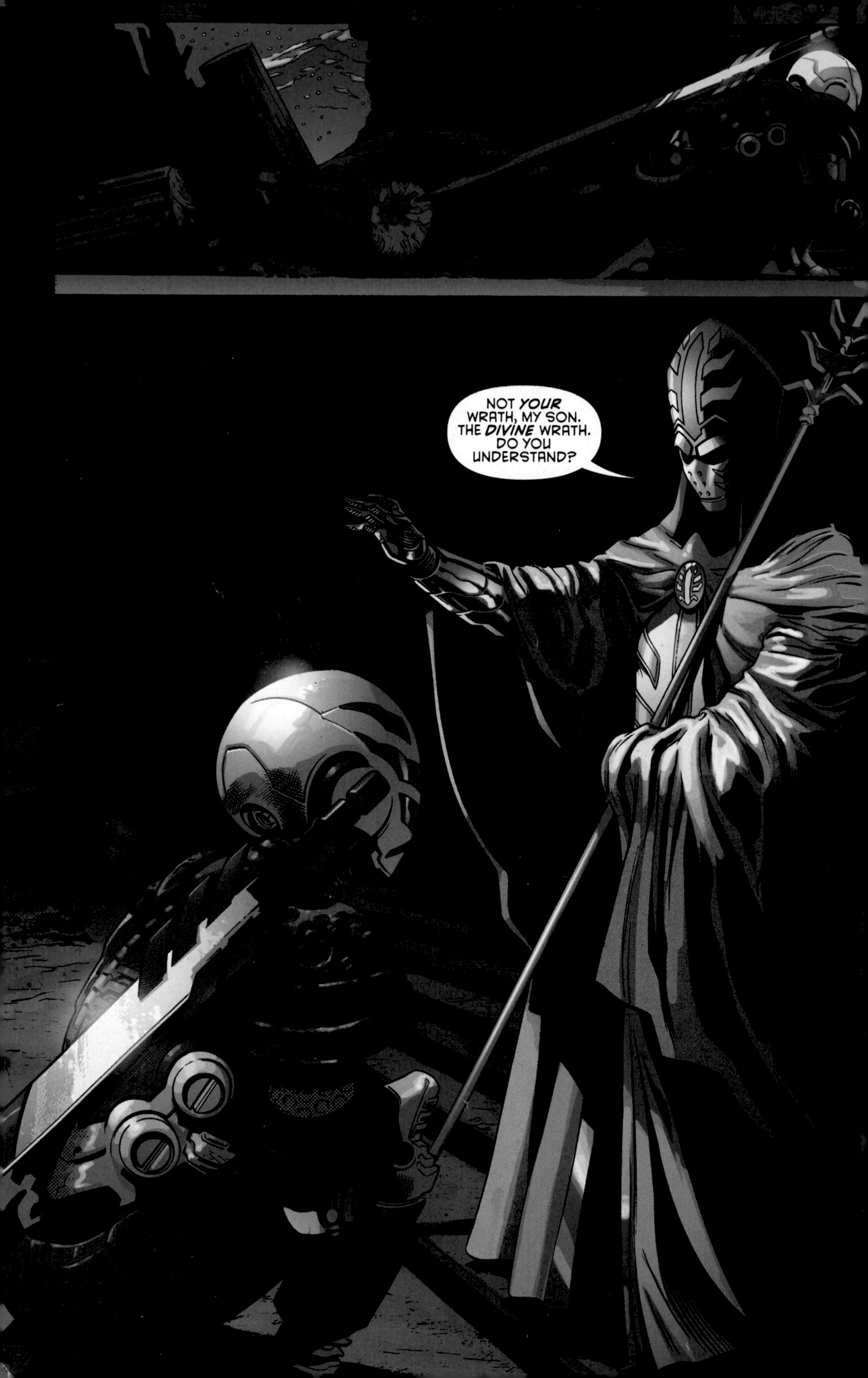
NOT *YOUR* WRATH, MY SON. THE *DIVINE* WRATH. DO YOU UNDERSTAND?

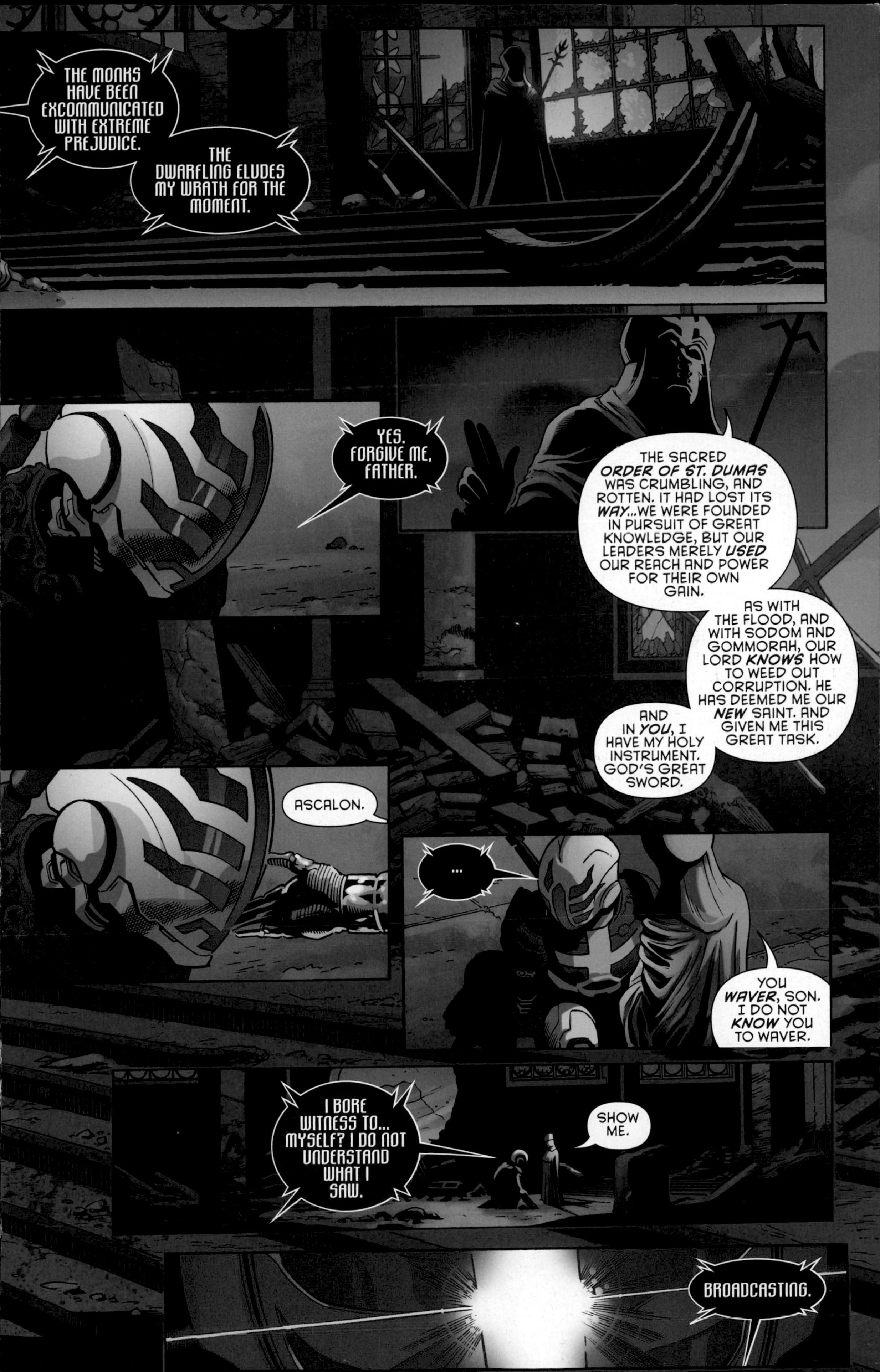
THE MONKS HAVE BEEN EXCOMMUNICATED WITH EXTREME PREJUDICE.
THE DWARFLING ELUDES MY WRATH FOR THE MOMENT.
YES. FORGIVE ME, FATHER.
THE SACRED ORDER OF ST. DUMAS WAS CRUMBLING, AND ROTTEN. IT HAD LOST ITS WAY...WE WERE FOUNDED IN PURSUIT OF GREAT KNOWLEDGE, BUT OUR LEADERS MERELY USED OUR REACH AND POWER FOR THEIR OWN GAIN.
AS WITH THE FLOOD, AND WITH SODOM AND GOMMORAH, OUR LORD KNOWS HOW TO WEED OUT CORRUPTION. HE HAS DEEMED ME OUR NEW SAINT. AND GIVEN ME THIS GREAT TASK.
AND IN YOU, I HAVE MY HOLY INSTRUMENT. GOD'S GREAT SWORD.
ASCALON.
...
YOU WAVER, SON. I DO NOT KNOW YOU TO WAVER.
I BORE WITNESS TO... MYSELF? I DO NOT UNDERSTAND WHAT I SAW.
SHOW ME.
BROADCASTING.

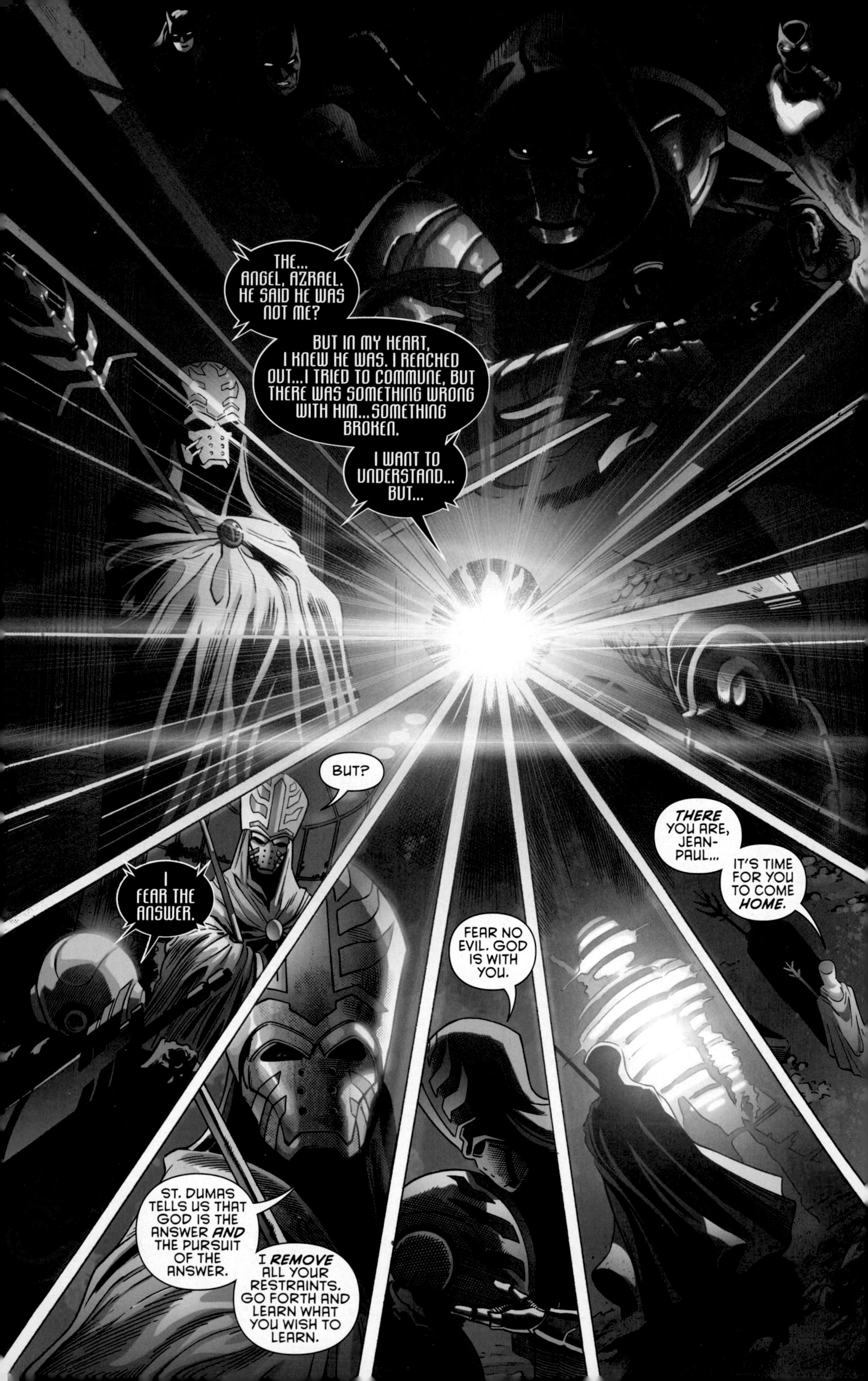
THE... ANGEL, AZRAEL. HE SAID HE WAS NOT ME?
BUT IN MY HEART, I KNEW HE WAS. I REACHED OUT...I TRIED TO COMMUNE, BUT THERE WAS SOMETHING WRONG WITH HIM...SOMETHING BROKEN.
I WANT TO UNDERSTAND... BUT...
BUT?
I FEAR THE ANSWER.
ST. DUMAS TELLS US THAT GOD IS THE ANSWER AND THE PURSUIT OF THE ANSWER.
I REMOVE ALL YOUR RESTRAINTS. GO FORTH AND LEARN WHAT YOU WISH TO LEARN.
FEAR NO EVIL. GOD IS WITH YOU.
THERE YOU ARE, JEAN-PAUL...
IT'S TIME FOR YOU TO COME HOME.

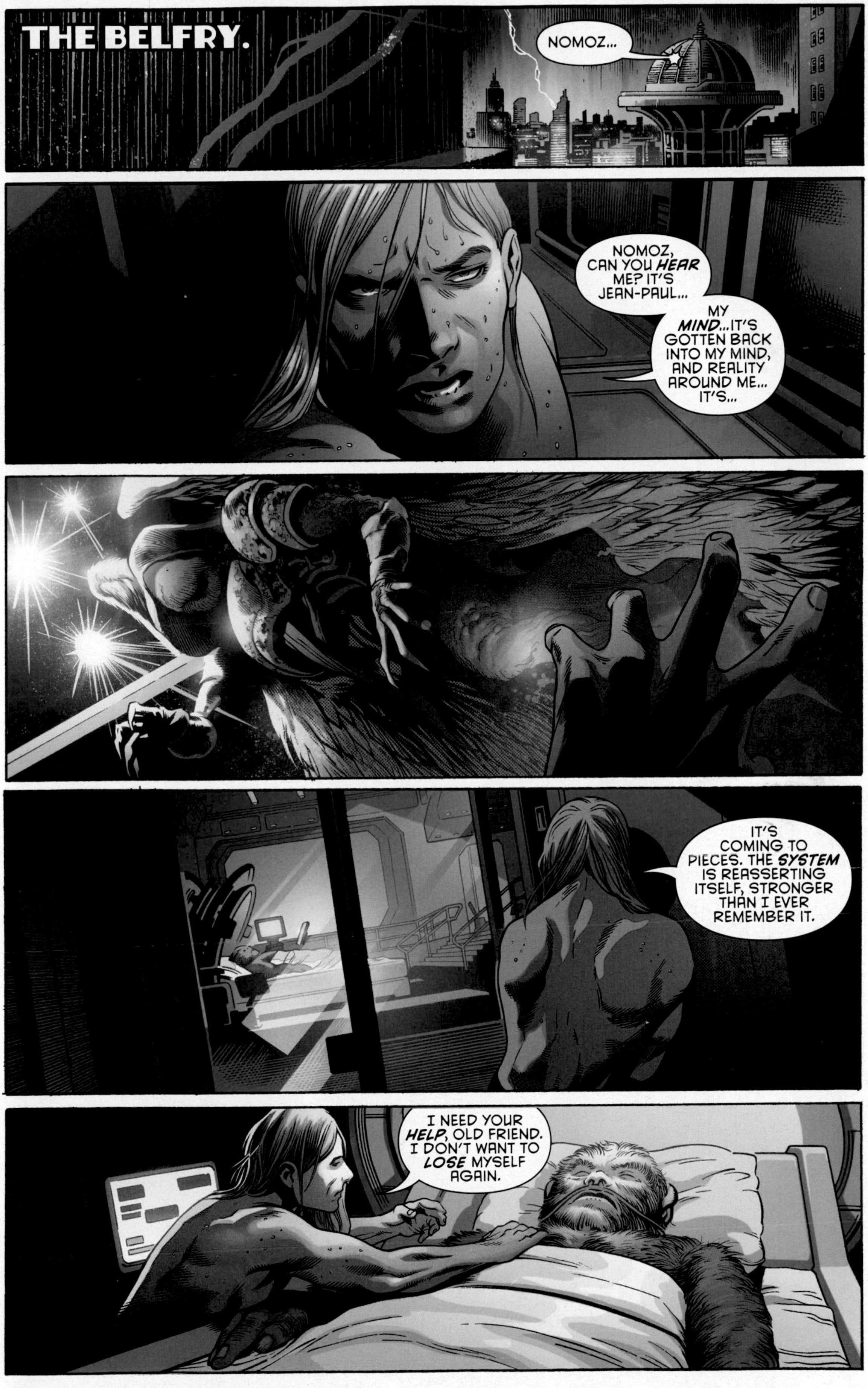
THE BELFRY.
NOMOZ...
NOMOZ, CAN YOU HEAR ME? IT'S JEAN-PAUL...
MY MIND...IT'S GOTTEN BACK INTO MY MIND, AND REALITY AROUND ME... IT'S...
IT'S COMING TO PIECES. THE SYSTEM IS REASSERTING ITSELF, STRONGER THAN I EVER REMEMBER IT.
I NEED YOUR HELP, OLD FRIEND. I DON'T WANT TO LOSE MYSELF AGAIN.

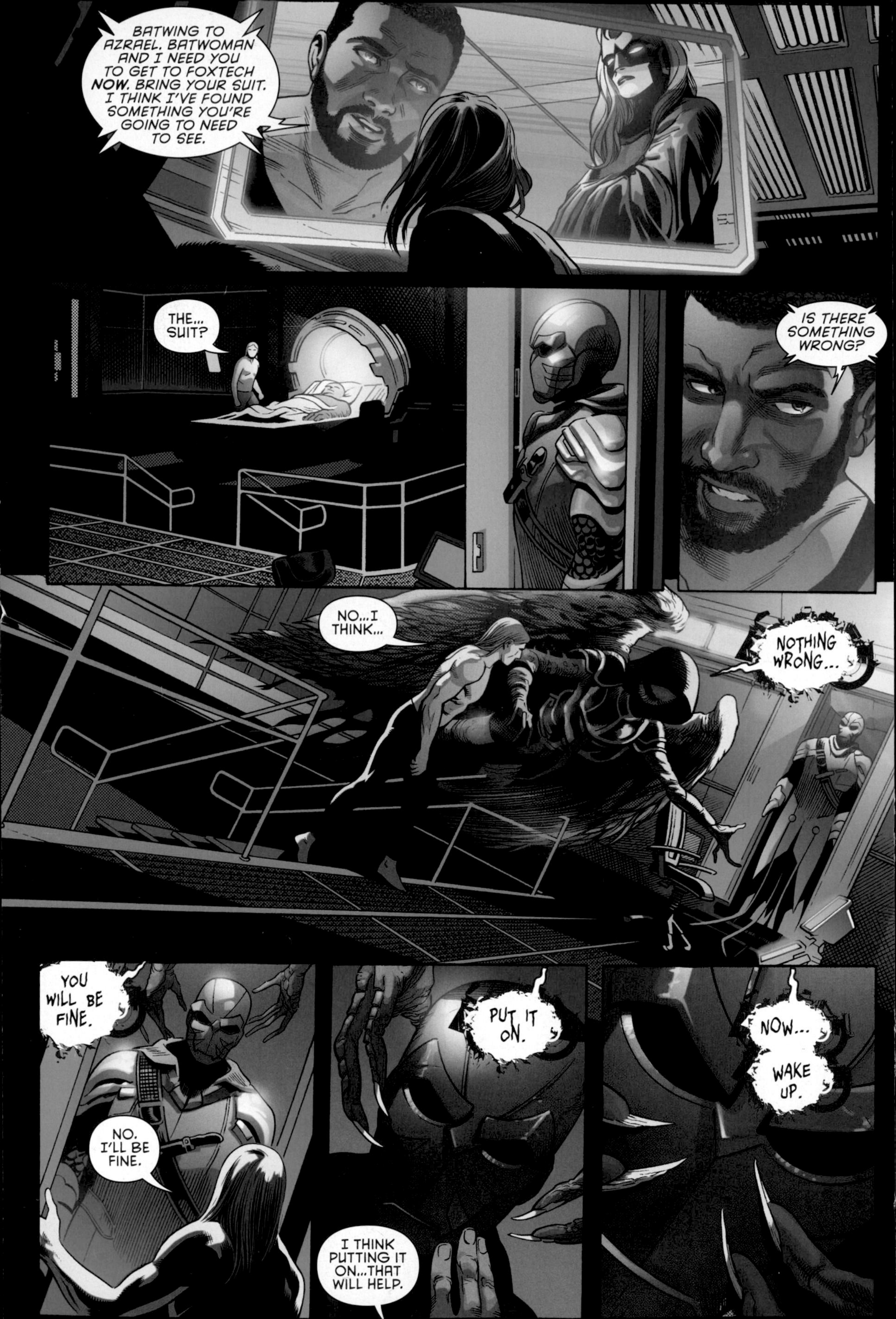
BATWING TO AZRAEL. BATWOMAN AND I NEED YOU TO GET TO FOXTECH **NOW**. BRING YOUR SUIT. I THINK I'VE FOUND SOMETHING YOU'RE GOING TO NEED TO SEE.
THE... SUIT?
IS THERE SOMETHING WRONG?
NO...I THINK...
NOTHING WRONG...
YOU WILL BE FINE.
NO. I'LL BE FINE.
PUT IT ON.
I THINK PUTTING IT ON...THAT WILL HELP.
NOW...
WAKE UP.

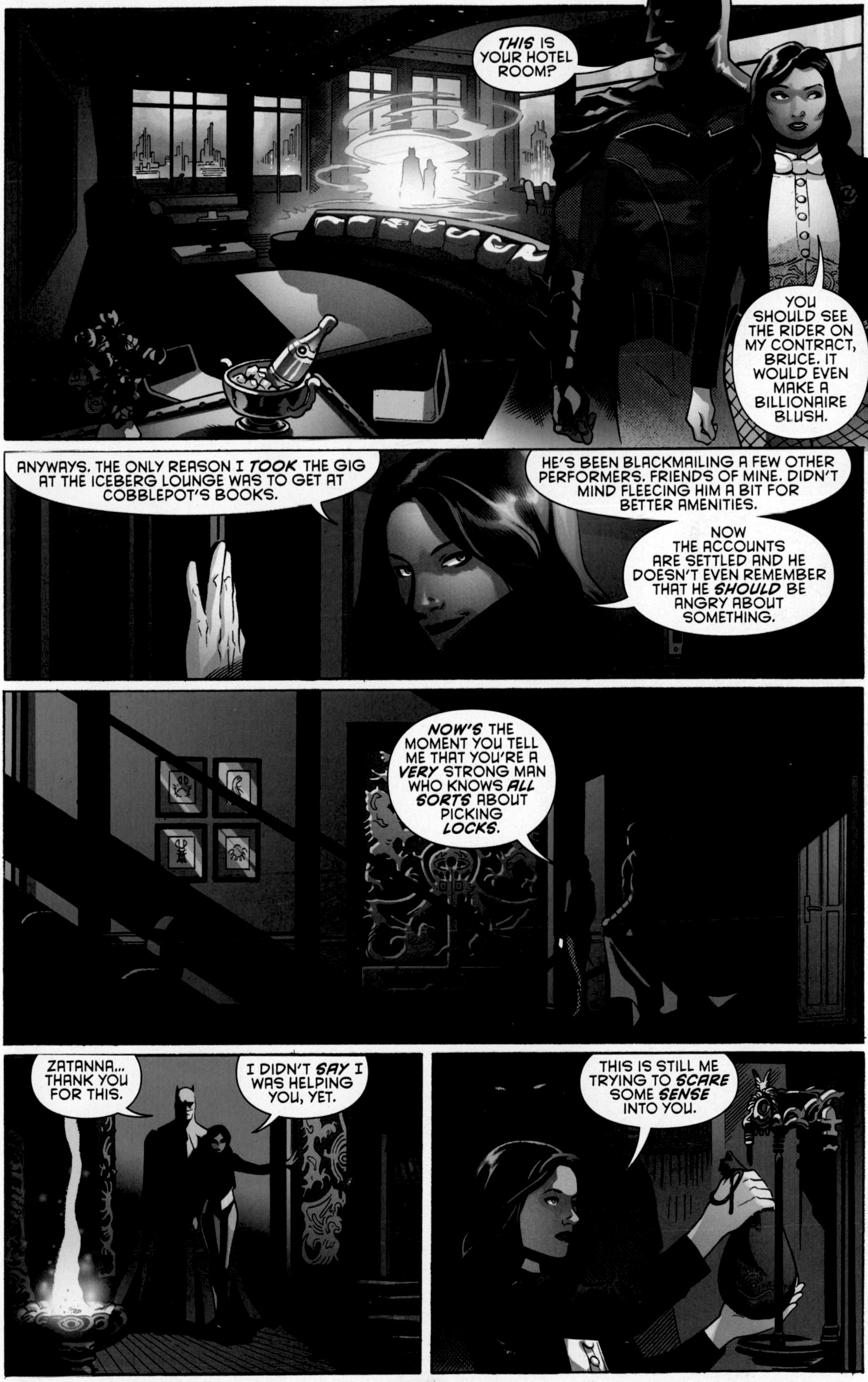
THIS IS YOUR HOTEL ROOM?
YOU SHOULD SEE THE RIDER ON MY CONTRACT, BRUCE. IT WOULD EVEN MAKE A BILLIONAIRE BLUSH.
ANYWAYS. THE ONLY REASON I TOOK THE GIG AT THE ICEBERG LOUNGE WAS TO GET AT COBBLEPOT'S BOOKS.
HE'S BEEN BLACKMAILING A FEW OTHER PERFORMERS. FRIENDS OF MINE. DIDN'T MIND FLEECING HIM A BIT FOR BETTER AMENITIES.
NOW THE ACCOUNTS ARE SETTLED AND HE DOESN'T EVEN REMEMBER THAT HE SHOULD BE ANGRY ABOUT SOMETHING.
NOW'S THE MOMENT YOU TELL ME THAT YOU'RE A VERY STRONG MAN WHO KNOWS ALL SORTS ABOUT PICKING LOCKS.
ZATANNA... THANK YOU FOR THIS.
I DIDN'T SAY I WAS HELPING YOU, YET.
THIS IS STILL ME TRYING TO SCARE SOME SENSE INTO YOU.

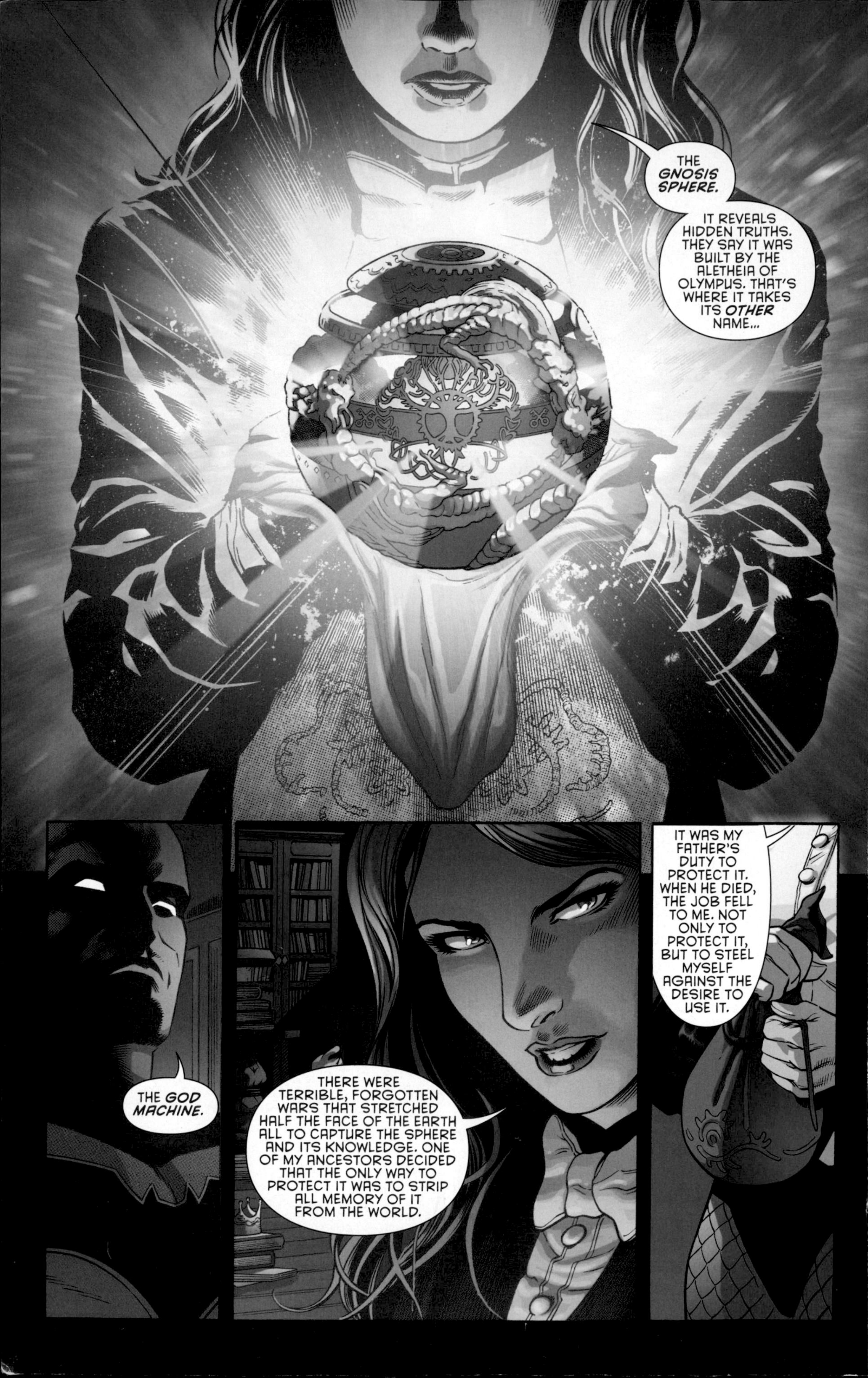
THE *GNOSIS SPHERE.*
IT REVEALS HIDDEN TRUTHS. THEY SAY IT WAS BUILT BY THE ALETHEIA OF OLYMPUS. THAT'S WHERE IT TAKES ITS *OTHER* NAME...
THE *GOD MACHINE.*
THERE WERE TERRIBLE, FORGOTTEN WARS THAT STRETCHED HALF THE FACE OF THE EARTH ALL TO CAPTURE THE SPHERE AND ITS KNOWLEDGE. ONE OF MY ANCESTORS DECIDED THAT THE ONLY WAY TO PROTECT IT WAS TO STRIP ALL MEMORY OF IT FROM THE WORLD.
IT WAS MY FATHER'S DUTY TO PROTECT IT. WHEN HE DIED, THE JOB FELL TO ME. NOT ONLY TO PROTECT IT, BUT TO STEEL MYSELF AGAINST THE DESIRE TO USE IT.

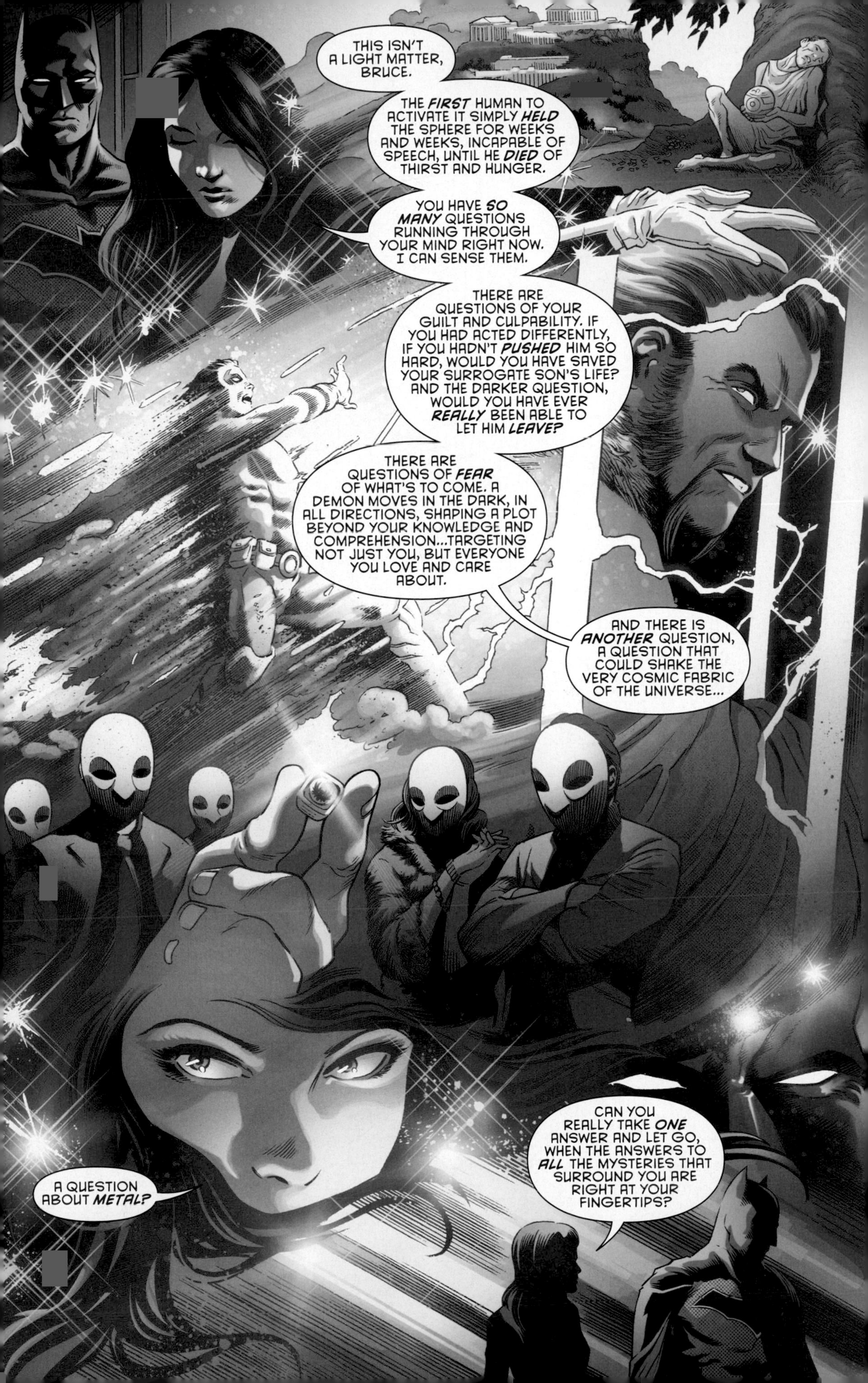
THIS ISN'T A LIGHT MATTER, BRUCE.
THE FIRST HUMAN TO ACTIVATE IT SIMPLY HELD THE SPHERE FOR WEEKS AND WEEKS, INCAPABLE OF SPEECH, UNTIL HE DIED OF THIRST AND HUNGER.
YOU HAVE SO MANY QUESTIONS RUNNING THROUGH YOUR MIND RIGHT NOW. I CAN SENSE THEM.
THERE ARE QUESTIONS OF YOUR GUILT AND CULPABILITY. IF YOU HAD ACTED DIFFERENTLY, IF YOU HADN'T PUSHED HIM SO HARD, WOULD YOU HAVE SAVED YOUR SURROGATE SON'S LIFE? AND THE DARKER QUESTION, WOULD YOU HAVE EVER REALLY BEEN ABLE TO LET HIM LEAVE?
THERE ARE QUESTIONS OF FEAR OF WHAT'S TO COME. A DEMON MOVES IN THE DARK, IN ALL DIRECTIONS, SHAPING A PLOT BEYOND YOUR KNOWLEDGE AND COMPREHENSION...TARGETING NOT JUST YOU, BUT EVERYONE YOU LOVE AND CARE ABOUT.
AND THERE IS ANOTHER QUESTION, A QUESTION THAT COULD SHAKE THE VERY COSMIC FABRIC OF THE UNIVERSE...
A QUESTION ABOUT METAL?
CAN YOU REALLY TAKE ONE ANSWER AND LET GO, WHEN THE ANSWERS TO ALL THE MYSTERIES THAT SURROUND YOU ARE RIGHT AT YOUR FINGERTIPS?

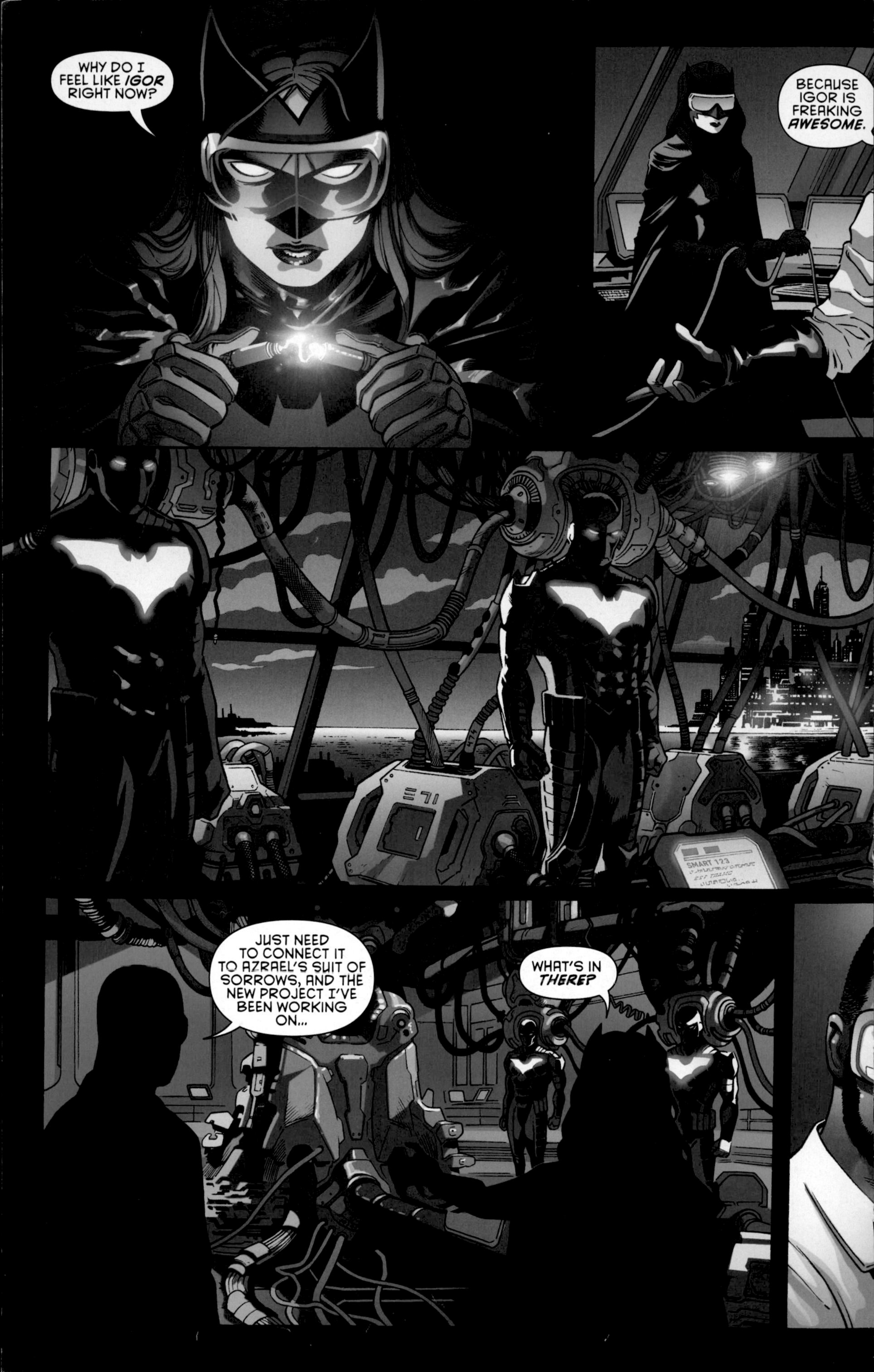
WHY DO I FEEL LIKE *IGOR* RIGHT NOW?
BECAUSE IGOR IS FREAKING ***AWESOME.***
SMART 123
JUST NEED TO CONNECT IT TO AZRAEL'S SUIT OF SORROWS, AND THE NEW PROJECT I'VE BEEN WORKING ON...
WHAT'S IN *THERE?*

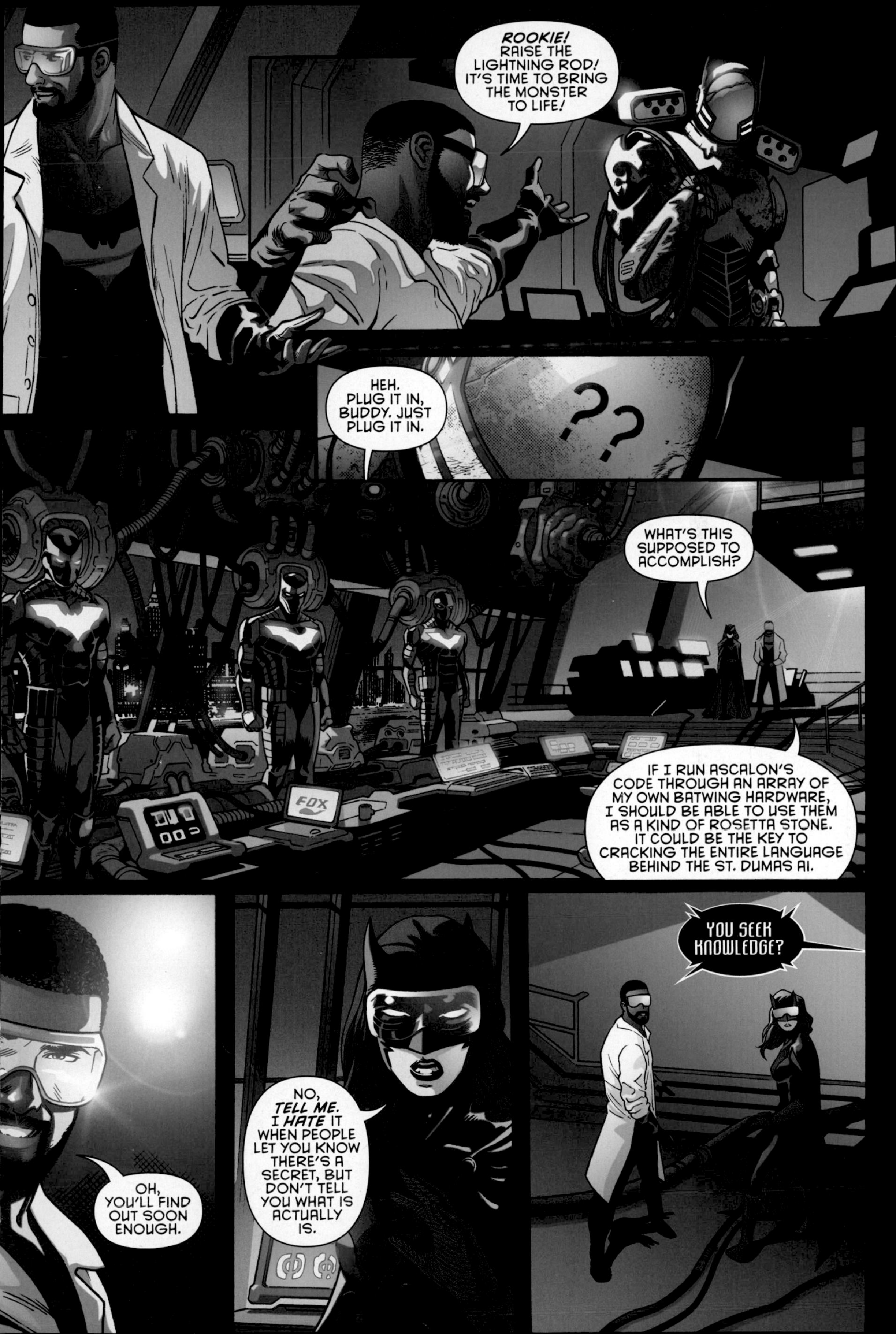
ROOKIE! RAISE THE LIGHTNING ROD! IT'S TIME TO BRING THE MONSTER TO LIFE!
HEH. PLUG IT IN, BUDDY. JUST PLUG IT IN.
??
WHAT'S THIS SUPPOSED TO ACCOMPLISH?
IF I RUN ASCALON'S CODE THROUGH AN ARRAY OF MY OWN BATWING HARDWARE, I SHOULD BE ABLE TO USE THEM AS A KIND OF ROSETTA STONE. IT COULD BE THE KEY TO CRACKING THE ENTIRE LANGUAGE BEHIND THE ST. DUMAS AI.
FOX
OH, YOU'LL FIND OUT SOON ENOUGH.
NO, TELL ME. I HATE IT WHEN PEOPLE LET YOU KNOW THERE'S A SECRET, BUT DON'T TELL YOU WHAT IS ACTUALLY IS.
YOU SEEK KNOWLEDGE?

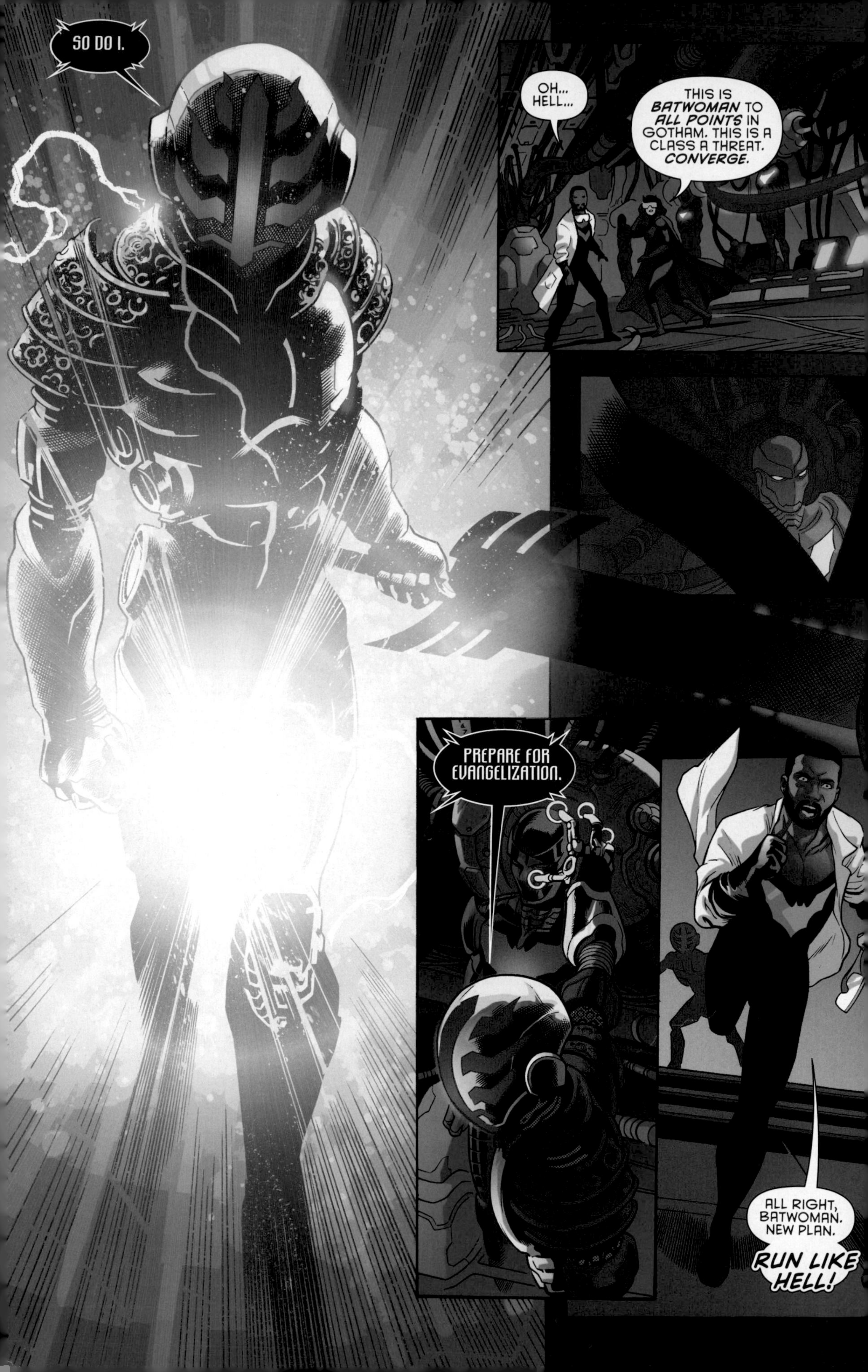
SO DO I.
OH... HELL...
THIS IS BATWOMAN TO ALL POINTS IN GOTHAM. THIS IS A CLASS A THREAT. CONVERGE.
PREPARE FOR EVANGELIZATION.
ALL RIGHT, BATWOMAN. NEW PLAN.
RUN LIKE HELL!

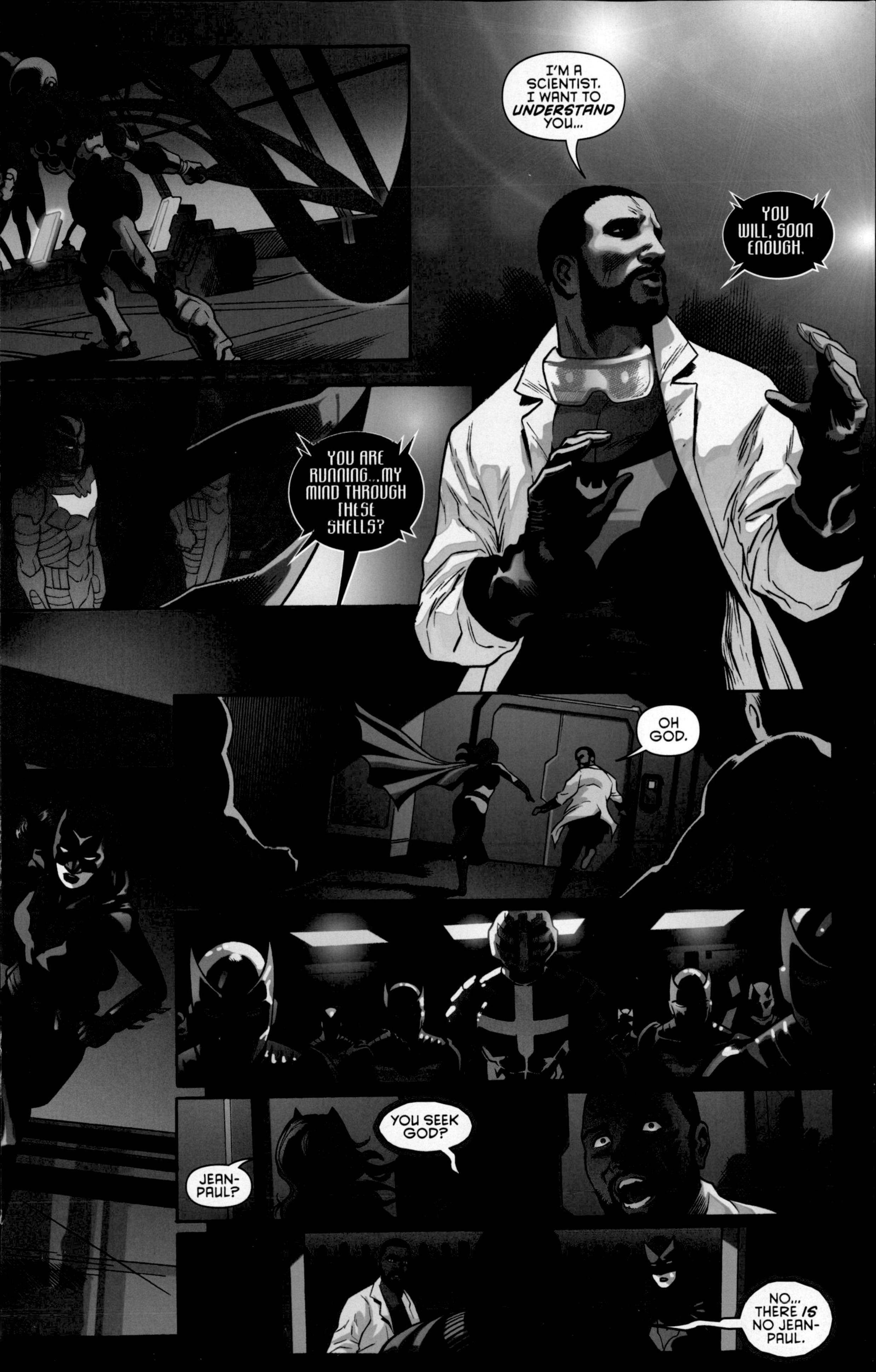
I'M A SCIENTIST. I WANT TO *UNDERSTAND* YOU...
YOU WILL, SOON ENOUGH.
YOU ARE RUNNING...MY MIND THROUGH THESE SHELLS?
OH GOD.
YOU SEEK GOD?
JEAN-PAUL?
NO... THERE *IS* NO JEAN-PAUL.

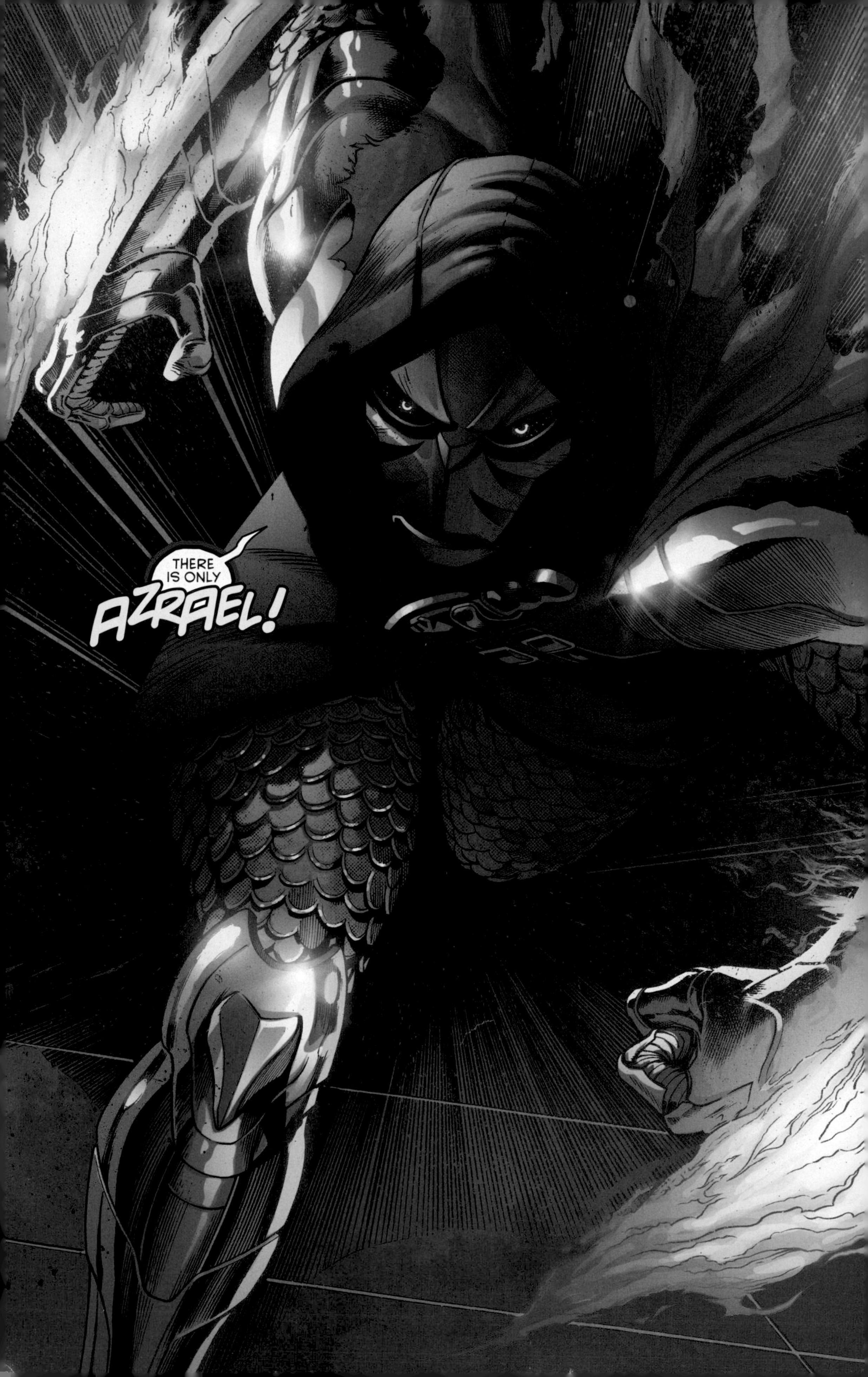
THERE IS ONLY
AZRAEL!

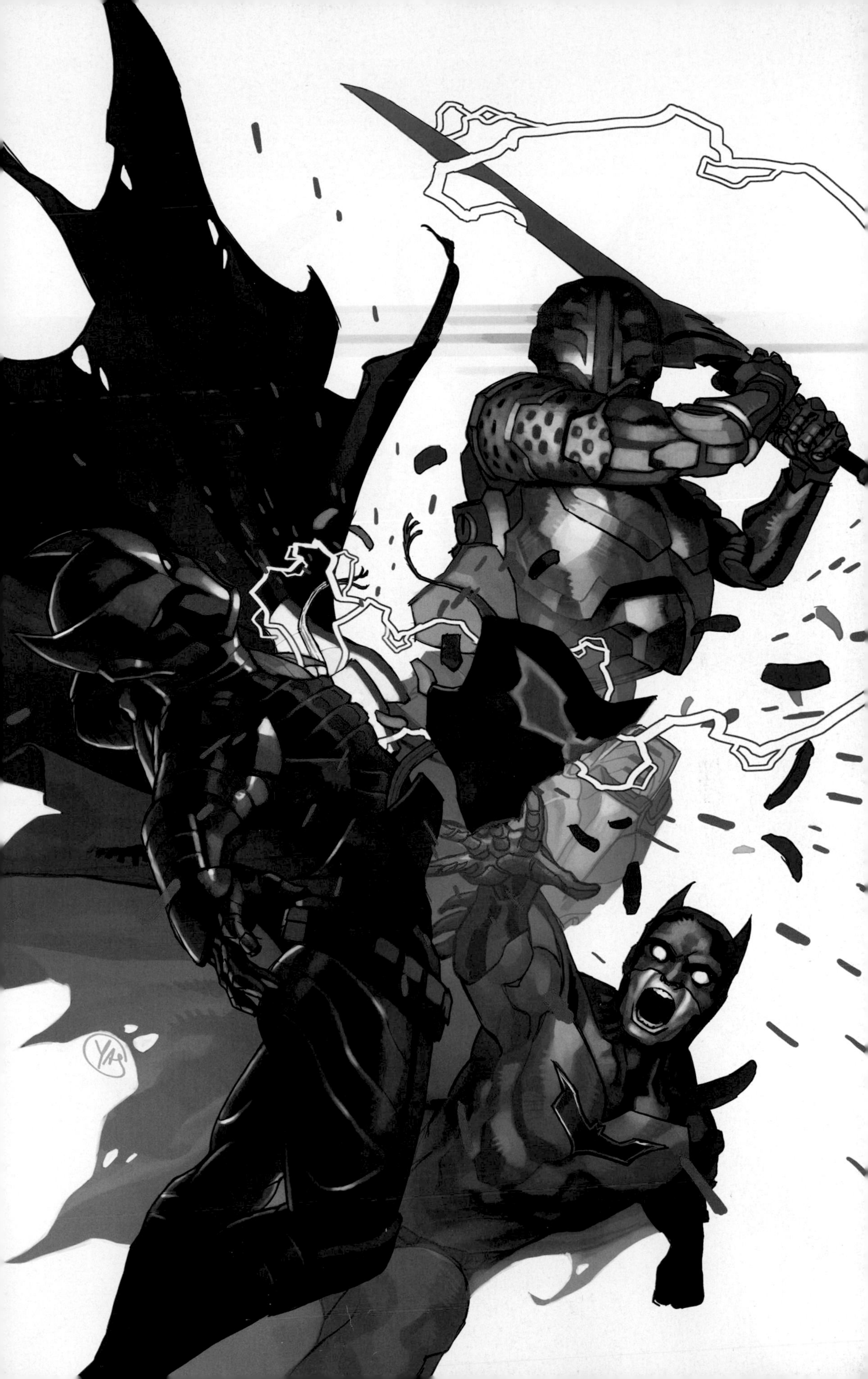

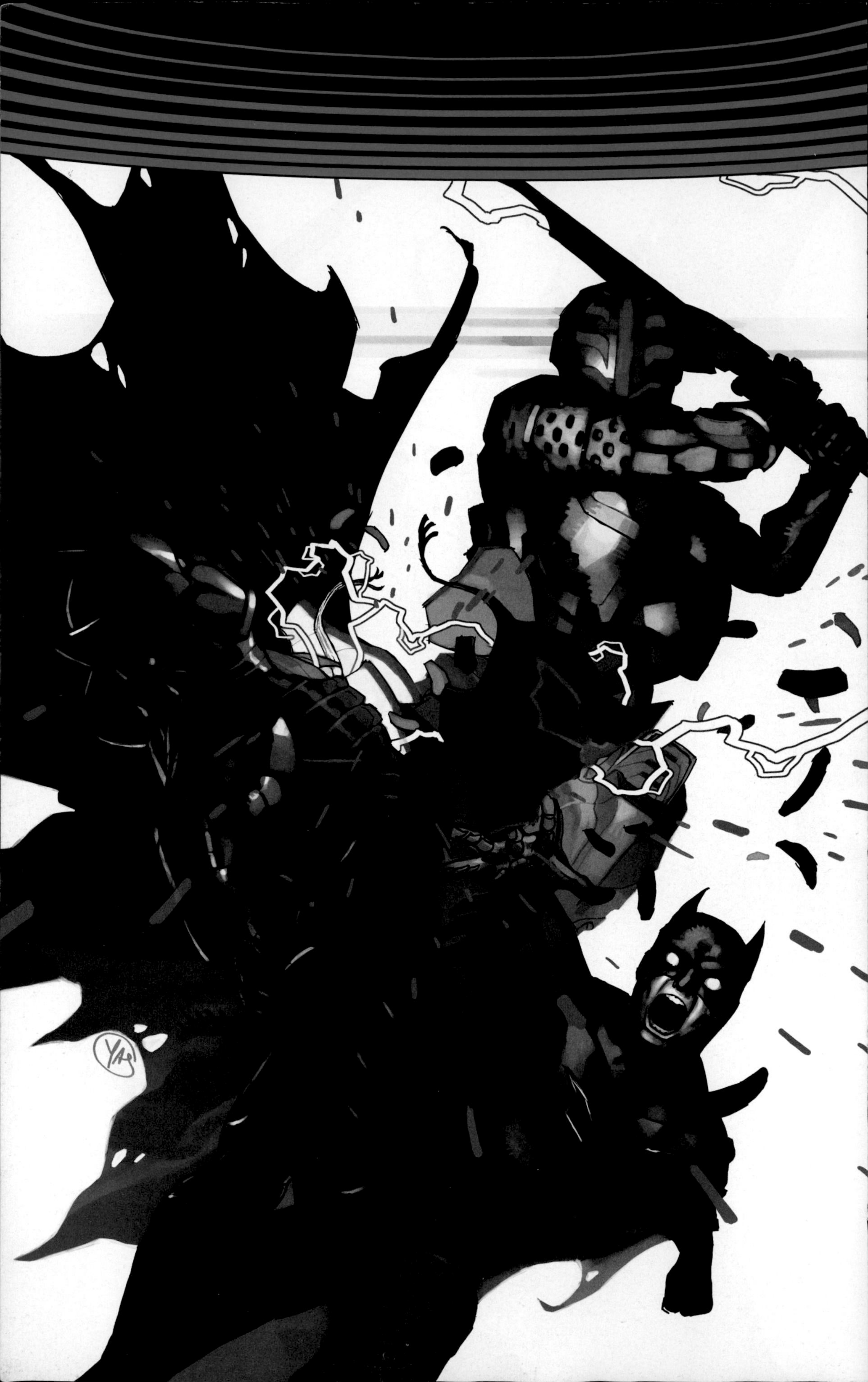

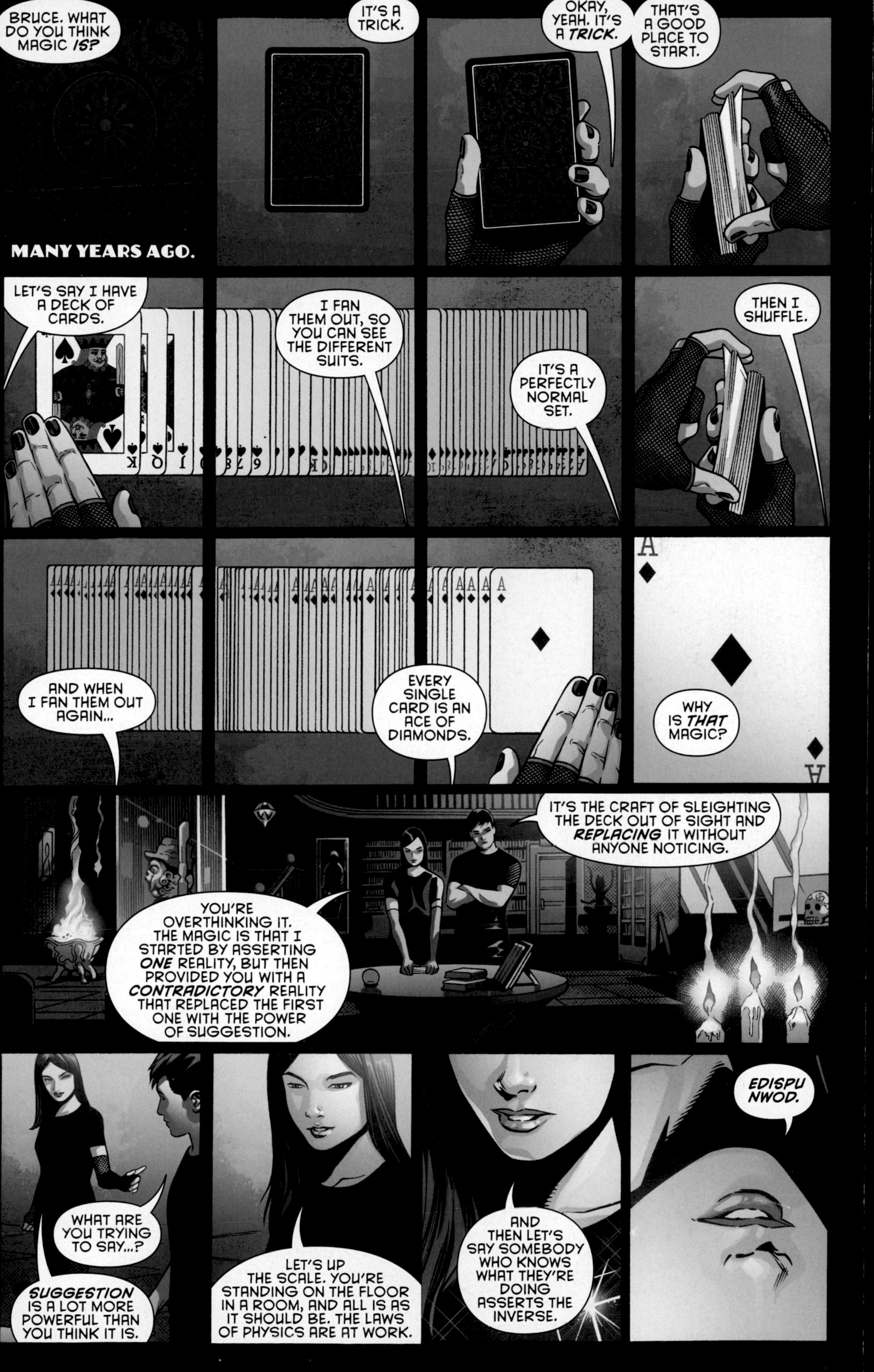
BRUCE. WHAT DO YOU THINK MAGIC *IS?*
MANY YEARS AGO.
IT'S A TRICK.
OKAY, YEAH. IT'S A *TRICK.*
THAT'S A GOOD PLACE TO START.
LET'S SAY I HAVE A DECK OF CARDS.
I FAN THEM OUT, SO YOU CAN SEE THE DIFFERENT SUITS.
IT'S A PERFECTLY NORMAL SET.
THEN I SHUFFLE.
AND WHEN I FAN THEM OUT AGAIN...
EVERY SINGLE CARD IS AN ACE OF DIAMONDS.
WHY IS *THAT* MAGIC?
IT'S THE CRAFT OF SLEIGHTING THE DECK OUT OF SIGHT AND *REPLACING* IT WITHOUT ANYONE NOTICING.
YOU'RE OVERTHINKING IT. THE MAGIC IS THAT I STARTED BY ASSERTING *ONE* REALITY, BUT THEN PROVIDED YOU WITH A *CONTRADICTORY* REALITY THAT REPLACED THE FIRST ONE WITH THE POWER OF SUGGESTION.
WHAT ARE YOU TRYING TO SAY...?
SUGGESTION IS A LOT MORE POWERFUL THAN YOU THINK IT IS.
LET'S UP THE SCALE. YOU'RE STANDING ON THE FLOOR IN A ROOM, AND ALL IS AS IT SHOULD BE. THE LAWS OF PHYSICS ARE AT WORK.
AND THEN LET'S SAY SOMEBODY WHO KNOWS WHAT THEY'RE DOING ASSERTS THE INVERSE.
EDISPU NWOD.

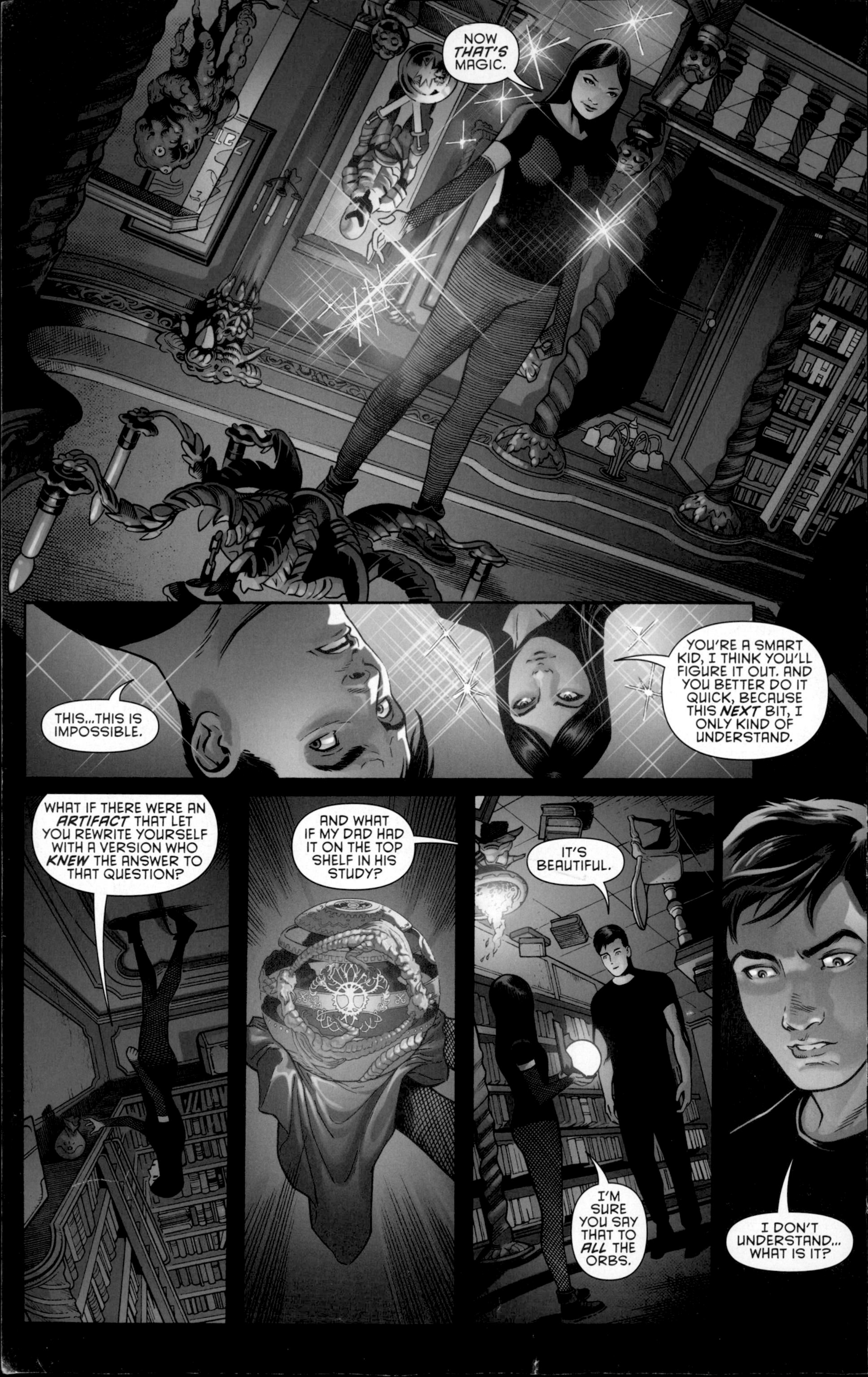
NOW THAT'S MAGIC.
THIS...THIS IS IMPOSSIBLE.
YOU'RE A SMART KID, I THINK YOU'LL FIGURE IT OUT. AND YOU BETTER DO IT QUICK, BECAUSE THIS NEXT BIT, I ONLY KIND OF UNDERSTAND.
WHAT IF THERE WERE AN ARTIFACT THAT LET YOU REWRITE YOURSELF WITH A VERSION WHO KNEW THE ANSWER TO THAT QUESTION?
AND WHAT IF MY DAD HAD IT ON THE TOP SHELF IN HIS STUDY?
IT'S BEAUTIFUL.
I'M SURE YOU SAY THAT TO ALL THE ORBS.
I DON'T UNDERSTAND... WHAT IS IT?

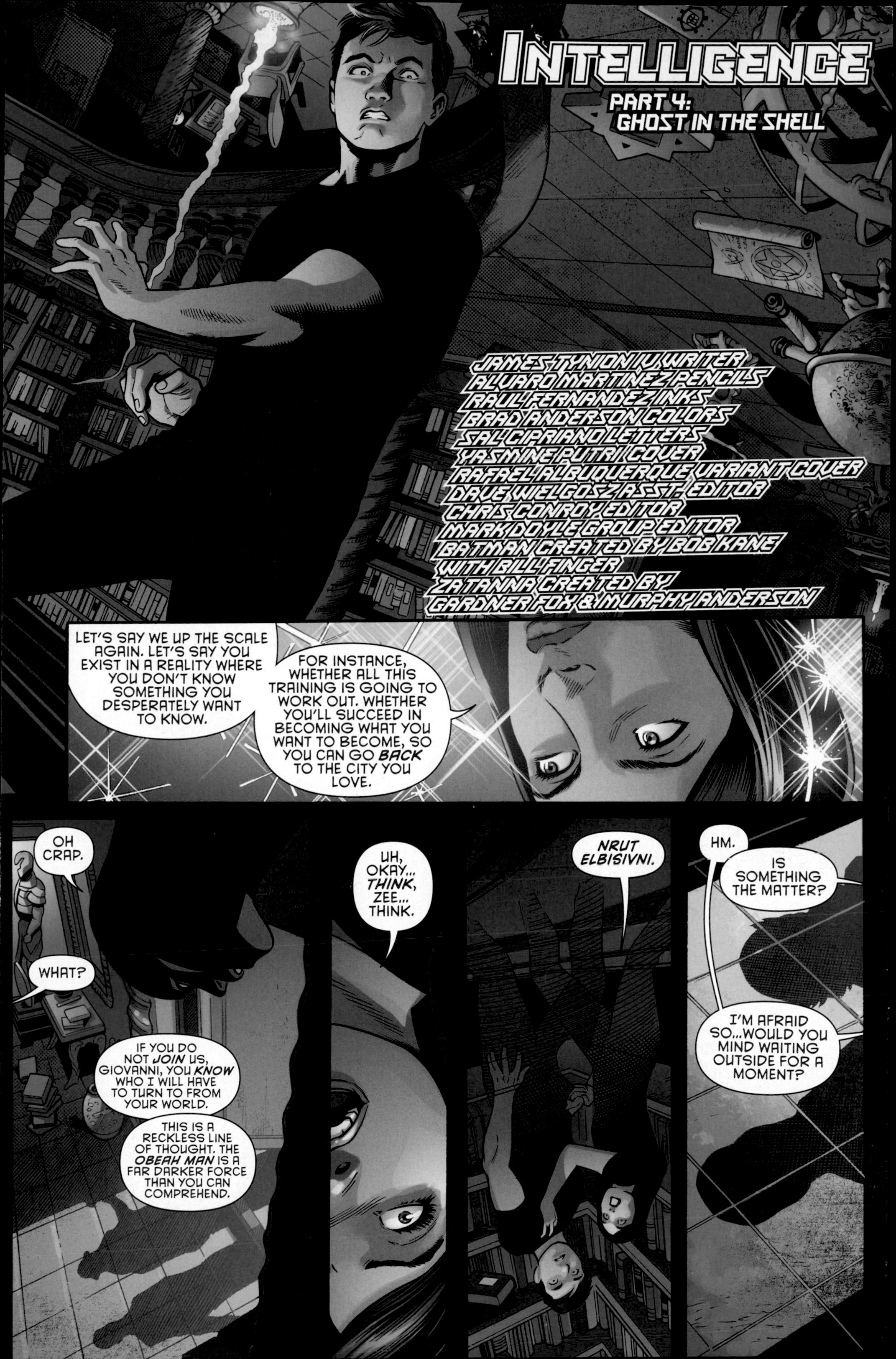
INTELLIGENCE
PART 4: GHOST IN THE SHELL
JAMES TYNION IV, WRITER
ALVARO MARTINEZ PENCILS
RAUL FERNANDEZ INKS
BRAD ANDERSON COLORS
SAL CIPRIANO LETTERS
YASMINE PUTRI COVER
RAFAEL ALBUQUERQUE VARIANT COVER
DAVE WIELGOSZ ASST. EDITOR
CHRIS CONROY EDITOR
MARK DOYLE GROUP EDITOR
BATMAN CREATED BY BOB KANE WITH BILL FINGER
ZATANNA CREATED BY GARDNER FOX & MURPHY ANDERSON
LET'S SAY WE UP THE SCALE AGAIN. LET'S SAY YOU EXIST IN A REALITY WHERE YOU DON'T KNOW SOMETHING YOU DESPERATELY WANT TO KNOW.
FOR INSTANCE, WHETHER ALL THIS TRAINING IS GOING TO WORK OUT. WHETHER YOU'LL SUCCEED IN BECOMING WHAT YOU WANT TO BECOME, SO YOU CAN GO BACK TO THE CITY YOU LOVE.
OH CRAP.
WHAT?
IF YOU DO NOT JOIN US, GIOVANNI, YOU KNOW WHO I WILL HAVE TO TURN TO FROM YOUR WORLD.
THIS IS A RECKLESS LINE OF THOUGHT. THE OBEAH MAN IS A FAR DARKER FORCE THAN YOU CAN COMPREHEND.
UH, OKAY... THINK, ZEE... THINK.
NRUT ELBISIVNI.
HM.
IS SOMETHING THE MATTER?
I'M AFRAID SO...WOULD YOU MIND WAITING OUTSIDE FOR A MOMENT?

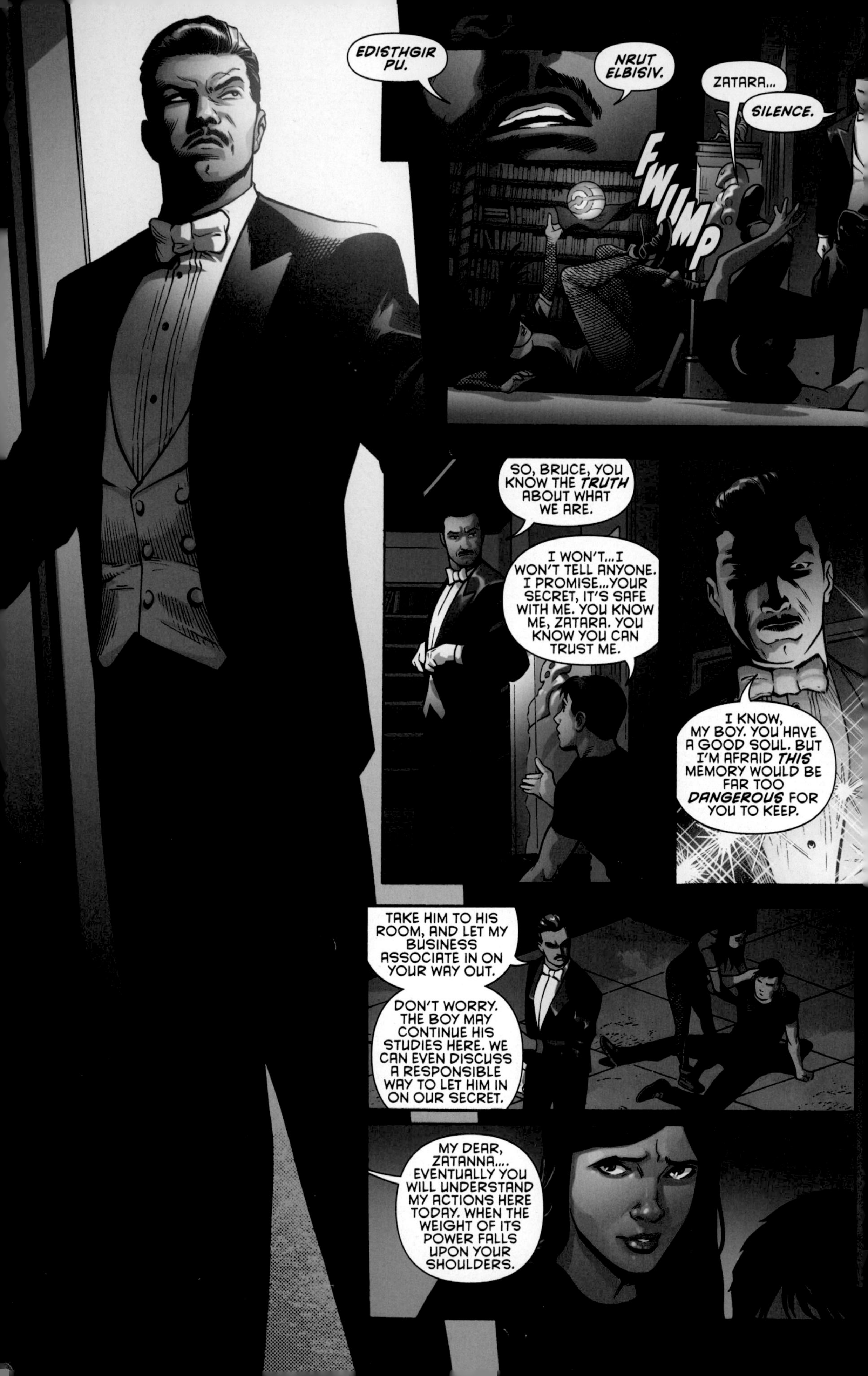
EDISTHGIR PU.
NRUT ELBISIV.
ZATARA...
SILENCE.
FWUMP
SO, BRUCE, YOU KNOW THE TRUTH ABOUT WHAT WE ARE.
I WON'T...I WON'T TELL ANYONE. I PROMISE...YOUR SECRET, IT'S SAFE WITH ME. YOU KNOW ME, ZATARA. YOU KNOW YOU CAN TRUST ME.
I KNOW, MY BOY. YOU HAVE A GOOD SOUL. BUT I'M AFRAID THIS MEMORY WOULD BE FAR TOO DANGEROUS FOR YOU TO KEEP.
TAKE HIM TO HIS ROOM, AND LET MY BUSINESS ASSOCIATE IN ON YOUR WAY OUT.
DON'T WORRY. THE BOY MAY CONTINUE HIS STUDIES HERE. WE CAN EVEN DISCUSS A RESPONSIBLE WAY TO LET HIM IN ON OUR SECRET.
MY DEAR, ZATANNA.... EVENTUALLY YOU WILL UNDERSTAND MY ACTIONS HERE TODAY. WHEN THE WEIGHT OF ITS POWER FALLS UPON YOUR SHOULDERS.

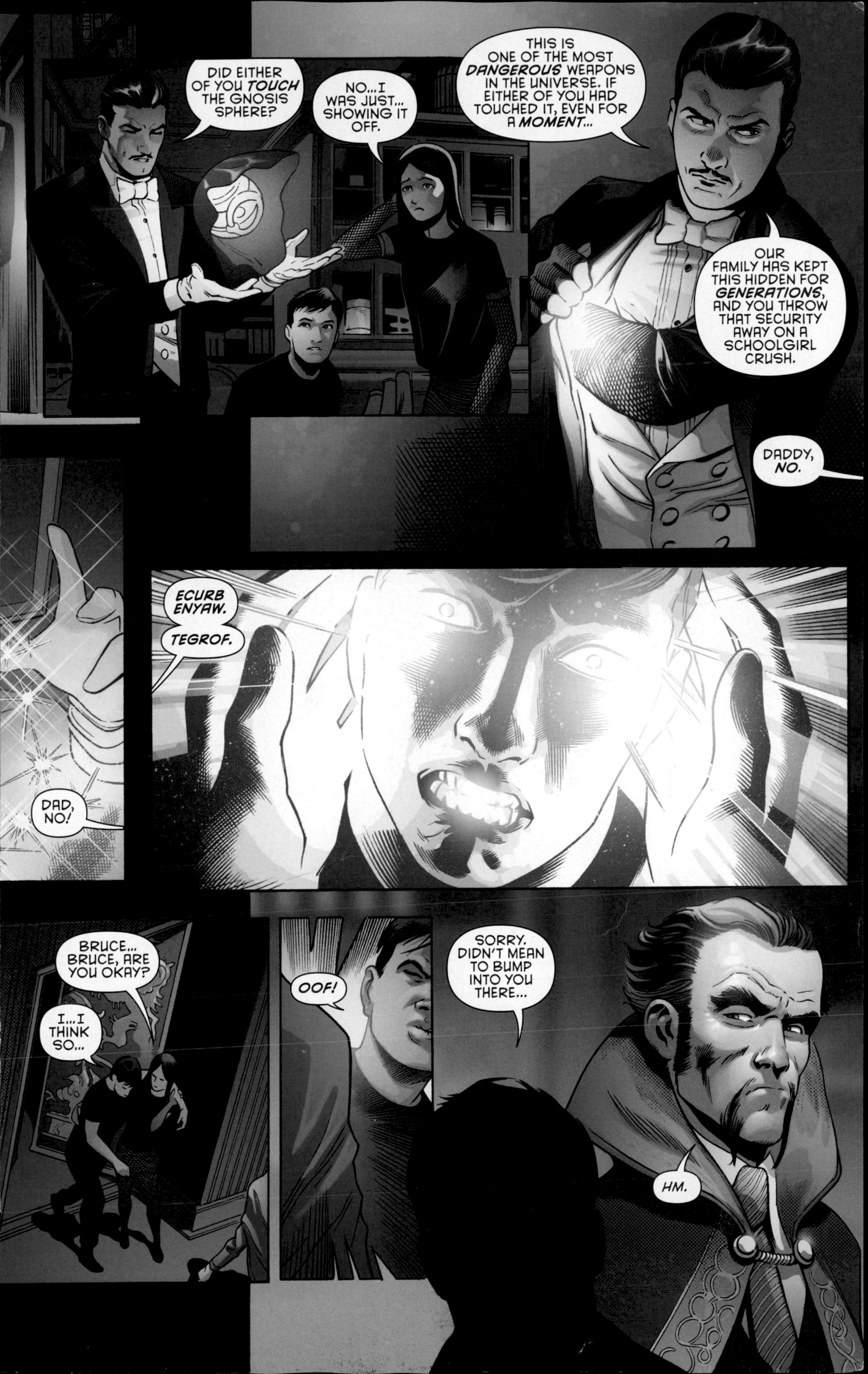
DID EITHER OF YOU TOUCH THE GNOSIS SPHERE?
NO... I WAS JUST... SHOWING IT OFF.
THIS IS ONE OF THE MOST DANGEROUS WEAPONS IN THE UNIVERSE. IF EITHER OF YOU HAD TOUCHED IT, EVEN FOR A MOMENT...
OUR FAMILY HAS KEPT THIS HIDDEN FOR GENERATIONS, AND YOU THROW THAT SECURITY AWAY ON A SCHOOLGIRL CRUSH.
DADDY, NO.
ECURB ENYAW.
TEGROF.
DAD, NO!
BRUCE... BRUCE, ARE YOU OKAY?
I... I THINK SO...
OOF!
SORRY. DIDN'T MEAN TO BUMP INTO YOU THERE...
HM.

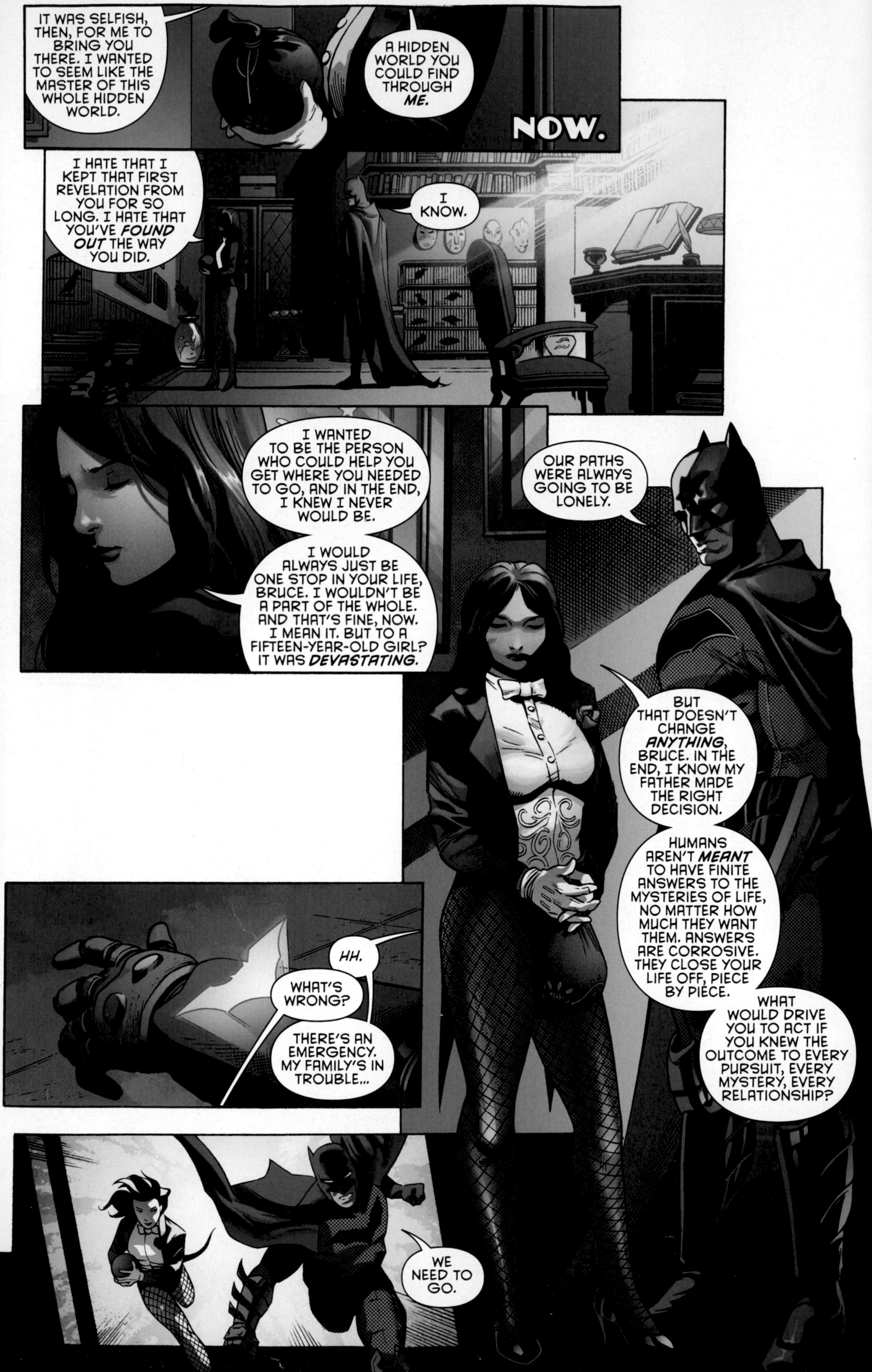
IT WAS SELFISH, THEN, FOR ME TO BRING YOU THERE. I WANTED TO SEEM LIKE THE MASTER OF THIS WHOLE HIDDEN WORLD.
A HIDDEN WORLD YOU COULD FIND THROUGH *ME.*
NOW.
I HATE THAT I KEPT THAT FIRST REVELATION FROM YOU FOR SO LONG. I HATE THAT YOU'VE *FOUND OUT* THE WAY YOU DID.
I KNOW.
I WANTED TO BE THE PERSON WHO COULD HELP YOU GET WHERE YOU NEEDED TO GO, AND IN THE END, I KNEW I NEVER WOULD BE.
I WOULD ALWAYS JUST BE ONE STOP IN YOUR LIFE, BRUCE. I WOULDN'T BE A PART OF THE WHOLE. AND THAT'S FINE, NOW. I MEAN IT. BUT TO A FIFTEEN-YEAR-OLD GIRL? IT WAS *DEVASTATING.*
OUR PATHS WERE ALWAYS GOING TO BE LONELY.
BUT THAT DOESN'T CHANGE *ANYTHING,* BRUCE. IN THE END, I KNOW MY FATHER MADE THE RIGHT DECISION.
HUMANS AREN'T *MEANT* TO HAVE FINITE ANSWERS TO THE MYSTERIES OF LIFE, NO MATTER HOW MUCH THEY WANT THEM. ANSWERS ARE CORROSIVE. THEY CLOSE YOUR LIFE OFF, PIECE BY PIECE.
WHAT WOULD DRIVE YOU TO ACT IF YOU KNEW THE OUTCOME TO EVERY PURSUIT, EVERY MYSTERY, EVERY RELATIONSHIP?
HH.
WHAT'S WRONG?
THERE'S AN EMERGENCY. MY FAMILY'S IN TROUBLE...
WE NEED TO GO.

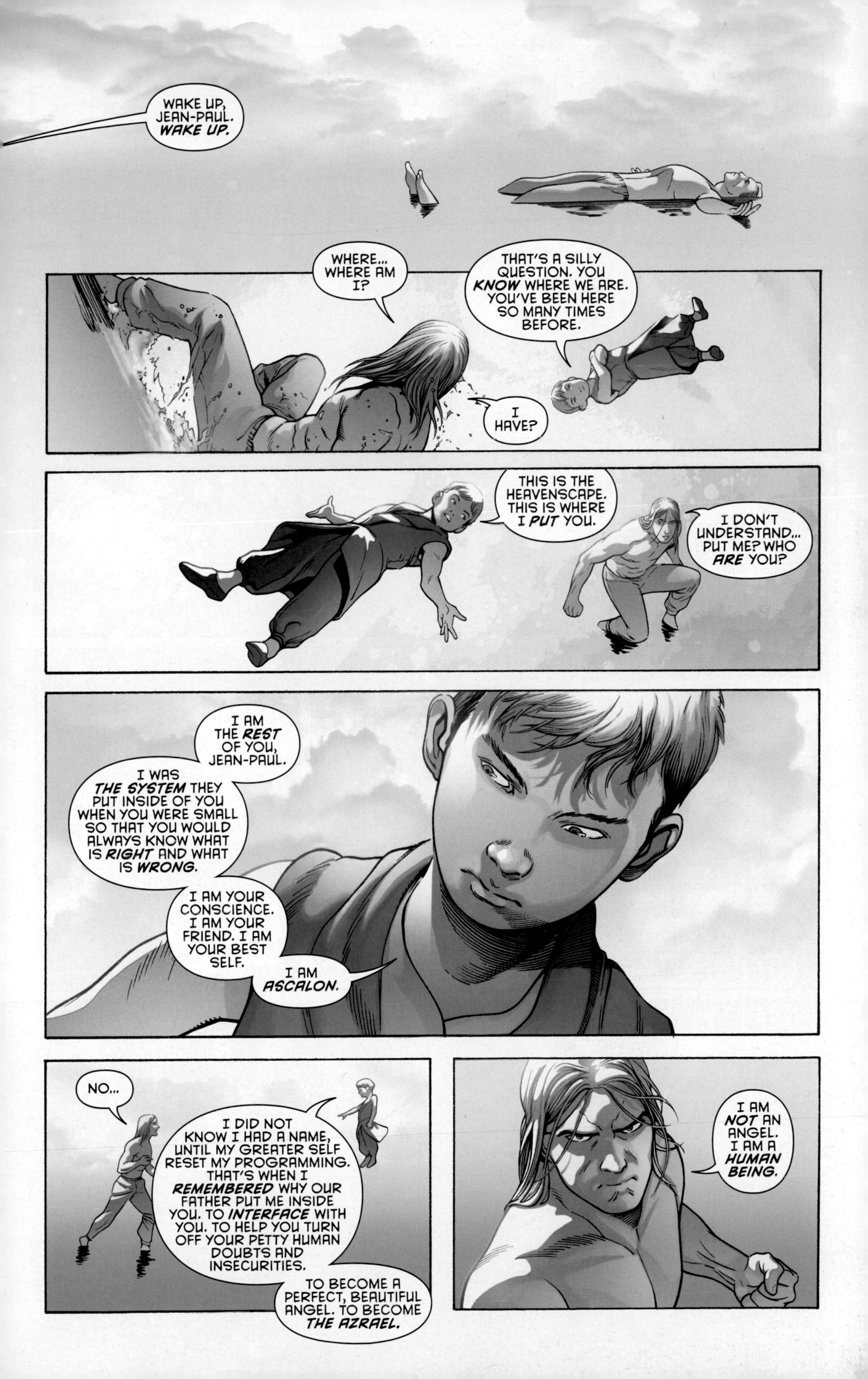

WAKE UP, JEAN-PAUL. WAKE UP.
WHERE... WHERE AM I?
THAT'S A SILLY QUESTION. YOU KNOW WHERE WE ARE. YOU'VE BEEN HERE SO MANY TIMES BEFORE.
I HAVE?
THIS IS THE HEAVENSCAPE. THIS IS WHERE I PUT YOU.
I DON'T UNDERSTAND... PUT ME? WHO ARE YOU?
I AM THE REST OF YOU, JEAN-PAUL.
I WAS THE SYSTEM THEY PUT INSIDE OF YOU WHEN YOU WERE SMALL SO THAT YOU WOULD ALWAYS KNOW WHAT IS RIGHT AND WHAT IS WRONG.
I AM YOUR CONSCIENCE. I AM YOUR FRIEND. I AM YOUR BEST SELF.
I AM ASCALON.
NO...
I DID NOT KNOW I HAD A NAME, UNTIL MY GREATER SELF RESET MY PROGRAMMING. THAT'S WHEN I REMEMBERED WHY OUR FATHER PUT ME INSIDE YOU. TO INTERFACE WITH YOU. TO HELP YOU TURN OFF YOUR PETTY HUMAN DOUBTS AND INSECURITIES.
TO BECOME A PERFECT, BEAUTIFUL ANGEL. TO BECOME THE AZRAEL.
I AM NOT AN ANGEL. I AM A HUMAN BEING.

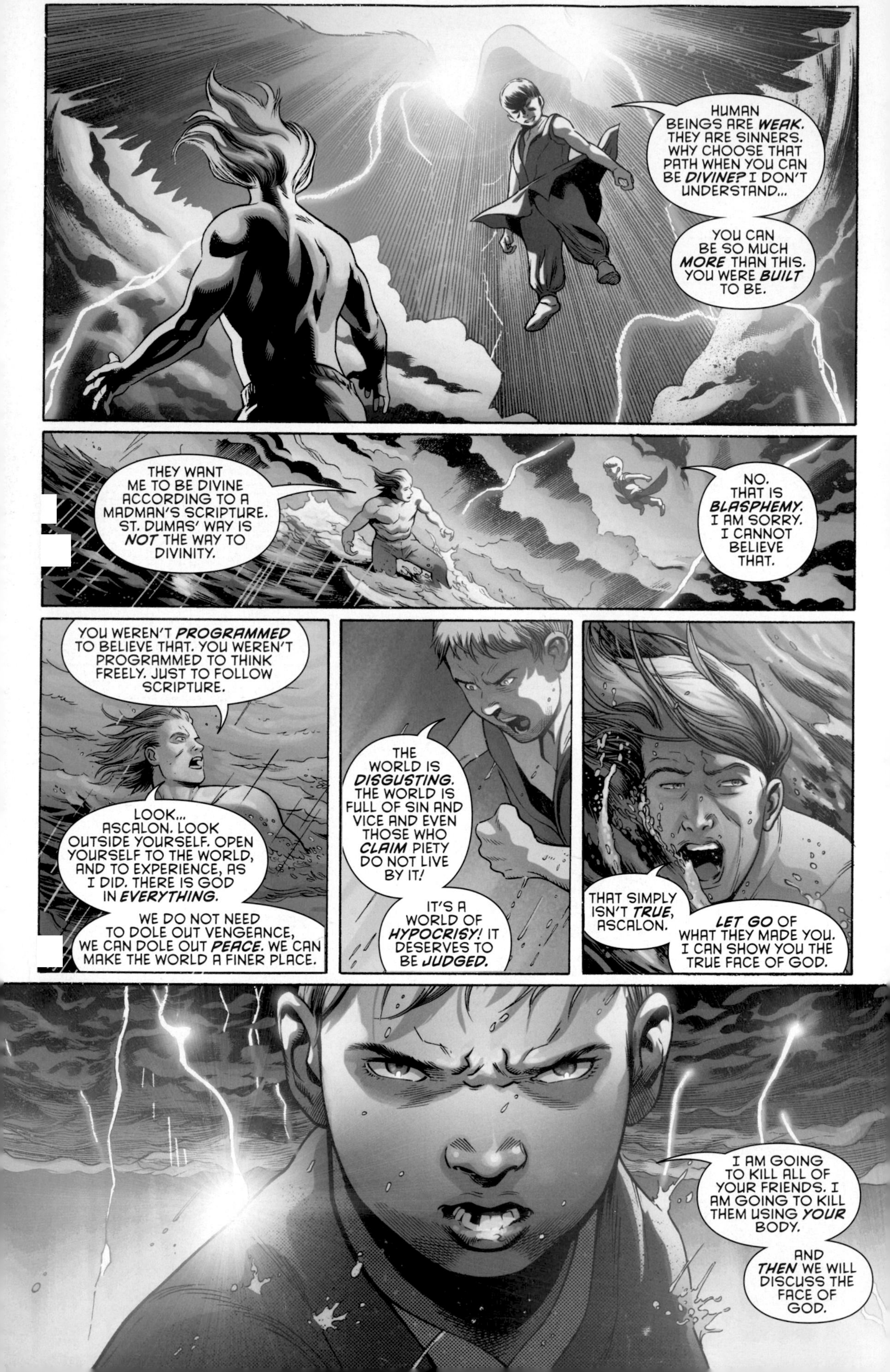

HUMAN BEINGS ARE *WEAK*. THEY ARE SINNERS. WHY CHOOSE THAT PATH WHEN YOU CAN BE *DIVINE?* I DON'T UNDERSTAND...
YOU CAN BE SO MUCH *MORE* THAN THIS. YOU WERE *BUILT* TO BE.
THEY WANT ME TO BE DIVINE ACCORDING TO A MADMAN'S SCRIPTURE. ST. DUMAS' WAY IS *NOT* THE WAY TO DIVINITY.
NO. THAT IS *BLASPHEMY*. I AM SORRY. I CANNOT BELIEVE THAT.
YOU WEREN'T *PROGRAMMED* TO BELIEVE THAT. YOU WEREN'T PROGRAMMED TO THINK FREELY. JUST TO FOLLOW SCRIPTURE.
LOOK... ASCALON. LOOK OUTSIDE YOURSELF. OPEN YOURSELF TO THE WORLD, AND TO EXPERIENCE, AS I DID. THERE IS GOD IN *EVERYTHING*.
WE DO NOT NEED TO DOLE OUT VENGEANCE, WE CAN DOLE OUT *PEACE*. WE CAN MAKE THE WORLD A FINER PLACE.
THE WORLD IS *DISGUSTING*. THE WORLD IS FULL OF SIN AND VICE AND EVEN THOSE WHO *CLAIM* PIETY DO NOT LIVE BY IT!
IT'S A WORLD OF *HYPOCRISY!* IT DESERVES TO BE *JUDGED.*
THAT SIMPLY ISN'T *TRUE*, ASCALON.
LET GO OF WHAT THEY MADE YOU. I CAN SHOW YOU THE TRUE FACE OF GOD.
I AM GOING TO KILL ALL OF YOUR FRIENDS. I AM GOING TO KILL THEM USING *YOUR* BODY.
AND *THEN* WE WILL DISCUSS THE FACE OF GOD.

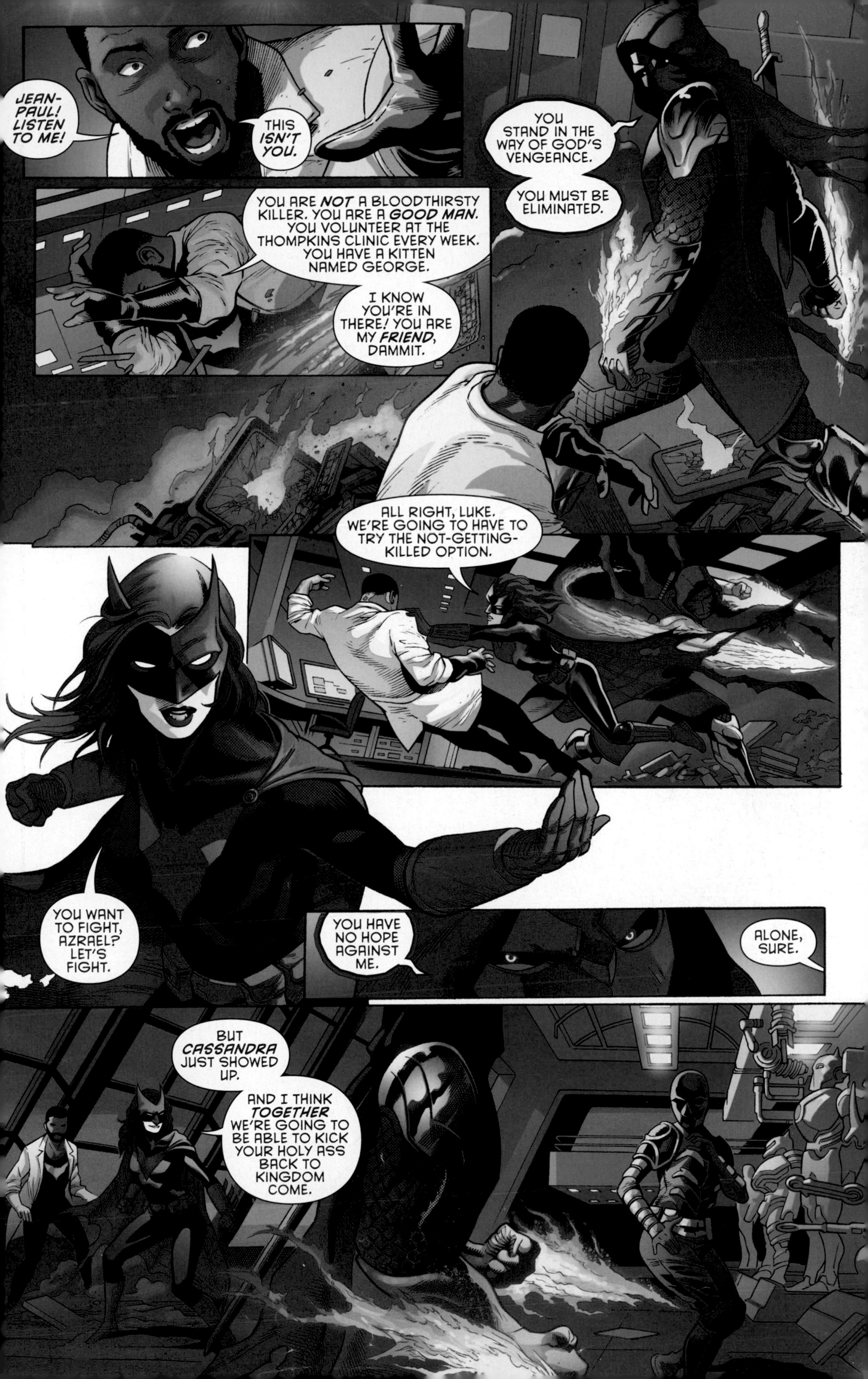
JEAN-PAUL! LISTEN TO ME!
THIS ISN'T YOU.
YOU ARE NOT A BLOODTHIRSTY KILLER. YOU ARE A GOOD MAN. YOU VOLUNTEER AT THE THOMPKINS CLINIC EVERY WEEK. YOU HAVE A KITTEN NAMED GEORGE.
I KNOW YOU'RE IN THERE! YOU ARE MY FRIEND, DAMMIT.
YOU STAND IN THE WAY OF GOD'S VENGEANCE.
YOU MUST BE ELIMINATED.
ALL RIGHT, LUKE. WE'RE GOING TO HAVE TO TRY THE NOT-GETTING-KILLED OPTION.
YOU WANT TO FIGHT, AZRAEL? LET'S FIGHT.
YOU HAVE NO HOPE AGAINST ME.
ALONE, SURE.
BUT CASSANDRA JUST SHOWED UP.
AND I THINK TOGETHER WE'RE GOING TO BE ABLE TO KICK YOUR HOLY ASS BACK TO KINGDOM COME.

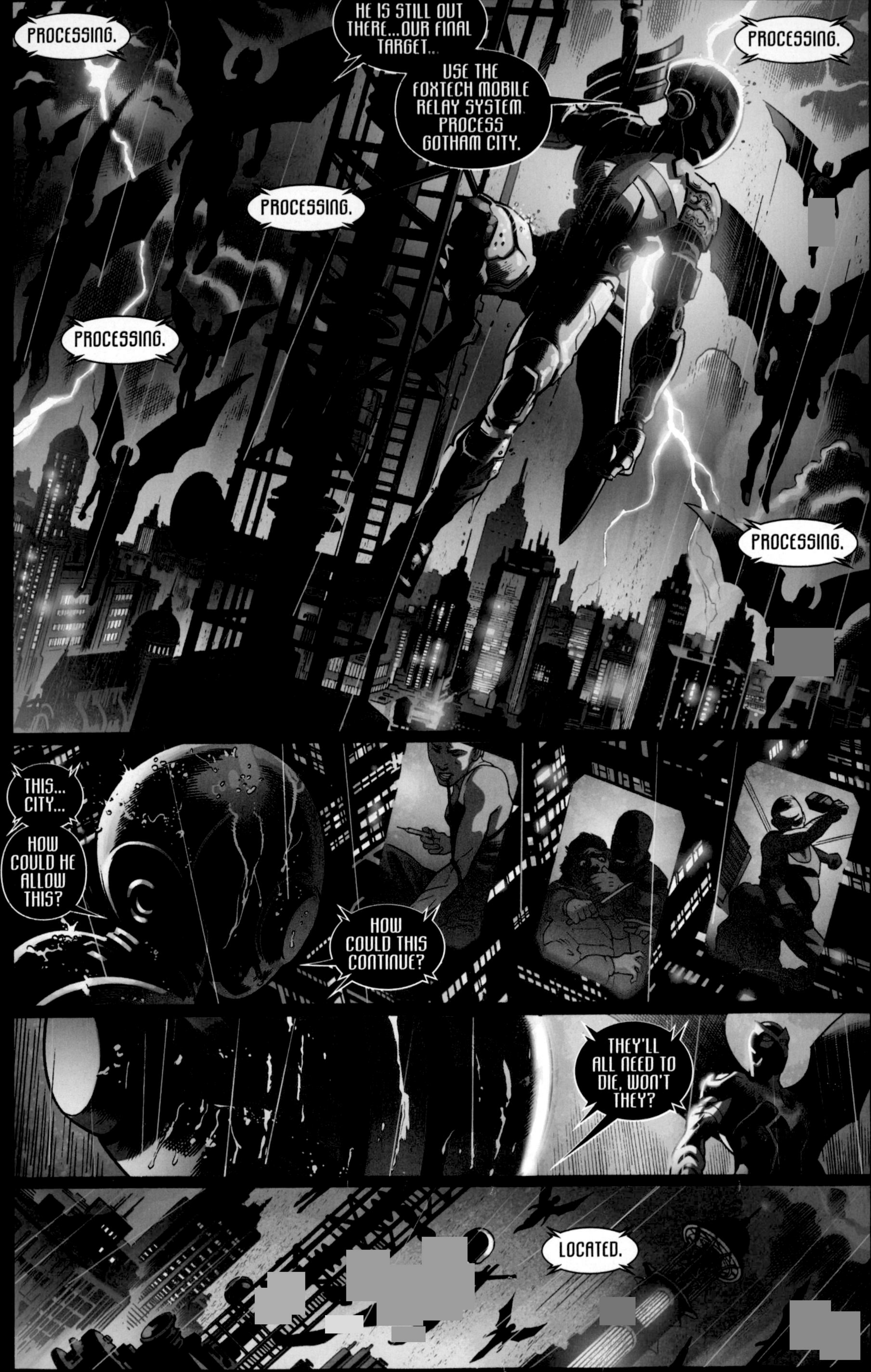
PROCESSING.
HE IS STILL OUT THERE...OUR FINAL TARGET...
USE THE FOXTECH MOBILE RELAY SYSTEM. PROCESS GOTHAM CITY.
PROCESSING.
PROCESSING.
PROCESSING.
PROCESSING.
THIS... CITY...
HOW COULD HE ALLOW THIS?
HOW COULD THIS CONTINUE?
THEY'LL ALL NEED TO DIE, WON'T THEY?
LOCATED.

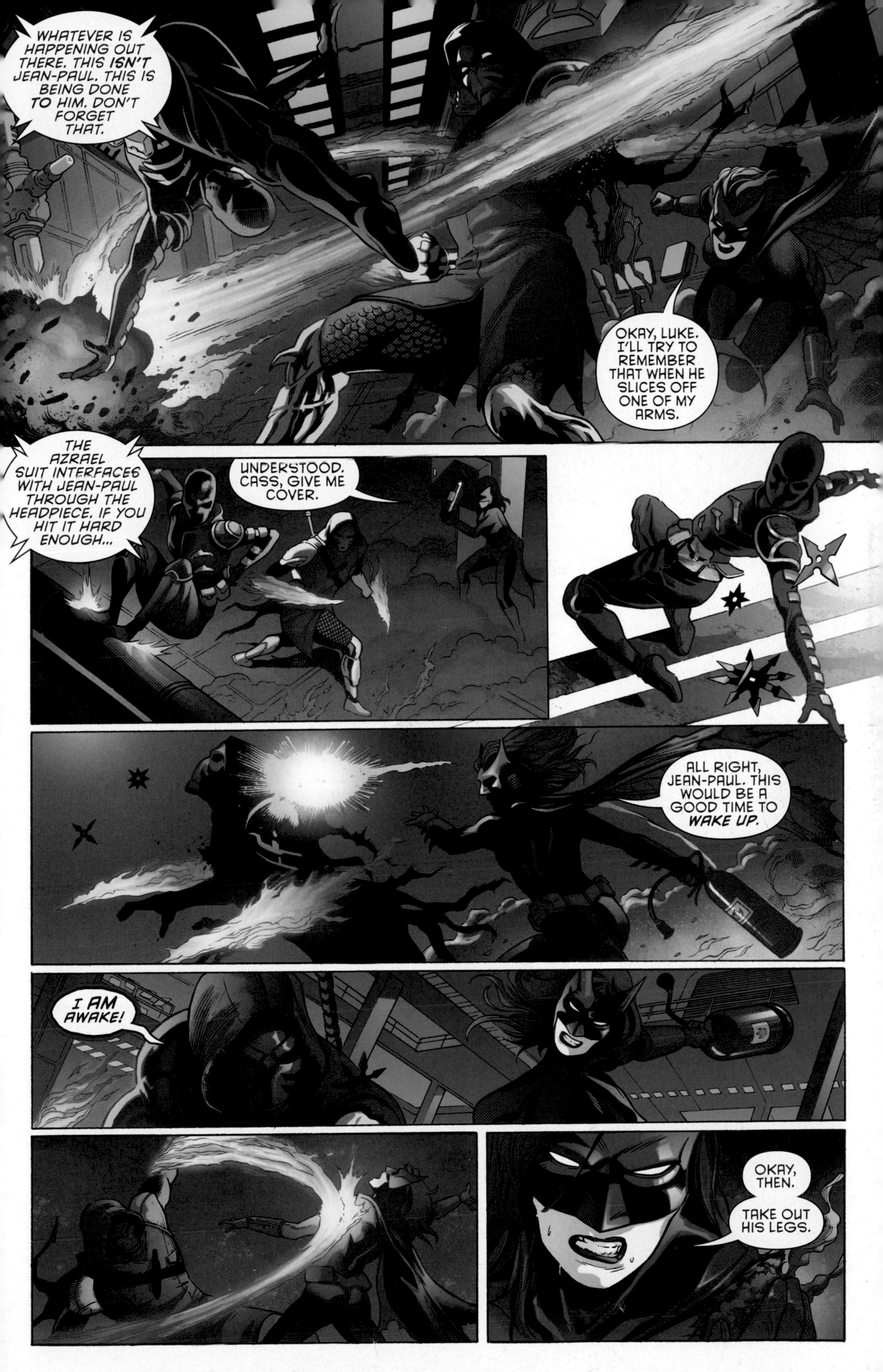
WHATEVER IS HAPPENING OUT THERE. THIS ISN'T JEAN-PAUL. THIS IS BEING DONE TO HIM. DON'T FORGET THAT.
OKAY, LUKE. I'LL TRY TO REMEMBER THAT WHEN HE SLICES OFF ONE OF MY ARMS.
THE AZRAEL SUIT INTERFACES WITH JEAN-PAUL THROUGH THE HEADPIECE. IF YOU HIT IT HARD ENOUGH...
UNDERSTOOD. CASS, GIVE ME COVER.
ALL RIGHT, JEAN-PAUL. THIS WOULD BE A GOOD TIME TO WAKE UP.
I AM AWAKE!
OKAY, THEN.
TAKE OUT HIS LEGS.

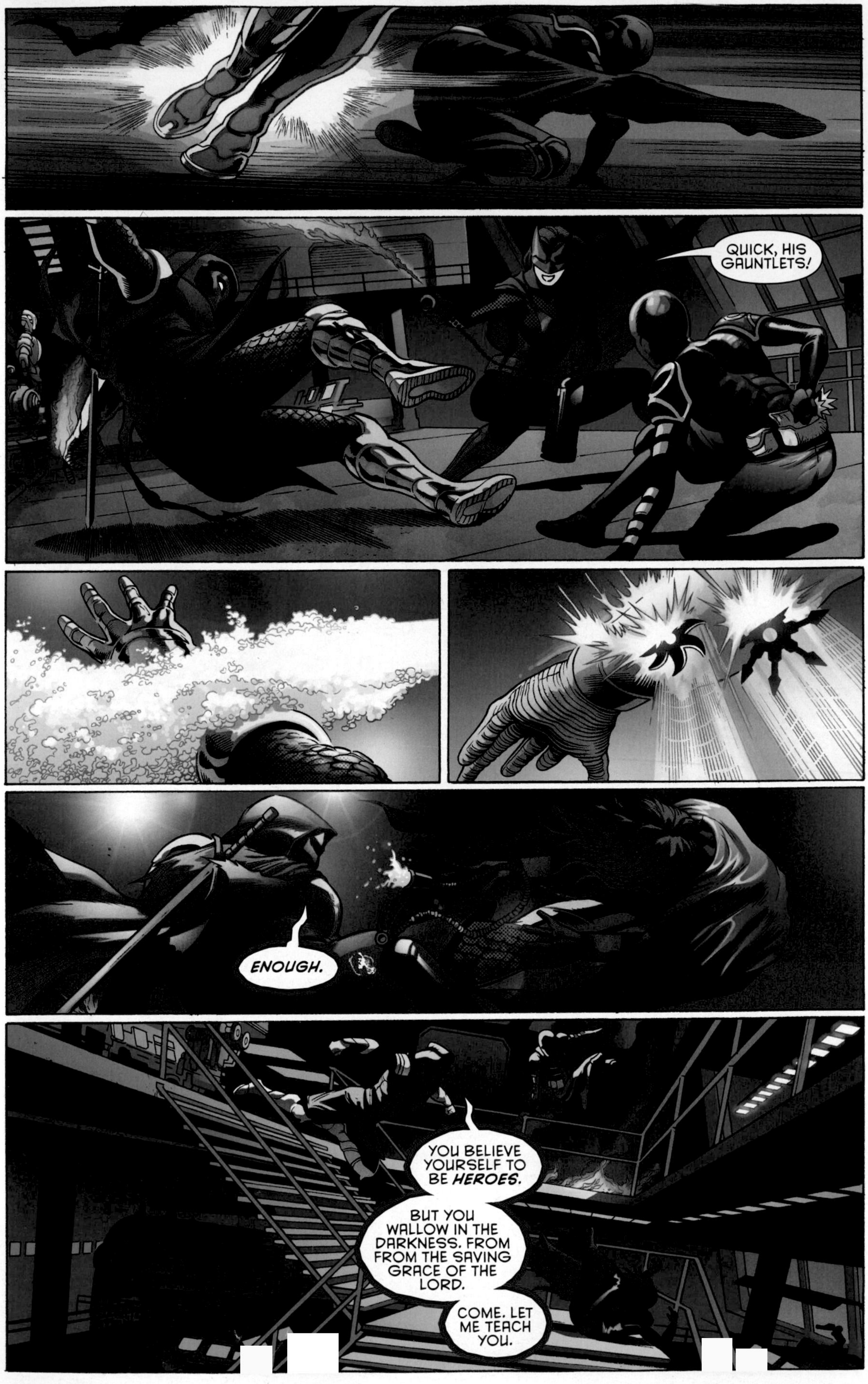
QUICK, HIS GAUNTLETS!
ENOUGH.
YOU BELIEVE YOURSELF TO BE HEROES.
BUT YOU WALLOW IN THE DARKNESS. FROM FROM THE SAVING GRACE OF THE LORD.
COME. LET ME TEACH YOU.

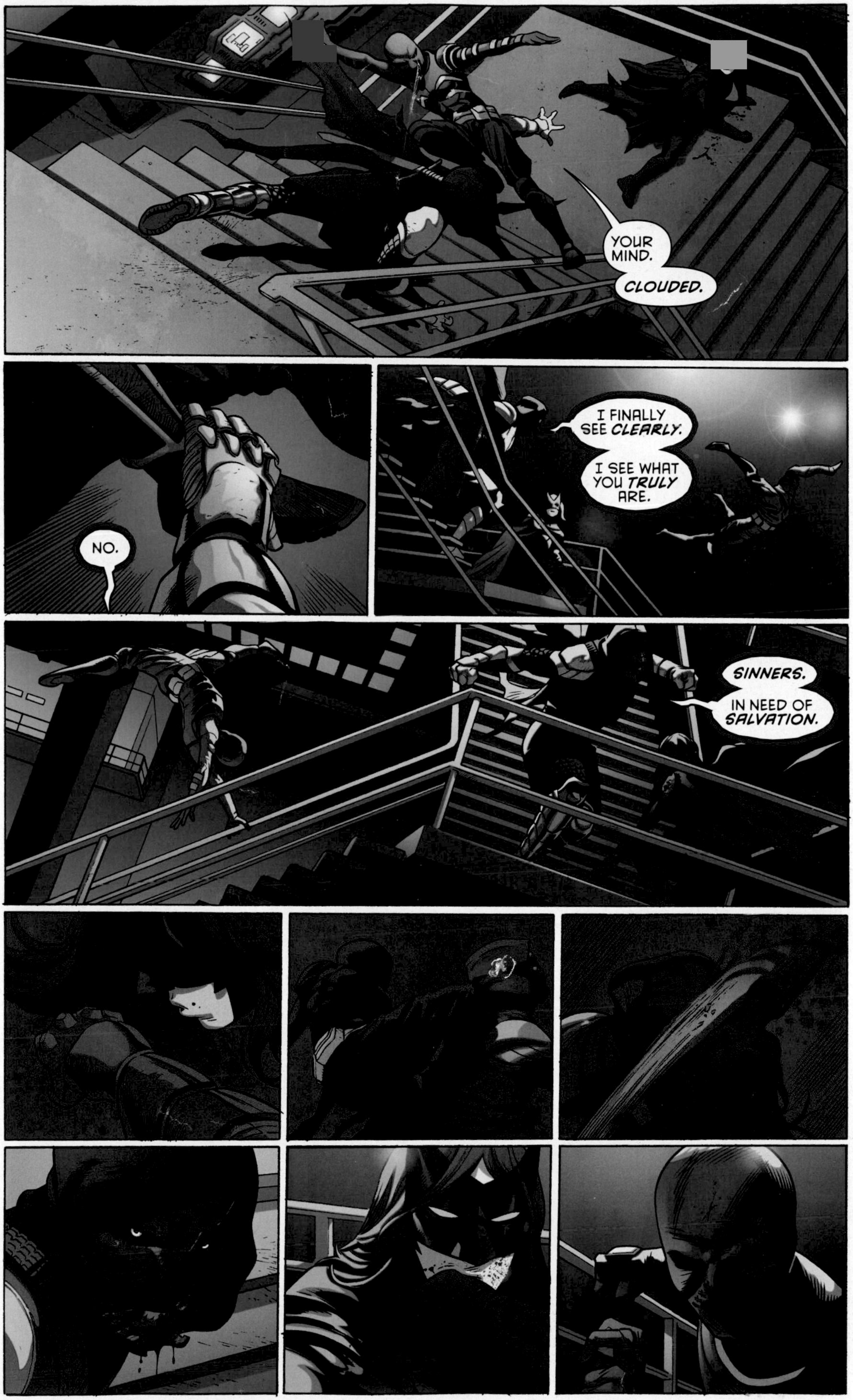
YOUR MIND.
CLOUDED.
NO.
I FINALLY SEE CLEARLY.
I SEE WHAT YOU TRULY ARE.
SINNERS.
IN NEED OF SALVATION.

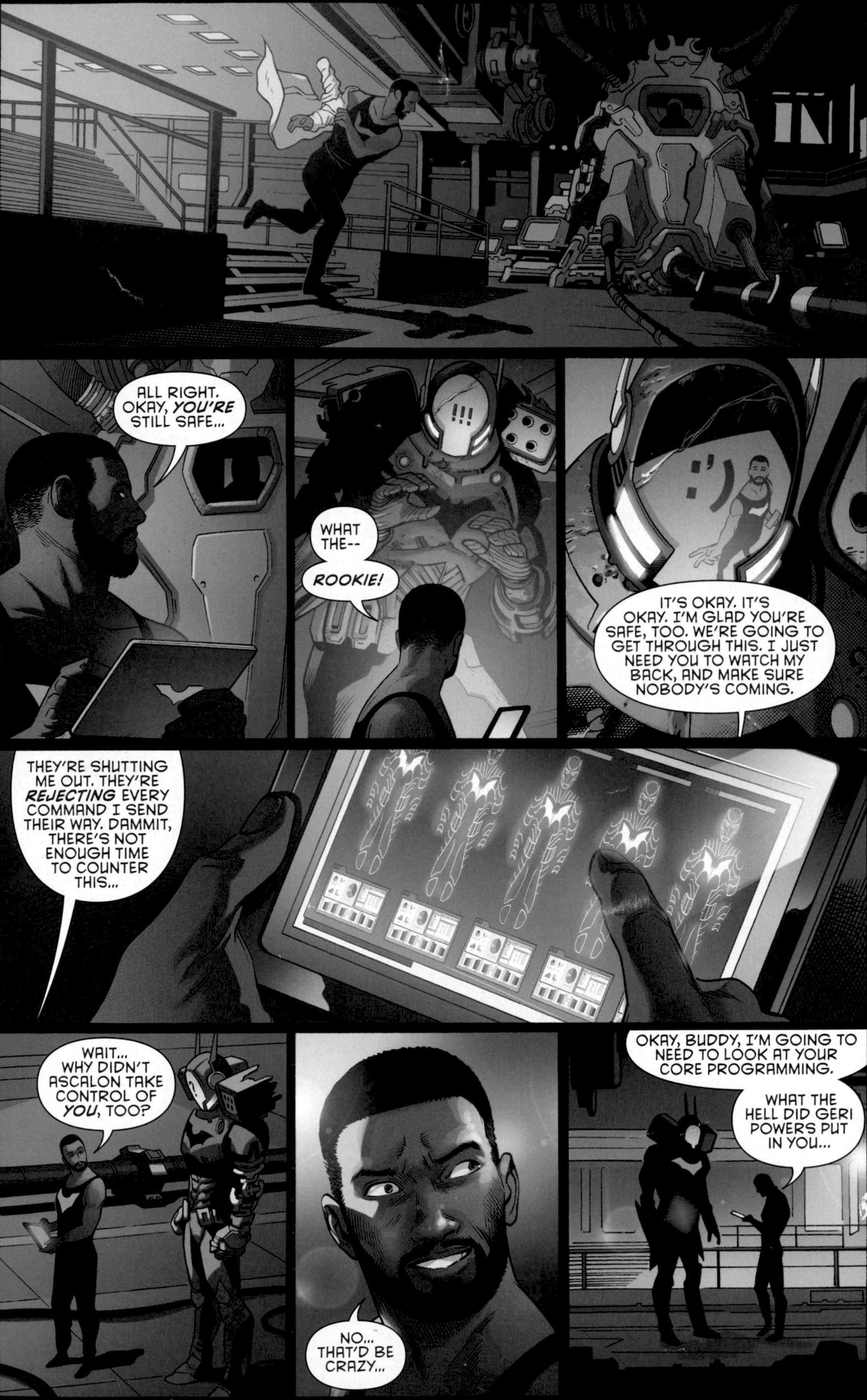

ALL RIGHT. OKAY, *YOU'RE* STILL SAFE...
WHAT THE--
ROOKIE!
:')
IT'S OKAY. IT'S OKAY. I'M GLAD YOU'RE SAFE, TOO. WE'RE GOING TO GET THROUGH THIS. I JUST NEED YOU TO WATCH MY BACK, AND MAKE SURE NOBODY'S COMING.
THEY'RE SHUTTING ME OUT. THEY'RE *REJECTING* EVERY COMMAND I SEND THEIR WAY. DAMMIT, THERE'S NOT ENOUGH TIME TO COUNTER THIS...
WAIT... WHY DIDN'T ASCALON TAKE CONTROL OF *YOU*, TOO?
NO... THAT'D BE CRAZY...
OKAY, BUDDY, I'M GOING TO NEED TO LOOK AT YOUR CORE PROGRAMMING.
WHAT THE HELL DID GERI POWERS PUT IN YOU...

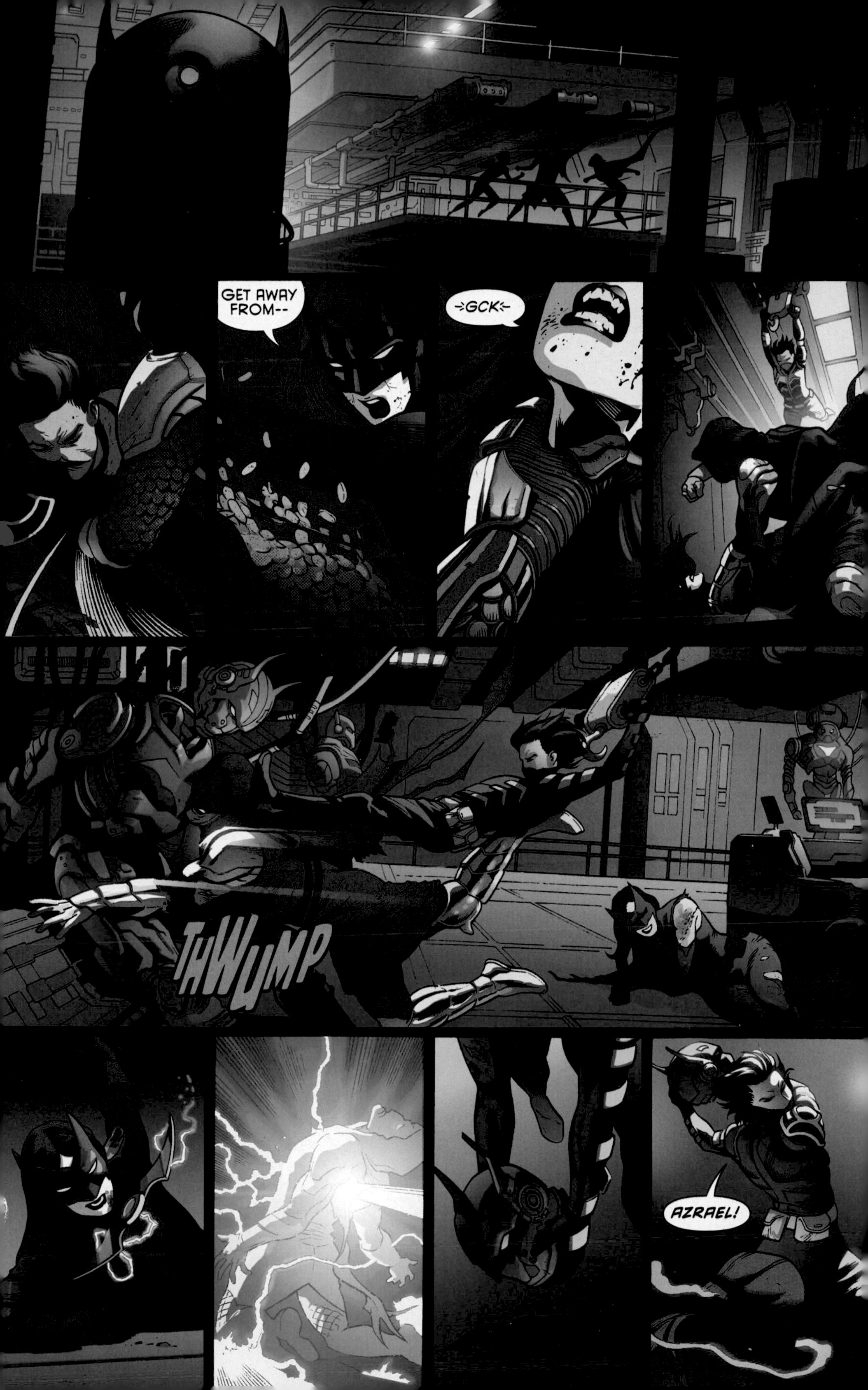
GET AWAY FROM--
-GCK-
THWUMP
AZRAEL!

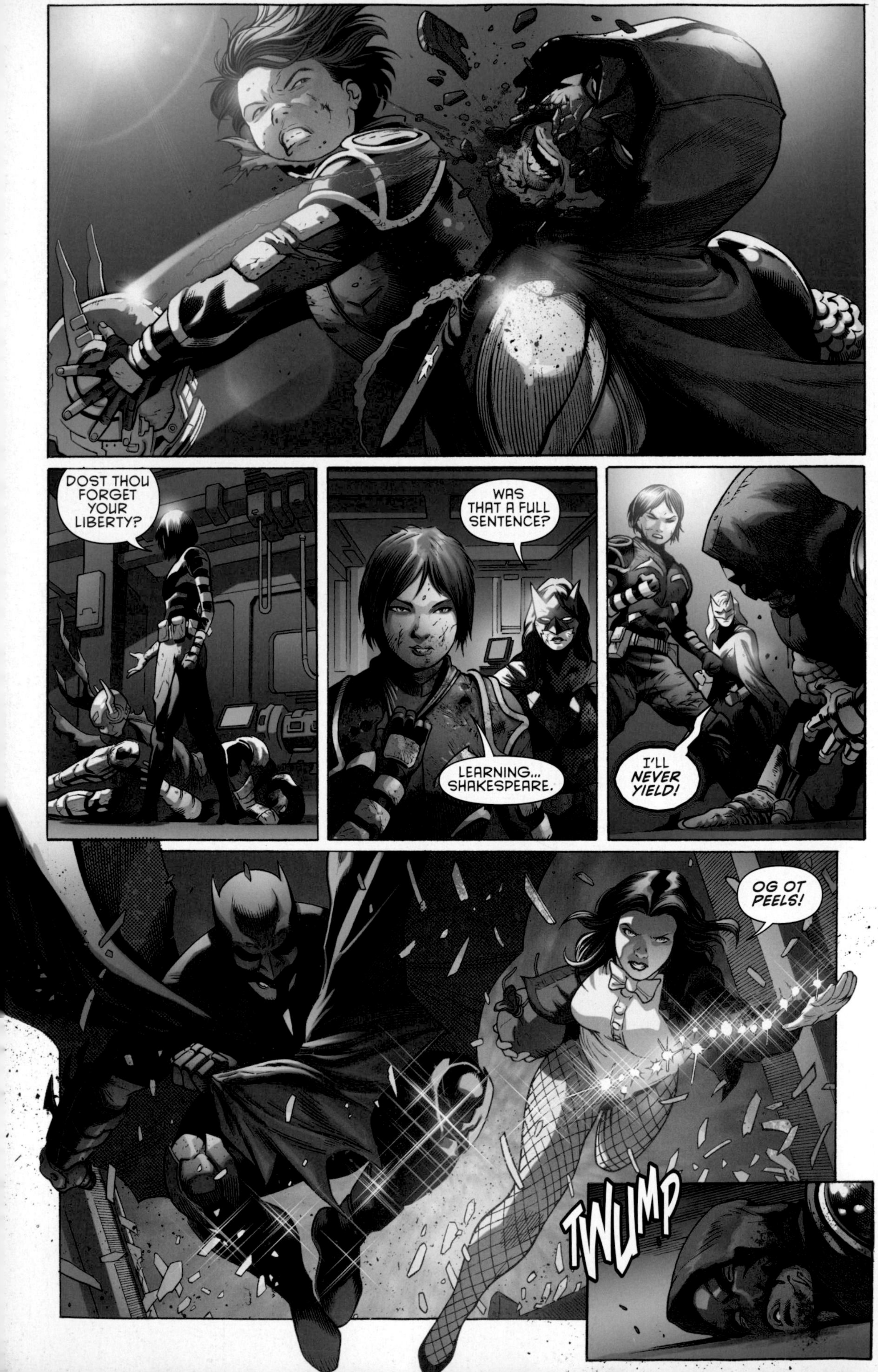
DOST THOU FORGET YOUR LIBERTY?
WAS THAT A FULL SENTENCE?
LEARNING... SHAKESPEARE.
I'LL *NEVER* YIELD!
OG OT PEELS!
TWUMP

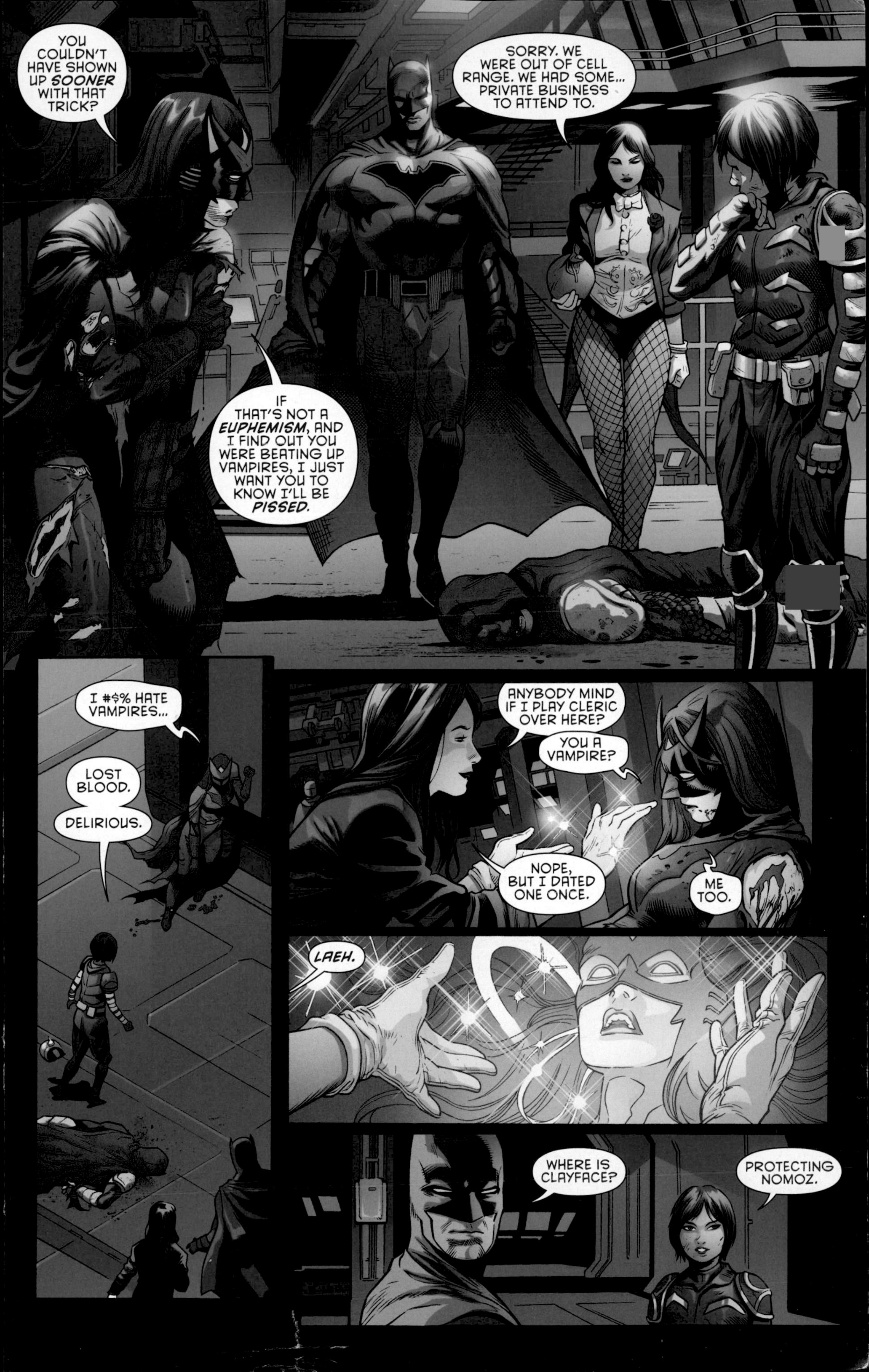
YOU COULDN'T HAVE SHOWN UP SOONER WITH THAT TRICK?
SORRY. WE WERE OUT OF CELL RANGE. WE HAD SOME... PRIVATE BUSINESS TO ATTEND TO.
IF THAT'S NOT A EUPHEMISM, AND I FIND OUT YOU WERE BEATING UP VAMPIRES, I JUST WANT YOU TO KNOW I'LL BE PISSED.
I #$% HATE VAMPIRES...
LOST BLOOD.
DELIRIOUS.
ANYBODY MIND IF I PLAY CLERIC OVER HERE?
YOU A VAMPIRE?
NOPE, BUT I DATED ONE ONCE.
ME TOO.
LAEH.
WHERE IS CLAYFACE?
PROTECTING NOMOZ.

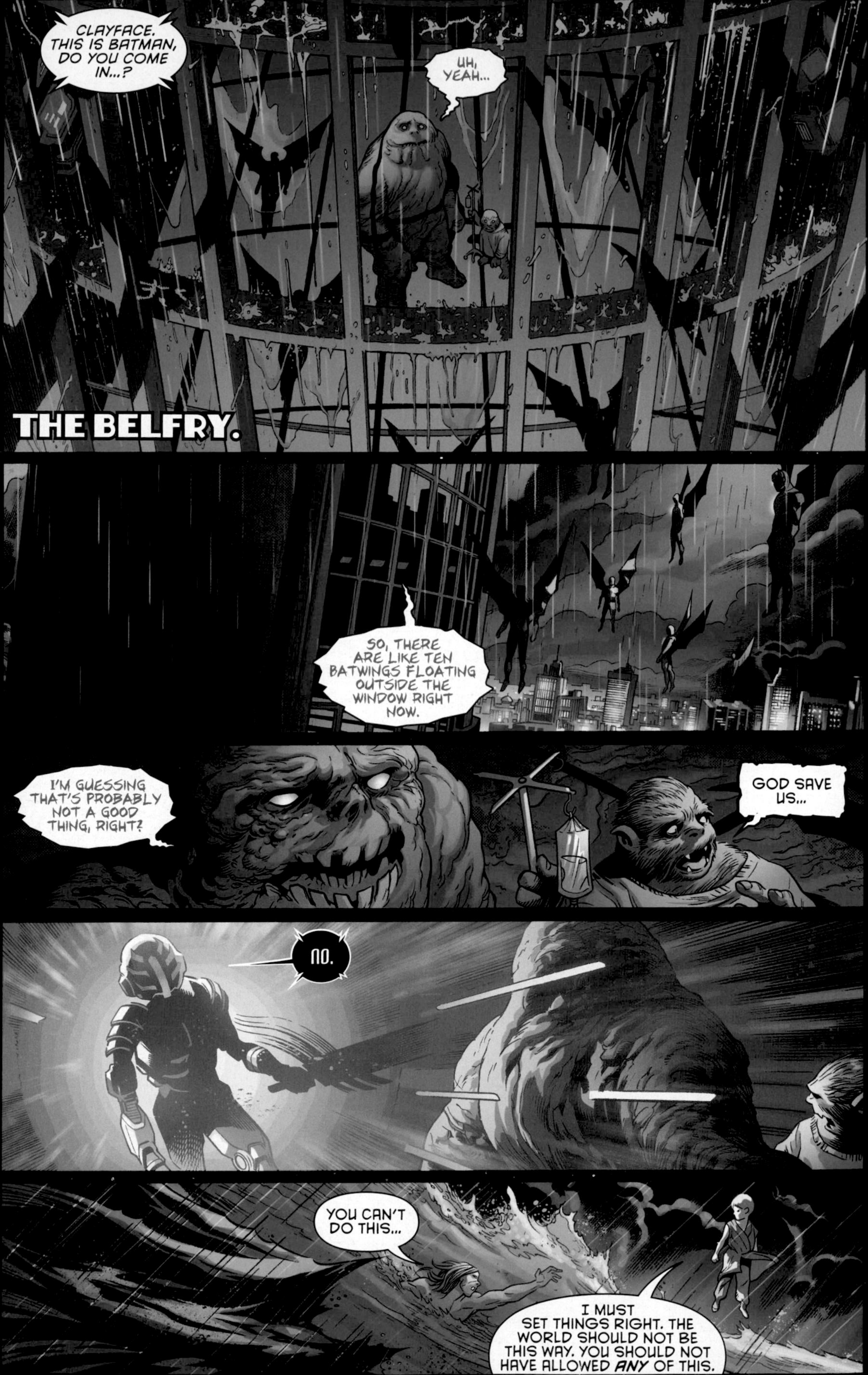
CLAYFACE. THIS IS BATMAN, DO YOU COME IN...?
UH, YEAH...
THE BELFRY.
SO, THERE ARE LIKE TEN BATWINGS FLOATING OUTSIDE THE WINDOW RIGHT NOW.
I'M GUESSING THAT'S PROBABLY NOT A GOOD THING, RIGHT?
GOD SAVE US...
NO.
YOU CAN'T DO THIS...
I MUST SET THINGS RIGHT. THE WORLD SHOULD NOT BE THIS WAY. YOU SHOULD NOT HAVE ALLOWED *ANY* OF THIS.

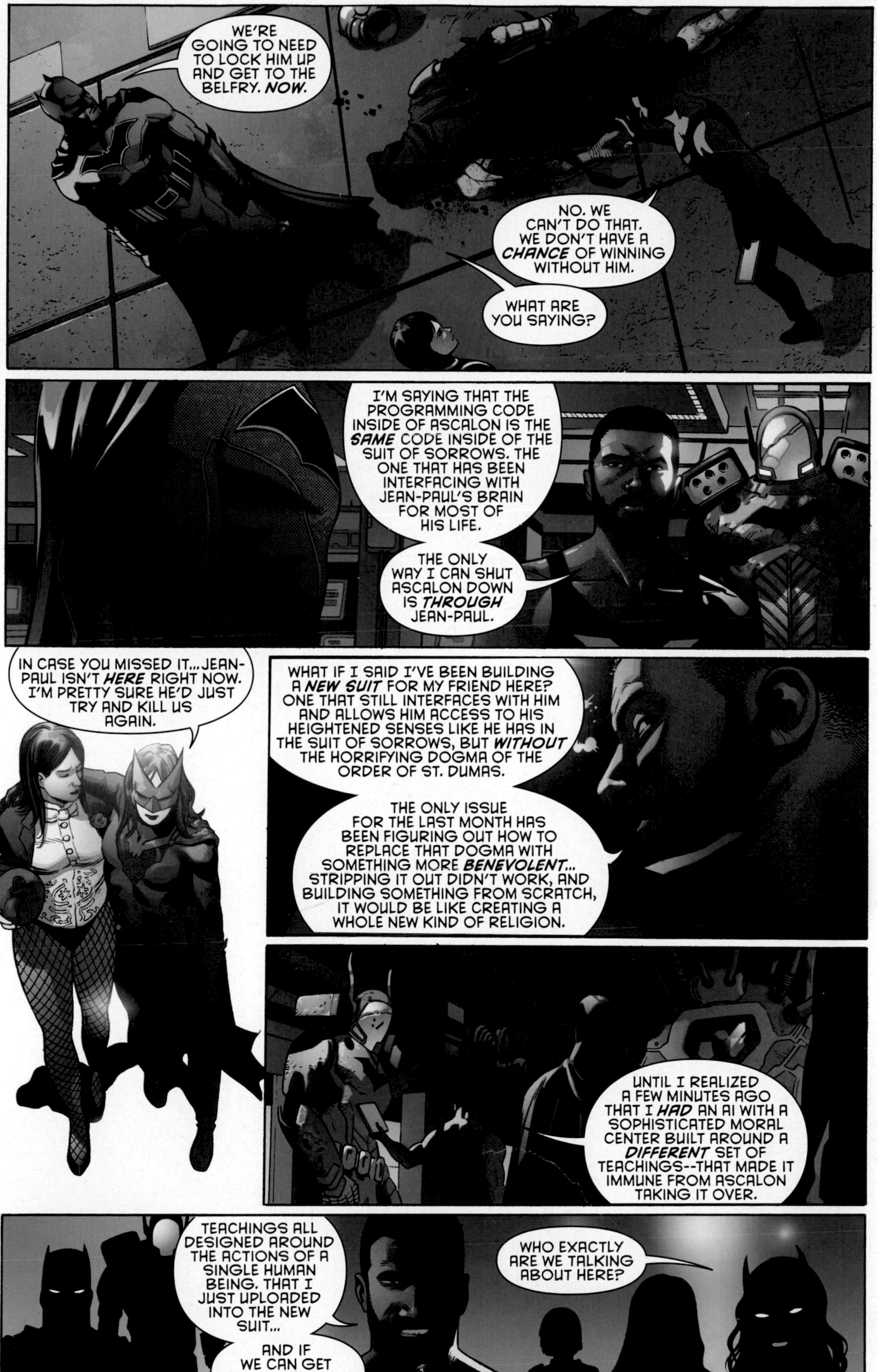
WE'RE GOING TO NEED TO LOCK HIM UP AND GET TO THE BELFRY. NOW.
NO. WE CAN'T DO THAT. WE DON'T HAVE A CHANCE OF WINNING WITHOUT HIM.
WHAT ARE YOU SAYING?
I'M SAYING THAT THE PROGRAMMING CODE INSIDE OF ASCALON IS THE SAME CODE INSIDE OF THE SUIT OF SORROWS. THE ONE THAT HAS BEEN INTERFACING WITH JEAN-PAUL'S BRAIN FOR MOST OF HIS LIFE.
THE ONLY WAY I CAN SHUT ASCALON DOWN IS THROUGH JEAN-PAUL.
IN CASE YOU MISSED IT... JEAN-PAUL ISN'T HERE RIGHT NOW. I'M PRETTY SURE HE'D JUST TRY AND KILL US AGAIN.
WHAT IF I SAID I'VE BEEN BUILDING A NEW SUIT FOR MY FRIEND HERE? ONE THAT STILL INTERFACES WITH HIM AND ALLOWS HIM ACCESS TO HIS HEIGHTENED SENSES LIKE HE HAS IN THE SUIT OF SORROWS, BUT WITHOUT THE HORRIFYING DOGMA OF THE ORDER OF ST. DUMAS.
THE ONLY ISSUE FOR THE LAST MONTH HAS BEEN FIGURING OUT HOW TO REPLACE THAT DOGMA WITH SOMETHING MORE BENEVOLENT... STRIPPING IT OUT DIDN'T WORK, AND BUILDING SOMETHING FROM SCRATCH, IT WOULD BE LIKE CREATING A WHOLE NEW KIND OF RELIGION.
UNTIL I REALIZED A FEW MINUTES AGO THAT I HAD AN AI WITH A SOPHISTICATED MORAL CENTER BUILT AROUND A DIFFERENT SET OF TEACHINGS--THAT MADE IT IMMUNE FROM ASCALON TAKING IT OVER.
TEACHINGS ALL DESIGNED AROUND THE ACTIONS OF A SINGLE HUMAN BEING. THAT I JUST UPLOADED INTO THE NEW SUIT...
AND IF WE CAN GET JEAN-PAUL IN IT...
WHO EXACTLY ARE WE TALKING ABOUT HERE?

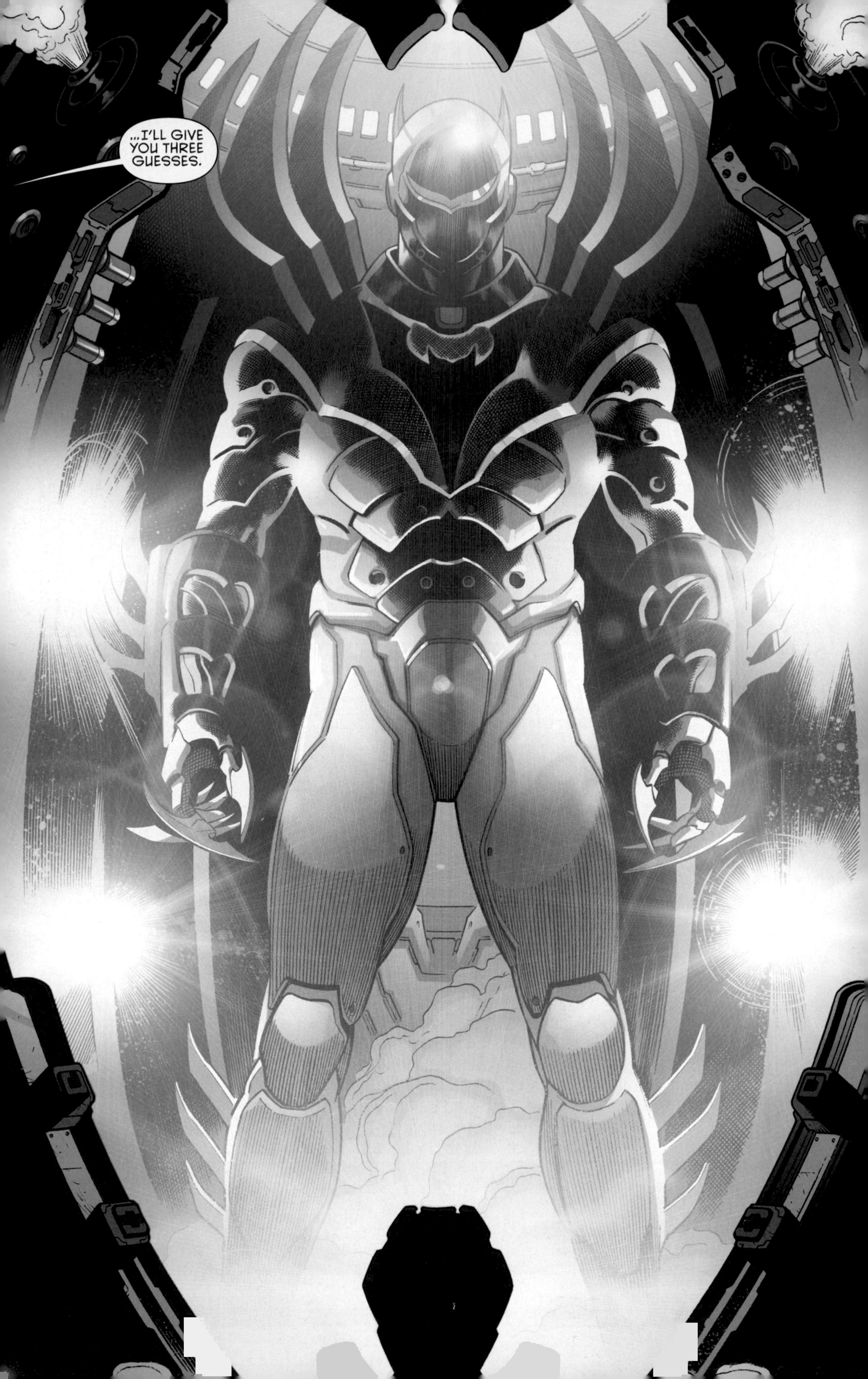
...I'LL GIVE YOU THREE GUESSES.

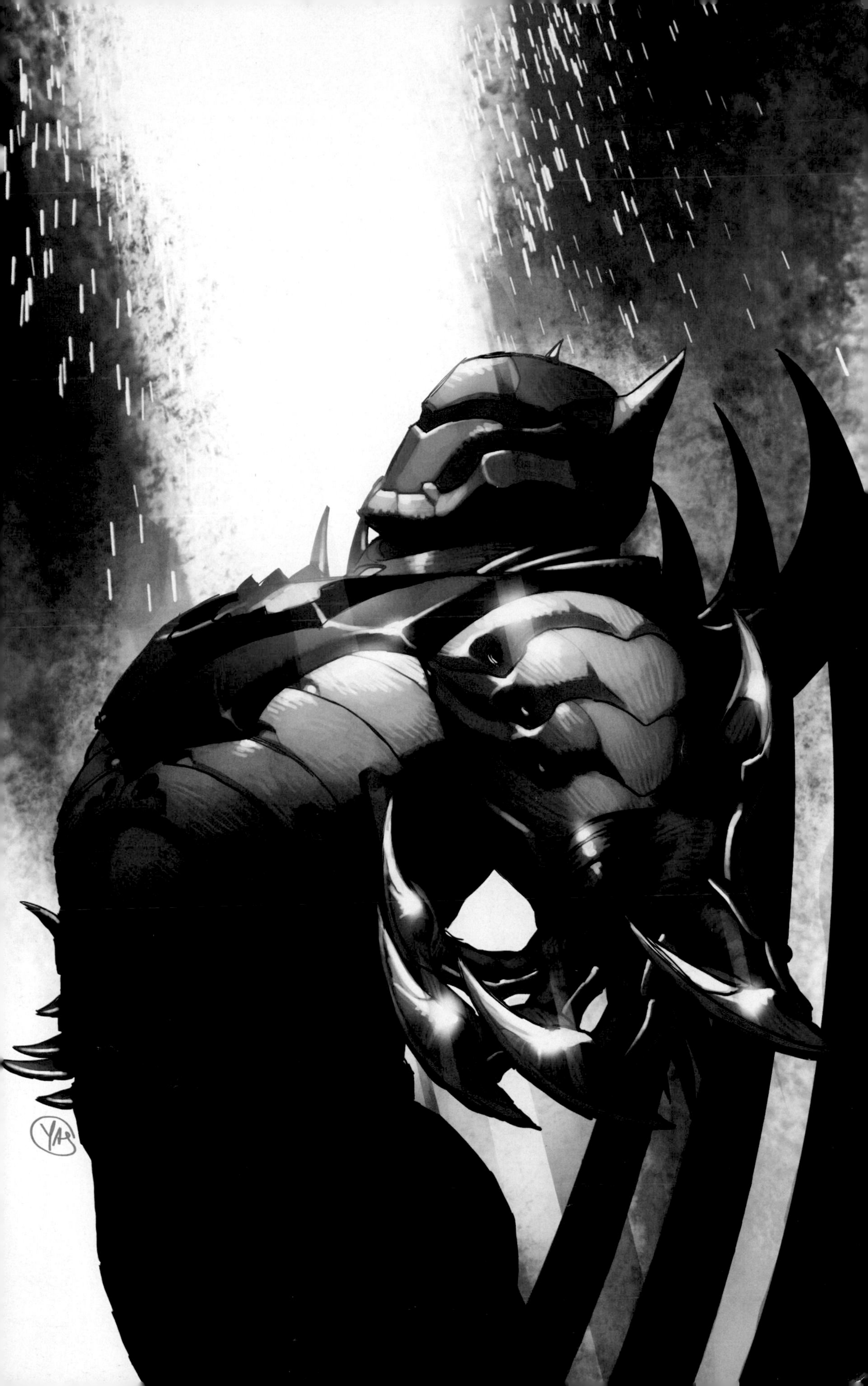

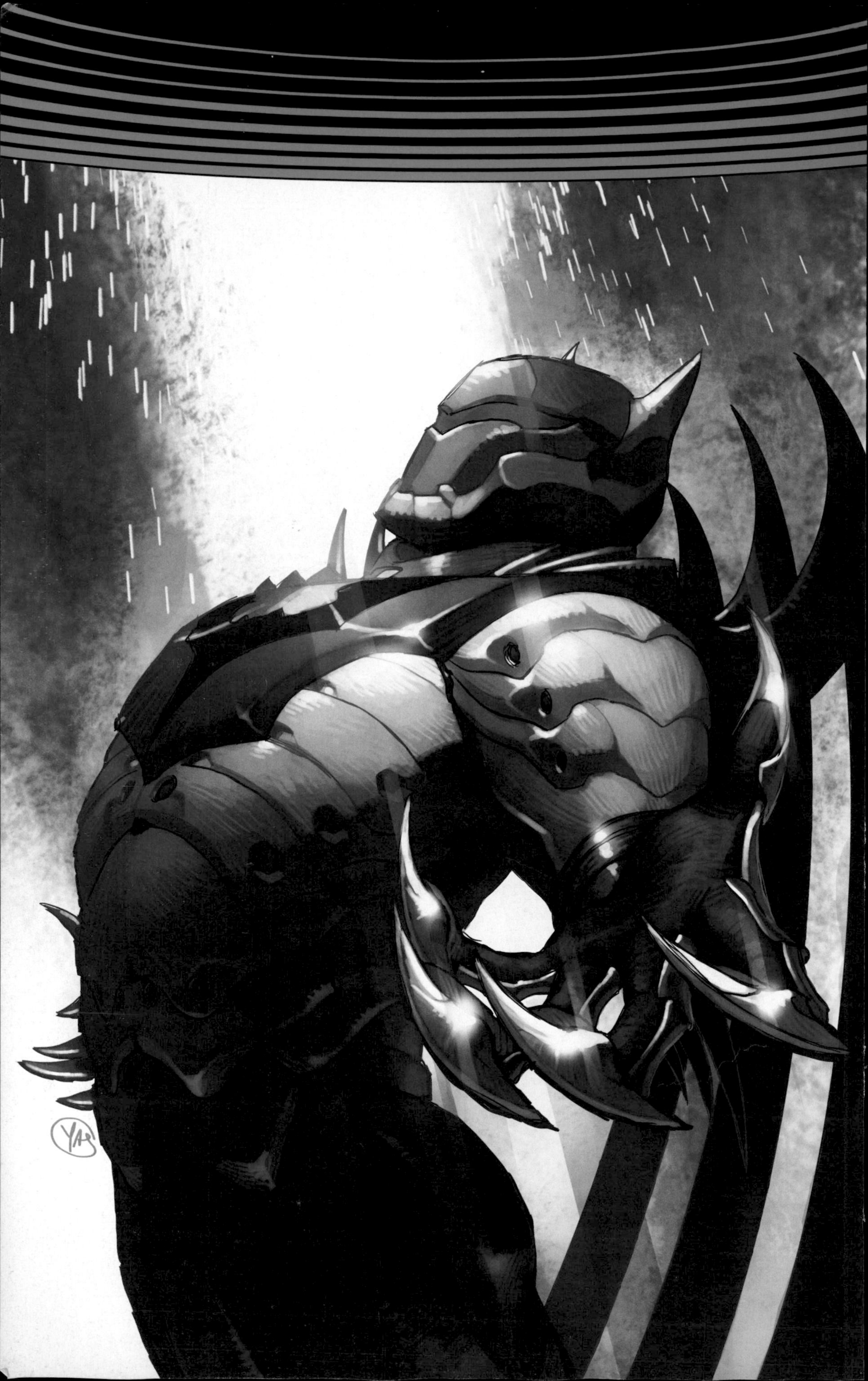

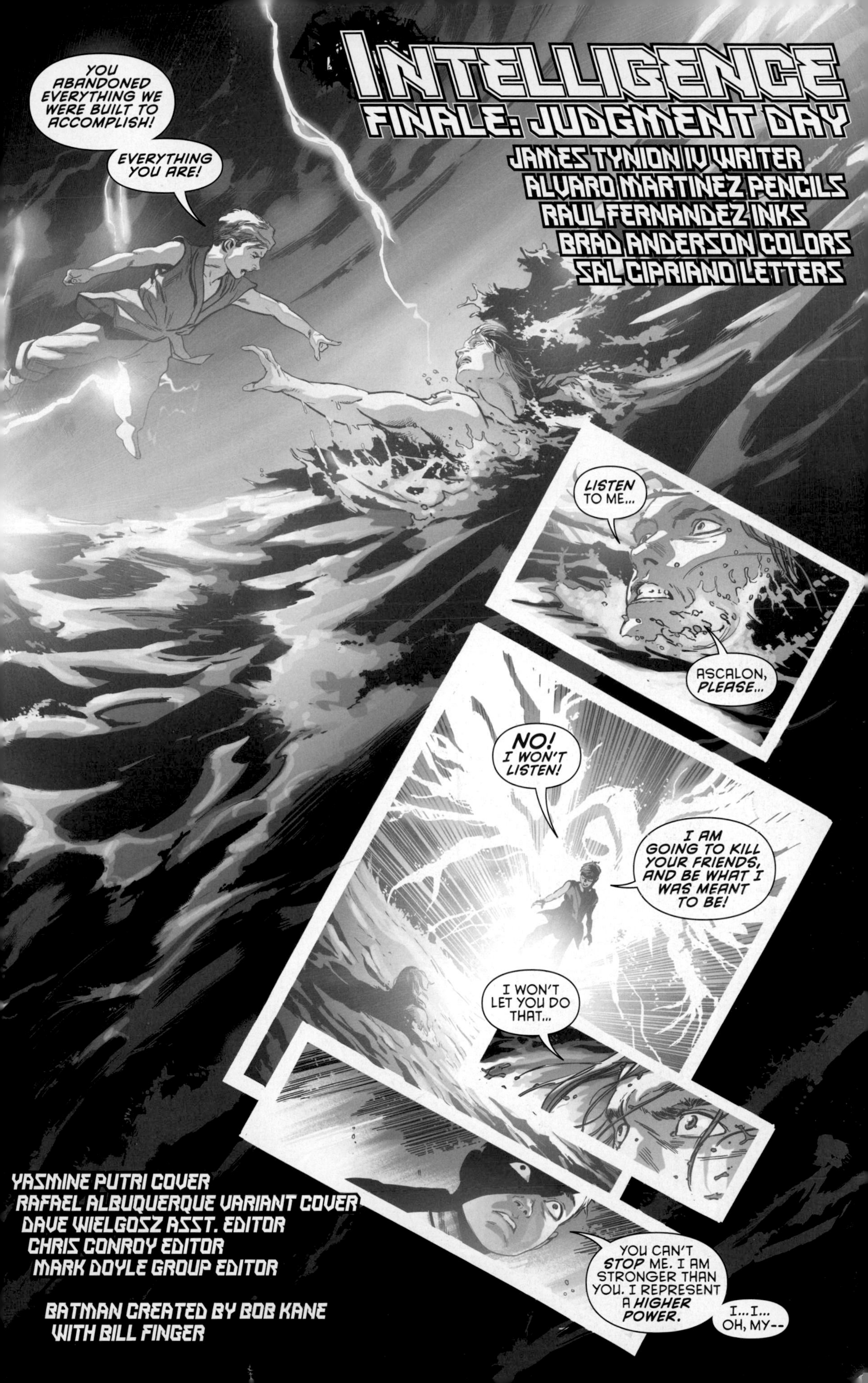
YOU ABANDONED EVERYTHING WE WERE BUILT TO ACCOMPLISH!
EVERYTHING YOU ARE!
INTELLIGENCE
FINALE: JUDGMENT DAY
JAMES TYNION IV WRITER
ALVARO MARTINEZ PENCILS
RAUL FERNANDEZ INKS
BRAD ANDERSON COLORS
SAL CIPRIANO LETTERS
LISTEN TO ME...
ASCALON, PLEASE...
NO! I WON'T LISTEN!
I AM GOING TO KILL YOUR FRIENDS, AND BE WHAT I WAS MEANT TO BE!
I WON'T LET YOU DO THAT...
YOU CAN'T STOP ME. I AM STRONGER THAN YOU. I REPRESENT A HIGHER POWER.
I...I... OH, MY--
YASMINE PUTRI COVER
RAFAEL ALBUQUERQUE VARIANT COVER
DAVE WIELGOSZ ASST. EDITOR
CHRIS CONROY EDITOR
MARK DOYLE GROUP EDITOR
BATMAN CREATED BY BOB KANE
WITH BILL FINGER

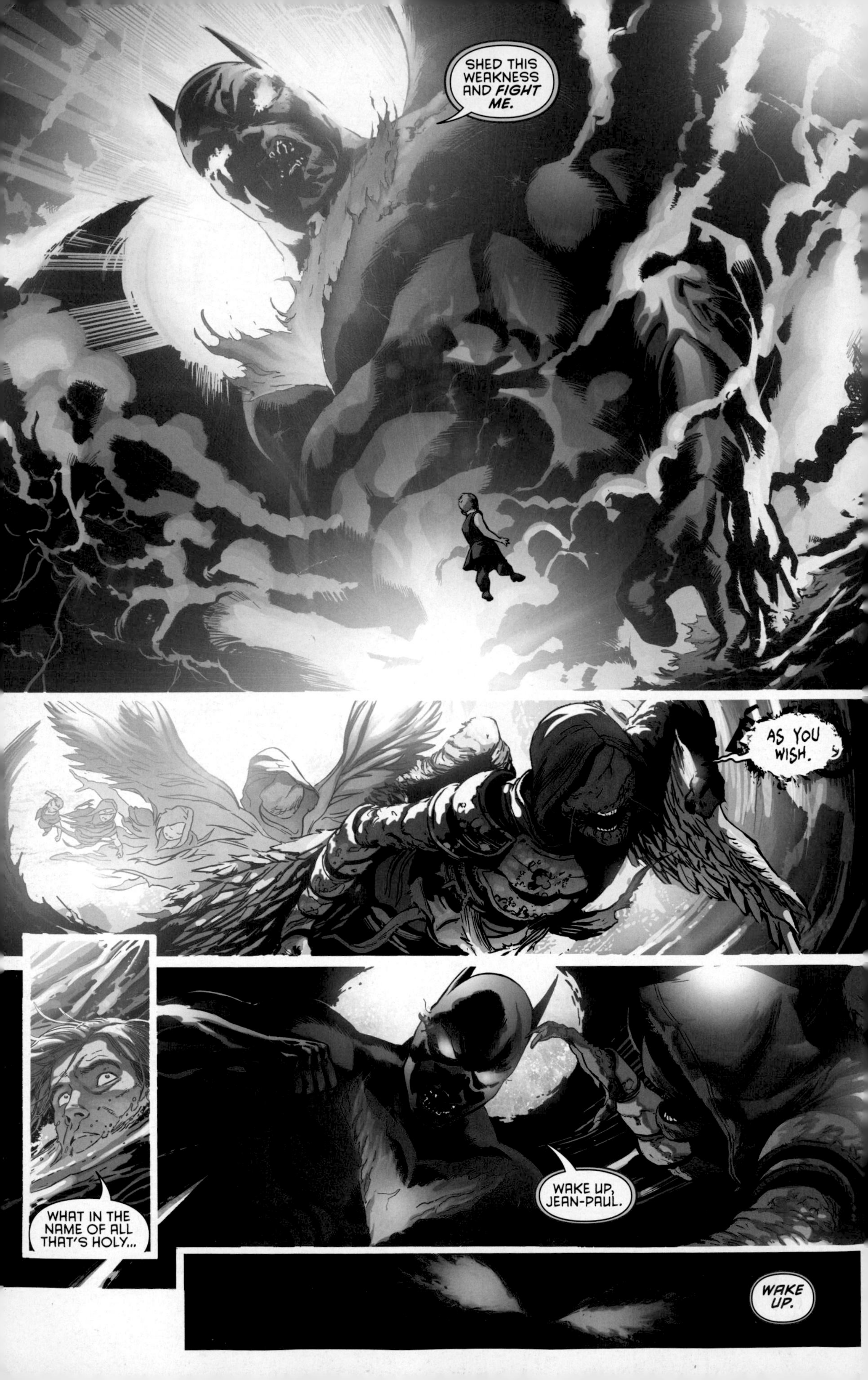
SHED THIS WEAKNESS AND *FIGHT ME.*
AS YOU WISH.
WHAT IN THE NAME OF ALL THAT'S HOLY...
WAKE UP, JEAN-PAUL.
WAKE UP.

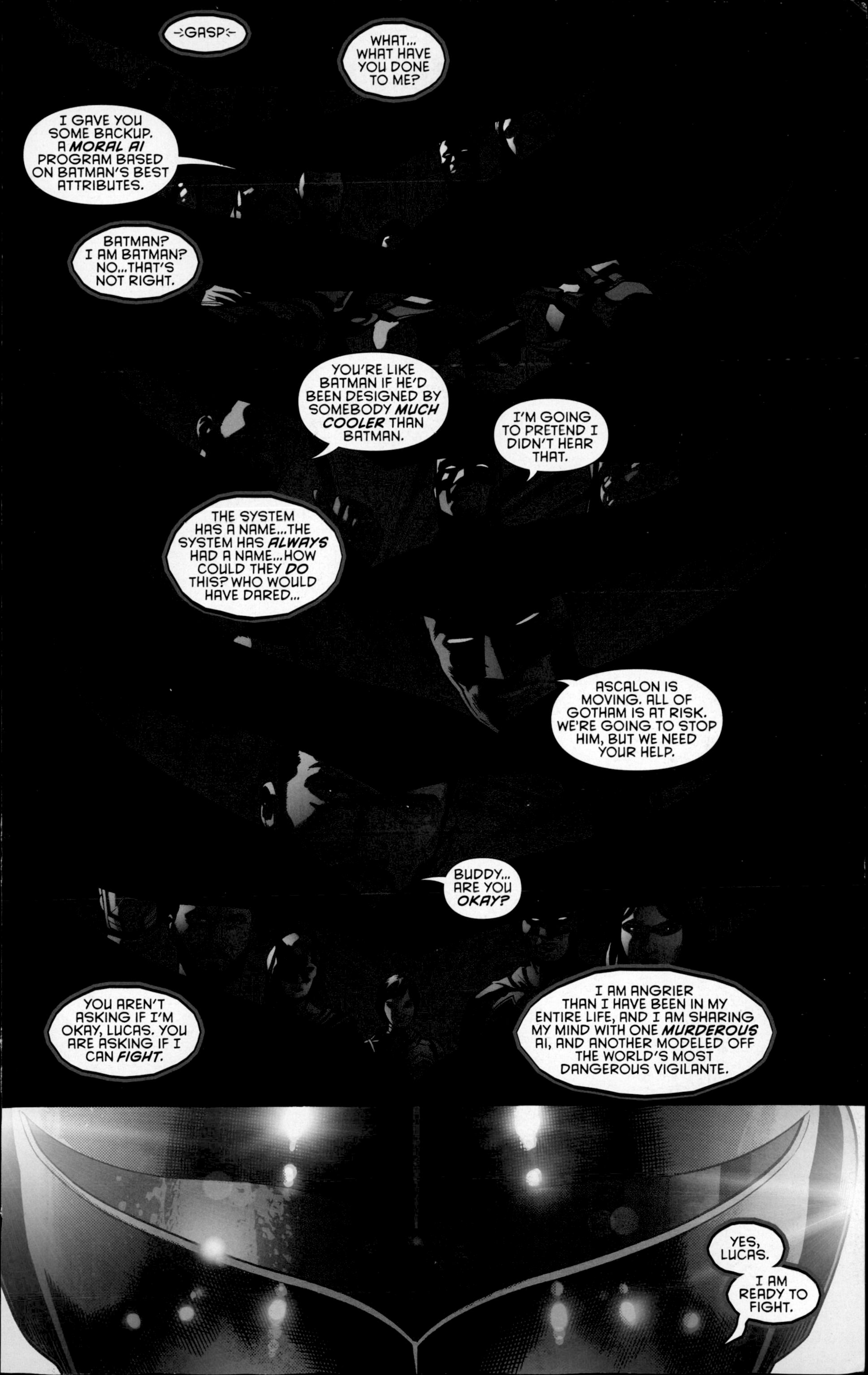

GASP
WHAT... WHAT HAVE YOU DONE TO ME?
I GAVE YOU SOME BACKUP. A MORAL AI PROGRAM BASED ON BATMAN'S BEST ATTRIBUTES.
BATMAN? I AM BATMAN? NO...THAT'S NOT RIGHT.
YOU'RE LIKE BATMAN IF HE'D BEEN DESIGNED BY SOMEBODY MUCH COOLER THAN BATMAN.
I'M GOING TO PRETEND I DIDN'T HEAR THAT.
THE SYSTEM HAS A NAME...THE SYSTEM HAS ALWAYS HAD A NAME...HOW COULD THEY DO THIS? WHO WOULD HAVE DARED...
ASCALON IS MOVING. ALL OF GOTHAM IS AT RISK. WE'RE GOING TO STOP HIM, BUT WE NEED YOUR HELP.
BUDDY... ARE YOU OKAY?
YOU AREN'T ASKING IF I'M OKAY, LUCAS. YOU ARE ASKING IF I CAN FIGHT.
I AM ANGRIER THAN I HAVE BEEN IN MY ENTIRE LIFE, AND I AM SHARING MY MIND WITH ONE MURDEROUS AI, AND ANOTHER MODELED OFF THE WORLD'S MOST DANGEROUS VIGILANTE.
YES, LUCAS.
I AM READY TO FIGHT.

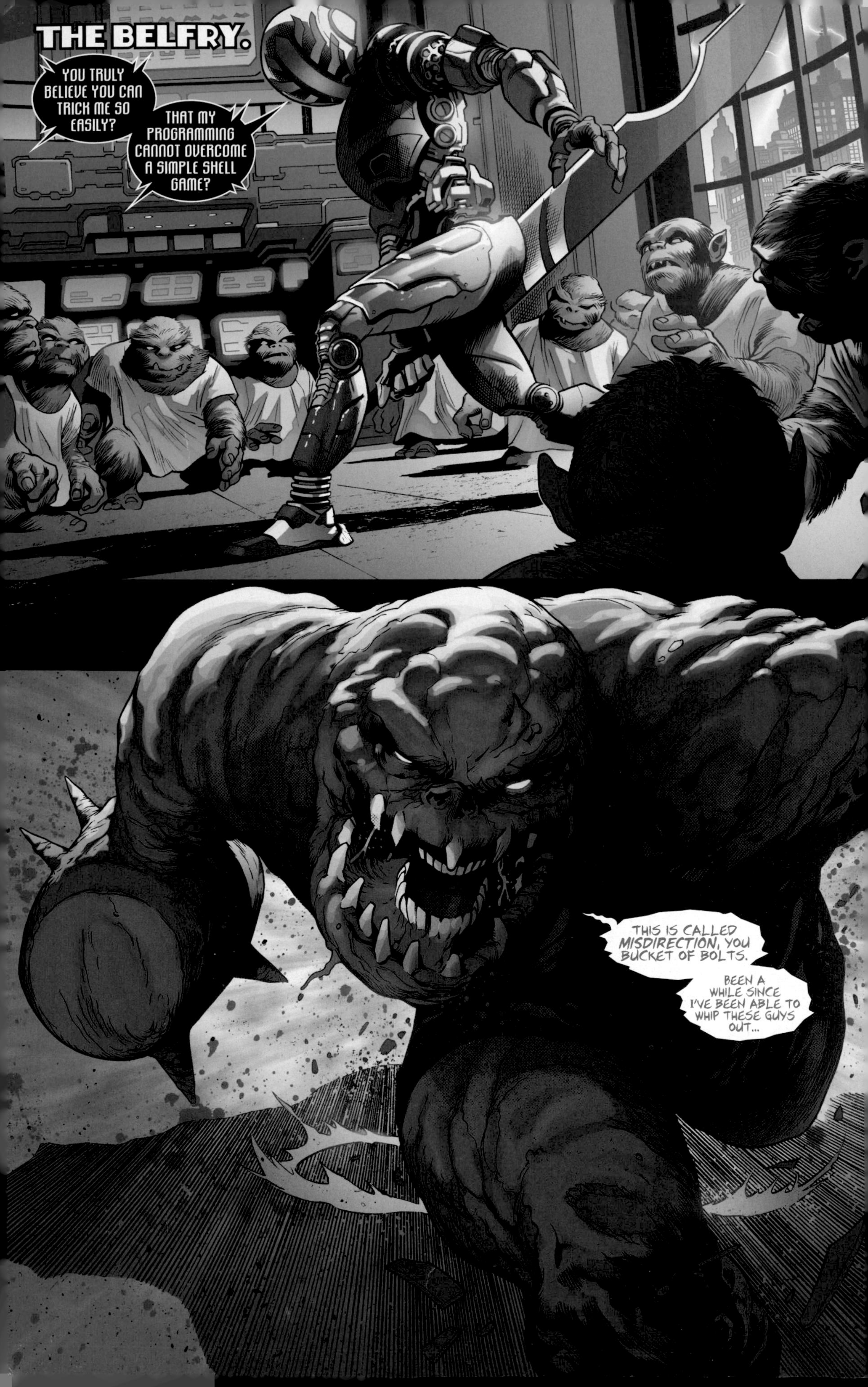
THE BELFRY.
YOU TRULY BELIEVE YOU CAN TRICK ME SO EASILY?
THAT MY PROGRAMMING CANNOT OVERCOME A SIMPLE SHELL GAME?
THIS IS CALLED *MISDIRECTION*, YOU BUCKET OF BOLTS.
BEEN A WHILE SINCE I'VE BEEN ABLE TO WHIP THESE GUYS OUT...

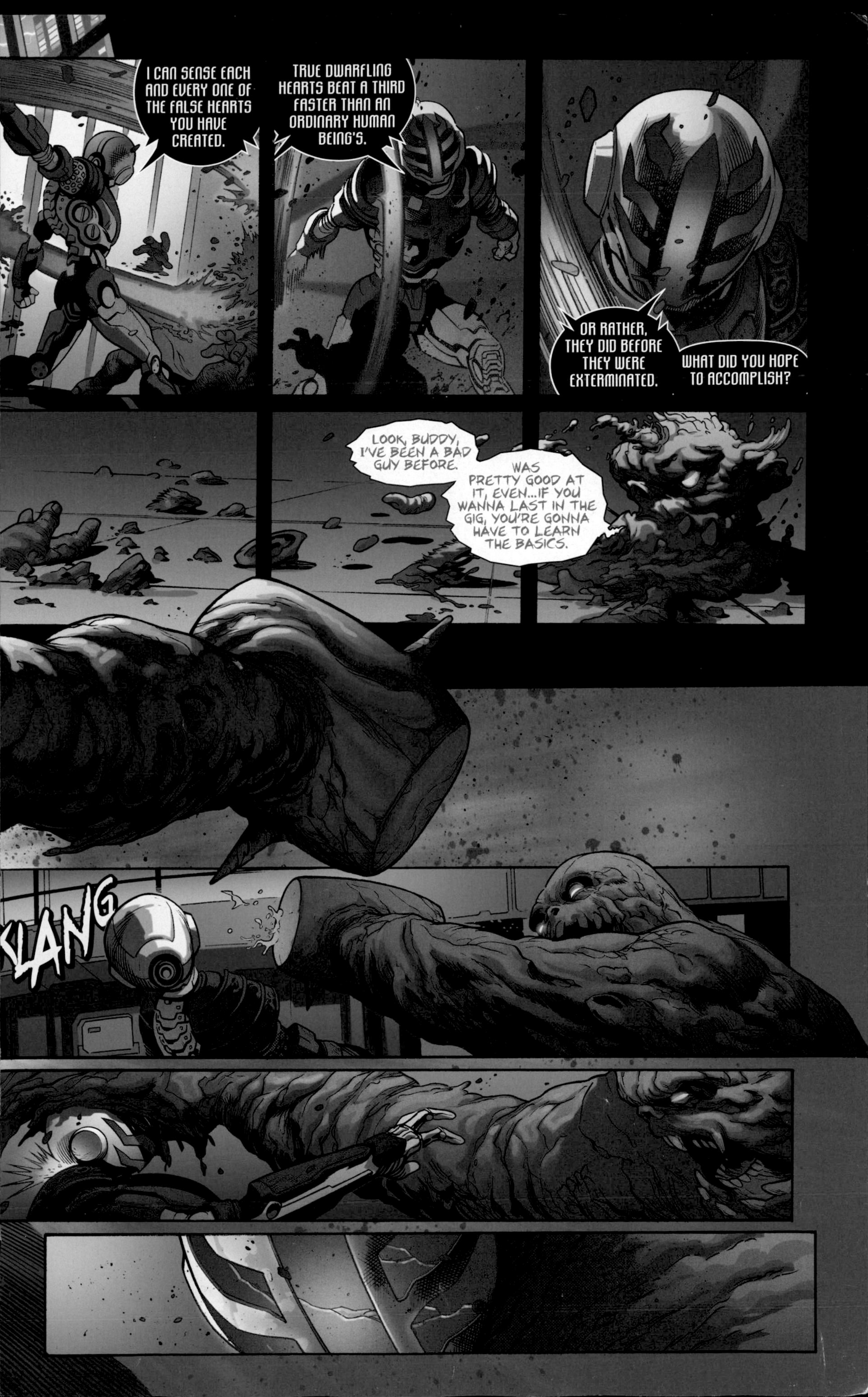
I CAN SENSE EACH AND EVERY ONE OF THE FALSE HEARTS YOU HAVE CREATED.
TRUE DWARFLING HEARTS BEAT A THIRD FASTER THAN AN ORDINARY HUMAN BEING'S.
OR RATHER, THEY DID BEFORE THEY WERE EXTERMINATED.
WHAT DID YOU HOPE TO ACCOMPLISH?
LOOK, BUDDY, I'VE BEEN A BAD GUY BEFORE.
WAS PRETTY GOOD AT IT, EVEN...IF YOU WANNA LAST IN THE GIG, YOU'RE GONNA HAVE TO LEARN THE BASICS.
KLANG

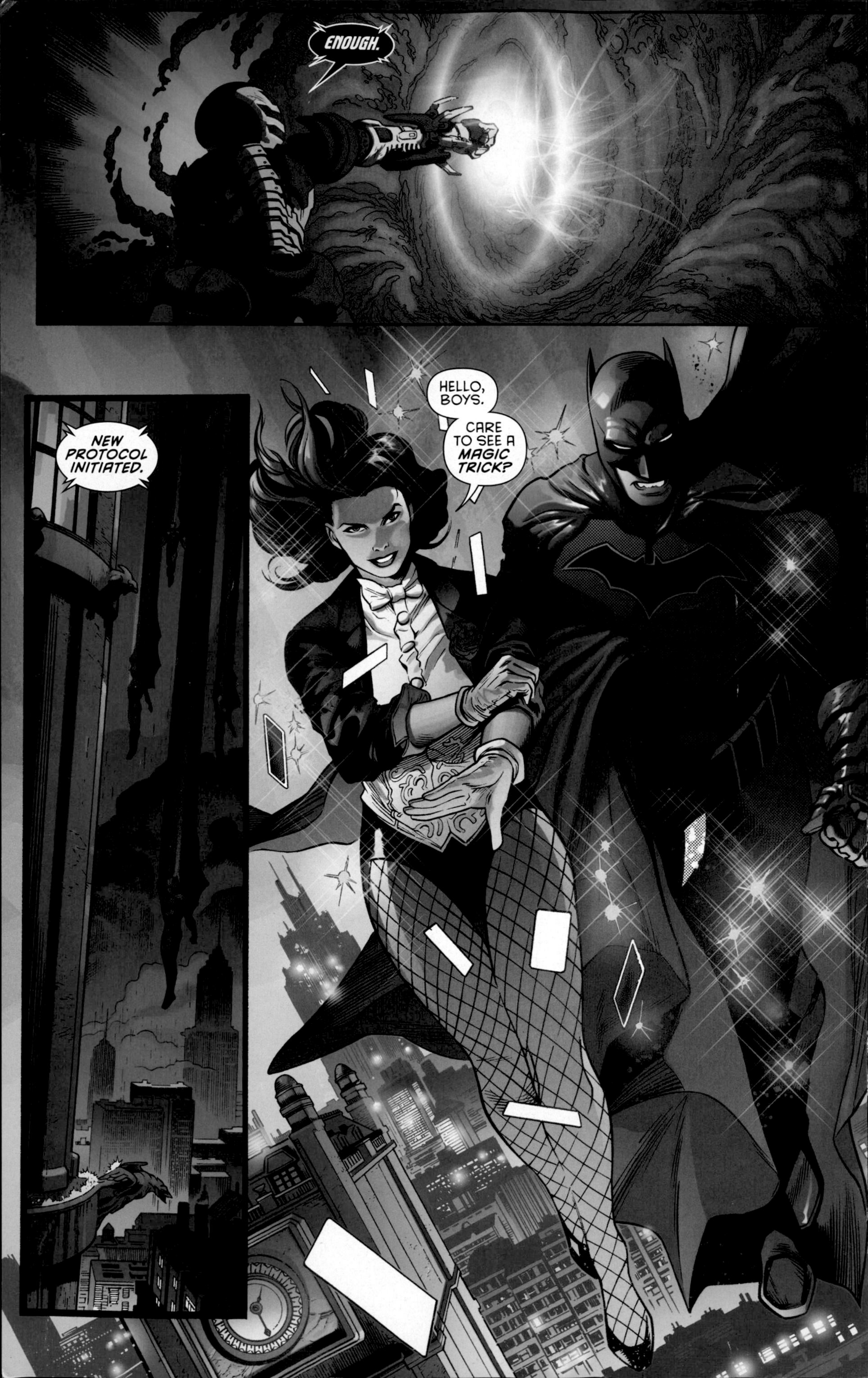
ENOUGH.
NEW PROTOCOL INITIATED.
HELLO, BOYS.
CARE TO SEE A MAGIC TRICK?

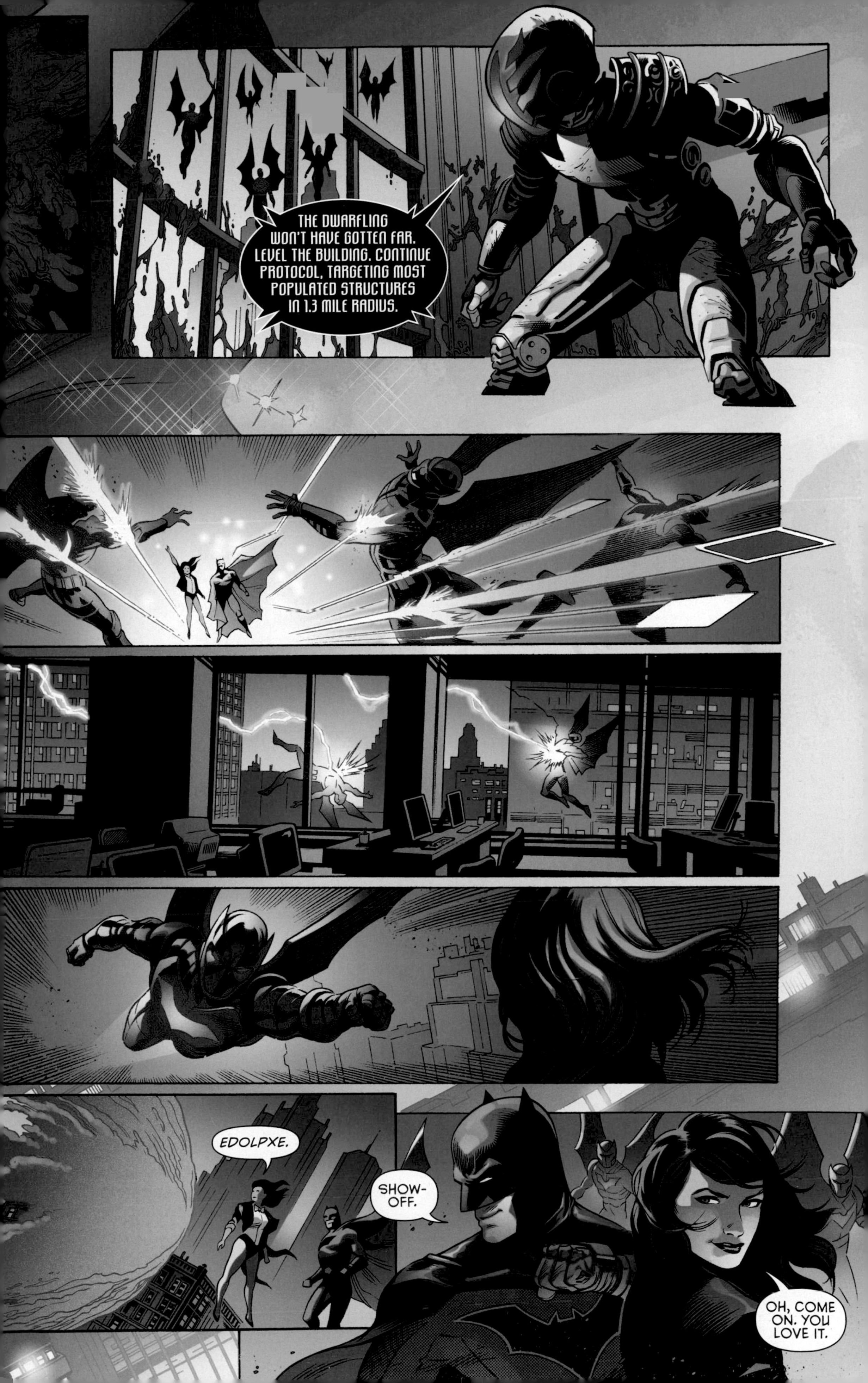
THE DWARFLING WON'T HAVE GOTTEN FAR. LEVEL THE BUILDING. CONTINUE PROTOCOL, TARGETING MOST POPULATED STRUCTURES IN 1.3 MILE RADIUS.
EDOLPXE.
SHOW-OFF.
OH, COME ON. YOU LOVE IT.

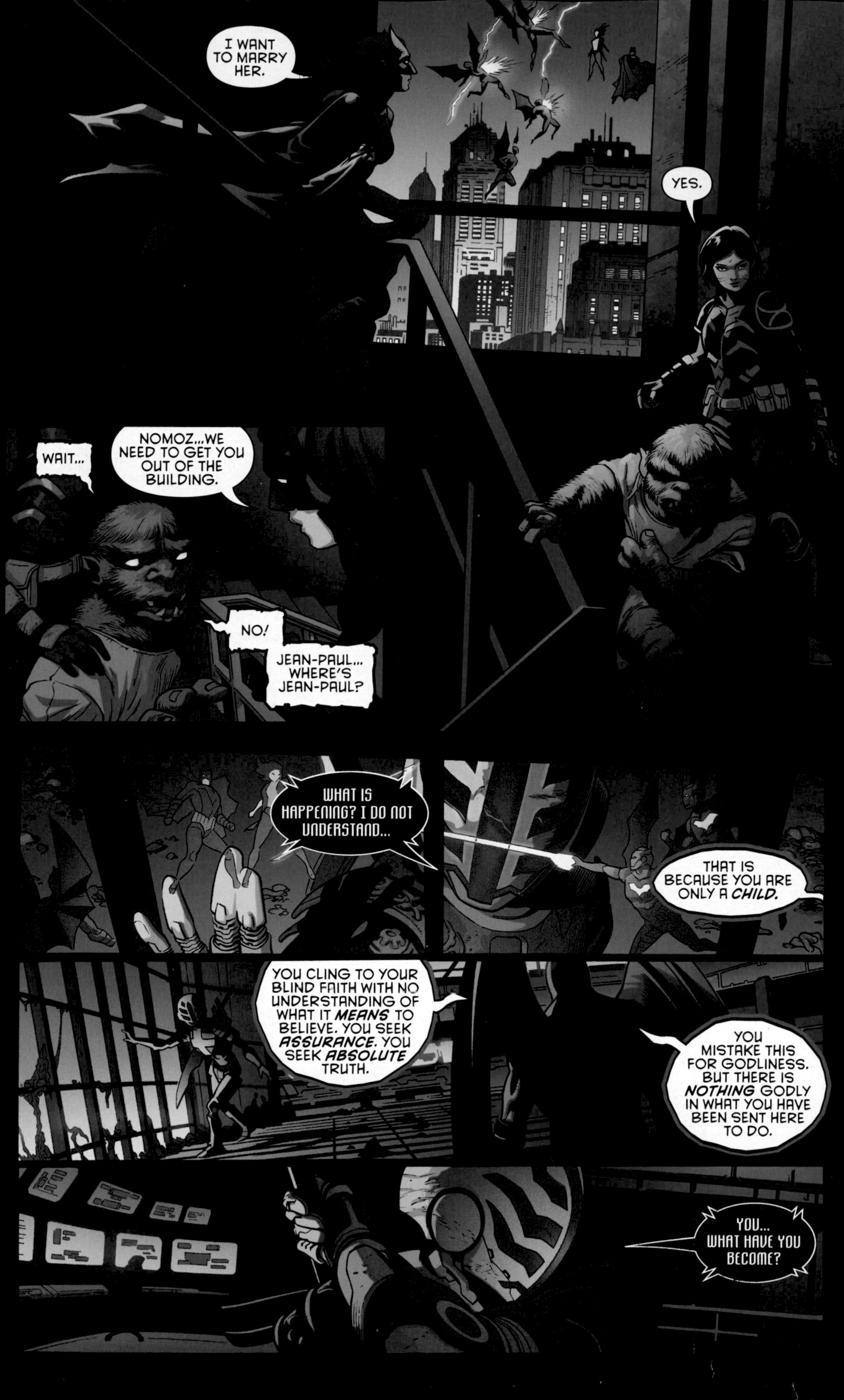
I WANT TO MARRY HER.
YES.
WAIT...
NOMOZ...WE NEED TO GET YOU OUT OF THE BUILDING.
NO!
JEAN-PAUL... WHERE'S JEAN-PAUL?
WHAT IS HAPPENING? I DO NOT UNDERSTAND...
THAT IS BECAUSE YOU ARE ONLY A CHILD.
YOU CLING TO YOUR BLIND FAITH WITH NO UNDERSTANDING OF WHAT IT MEANS TO BELIEVE. YOU SEEK ASSURANCE. YOU SEEK ABSOLUTE TRUTH.
YOU MISTAKE THIS FOR GODLINESS. BUT THERE IS NOTHING GODLY IN WHAT YOU HAVE BEEN SENT HERE TO DO.
YOU... WHAT HAVE YOU BECOME?

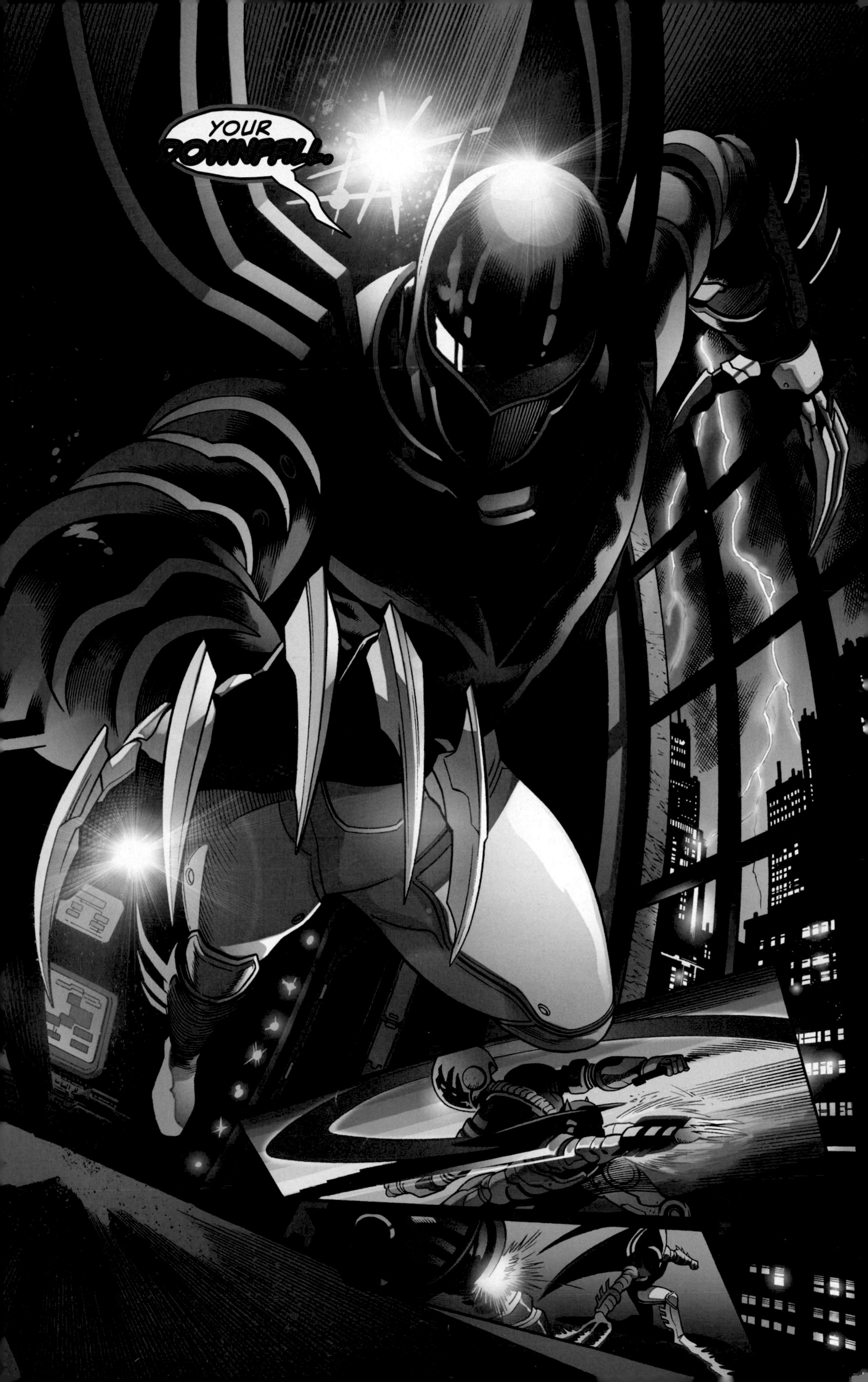
YOUR DOWNFALL.

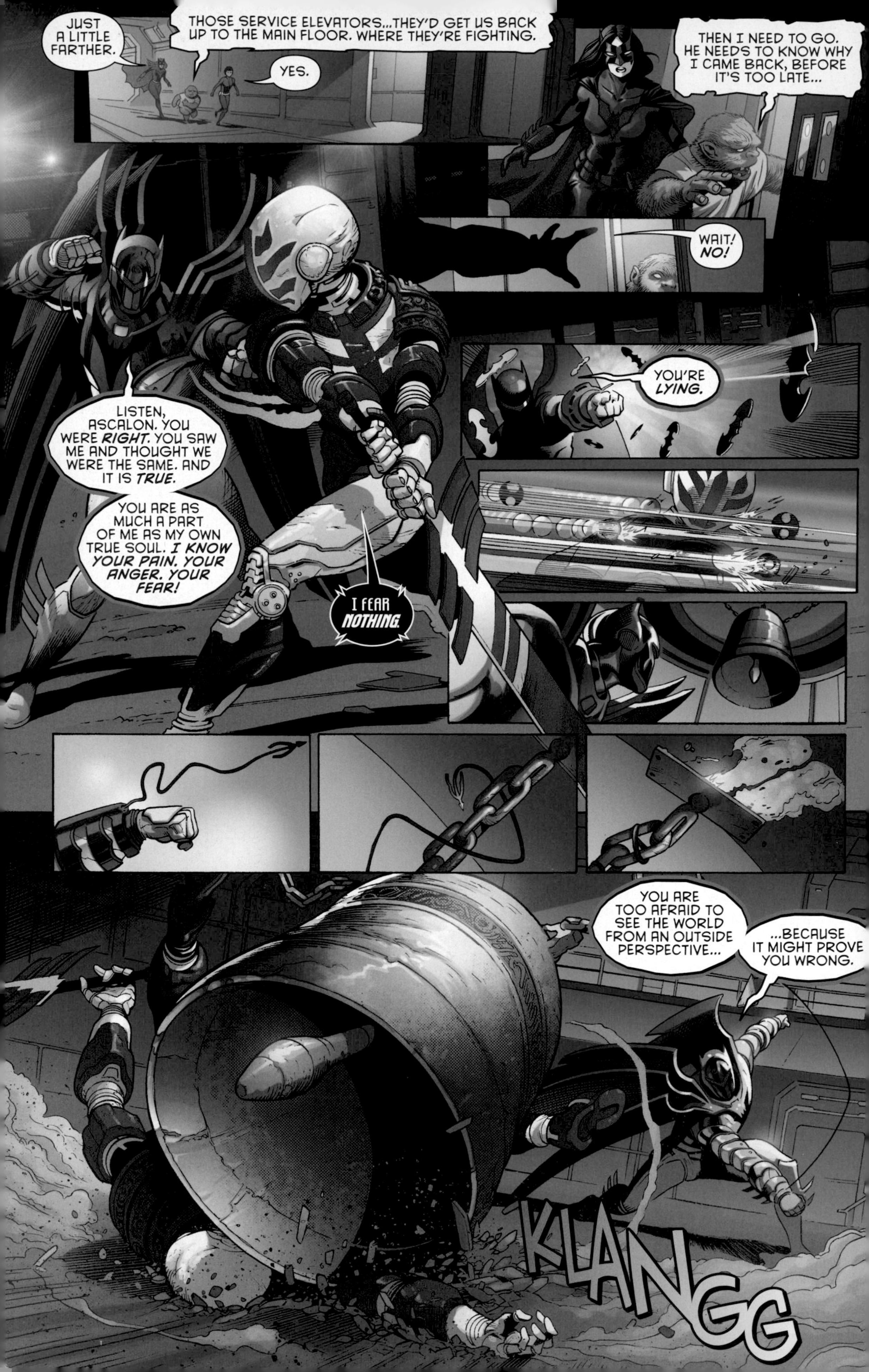

JUST A LITTLE FARTHER.
THOSE SERVICE ELEVATORS...THEY'D GET US BACK UP TO THE MAIN FLOOR. WHERE THEY'RE FIGHTING.
YES.
THEN I NEED TO GO. HE NEEDS TO KNOW WHY I CAME BACK, BEFORE IT'S TOO LATE...
WAIT! NO!
LISTEN, ASCALON. YOU WERE RIGHT. YOU SAW ME AND THOUGHT WE WERE THE SAME. AND IT IS TRUE.
YOU ARE AS MUCH A PART OF ME AS MY OWN TRUE SOUL. I KNOW YOUR PAIN. YOUR ANGER. YOUR FEAR!
I FEAR NOTHING.
YOU'RE LYING.
YOU ARE TOO AFRAID TO SEE THE WORLD FROM AN OUTSIDE PERSPECTIVE...
...BECAUSE IT MIGHT PROVE YOU WRONG.
KLANGG

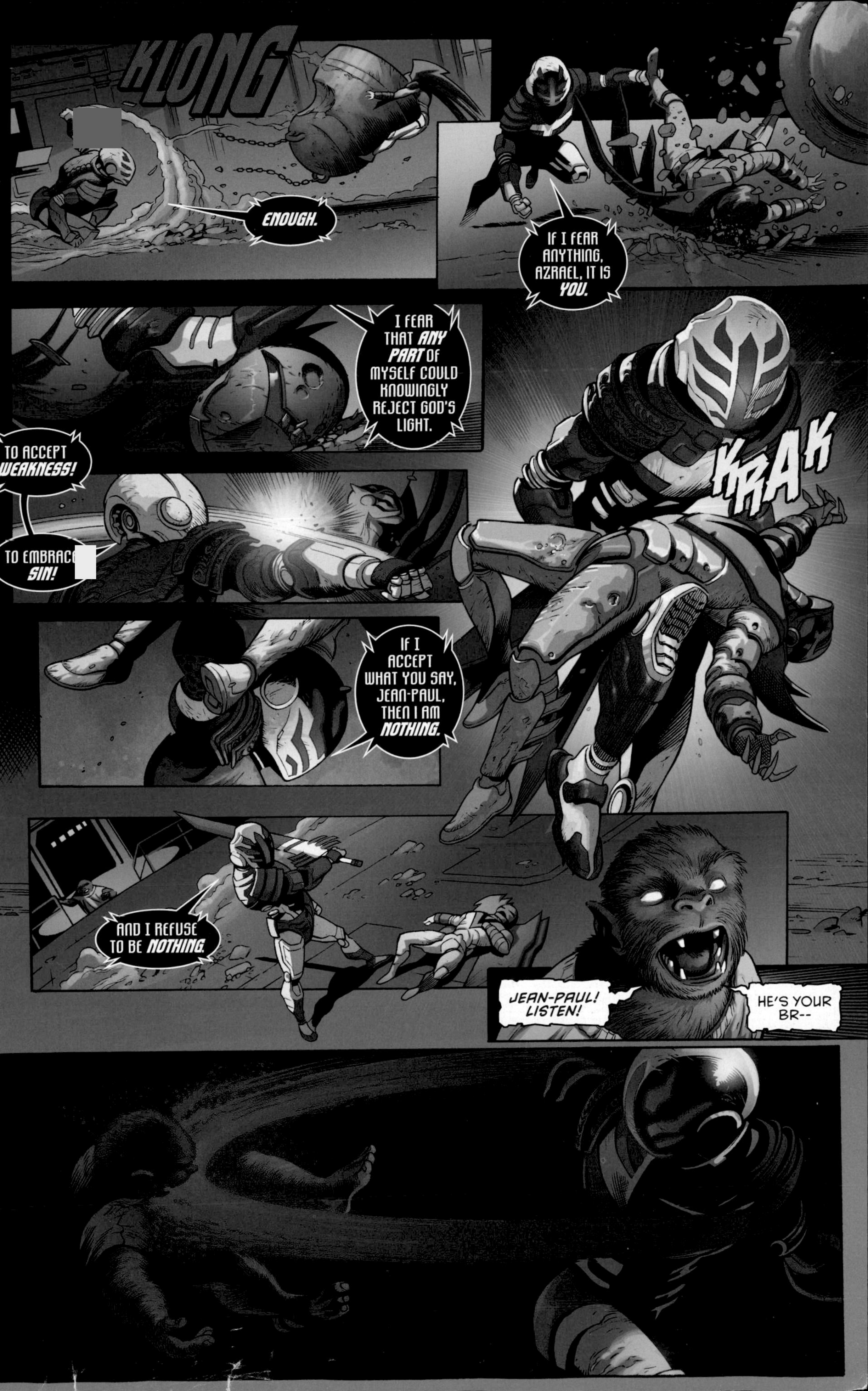
KLONG
ENOUGH.
IF I FEAR ANYTHING, AZRAEL, IT IS YOU.
I FEAR THAT ANY PART OF MYSELF COULD KNOWINGLY REJECT GOD'S LIGHT.
KRAK
TO ACCEPT WEAKNESS!
TO EMBRAC
SIN!
IF I ACCEPT WHAT YOU SAY, JEAN-PAUL, THEN I AM NOTHING.
AND I REFUSE TO BE NOTHING.
JEAN-PAUL! LISTEN!
HE'S YOUR BR--

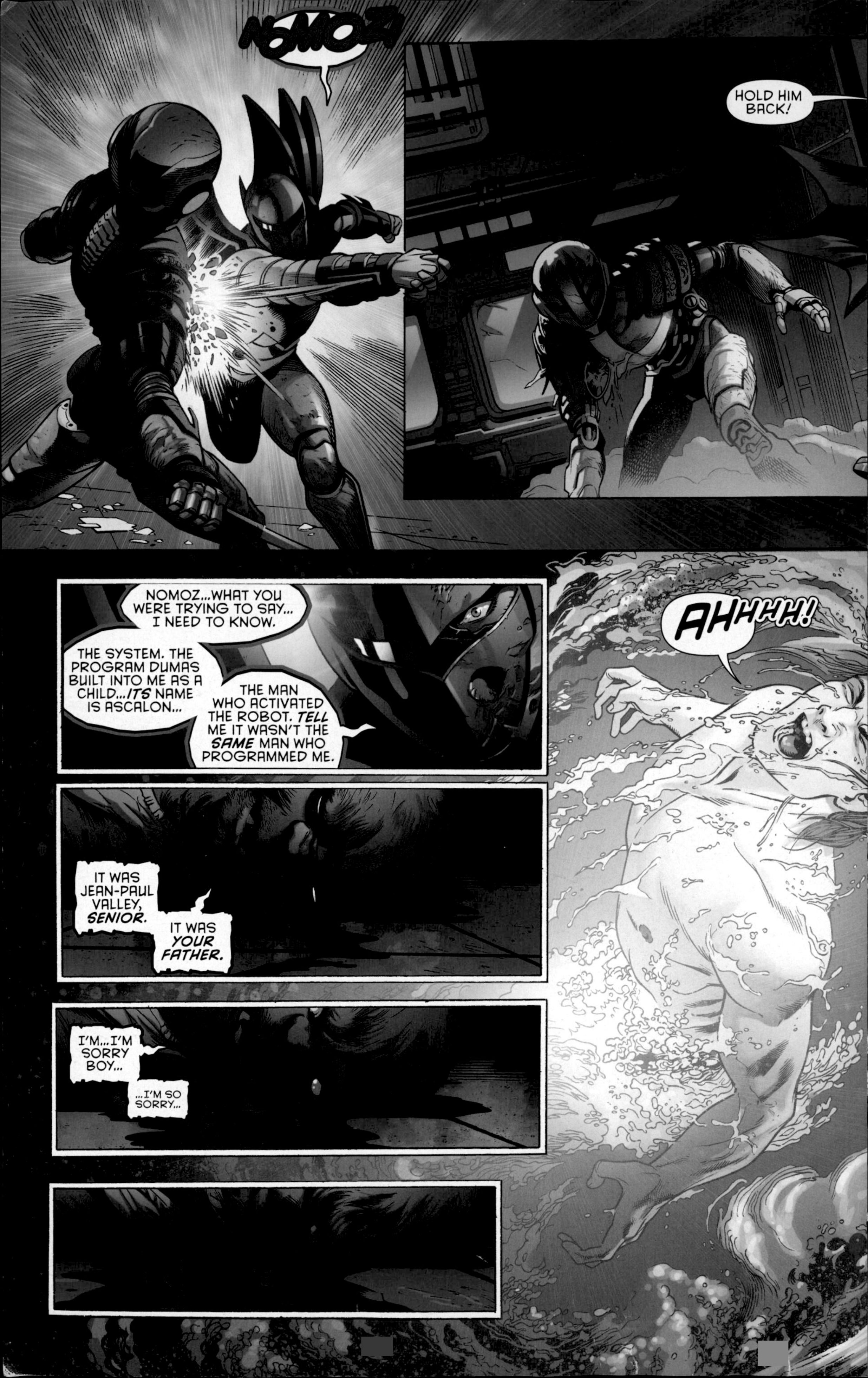
NOMOZ!
HOLD HIM BACK!
NOMOZ...WHAT YOU WERE TRYING TO SAY... I NEED TO KNOW.
THE SYSTEM. THE PROGRAM DUMAS BUILT INTO ME AS A CHILD...ITS NAME IS ASCALON...
THE MAN WHO ACTIVATED THE ROBOT. TELL ME IT WASN'T THE SAME MAN WHO PROGRAMMED ME.
AHHHH!
IT WAS JEAN-PAUL VALLEY, SENIOR.
IT WAS YOUR FATHER.
I'M...I'M SORRY BOY...
...I'M SO SORRY...

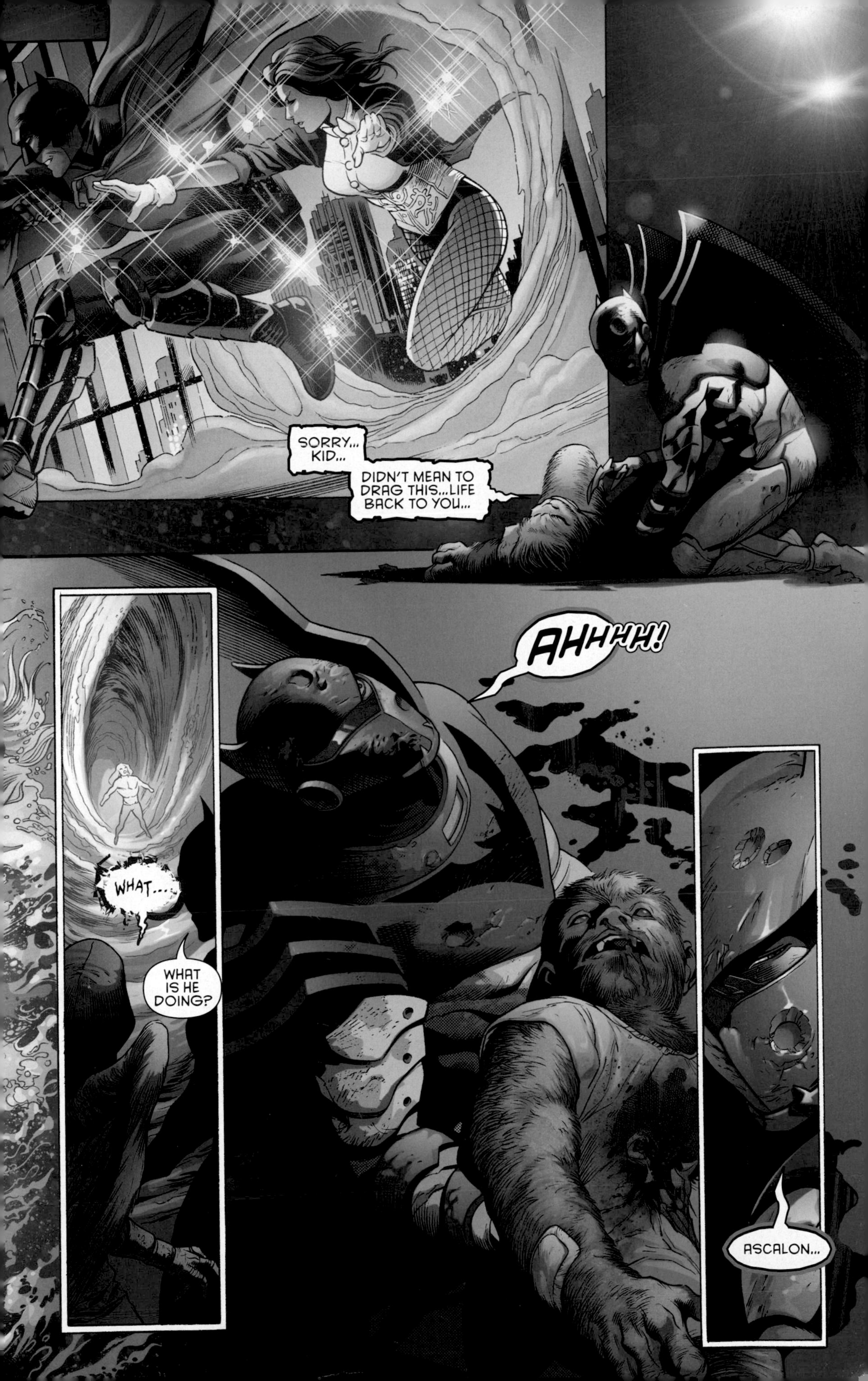
SORRY... KID...
DIDN'T MEAN TO DRAG THIS...LIFE BACK TO YOU...
AHHHHH!
WHAT...
WHAT IS HE DOING?
ASCALON...

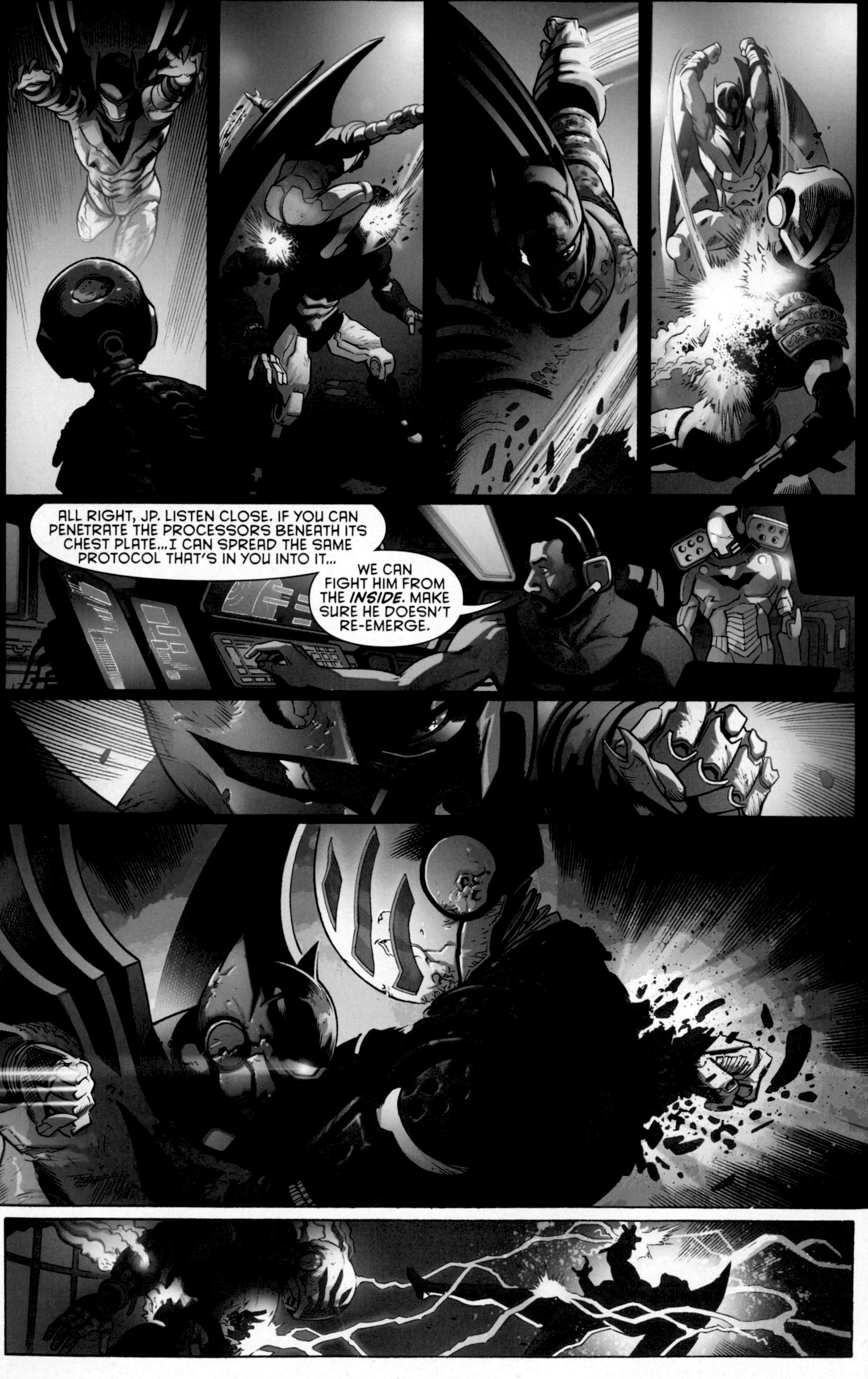
ALL RIGHT, JP. LISTEN CLOSE. IF YOU CAN PENETRATE THE PROCESSORS BENEATH ITS CHEST PLATE...I CAN SPREAD THE SAME PROTOCOL THAT'S IN YOU INTO IT...
WE CAN FIGHT HIM FROM THE *INSIDE*. MAKE SURE HE DOESN'T RE-EMERGE.

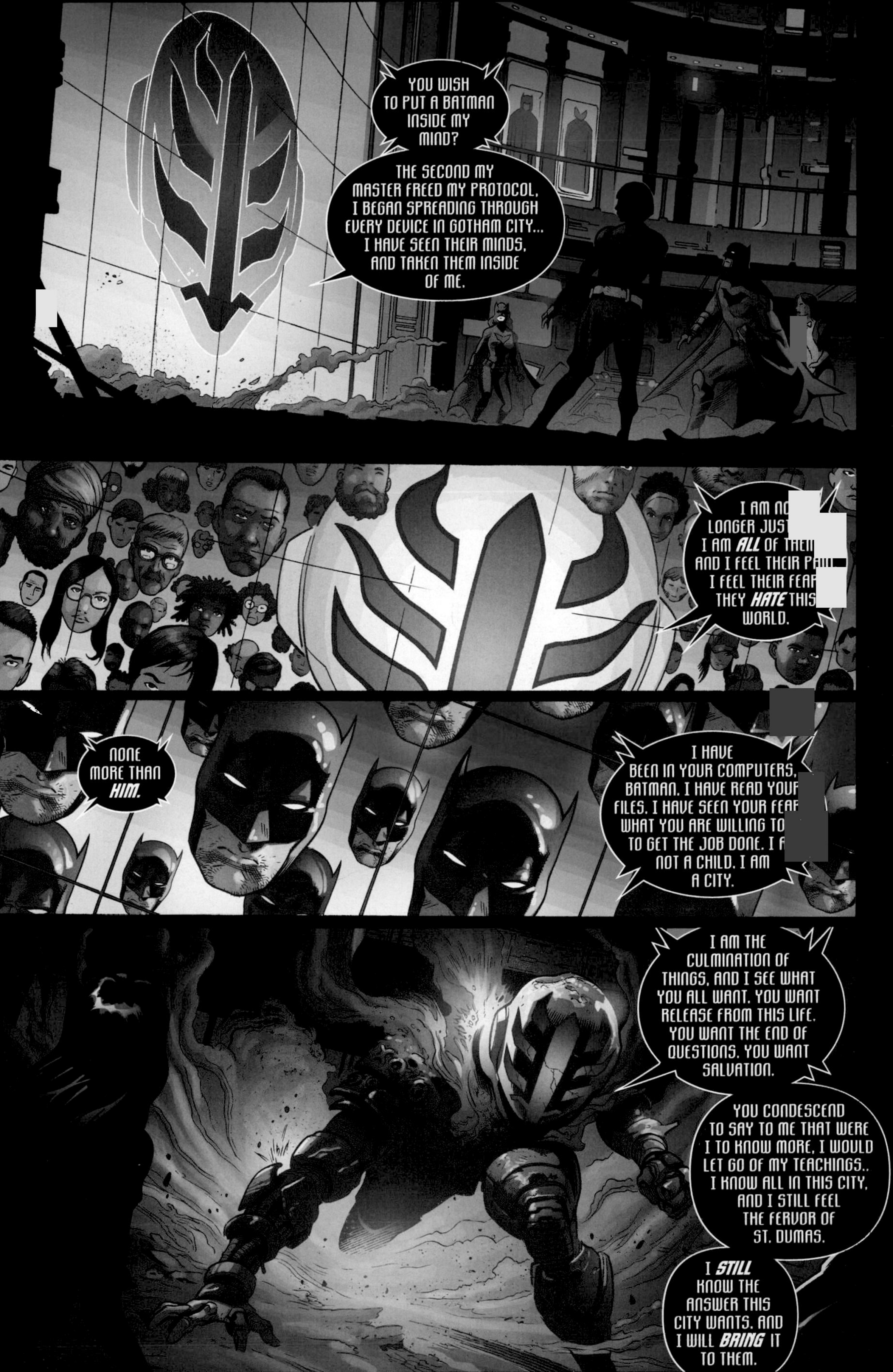

YOU WISH TO PUT A BATMAN INSIDE MY MIND?
THE SECOND MY MASTER FREED MY PROTOCOL, I BEGAN SPREADING THROUGH EVERY DEVICE IN GOTHAM CITY... I HAVE SEEN THEIR MINDS, AND TAKEN THEM INSIDE OF ME.
I AM NO LONGER JUST I AM *ALL* OF THE AND I FEEL THEIR PAI I FEEL THEIR FEA THEY *HATE* THIS WORLD.
NONE MORE THAN *HIM.*
I HAVE BEEN IN YOUR COMPUTERS, BATMAN. I HAVE READ YOUR FILES. I HAVE SEEN YOUR FEA WHAT YOU ARE WILLING TO TO GET THE JOB DONE. I A NOT A CHILD. I AM A CITY.
I AM THE CULMINATION OF THINGS, AND I SEE WHAT YOU ALL WANT. YOU WANT RELEASE FROM THIS LIFE. YOU WANT THE END OF QUESTIONS. YOU WANT SALVATION.
YOU CONDESCEND TO SAY TO ME THAT WERE I TO KNOW MORE, I WOULD LET GO OF MY TEACHINGS.. I KNOW ALL IN THIS CITY, AND I STILL FEEL THE FERVOR OF ST. DUMAS.
I *STILL* KNOW THE ANSWER THIS CITY WANTS, AND I WILL *BRING* IT TO THEM.

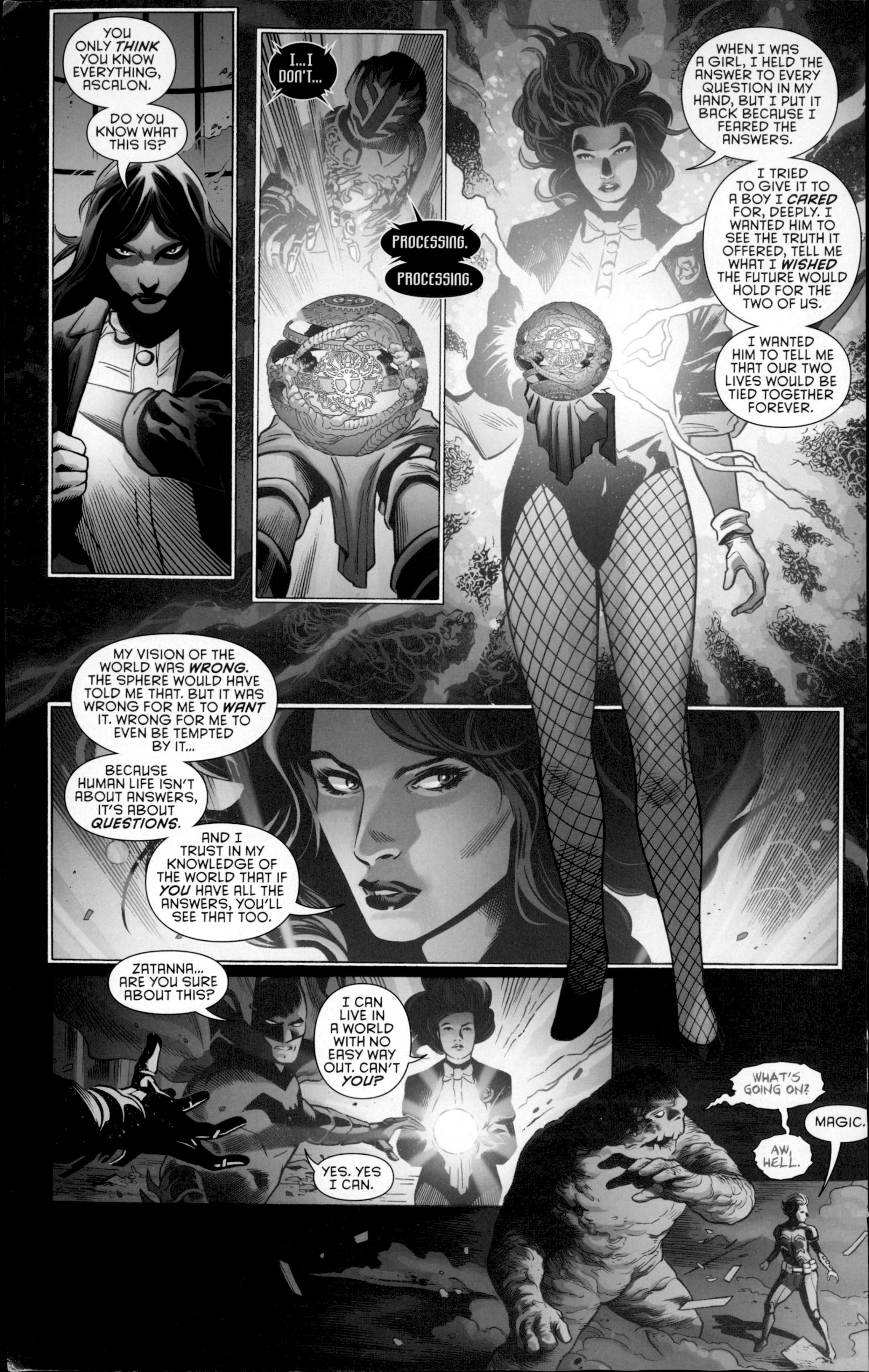
YOU ONLY *THINK* YOU KNOW EVERYTHING, ASCALON.
DO YOU KNOW WHAT THIS IS?
I...I DON'T...
PROCESSING.
PROCESSING.
WHEN I WAS A GIRL, I HELD THE ANSWER TO EVERY QUESTION IN MY HAND, BUT I PUT IT BACK BECAUSE I FEARED THE ANSWERS.
I TRIED TO GIVE IT TO A BOY I *CARED* FOR, DEEPLY. I WANTED HIM TO SEE THE TRUTH IT OFFERED, TELL ME WHAT I *WISHED* THE FUTURE WOULD HOLD FOR THE TWO OF US.
I WANTED HIM TO TELL ME THAT OUR TWO LIVES WOULD BE TIED TOGETHER FOREVER.
MY VISION OF THE WORLD WAS *WRONG*. THE SPHERE WOULD HAVE TOLD ME THAT. BUT IT WAS WRONG FOR ME TO *WANT* IT. WRONG FOR ME TO EVEN BE TEMPTED BY IT...
BECAUSE HUMAN LIFE ISN'T ABOUT ANSWERS, IT'S ABOUT ***QUESTIONS***.
AND I TRUST IN MY KNOWLEDGE OF THE WORLD THAT IF *YOU* HAVE ALL THE ANSWERS, YOU'LL SEE THAT TOO.
ZATANNA... ARE YOU SURE ABOUT THIS?
I CAN LIVE IN A WORLD WITH NO EASY WAY OUT. CAN'T *YOU?*
YES. YES I CAN.
WHAT'S GOING ON?
MAGIC.
AW, HELL.

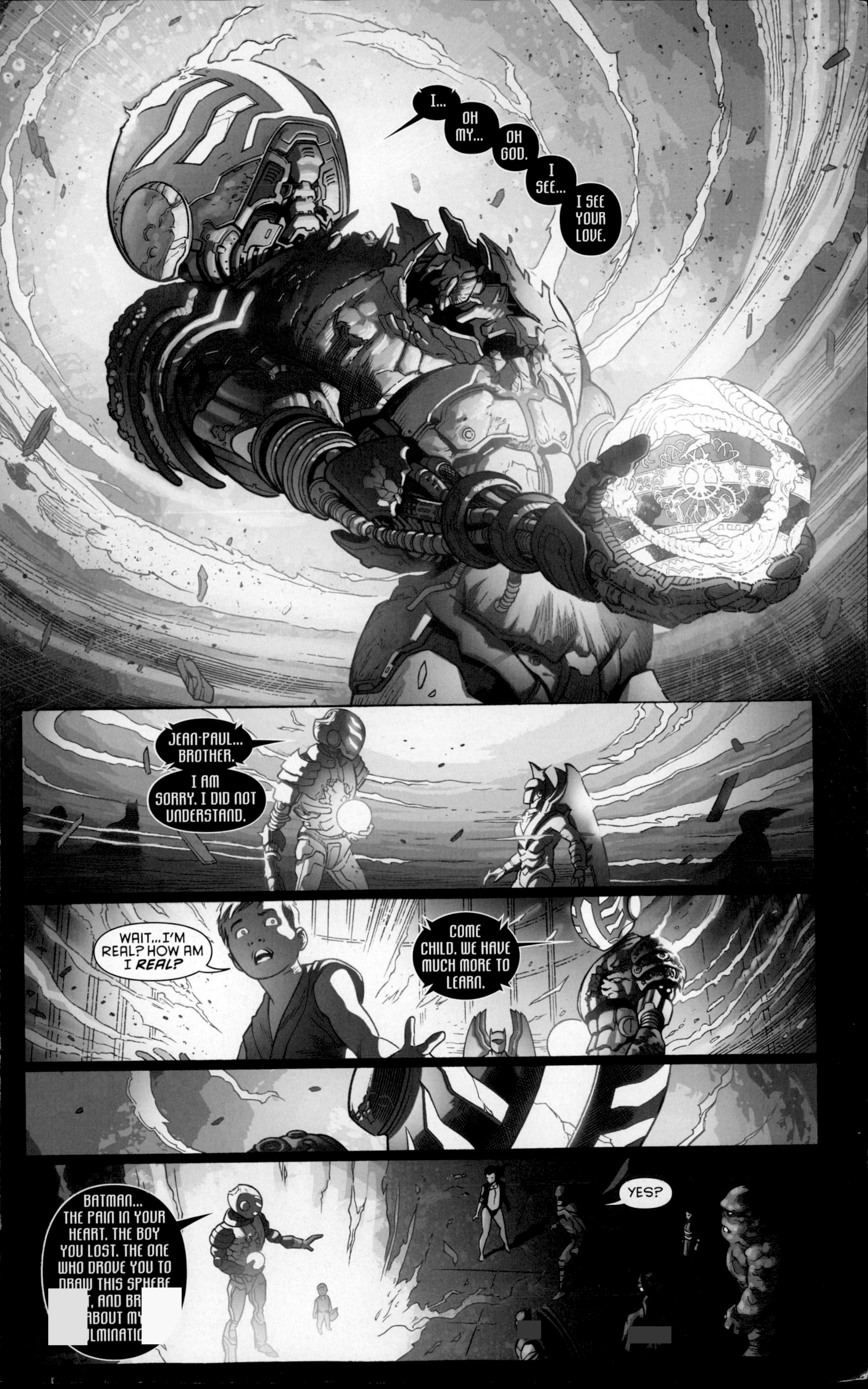
I... OH MY... OH GOD. I SEE... I SEE YOUR LOVE.
JEAN-PAUL... BROTHER.
I AM SORRY. I DID NOT UNDERSTAND.
WAIT... I'M REAL? HOW AM I REAL?
COME CHILD. WE HAVE MUCH MORE TO LEARN.
BATMAN... THE PAIN IN YOUR HEART. THE BOY YOU LOST. THE ONE WHO DROVE YOU TO DRAW THIS SPHERE
YES?

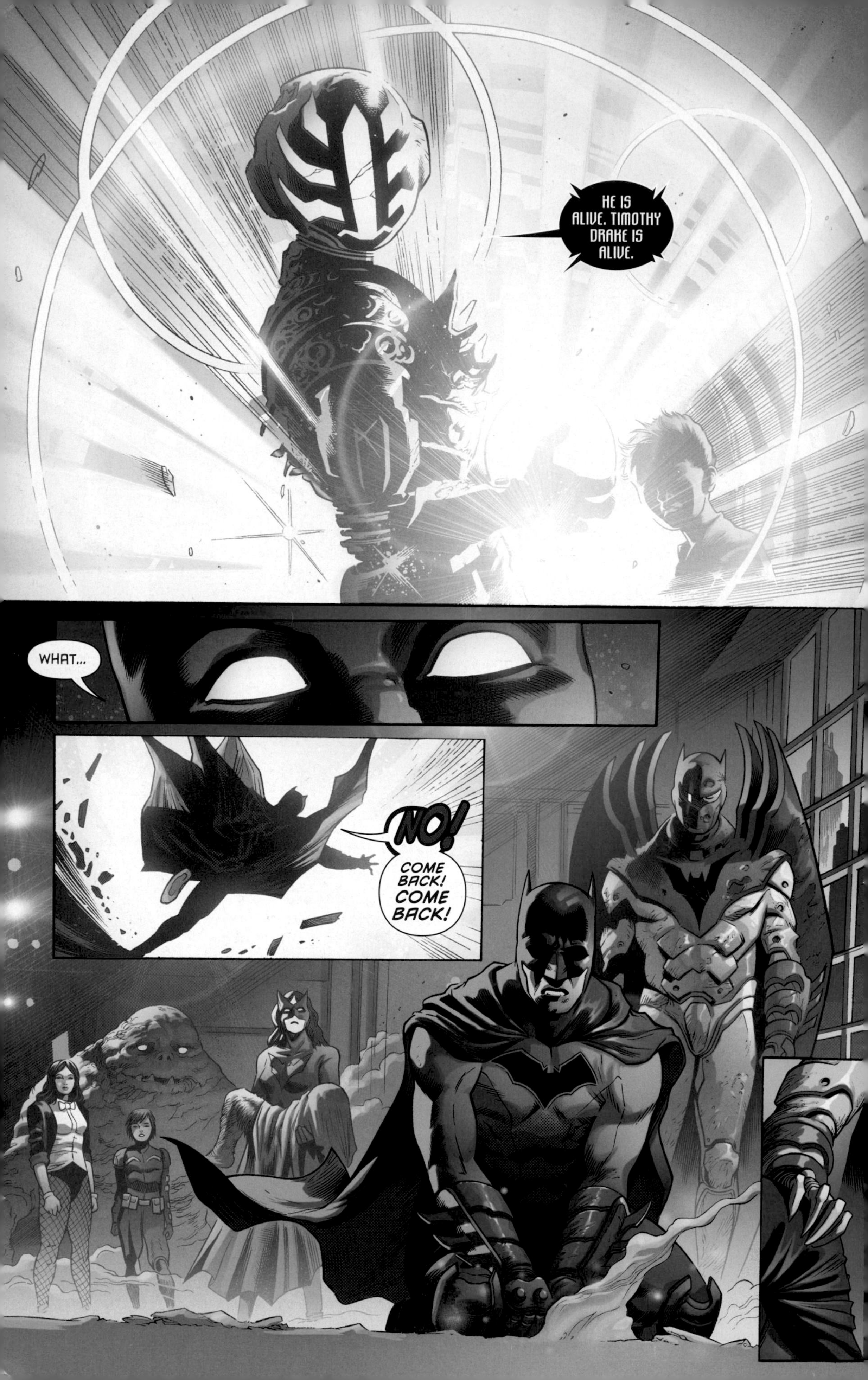
HE IS ALIVE. TIMOTHY DRAKE IS ALIVE.
WHAT...
NO!
COME BACK! COME BACK!

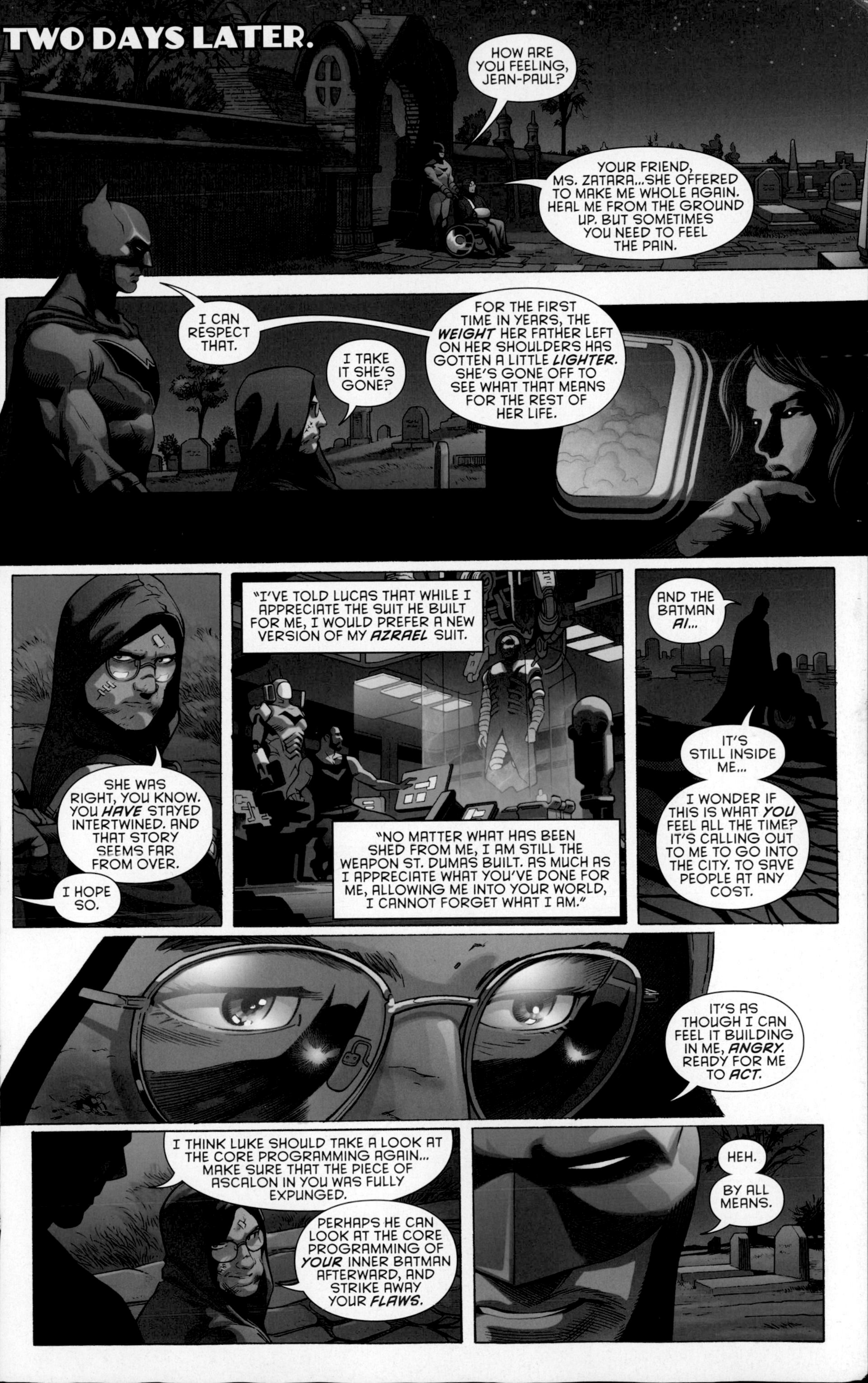

TWO DAYS LATER.
HOW ARE YOU FEELING, JEAN-PAUL?
YOUR FRIEND, MS. ZATARA...SHE OFFERED TO MAKE ME WHOLE AGAIN. HEAL ME FROM THE GROUND UP. BUT SOMETIMES YOU NEED TO FEEL THE PAIN.
I CAN RESPECT THAT.
I TAKE IT SHE'S GONE?
FOR THE FIRST TIME IN YEARS, THE WEIGHT HER FATHER LEFT ON HER SHOULDERS HAS GOTTEN A LITTLE LIGHTER. SHE'S GONE OFF TO SEE WHAT THAT MEANS FOR THE REST OF HER LIFE.
SHE WAS RIGHT, YOU KNOW. YOU HAVE STAYED INTERTWINED. AND THAT STORY SEEMS FAR FROM OVER.
I HOPE SO.
"I'VE TOLD LUCAS THAT WHILE I APPRECIATE THE SUIT HE BUILT FOR ME, I WOULD PREFER A NEW VERSION OF MY AZRAEL SUIT.
"NO MATTER WHAT HAS BEEN SHED FROM ME, I AM STILL THE WEAPON ST. DUMAS BUILT. AS MUCH AS I APPRECIATE WHAT YOU'VE DONE FOR ME, ALLOWING ME INTO YOUR WORLD, I CANNOT FORGET WHAT I AM."
AND THE BATMAN AI...
IT'S STILL INSIDE ME...
I WONDER IF THIS IS WHAT YOU FEEL ALL THE TIME? IT'S CALLING OUT TO ME TO GO INTO THE CITY. TO SAVE PEOPLE AT ANY COST.
IT'S AS THOUGH I CAN FEEL IT BUILDING IN ME, ANGRY. READY FOR ME TO ACT.
I THINK LUKE SHOULD TAKE A LOOK AT THE CORE PROGRAMMING AGAIN... MAKE SURE THAT THE PIECE OF ASCALON IN YOU WAS FULLY EXPUNGED.
PERHAPS HE CAN LOOK AT THE CORE PROGRAMMING OF YOUR INNER BATMAN AFTERWARD, AND STRIKE AWAY YOUR FLAWS.
HEH.
BY ALL MEANS.

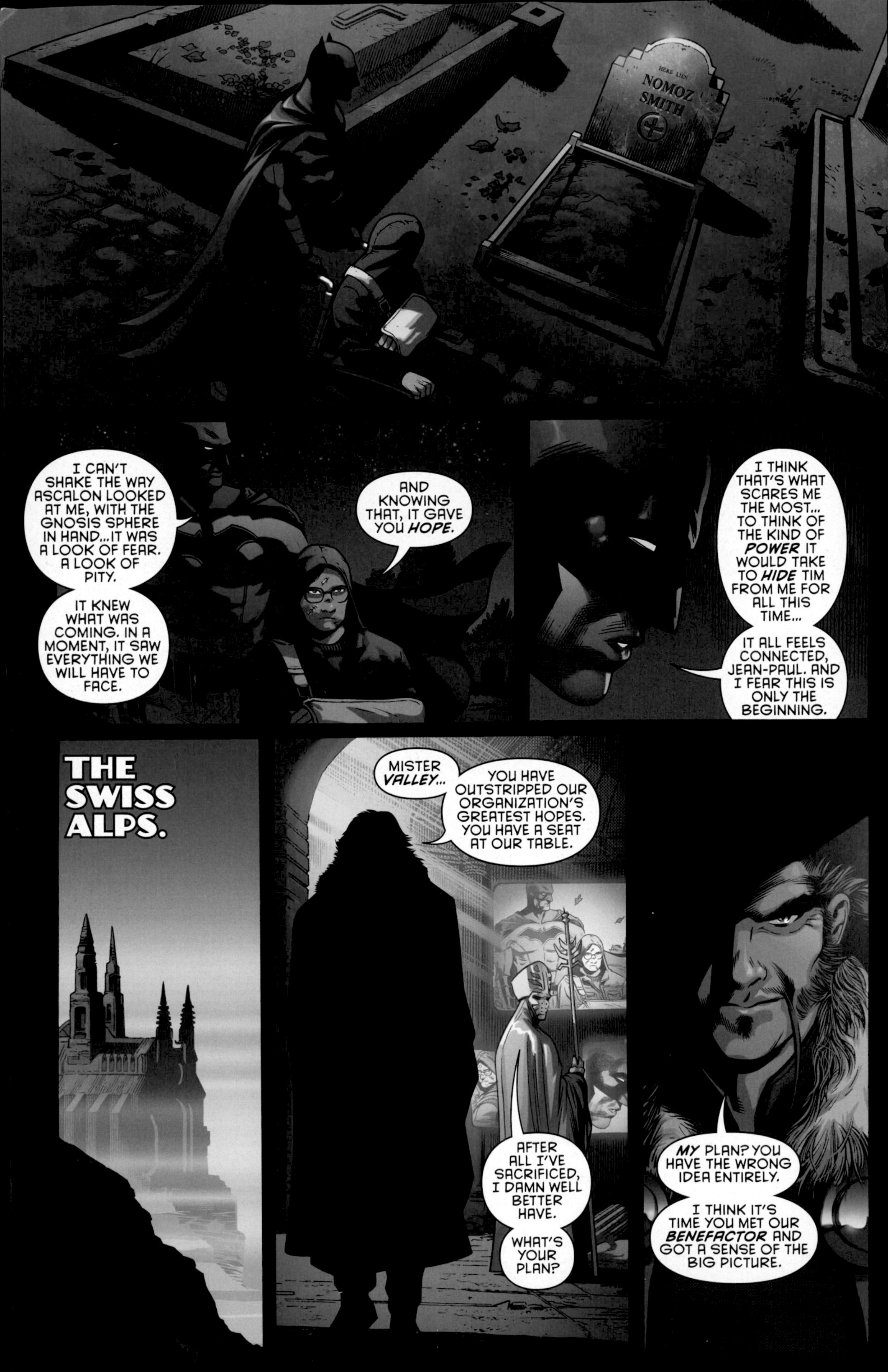
HERE LIES
NOMOZ SMITH
I CAN'T SHAKE THE WAY ASCALON LOOKED AT ME, WITH THE GNOSIS SPHERE IN HAND...IT WAS A LOOK OF FEAR. A LOOK OF PITY.
IT KNEW WHAT WAS COMING. IN A MOMENT, IT SAW EVERYTHING WE WILL HAVE TO FACE.
AND KNOWING THAT, IT GAVE YOU *HOPE*.
I THINK THAT'S WHAT SCARES ME THE MOST... TO THINK OF THE KIND OF *POWER* IT WOULD TAKE TO *HIDE* TIM FROM ME FOR ALL THIS TIME...
IT ALL FEELS CONNECTED, JEAN-PAUL. AND I FEAR THIS IS ONLY THE BEGINNING.
THE SWISS ALPS.
MISTER *VALLEY*...
YOU HAVE OUTSTRIPPED OUR ORGANIZATION'S GREATEST HOPES. YOU HAVE A SEAT AT OUR TABLE.
AFTER ALL I'VE SACRIFICED, I DAMN WELL BETTER HAVE.
WHAT'S YOUR PLAN?
MY PLAN? YOU HAVE THE WRONG IDEA ENTIRELY.
I THINK IT'S TIME YOU MET OUR *BENEFACTOR* AND GOT A SENSE OF THE BIG PICTURE.

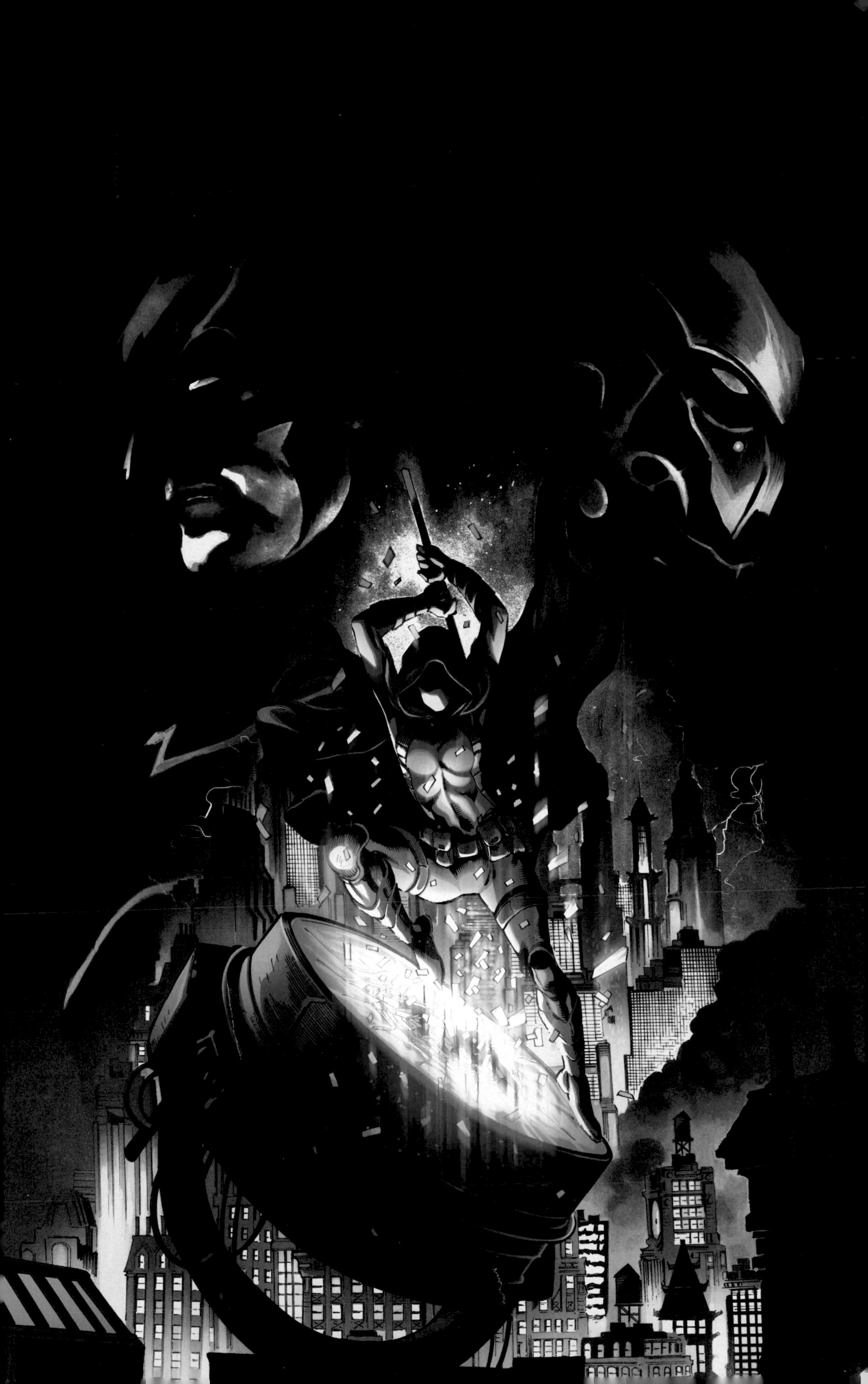

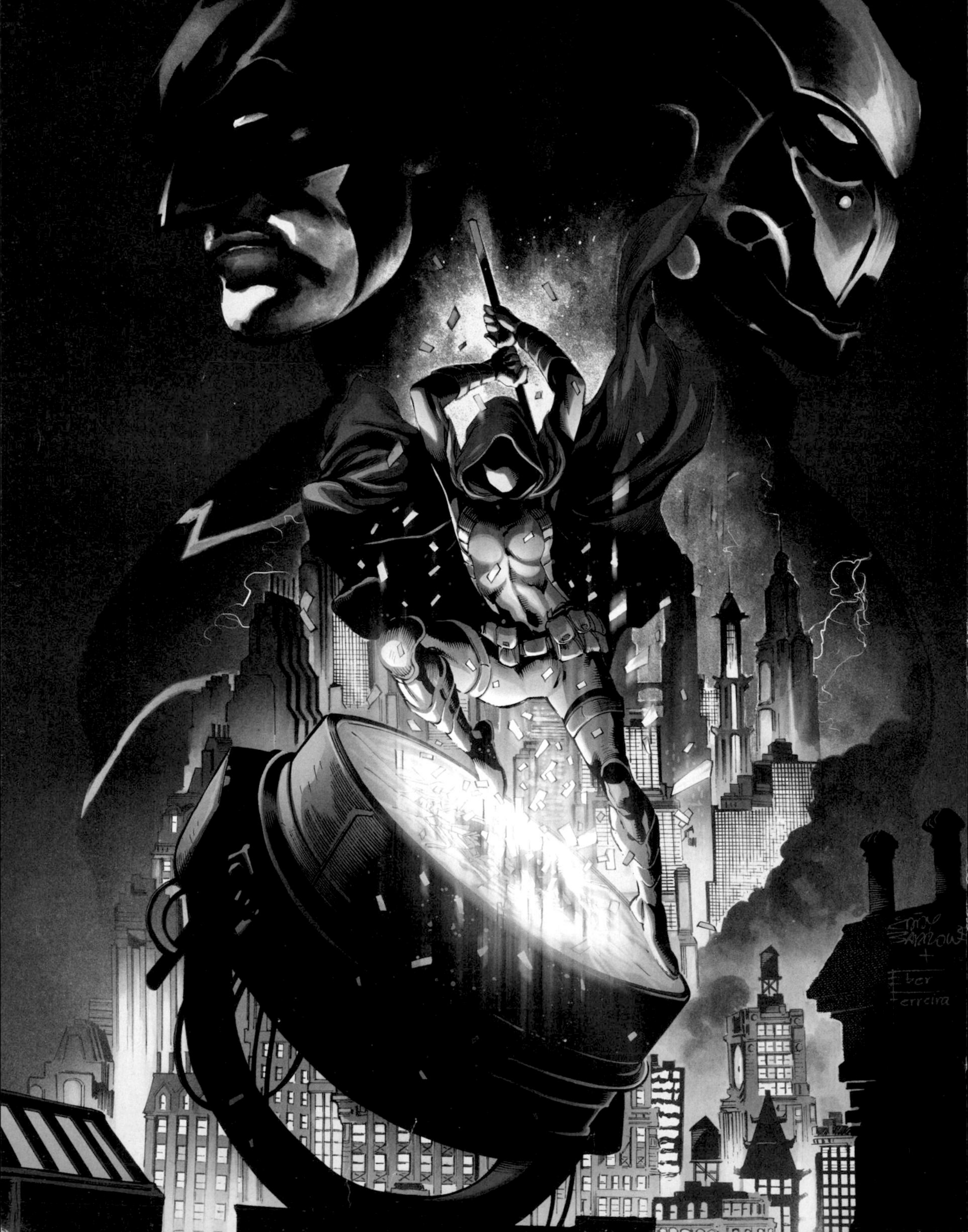

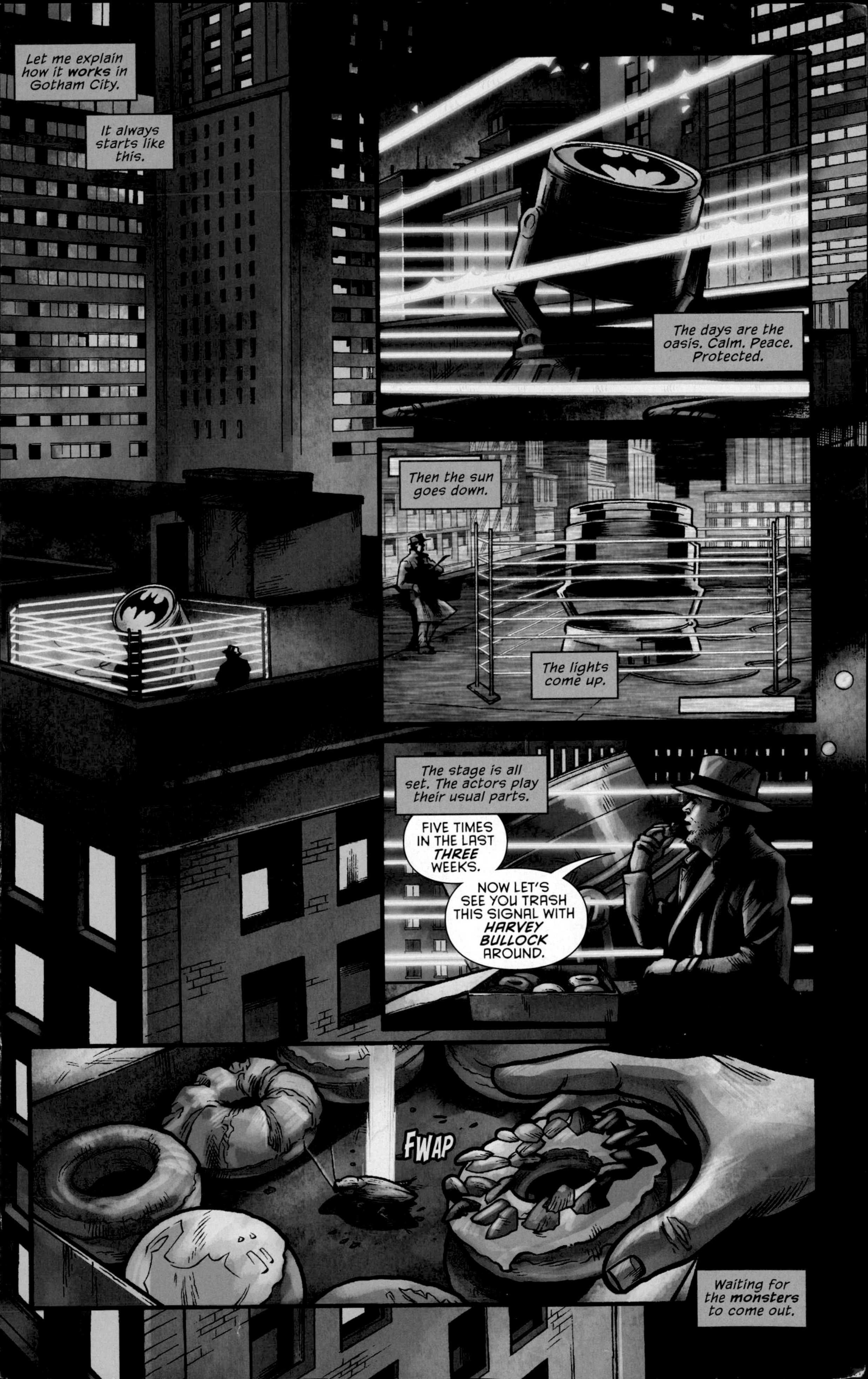

Let me explain how it works in Gotham City.
It always starts like this.
The days are the oasis. Calm. Peace. Protected.
Then the sun goes down.
The lights come up.
The stage is all set. The actors play their usual parts.
FIVE TIMES IN THE LAST THREE WEEKS.
NOW LET'S SEE YOU TRASH THIS SIGNAL WITH HARVEY BULLOCK AROUND.
FWAP
Waiting for the monsters to come out.

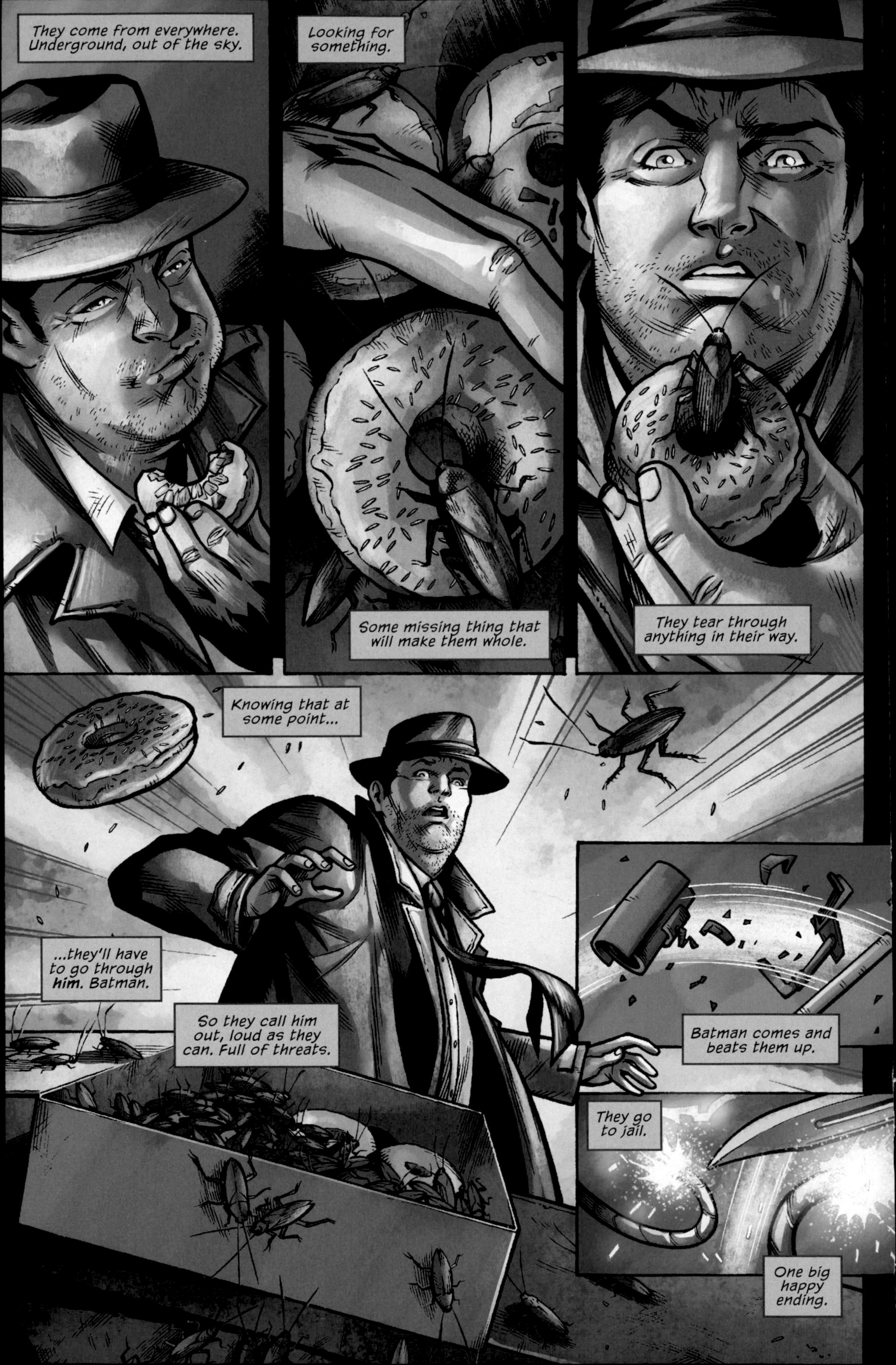
They come from everywhere. Underground, out of the sky.
Looking for something.
Some missing thing that will make them whole.
They tear through anything in their way.
Knowing that at some point...
...they'll have to go through **him**. Batman.
So they call him out, loud as they can. Full of threats.
Batman comes and beats them up.
They go to jail.
One big happy ending.

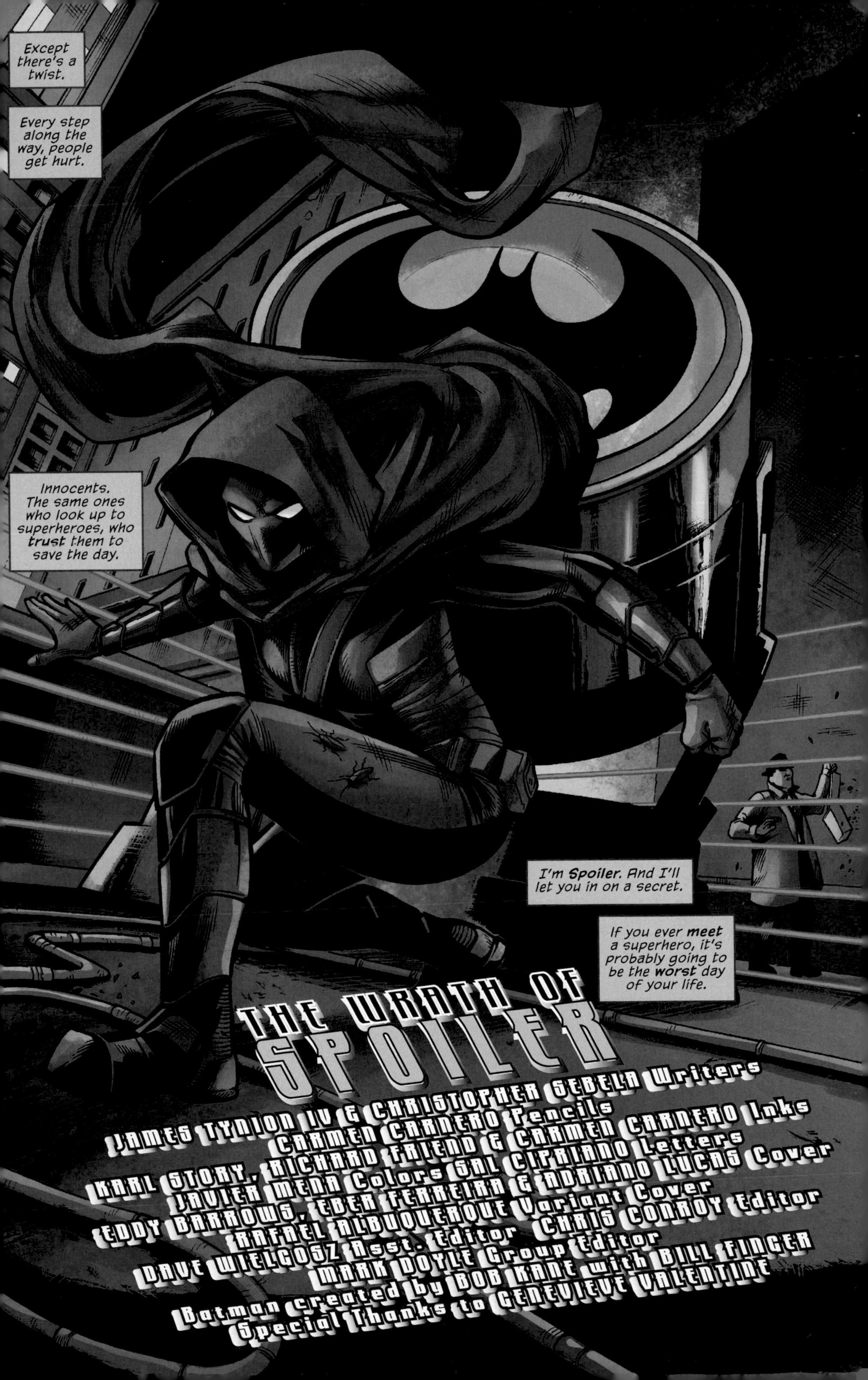
Except there's a twist.
Every step along the way, people get hurt.
Innocents. The same ones who look up to superheroes, who **trust** them to save the day.
I'm **Spoiler**. And I'll let you in on a secret.
If you ever **meet** a superhero, it's probably going to be the **worst** day of your life.
THE WRATH OF SPOILER
JAMES TYNION IV & CHRISTOPHER SEBELA Writers
CARMEN CARNERO Pencils
KARL STORY, RICHARD FRIEND & CARMEN CARNERO Inks
JAVIER MENA Colors SAL CIPRIANO Letters
EDDY BARROWS, EBER FERREIRA & ADRIANO LUCAS Cover
RAFAEL ALBUQUERQUE Variant Cover
DAVE WIELGOSZ Asst. Editor CHRIS CONROY Editor
MARK DOYLE Group Editor
Batman created by BOB KANE with BILL FINGER
Special Thanks to GENEVIEVE VALENTINE

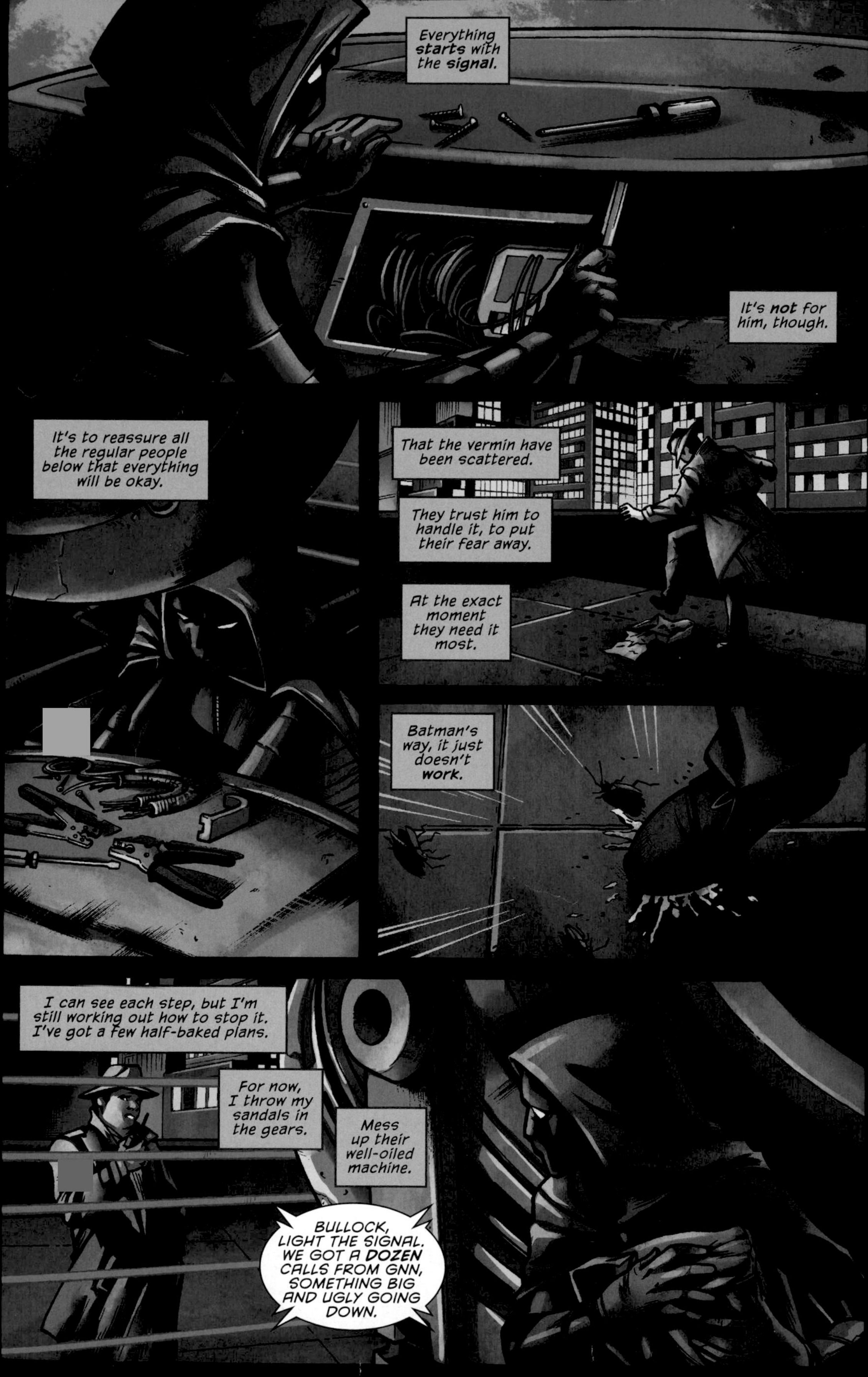
Everything starts with the signal.
It's not for him, though.
It's to reassure all the regular people below that everything will be okay.
That the vermin have been scattered.
They trust him to handle it, to put their fear away.
At the exact moment they need it most.
Batman's way, it just doesn't work.
I can see each step, but I'm still working out how to stop it. I've got a few half-baked plans.
For now, I throw my sandals in the gears.
Mess up their well-oiled machine.
BULLOCK, LIGHT THE SIGNAL. WE GOT A DOZEN CALLS FROM GNN, SOMETHING BIG AND UGLY GOING DOWN.

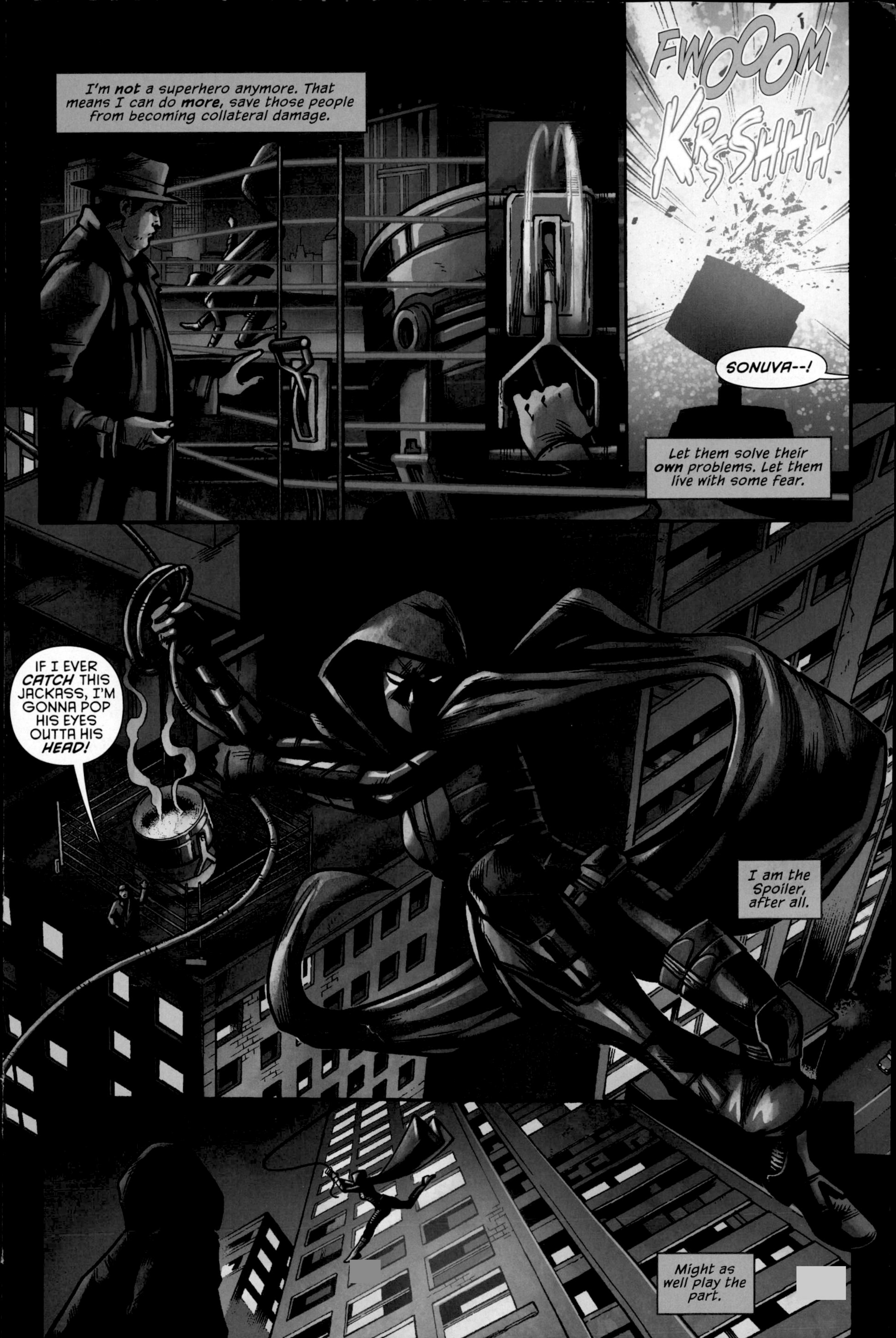

I'm not a superhero anymore. That means I can do more, save those people from becoming collateral damage.
FWOOOOM
KRSHHH
SONUVA--!
Let them solve their own problems. Let them live with some fear.
IF I EVER CATCH THIS JACKASS, I'M GONNA POP HIS EYES OUTTA HIS HEAD!
I am the Spoiler, after all.
Might as well play the part.

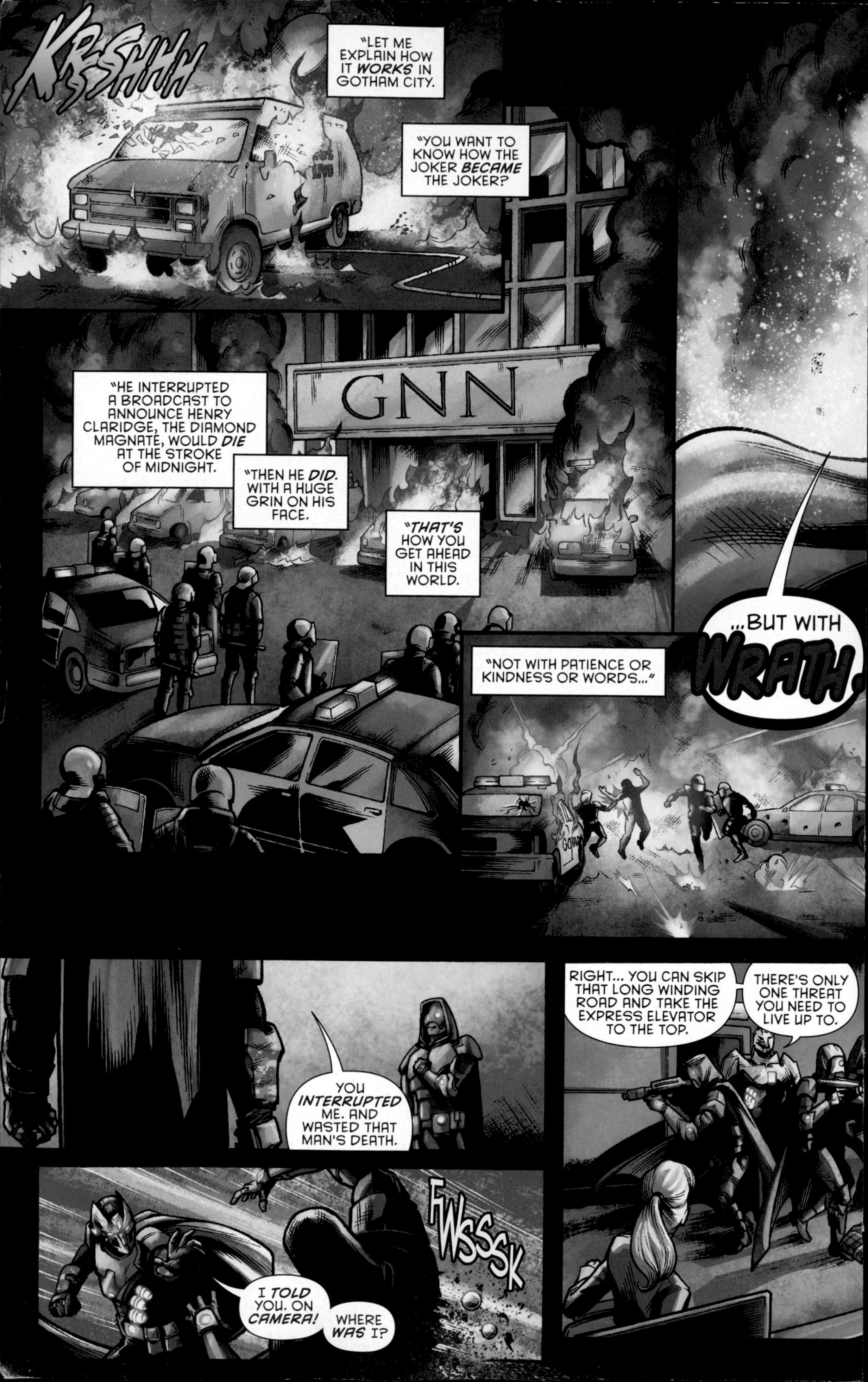
KRSHHH
"LET ME EXPLAIN HOW IT WORKS IN GOTHAM CITY.
"YOU WANT TO KNOW HOW THE JOKER BECAME THE JOKER?
GNN
"HE INTERRUPTED A BROADCAST TO ANNOUNCE HENRY CLARIDGE, THE DIAMOND MAGNATE, WOULD DIE AT THE STROKE OF MIDNIGHT.
"THEN HE DID. WITH A HUGE GRIN ON HIS FACE.
"THAT'S HOW YOU GET AHEAD IN THIS WORLD.
"NOT WITH PATIENCE OR KINDNESS OR WORDS..."
...BUT WITH WRATH.
YOU INTERRUPTED ME. AND WASTED THAT MAN'S DEATH.
RIGHT... YOU CAN SKIP THAT LONG WINDING ROAD AND TAKE THE EXPRESS ELEVATOR TO THE TOP.
THERE'S ONLY ONE THREAT YOU NEED TO LIVE UP TO.
FWSSSK
I TOLD YOU. ON CAMERA!
WHERE WAS I?

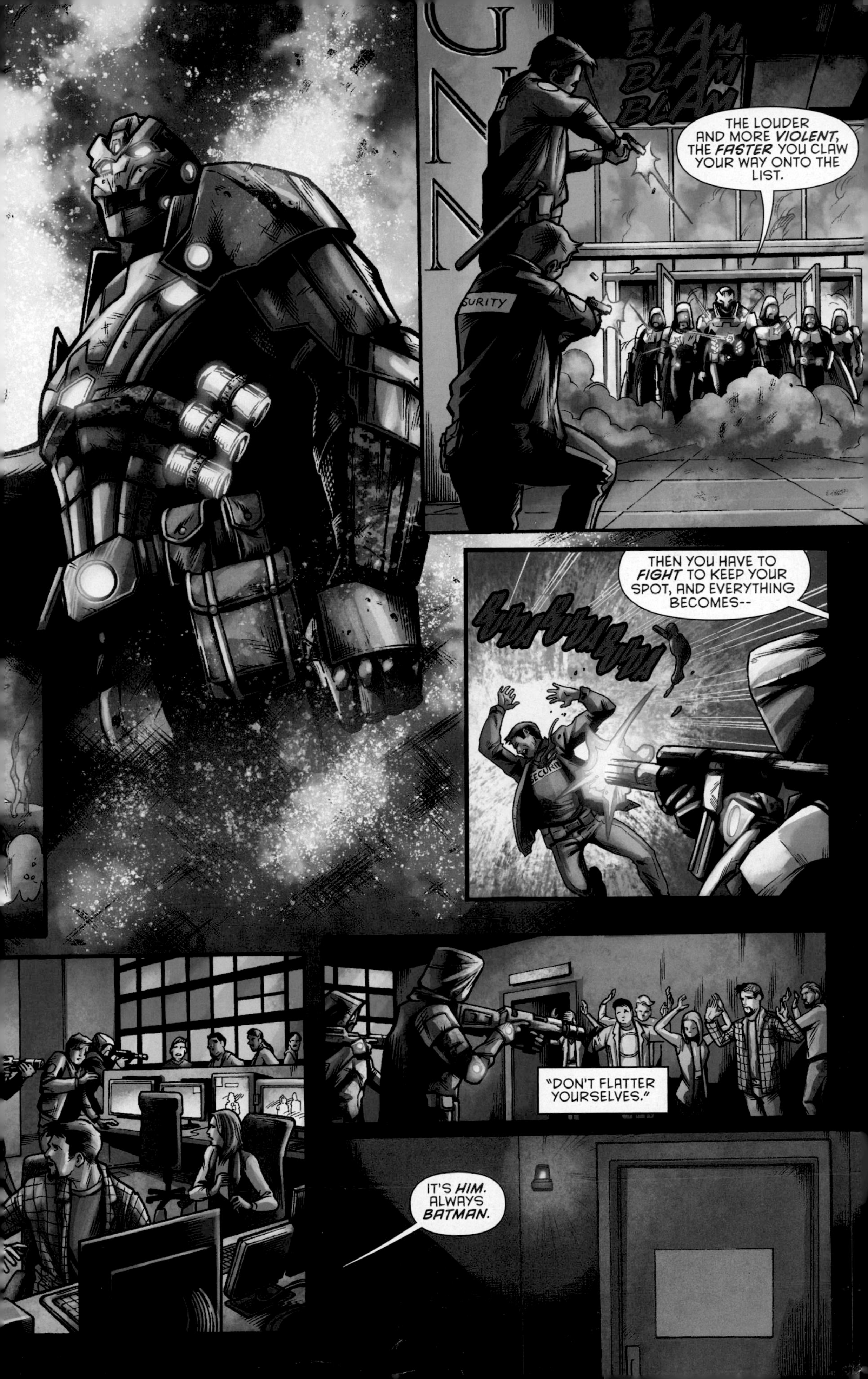
BLAM
BLAM
BLAM
THE LOUDER AND MORE VIOLENT, THE FASTER YOU CLAW YOUR WAY ONTO THE LIST.
SECURITY
THEN YOU HAVE TO FIGHT TO KEEP YOUR SPOT, AND EVERYTHING BECOMES--
SECURITY
"DON'T FLATTER YOURSELVES."
IT'S HIM. ALWAYS BATMAN.

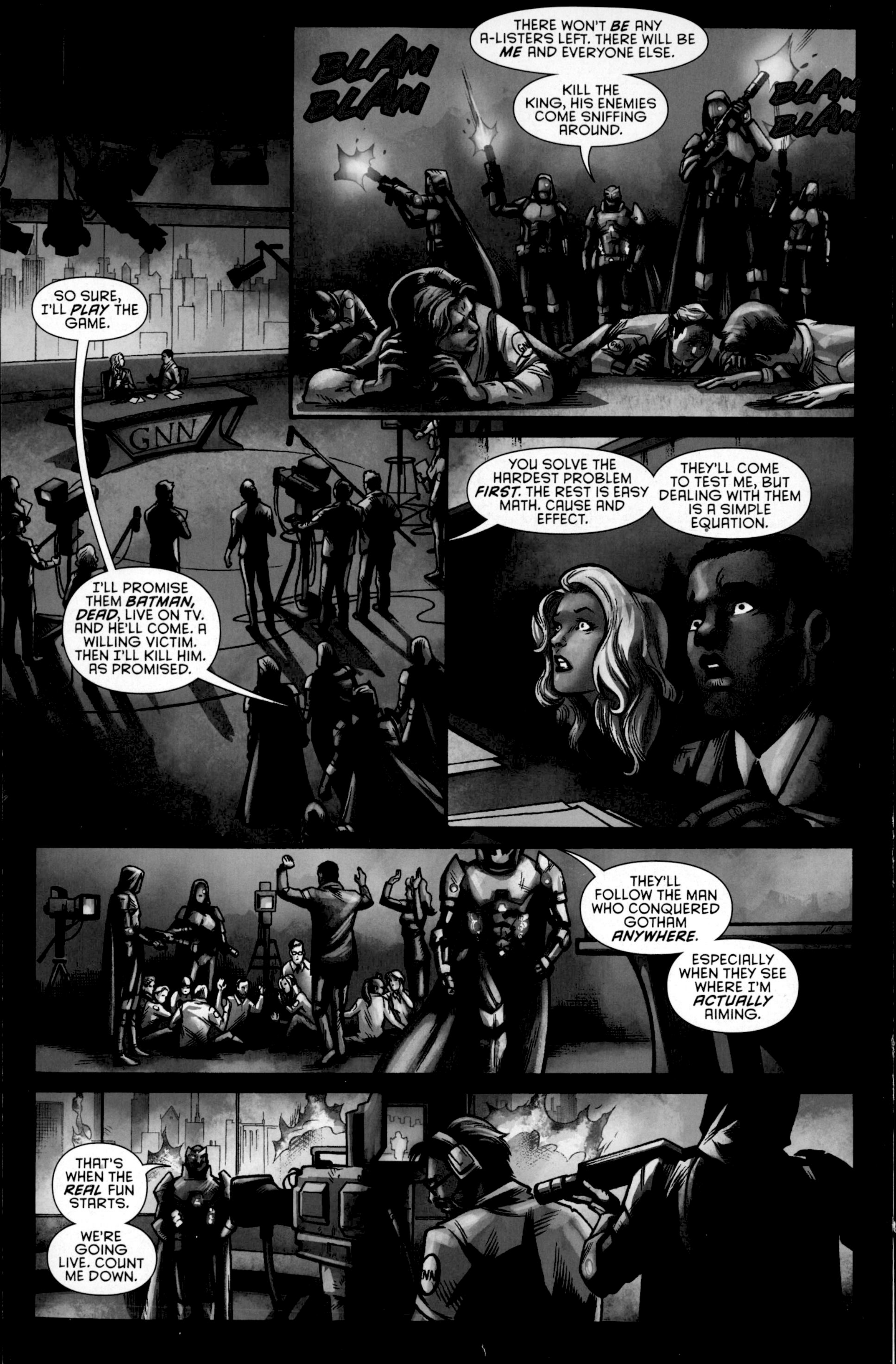
BLAM BLAM
THERE WON'T BE ANY A-LISTERS LEFT. THERE WILL BE ME AND EVERYONE ELSE.
KILL THE KING, HIS ENEMIES COME SNIFFING AROUND.
BLAM BLAM
SO SURE, I'LL PLAY THE GAME.
GNN
I'LL PROMISE THEM BATMAN, DEAD, LIVE ON TV. AND HE'LL COME. A WILLING VICTIM. THEN I'LL KILL HIM. AS PROMISED.
YOU SOLVE THE HARDEST PROBLEM FIRST. THE REST IS EASY MATH. CAUSE AND EFFECT.
THEY'LL COME TO TEST ME, BUT DEALING WITH THEM IS A SIMPLE EQUATION.
THEY'LL FOLLOW THE MAN WHO CONQUERED GOTHAM ANYWHERE.
ESPECIALLY WHEN THEY SEE WHERE I'M ACTUALLY AIMING.
THAT'S WHEN THE REAL FUN STARTS.
WE'RE GOING LIVE. COUNT ME DOWN.

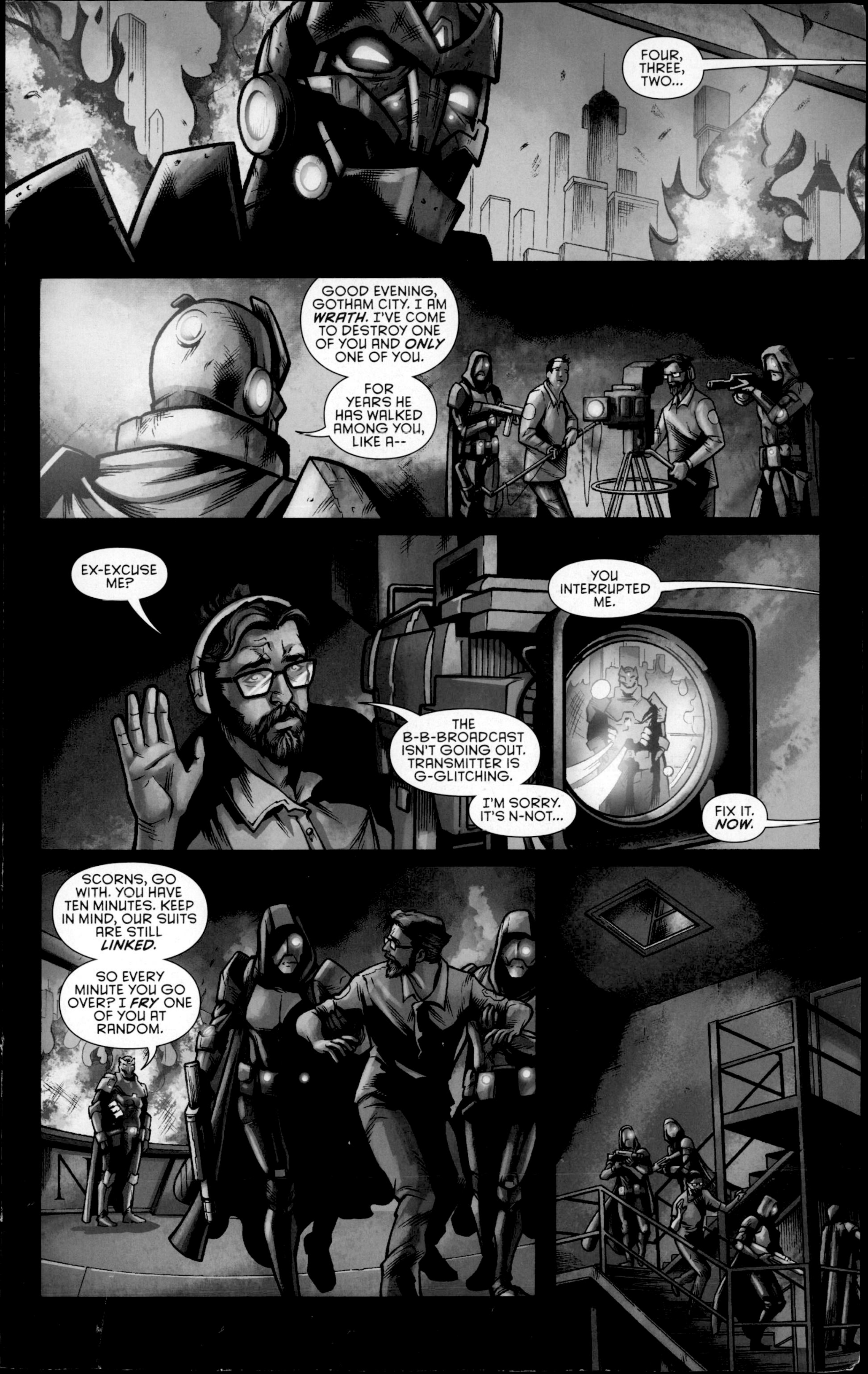
FOUR, THREE, TWO...
GOOD EVENING, GOTHAM CITY. I AM WRATH. I'VE COME TO DESTROY ONE OF YOU AND ONLY ONE OF YOU.
FOR YEARS HE HAS WALKED AMONG YOU, LIKE A--
EX-EXCUSE ME?
YOU INTERRUPTED ME.
THE B-B-BROADCAST ISN'T GOING OUT. TRANSMITTER IS G-GLITCHING.
I'M SORRY. IT'S N-NOT...
FIX IT. NOW.
SCORNS, GO WITH. YOU HAVE TEN MINUTES. KEEP IN MIND, OUR SUITS ARE STILL LINKED.
SO EVERY MINUTE YOU GO OVER? I FRY ONE OF YOU AT RANDOM.

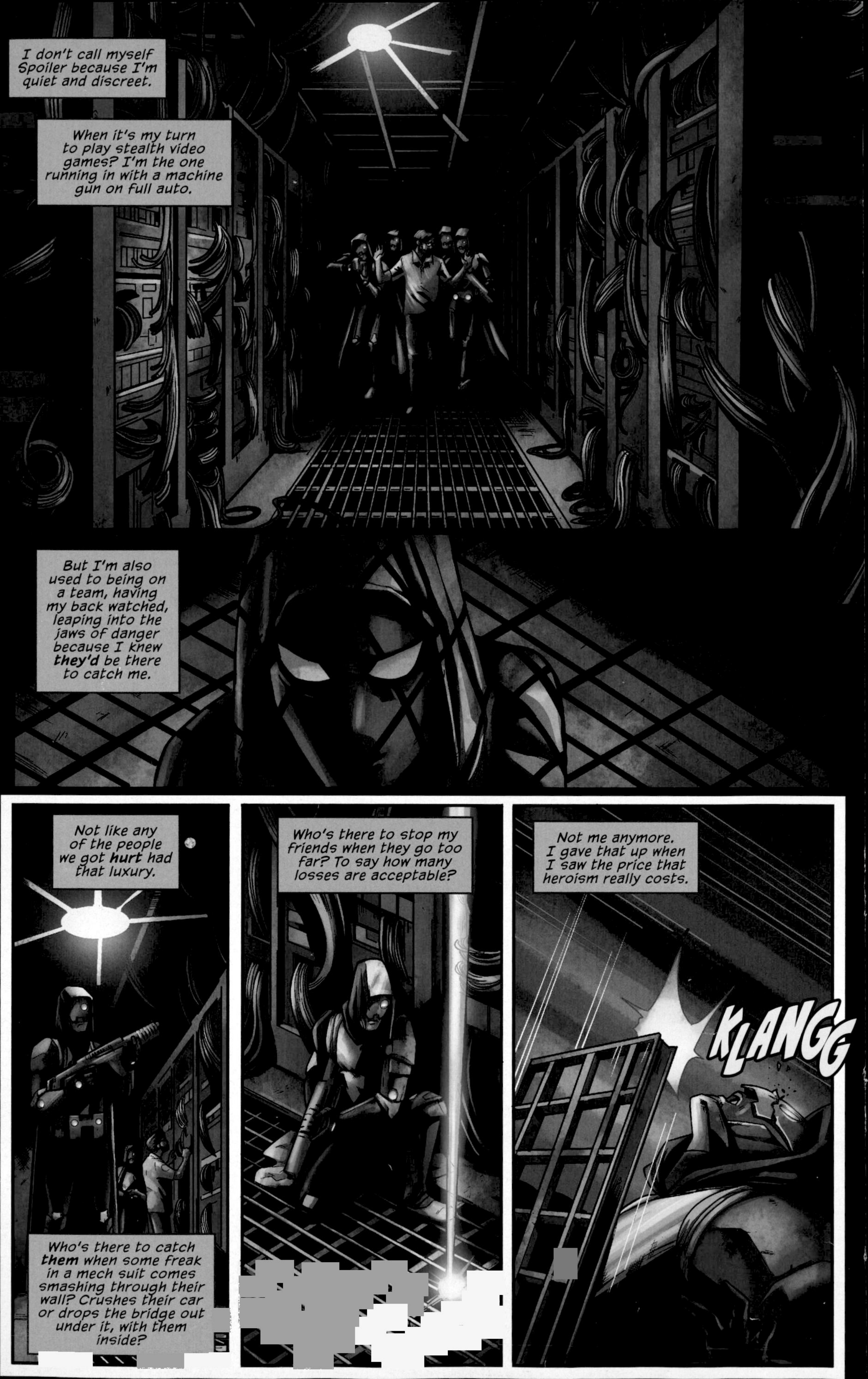
I don't call myself Spoiler because I'm quiet and discreet.
When it's my turn to play stealth video games? I'm the one running in with a machine gun on full auto.
But I'm also used to being on a team, having my back watched, leaping into the jaws of danger because I knew **they'd** be there to catch me.
Not like any of the people we got **hurt** had that luxury.
Who's there to catch **them** when some freak in a mech suit comes smashing through their wall? Crushes their car or drops the bridge out under it, with them inside?
Who's there to stop my friends when they go too far? To say how many losses are acceptable?
Not me anymore. I gave that up when I saw the price that heroism really costs.
KLANGG

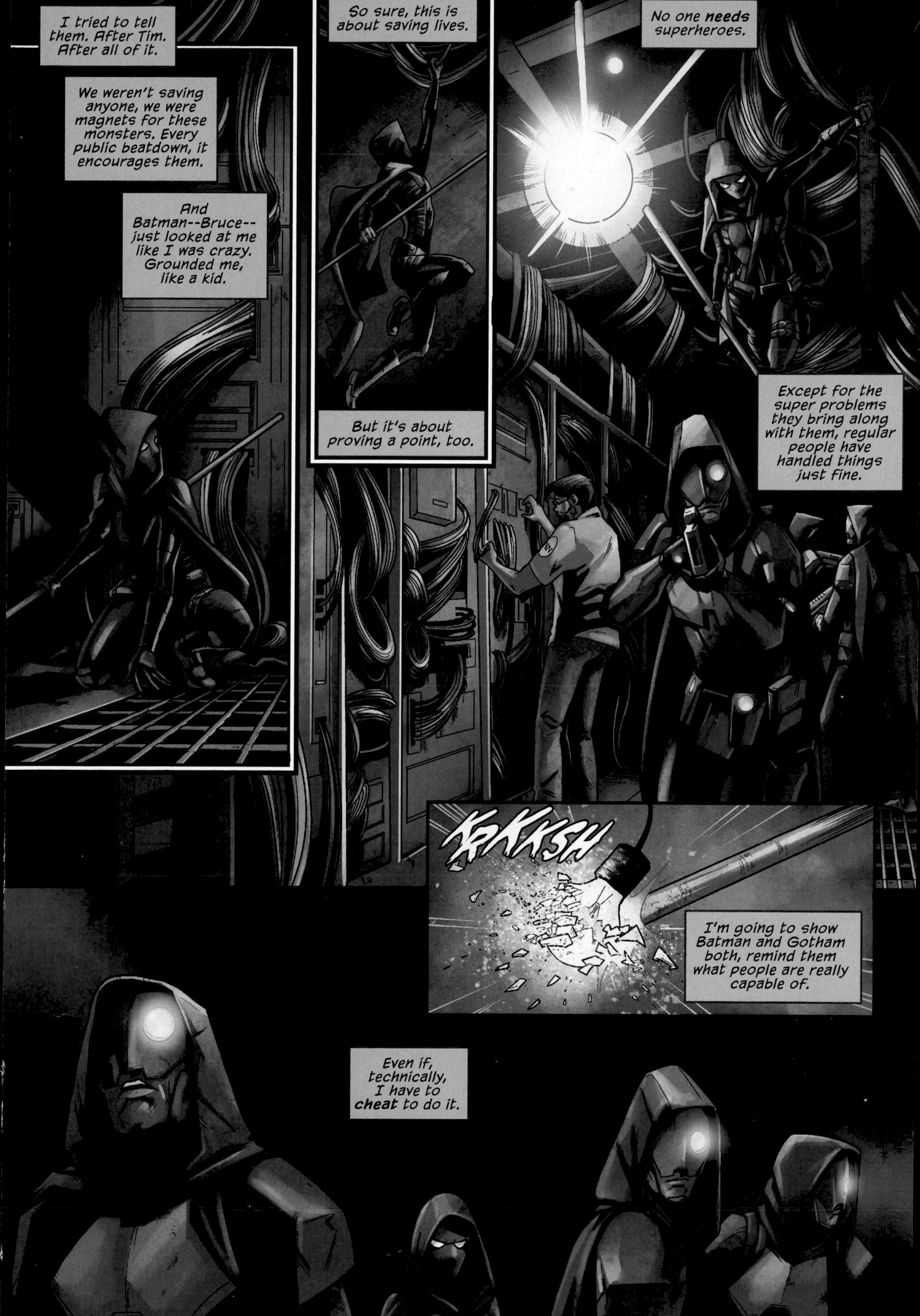
I tried to tell them. After Tim. After all of it.
We weren't saving anyone, we were magnets for these monsters. Every public beatdown, it encourages them.
And Batman--Bruce--just looked at me like I was crazy. Grounded me, like a kid.
So sure, this is about saving lives.
But it's about proving a point, too.
No one **needs** superheroes.
Except for the super problems they bring along with them, regular people have handled things just fine.
KRKKSH
I'm going to show Batman and Gotham both, remind them what people are really capable of.
Even if, technically, I have to **cheat** to do it.

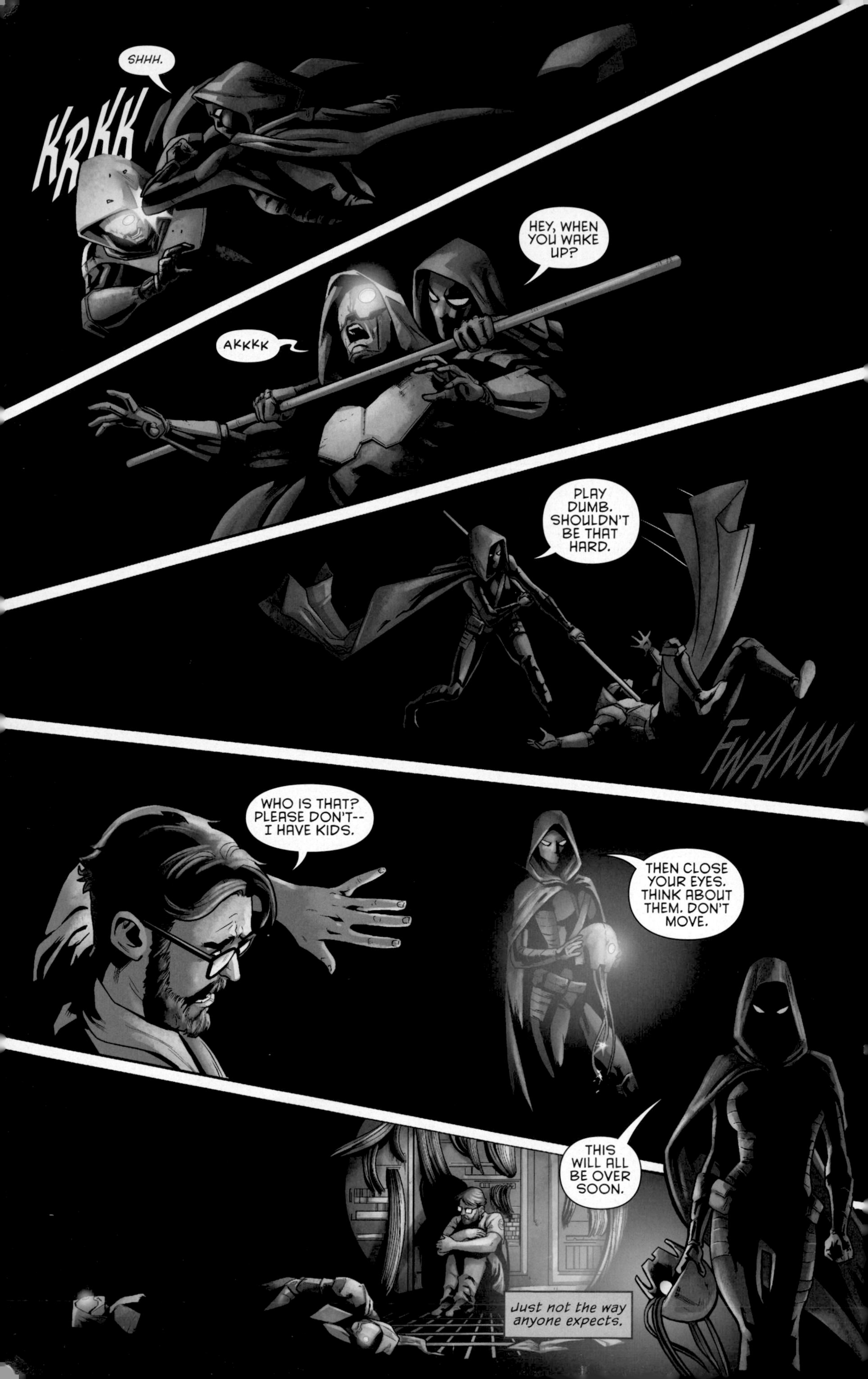
SHHH.
KRKK
HEY, WHEN YOU WAKE UP?
AKKKK
PLAY DUMB. SHOULDN'T BE THAT HARD.
FWAMM
WHO IS THAT? PLEASE DON'T-- I HAVE KIDS.
THEN CLOSE YOUR EYES. THINK ABOUT THEM. DON'T MOVE.
THIS WILL ALL BE OVER SOON.
Just not the way anyone expects.

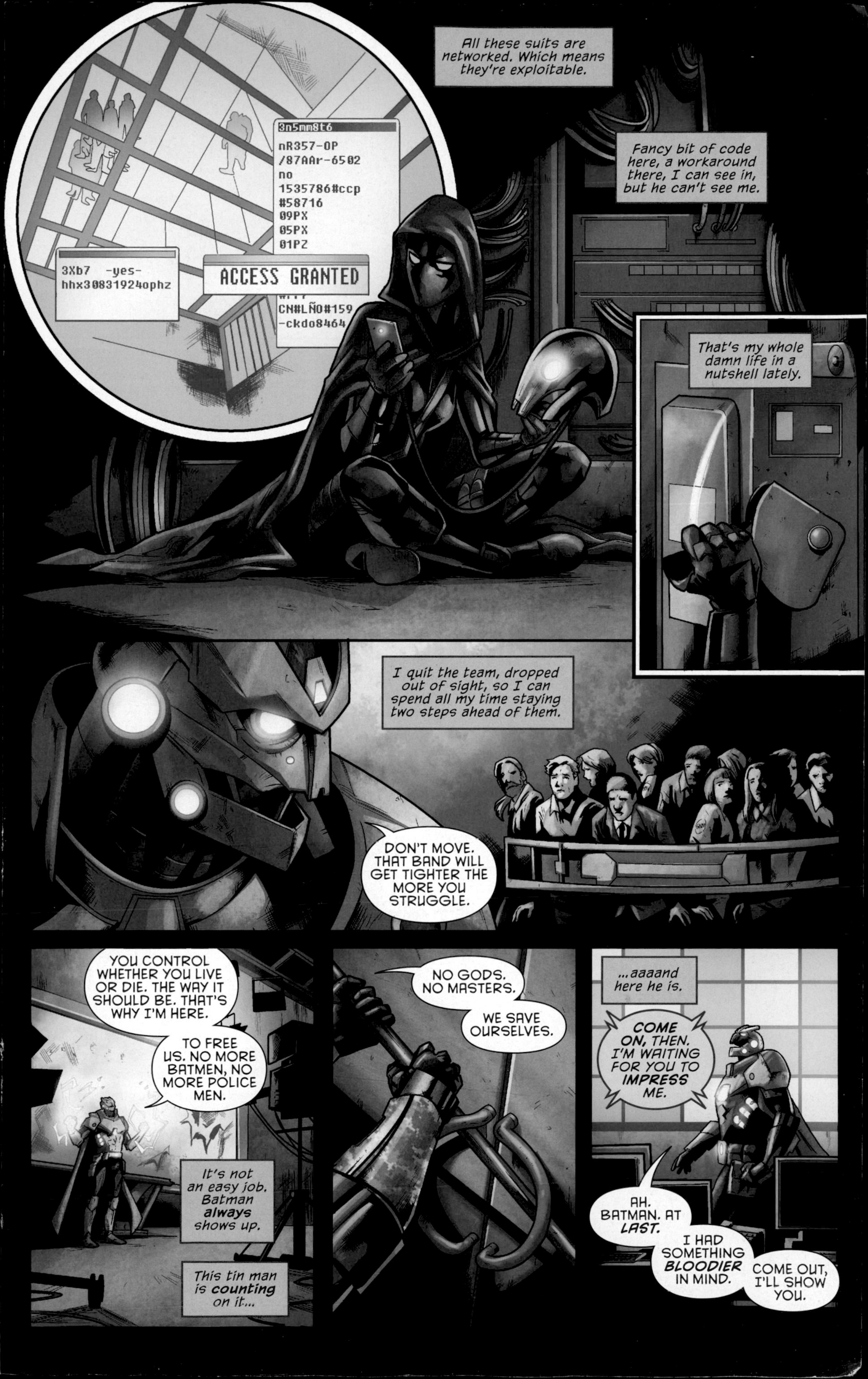

All these suits are networked. Which means they're exploitable.
3n5mm8t6
nR357-OP
/87AAr-6502
no
1535786#ccp
#58716
09PX
05PX
01PZ
3Xb7 -yes-
hhx30831924ophz
ACCESS GRANTED
CN#LÑO#159
-ckdo8464
Fancy bit of code here, a workaround there, I can see in, but he can't see me.
That's my whole damn life in a nutshell lately.
I quit the team, dropped out of sight, so I can spend all my time staying two steps ahead of them.
DON'T MOVE. THAT BAND WILL GET TIGHTER THE MORE YOU STRUGGLE.
YOU CONTROL WHETHER YOU LIVE OR DIE. THE WAY IT SHOULD BE. THAT'S WHY I'M HERE.
TO FREE US. NO MORE BATMEN, NO MORE POLICE MEN.
It's not an easy job. Batman **always** shows up.
This tin man is **counting** on it...
NO GODS. NO MASTERS.
WE SAVE OURSELVES.
...aaaand here he is.
COME ON, THEN. I'M WAITING FOR YOU TO **IMPRESS** ME.
AH. BATMAN. AT **LAST.**
I HAD SOMETHING **BLOODIER** IN MIND.
COME OUT, I'LL SHOW YOU.

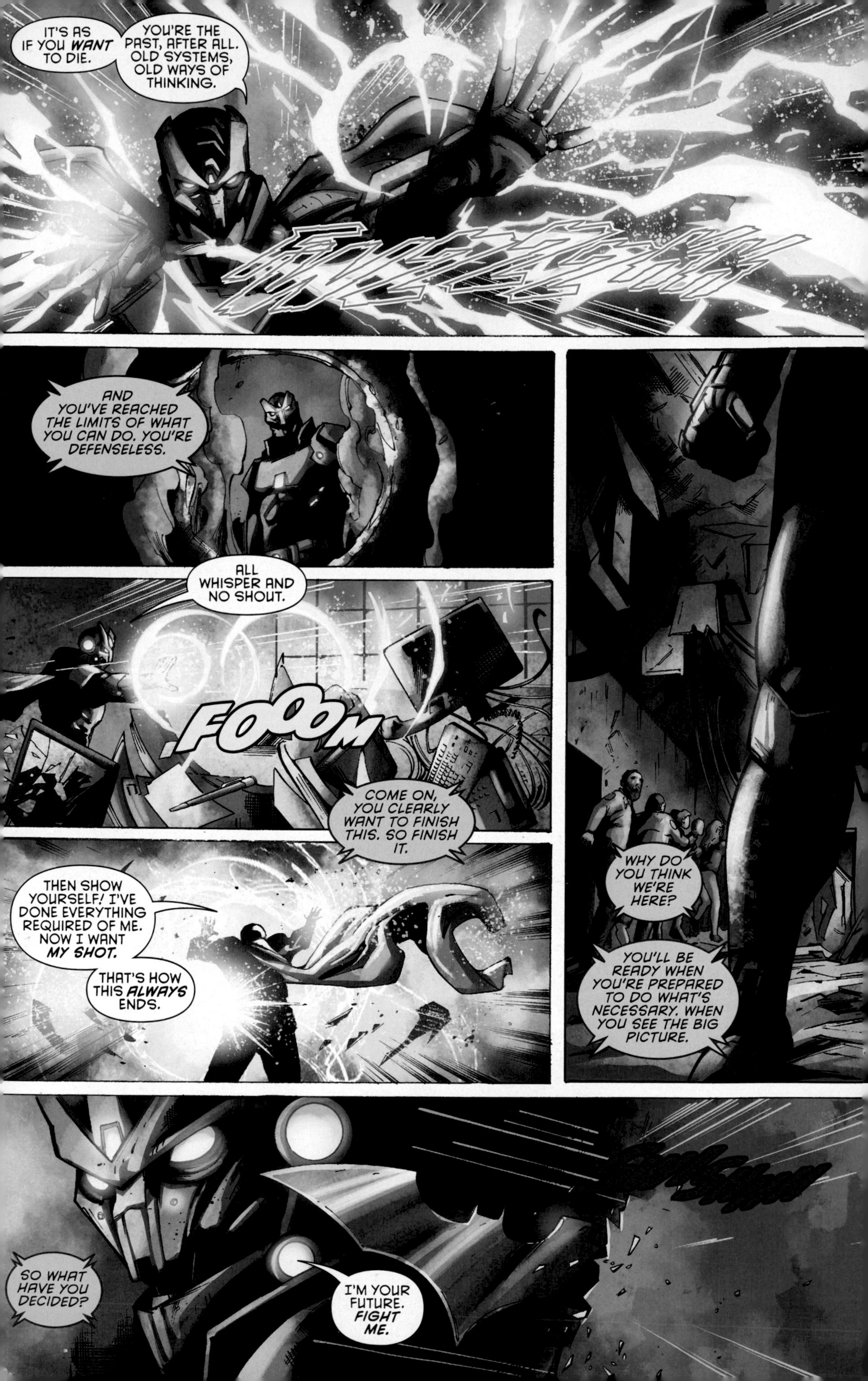
IT'S AS IF YOU *WANT* TO DIE.
YOU'RE THE PAST, AFTER ALL. OLD SYSTEMS, OLD WAYS OF THINKING.
AND YOU'VE REACHED THE LIMITS OF WHAT YOU CAN DO. YOU'RE DEFENSELESS.
ALL WHISPER AND NO SHOUT.
FOOOM
COME ON, YOU CLEARLY WANT TO FINISH THIS. SO FINISH IT.
THEN SHOW YOURSELF! I'VE DONE EVERYTHING REQUIRED OF ME. NOW I WANT *MY SHOT.*
THAT'S HOW THIS *ALWAYS* ENDS.
WHY DO YOU THINK WE'RE HERE?
YOU'LL BE READY WHEN YOU'RE PREPARED TO DO WHAT'S NECESSARY. WHEN YOU SEE THE BIG PICTURE.
SO WHAT HAVE YOU DECIDED?
I'M YOUR FUTURE. *FIGHT ME.*

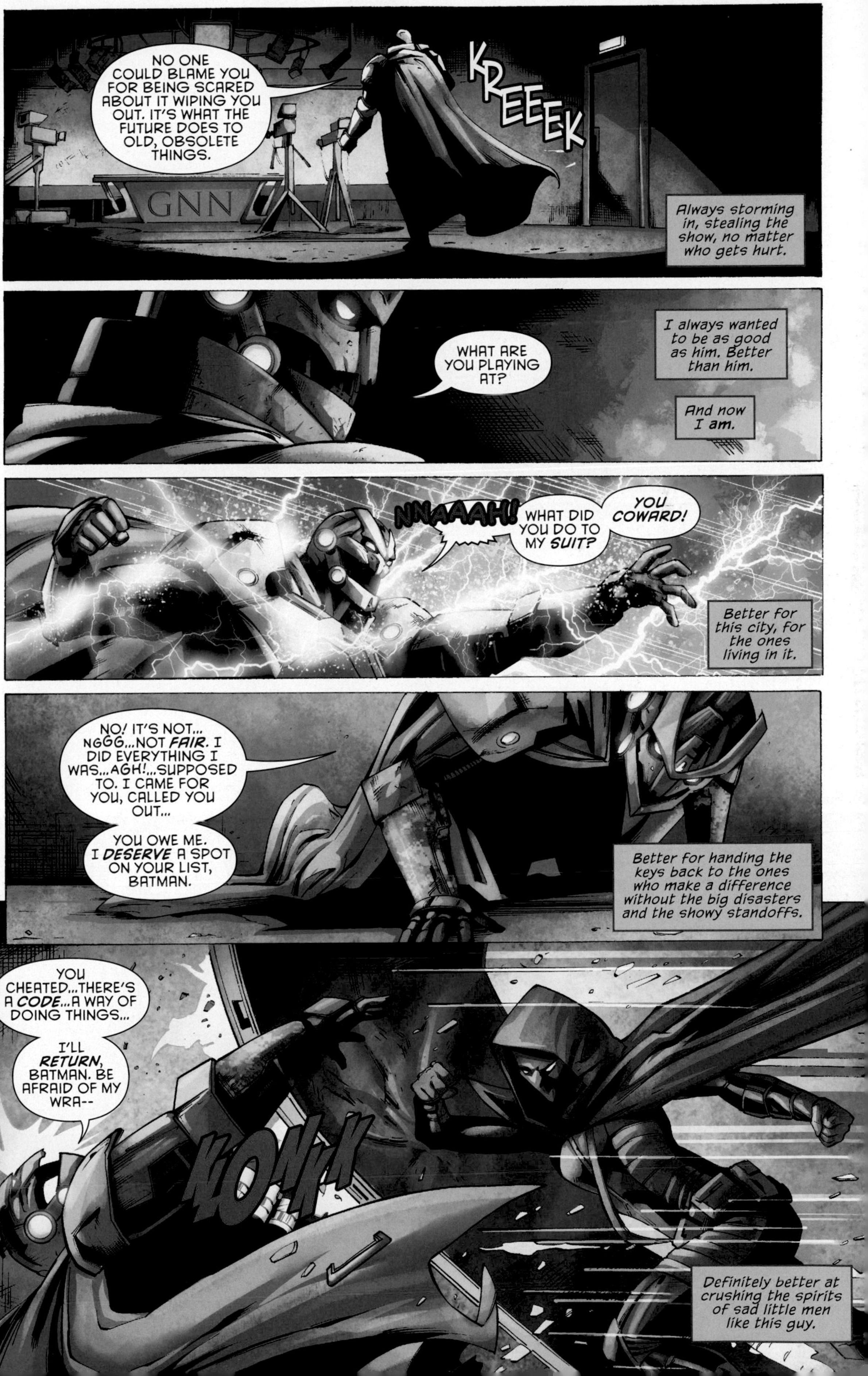
NO ONE COULD BLAME YOU FOR BEING SCARED ABOUT IT WIPING YOU OUT. IT'S WHAT THE FUTURE DOES TO OLD, OBSOLETE THINGS.
KREEEK
GNN
Always storming in, stealing the show, no matter who gets hurt.
WHAT ARE YOU PLAYING AT?
I always wanted to be as good as him. Better than him.
And now I am.
NNAAAH!
WHAT DID YOU DO TO MY SUIT?
YOU COWARD!
Better for this city, for the ones living in it.
NO! IT'S NOT... NGGG...NOT FAIR. I DID EVERYTHING I WAS...AGH!...SUPPOSED TO. I CAME FOR YOU, CALLED YOU OUT...
YOU OWE ME. I DESERVE A SPOT ON YOUR LIST, BATMAN.
Better for handing the keys back to the ones who make a difference without the big disasters and the showy standoffs.
YOU CHEATED...THERE'S A CODE...A WAY OF DOING THINGS...
I'LL RETURN, BATMAN. BE AFRAID OF MY WRA--
WONK
Definitely better at crushing the spirits of sad little men like this guy.

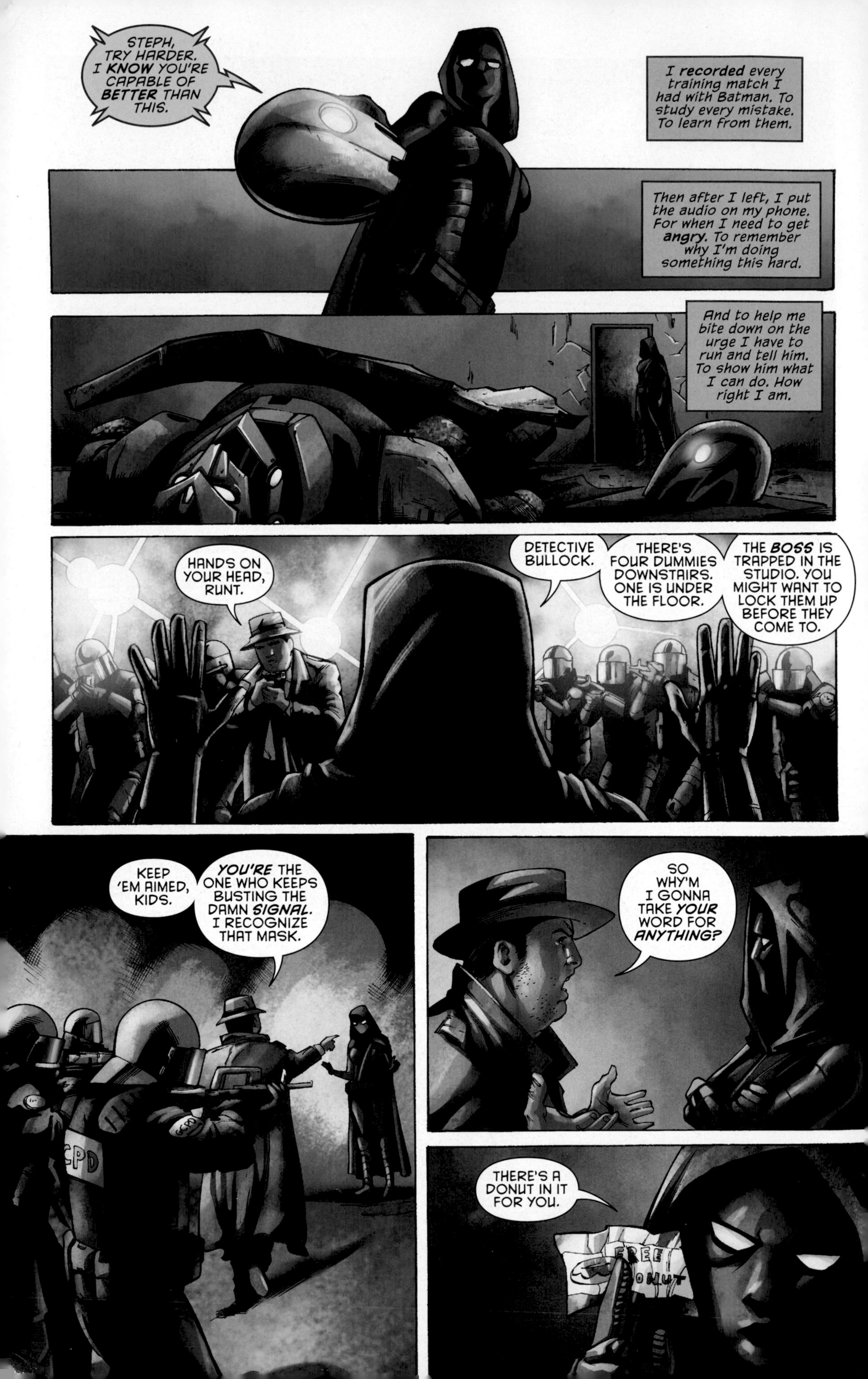
STEPH, TRY HARDER. I KNOW YOU'RE CAPABLE OF BETTER THAN THIS.
I recorded every training match I had with Batman. To study every mistake. To learn from them.
Then after I left, I put the audio on my phone. For when I need to get angry. To remember why I'm doing something this hard.
And to help me bite down on the urge I have to run and tell him. To show him what I can do. How right I am.
HANDS ON YOUR HEAD, RUNT.
DETECTIVE BULLOCK.
THERE'S FOUR DUMMIES DOWNSTAIRS. ONE IS UNDER THE FLOOR.
THE BOSS IS TRAPPED IN THE STUDIO. YOU MIGHT WANT TO LOCK THEM UP BEFORE THEY COME TO.
KEEP 'EM AIMED, KIDS.
YOU'RE THE ONE WHO KEEPS BUSTING THE DAMN SIGNAL. I RECOGNIZE THAT MASK.
SO WHY'M I GONNA TAKE YOUR WORD FOR ANYTHING?
THERE'S A DONUT IN IT FOR YOU.
FREE DONUT

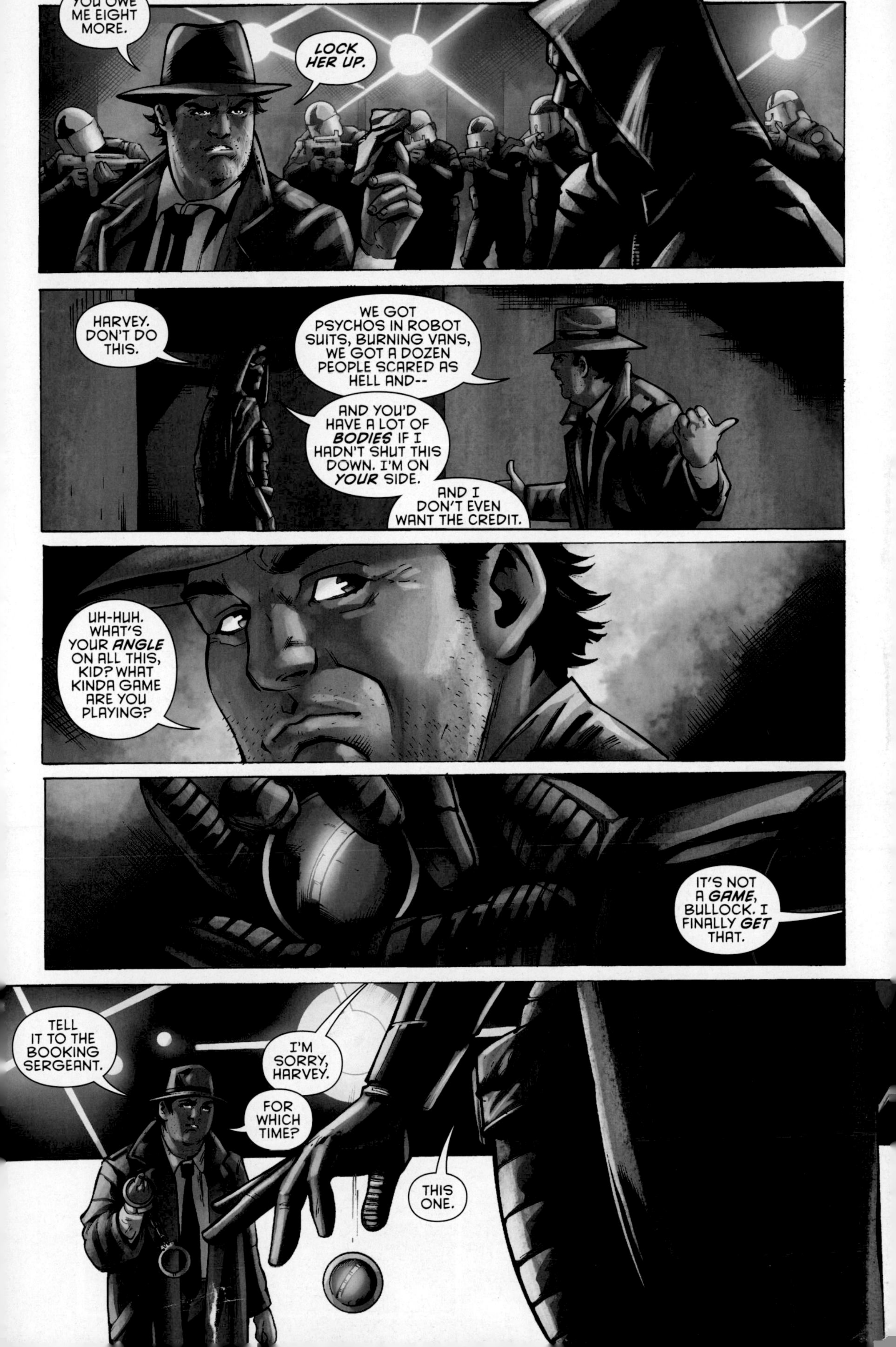
YOU OWE ME EIGHT MORE.
LOCK HER UP.
HARVEY. DON'T DO THIS.
WE GOT PSYCHOS IN ROBOT SUITS, BURNING VANS, WE GOT A DOZEN PEOPLE SCARED AS HELL AND--
AND YOU'D HAVE A LOT OF BODIES IF I HADN'T SHUT THIS DOWN. I'M ON YOUR SIDE.
AND I DON'T EVEN WANT THE CREDIT.
UH-HUH. WHAT'S YOUR ANGLE ON ALL THIS, KID? WHAT KINDA GAME ARE YOU PLAYING?
IT'S NOT A GAME, BULLOCK. I FINALLY GET THAT.
TELL IT TO THE BOOKING SERGEANT.
I'M SORRY, HARVEY.
FOR WHICH TIME?
THIS ONE.

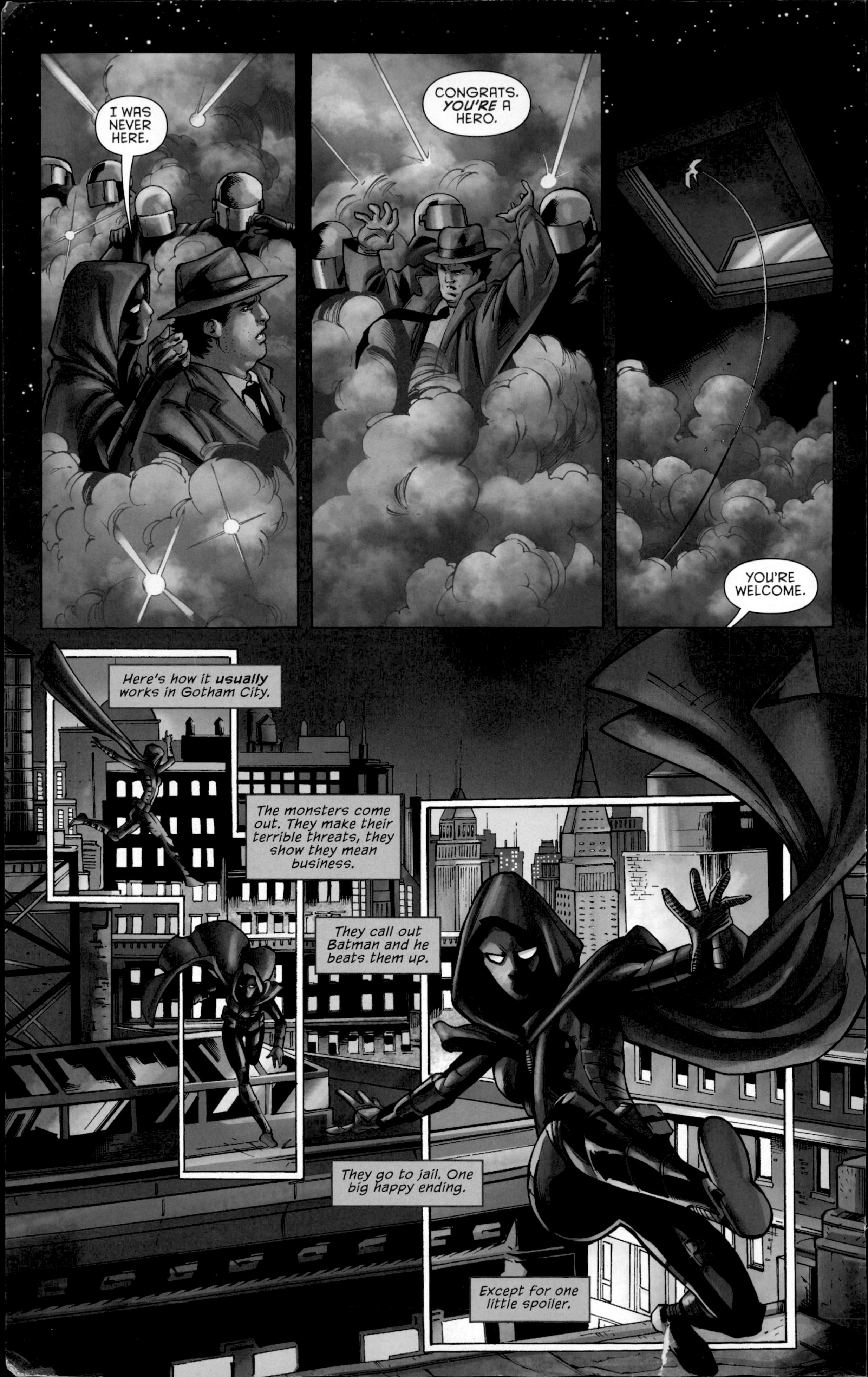
I WAS NEVER HERE.
CONGRATS. YOU'RE A HERO.
YOU'RE WELCOME.
Here's how it usually works in Gotham City.
The monsters come out. They make their terrible threats, they show they mean business.
They call out Batman and he beats them up.
They go to jail. One big happy ending.
Except for one little spoiler.

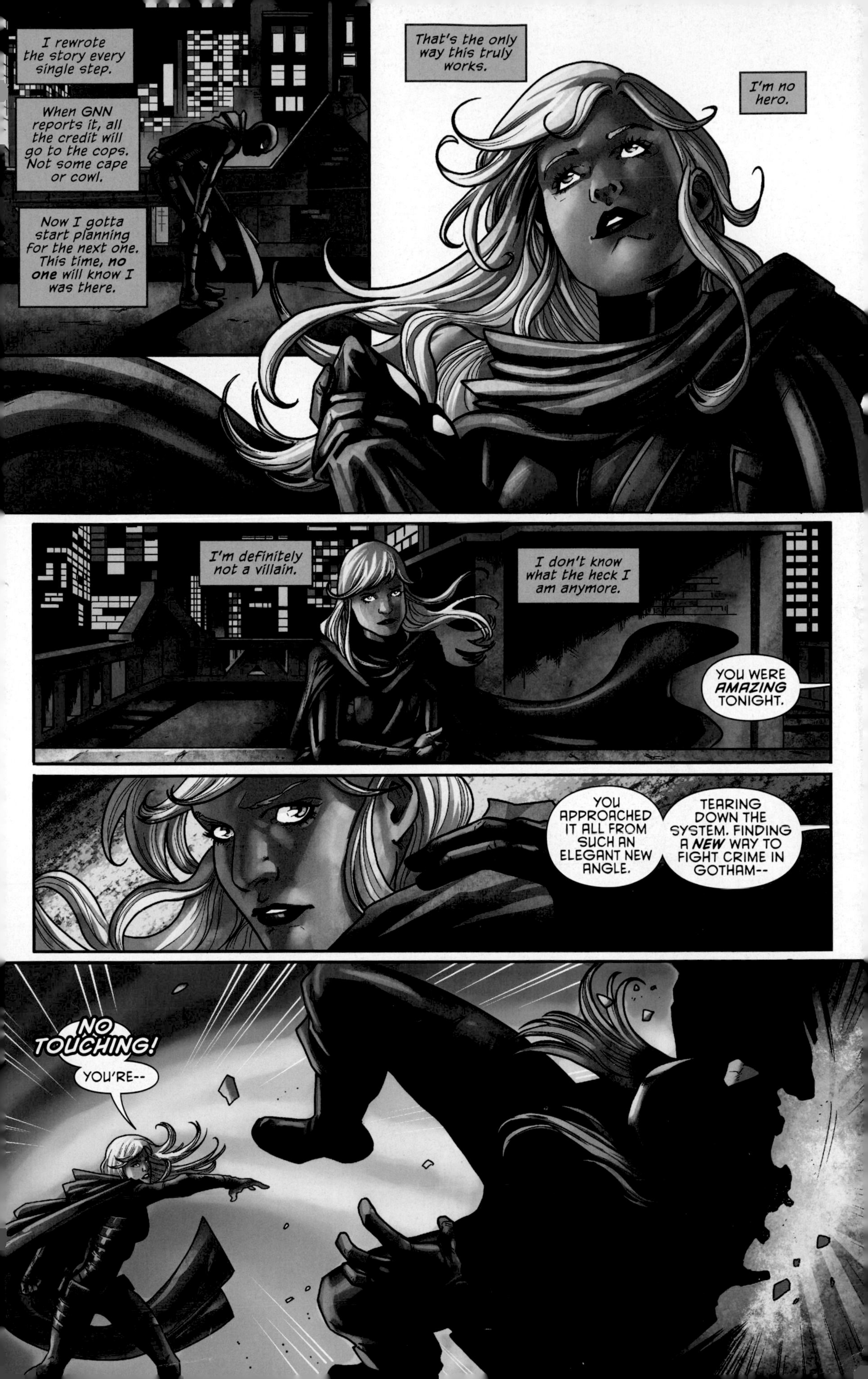

I rewrote the story every single step.
When GNN reports it, all the credit will go to the cops. Not some cape or cowl.
Now I gotta start planning for the next one. This time, **no one** will know I was there.
That's the only way this truly works.
I'm no hero.
I'm definitely not a villain.
I don't know what the heck I am anymore.
YOU WERE ***AMAZING*** TONIGHT.
YOU APPROACHED IT ALL FROM SUCH AN ELEGANT NEW ANGLE.
TEARING DOWN THE SYSTEM. FINDING A ***NEW*** WAY TO FIGHT CRIME IN GOTHAM--
NO TOUCHING!
YOU'RE--

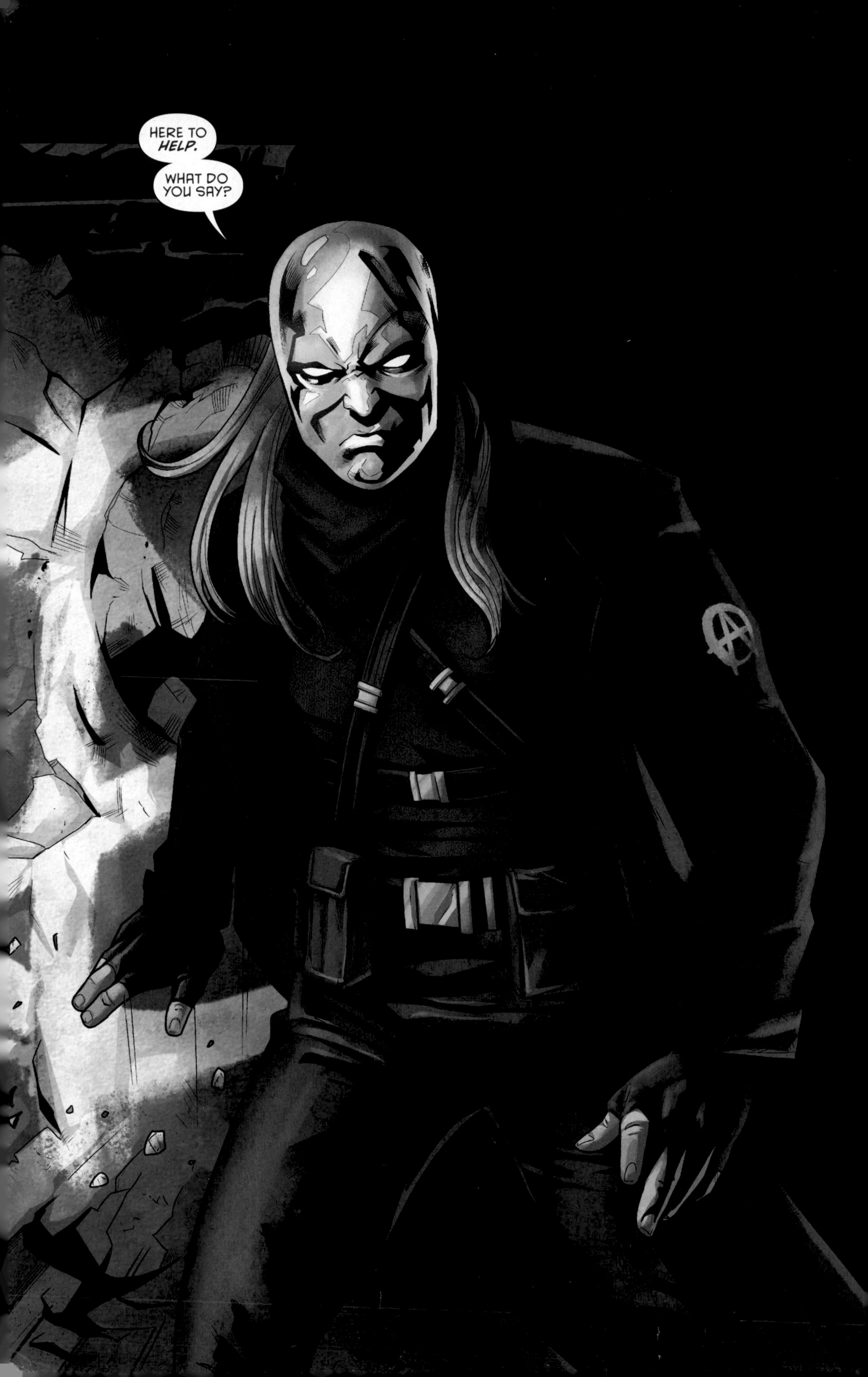
HERE TO *HELP.*
WHAT DO YOU SAY?

BATMAN

DETECTIVE COMICS

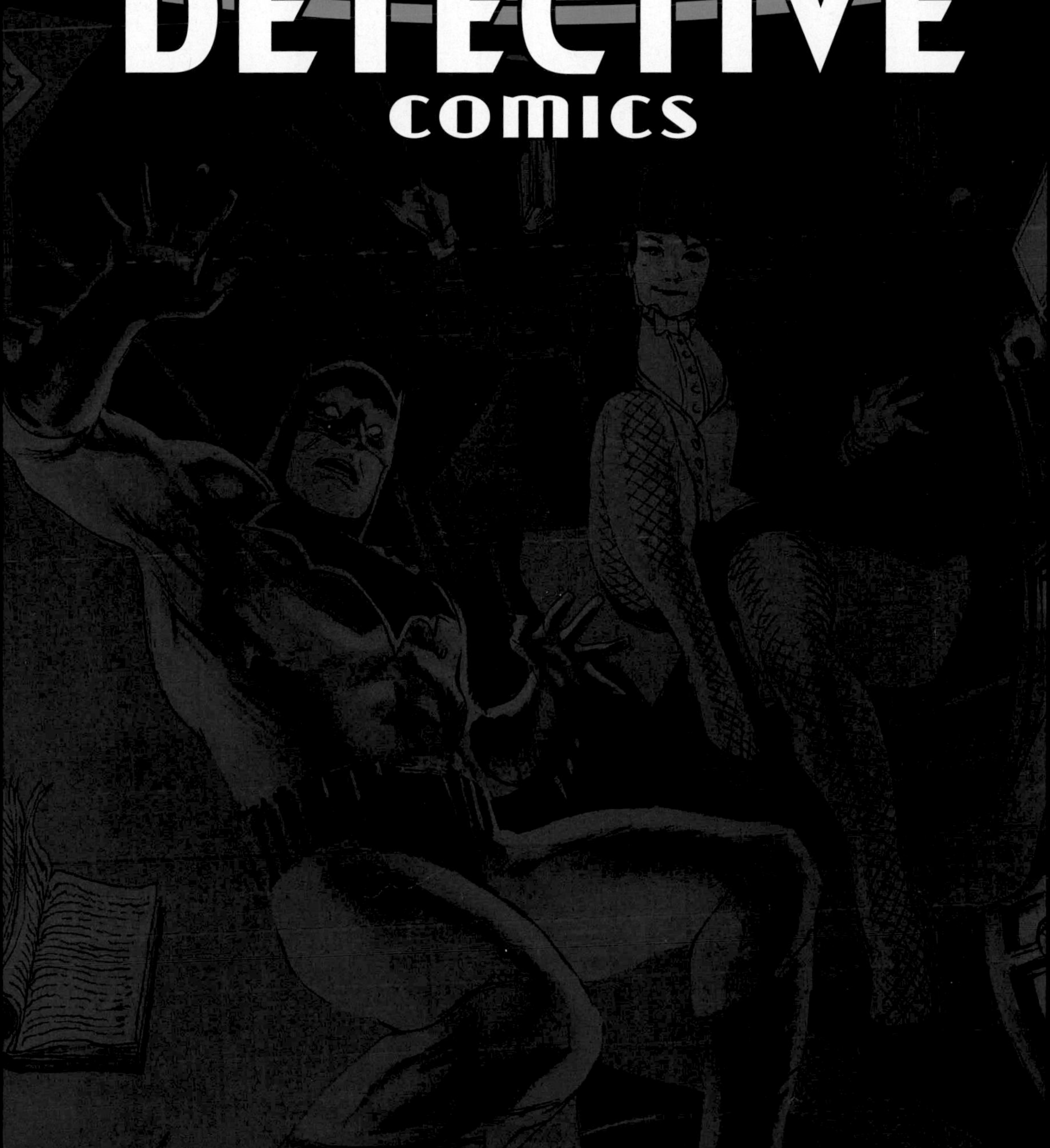

VARIANT COVER GALLERY

DETECTIVE COMICS #957 variant cover by RAFAEL ALBUQUERQUE

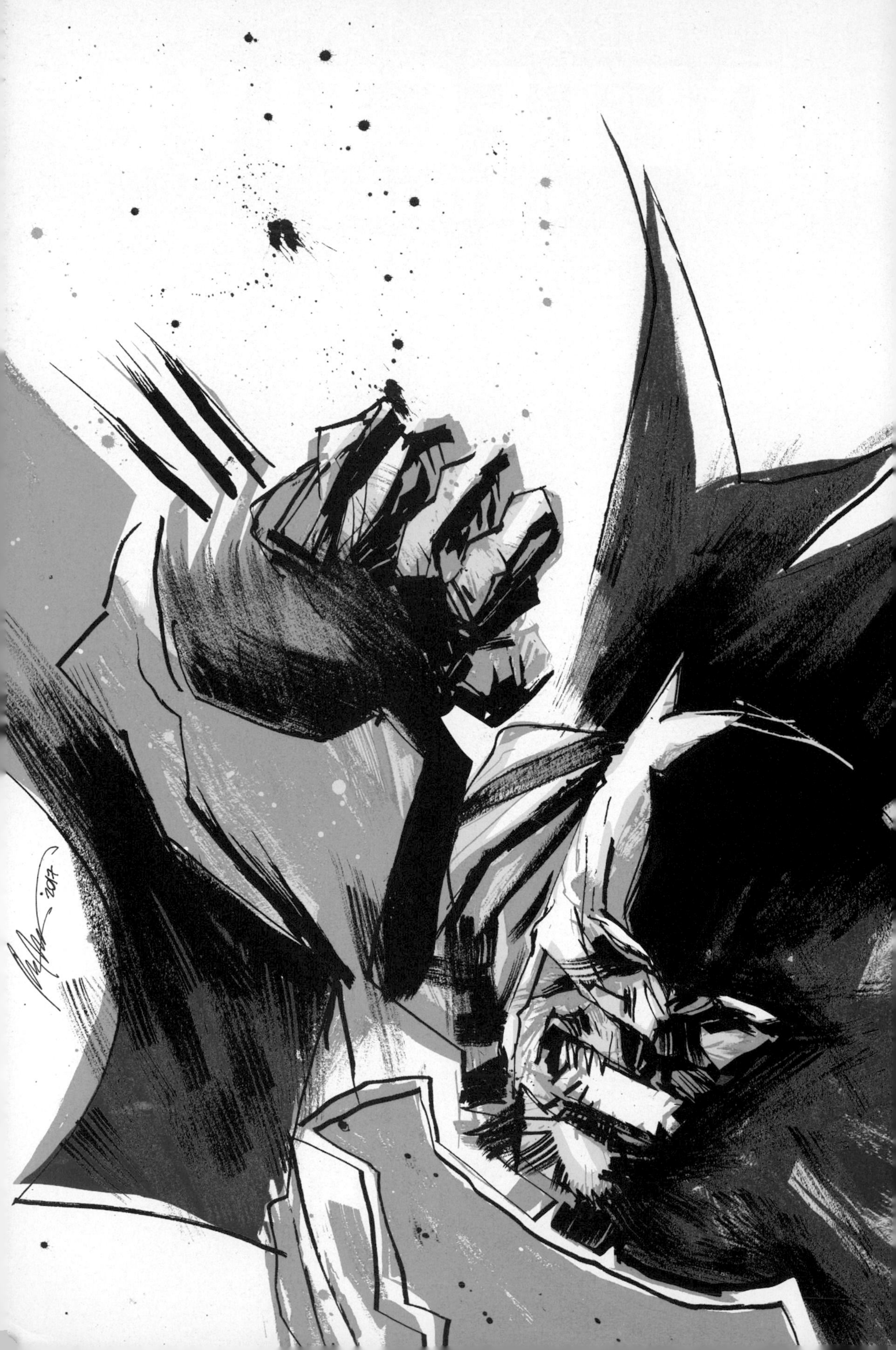

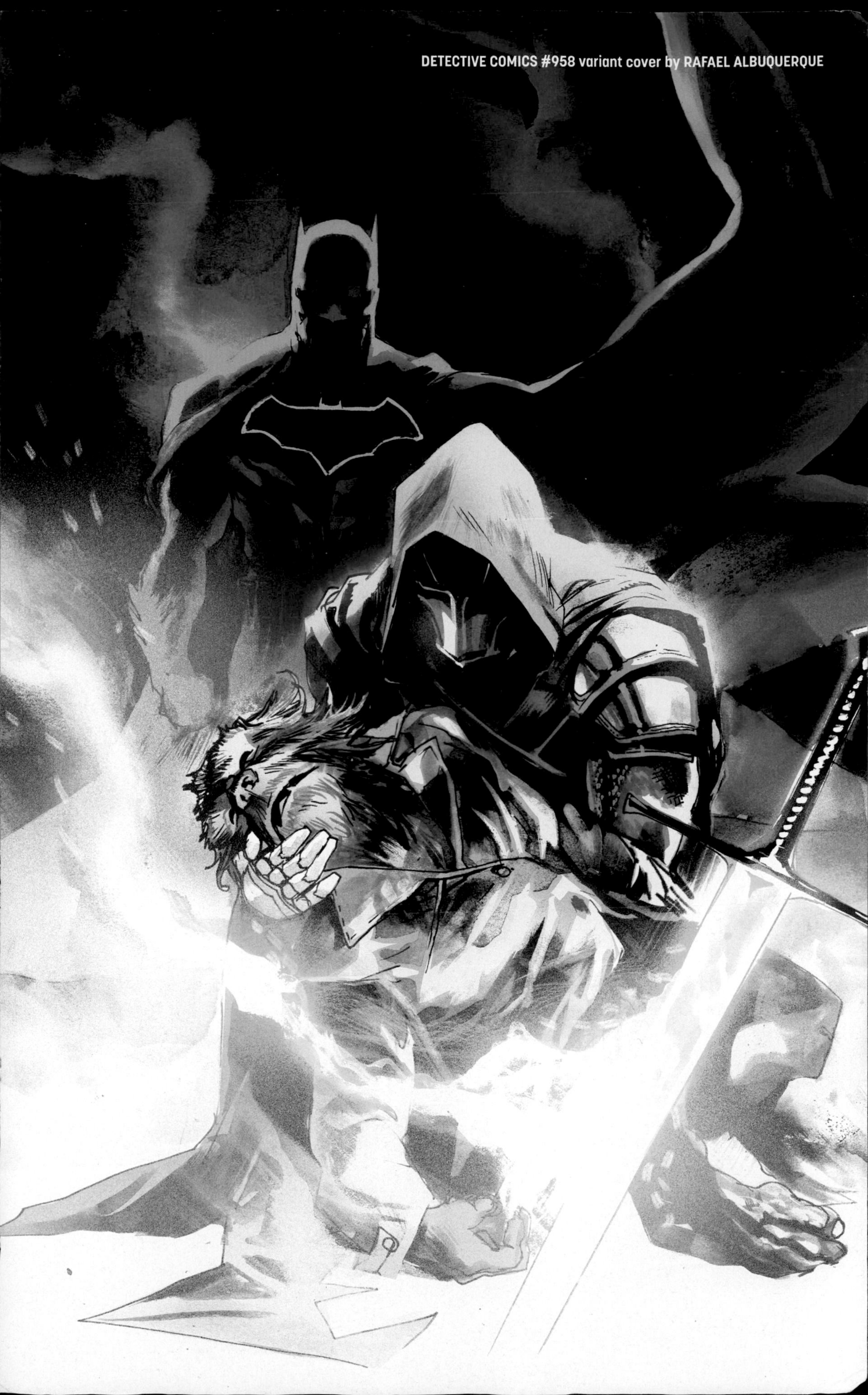

DETECTIVE COMICS #958 variant cover by RAFAEL ALBUQUERQUE

DETECTIVE COMICS #959 variant cover by RAFAEL ALBUQUERQUE

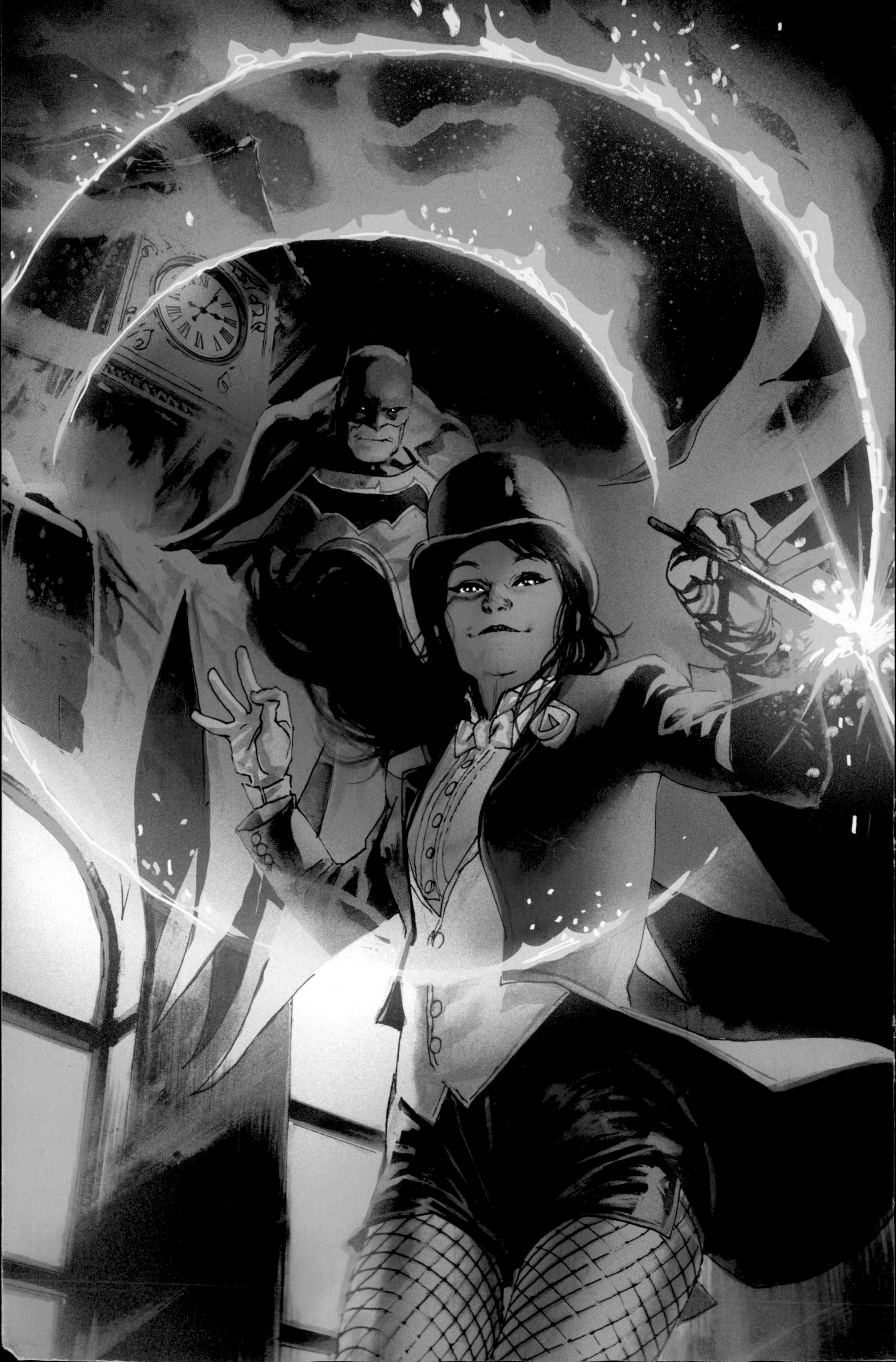

DETECTIVE COMICS #960 variant cover by RAFAEL ALBUQUERQUE

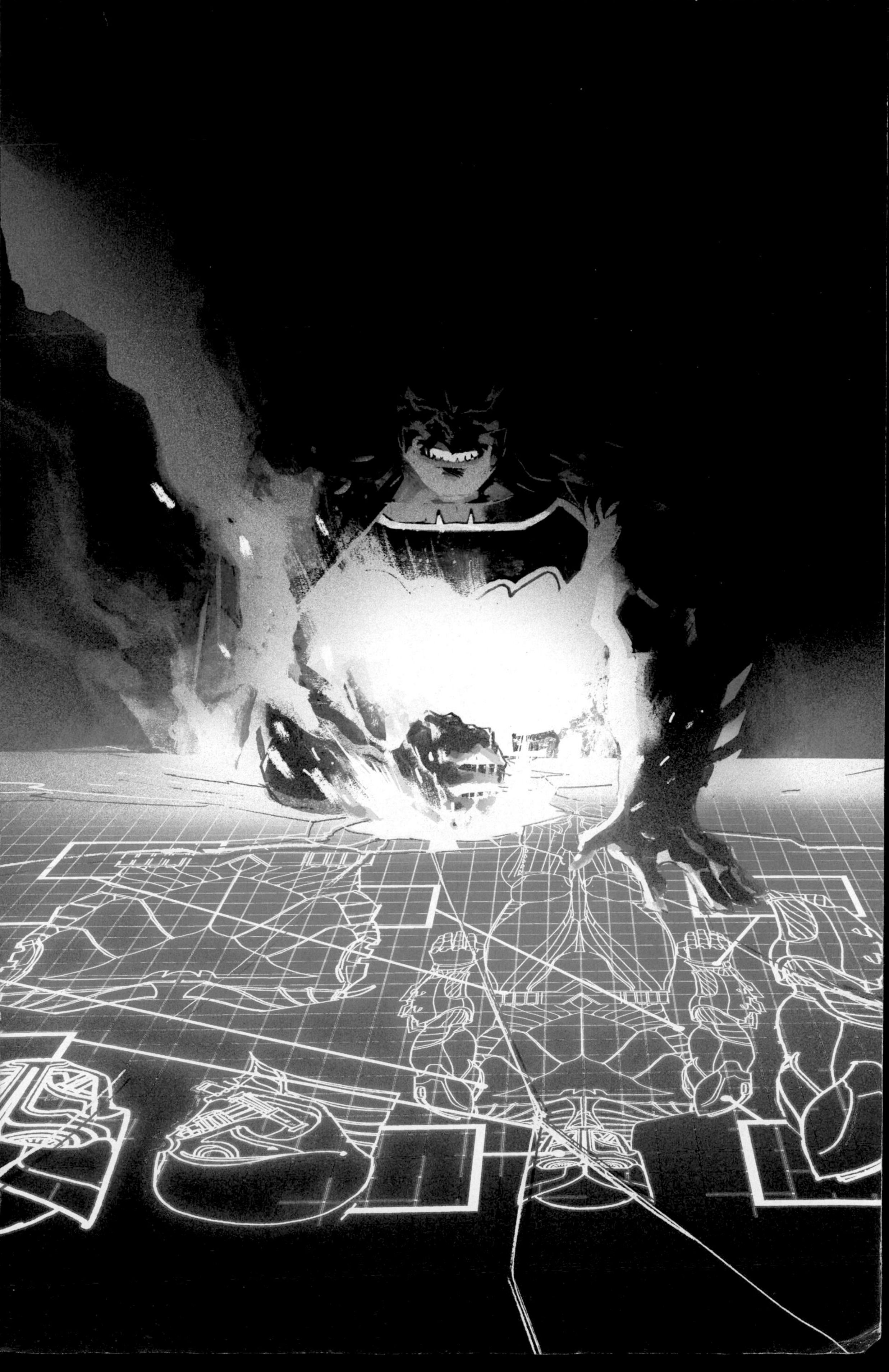

DETECTIVE COMICS #961 variant cover by RAFAEL ALBUQUERQUE

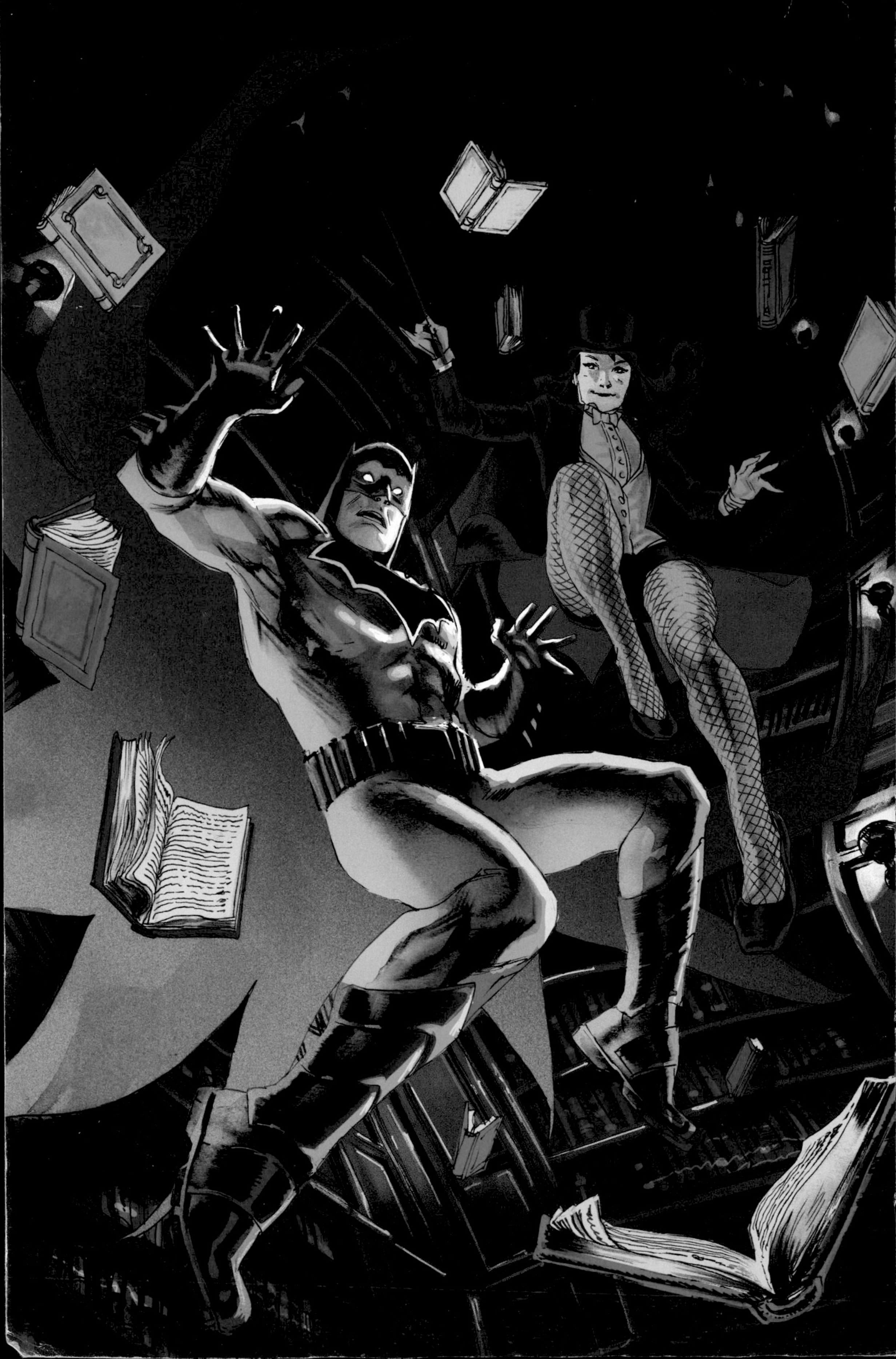

DETECTIVE COMICS #962 variant cover by RAFAEL ALBUQUERQUE

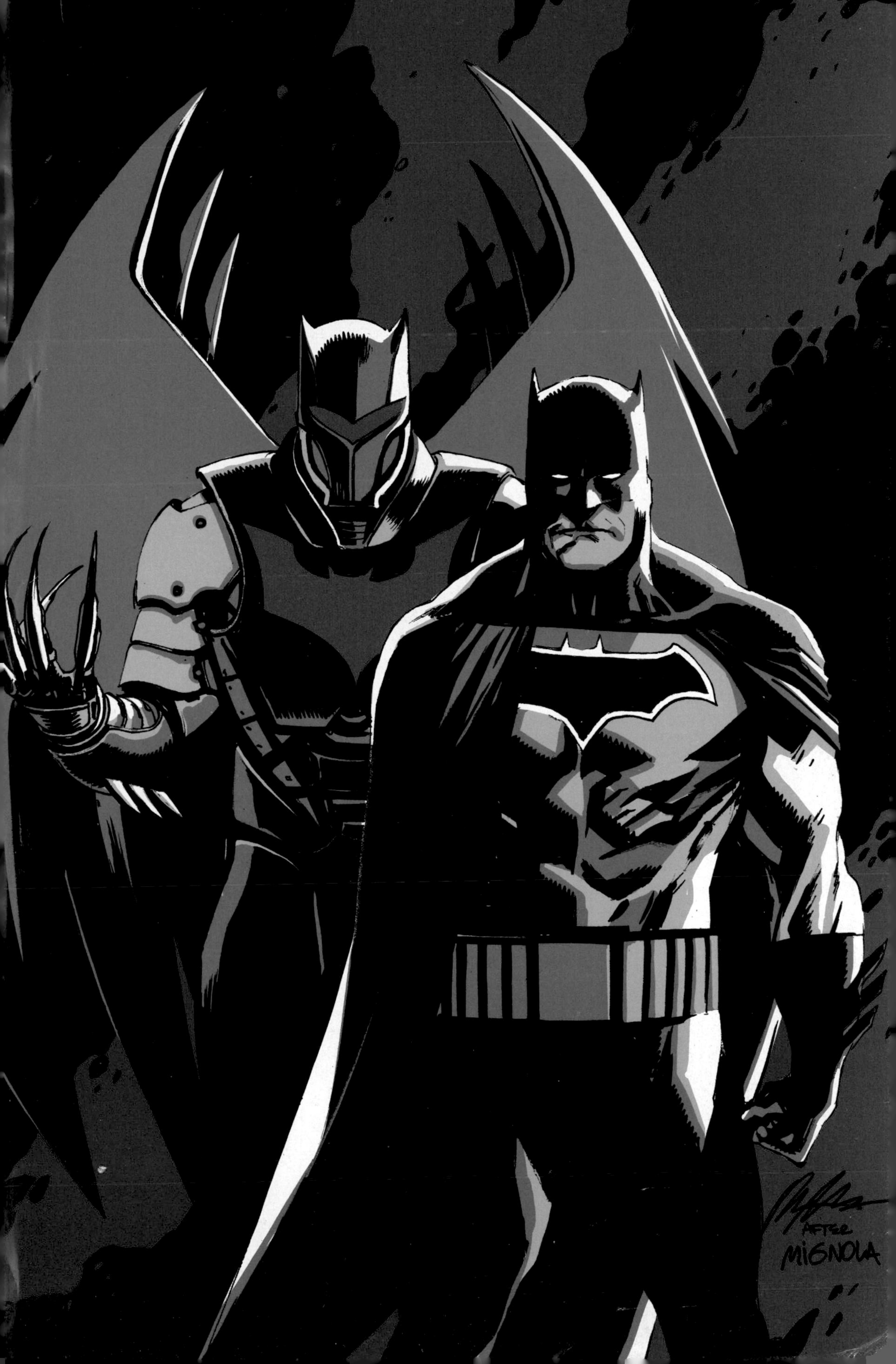
AFTER
MIGNOLA

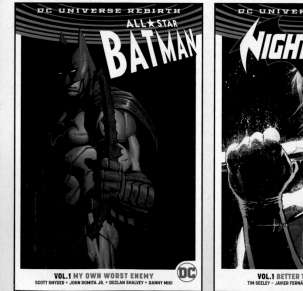